BAD SUBJECTS

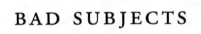

FRANCE OVERSEAS: STUDIES IN EMPIRE AND DECOLONIZATION

Series editors: A. J. B. Johnston, James D. Le Sueur

Founding editor: Tyler Stovall (1954–2021)

BAD SUBJECTS

Libertine Lives in the French Atlantic, 1619–1814

JENNIFER J. DAVIS

UNIVERSITY OF NEBRASKA PRESS   LINCOLN

The University of Nebraska Press is part of a land-
grant institution with campuses and programs on the
past, present, and future homelands of the Pawnee,
Ponca, Otoe-Missouria, Omaha, Dakota, Lakota, Kaw,
Cheyenne, and Arapaho Peoples, as well as those of the
relocated Ho-Chunk, Sac and Fox, and Iowa Peoples.

Financial support was provided by the Office of the
Vice President for Research and Partnerships and
the Office of the Provost, University of Oklahoma.

Library of Congress Control Number: 2022043605

Set and designed in Adobe Garamond by N. Putens.

CONTENTS

ILLUSTRATIONS

ACKNOWLEDGMENTS

What a profound joy to reflect on the people and institutional supports that sustained the research and writing of this book.

First I want to express my thanks to my family, who have lived with libertines for over a decade and supported me throughout the entire process, even when that required late-night writing jags or travel to French archives. My husband, Rangar Cline, is an intrepid partner both at home and abroad. He scouts out the best parks and playgrounds in France, tracks down fantastic bookstores and free concerts, and composes the most delicious meals from Sunday market fare. My second debt is to the gifted teachers who have helped us raise our children. A special note of thanks to early childhood educators *extraordinaires* Carol Jacob, Dan Boone, Noah Boone, and Kate Vincent, who taught our kids the most important things—curiosity, cooperation, the alphabet, and the joys of dumb jokes.

Speaking of the most important things, this book is only possible thanks to the daily labors of the archivists and librarians in France, Canada, and the United States who have conserved personal and state records across the centuries despite wars, civil unrest, fires, foreign occupations, political upheaval, and technological revolutions. In Quebec City I was particularly fortunate to make the acquaintance of M. Reynald Lessard, whose expertise in the French colonial records provided invaluable direction to my research. In Paris, Rochefort, Aix-en-Provence and Marseilles, I have been incredibly lucky to work with teams of gifted professionals dedicated to providing access to France's cultural patrimony. Closer to home, the librarians at the University of Oklahoma and the Interlibrary Loan service have made sure that I have all the resources I need to conduct research and teach. A special note of thanks to Dr. JoAnn Palmieri, the curator of OU's History of Science Collections, for providing access to critical ILL materials that arrived in March 2020 as the world shut down.

This book required multiple trips to archives and libraries in three countries. Funding from the Junior Faculty Summer Research Fellowship and the Arts and Humanities Faculty Fellowship at the University of Oklahoma financed portions of these trips. A short-term fellowship from the Huntington Library in San Marino, California, provided access to essential archival materials for chapter 4. I completed much of the research during a year-long sabbatical, part of which my family and I spent in Paris. I wrote the first draft of this manuscript while teaching remotely in Jerusalem during my husband's sabbatical. For that flexibility I am grateful to the History Department, the College of Arts and Sciences, and the provost at the University of Oklahoma. I am so glad I can count Megan Elwood Madden, planetary geologist and current director of OU's Center for Faculty Excellence, as one of my closest friends. I depend on our regular walks to keep my sanity and am grateful for her leadership in making the university a more inclusive place for all people to learn and work. She may not remember it, but she played a pivotal role in the publication process when she asked me in 2020, "What would it take for you to finish that book you've been working on?" and I realized that the answer was a writing group.

I have found the History Department at the University of Oklahoma to be an exceptionally supportive intellectual home. My department chairs, first Rob Griswold and then James S. Hart, encouraged me at a critical moment to take the time to write the best version of this book, even if that meant spending years more in research. The current department chair, Elyssa Faison, has been a staunch advocate for faculty throughout the pandemic who has worked to ensure that the university address the particular challenges faced by scholars who are parents of young children. I am so grateful for the friendship, writing advice, and mad culinary skills of my colleagues, especially Sandie Holguín, Jane Wickersham,

Melissa Stockdale, Steve Bradford, Sarah Hines, Noam Stillman, Bala Saho, Rhona Seidelman, Paul Gilje, Kathy Brosnan, Alan Levenson, Dan Snell, Judith Lewis-Phillips, and Lauren Duval. It is endlessly rewarding to teach history alongside superstars including Jenn Holland, Anne Hyde, Roberta Magnusson, Janet Ward, David Wrobel, Adam Malka, Shmuel Shepkaru, Katy Schumaker, Jay Casey, Raphael Folsom, Ben Keppel, Lizzie Grennan Browning, Warren Metcalf, Carsten Schapkow, Garret Olberding, Cori Simon, Stephen Norwood, David Chappell, Ronnie Grinberg, Jim Cane-Carrasco, Lewis Eliot, and Miriam Gross. In addition to these colleagues, I learn so much from my students at the University of Oklahoma. Graduate students in History, History of Science, and French, including Bethany Mowry, Justin Wollenberg, Heather Walser, Michael Baliff, Hannah Zinn, Victoria Funk, Amy Bergseth, Camille Testa, Kirsty Lawson Gaither, Nisrine Slitine El Mghari, Kelsey Madsen, Rokiatou Soumare, Latifah Zoulagh and Marie-Anne Baissac, ensure that I am part of wide-ranging conversations about global France. I am particularly grateful to those undergraduate students who joined courses on the French Revolution, Atlantic Revolutions, Marie-Antoinette, and a Dream Course on France and Haiti in Revolution over the past ten years.

In 2020, I joined a writing group organized by ou's Center for Faculty Excellence and Michelle Eodice that ensured I would spend time writing nearly every day. Then, early in 2021, Sarah Griswold invited me to join a French history writing group that she was organizing with Jessica Pearson, Nicole Bauer, Melissa Byrnes, and Peter Soppelsa. Regularly meeting the "I-35 Frenchies" on Zoom to workshop our book chapters and articles proved to be one of the bright spots of the pandemic era. It is no exaggeration to say that I would not have finished this book without them. I am so grateful for their robust feedback on the book's final chapter.

This book spans centuries and encompasses a vast geographic expanse. Maintaining that scope was only possible thanks to the tremendous intellectual generosity of a formidable group of scholars. These individuals have listened to bits and pieces of this book in conference presentations over the years, challenged me to clarify key points, and shared their own archival photographs with me. A few have even read the entire manuscript of this book prior to publication. I honestly do not know what I would have done without their wise counsel. Deepest thanks to Julie Hardwick, Nina Kushner, Andrew Israel Ross, Alyssa Goldstein Sepinwall, Mary Gayne, Heidi Keller-Lapp, Darryl Dee, Julia Landweber, Matthew Gerber, Lisa Jane Graham, Cathy McClive, Elizabeth Heath, Jennifer Heuer, Malick Ghachem, Jennifer L. Palmer, Michael Winston, Kolleen Guy, Julia Gaffield, Matthew Kruer, Susan Marie Mokhberi, Jeremy Popkin, Lorelle Semley, Anne Verjus, Brett Rushforth, Katie Hickerson, Robert Scafe, Julia Abramson, Caroline Séquin, Andrew Jainchill, Catherine E. Kelly, Jennifer Boittin, and Jacqueline Couti. Their insights improved this book immeasurably. I take full responsibility for any remaining errors and omissions.

Finally, for bringing my ideas to the printed page, many thanks to editor in chief Bridget Barry, copyeditor Emily Shelton, and the entire editorial team at the University of Nebraska Press.

BAD SUBJECTS

Introduction

Bad Subjects in the French Atlantic World

The twenty-first-century transatlantic trials of Dominque Strauss-Kahn, the prominent French politician and former head of the International Monetary Fund, momentarily rekindled our interest in libertines. Tried for the sexual assault and attempted rape of a hotel employee in the state of New York and for aggravated pimping at the Carlton hotel in the French city of Lille, Strauss-Kahn's court cases attracted sustained media coverage and inspired far-ranging conversations about sexual assault and solicitation in France and the United States.[1] While prosecutors in both countries represented Strauss-Kahn's actions as crimes, the defendant swatted away such accusations. He was no criminal, he maintained. What the prosecution called sexual assault in New York, Strauss-Kahn termed "inappropriate" and a misunderstanding. What the prosecution called pimping and assault in Lille, Strauss-Kahn characterized with equanimity as libertine evenings. Sex acts between consenting adults, he reminded judges during testimony in the Carlton Case, were not illegal.[2] If some of the women attending these gatherings had been prostitutes, he claimed not to have known it, thus undercutting the French state's central charge.[3] Several of the women testified that Strauss-Kahn's behavior at these gatherings amounted to "butchery" and "slaughter," addressing both the violence of his copulation technique and his refusal to wear a condom to reduce the risk of venereal disease.[4] But the courts' decisions in both France and the United States indicate that Strauss-Kahn's defense worked. In the United States, Strauss-Kahn settled out of court with Nafissatou Diallo, the woman who had accused him of attempted rape. And in France Strauss-Kahn was ultimately acquitted on all charges.[5] The prosecutor Frédéric Fèvre concurred that the state had failed to demonstrate that Strauss-Kahn had materially benefited from the prostitution of these women. At the end of the day, the prosecutor's goal was to enforce the law, not a moral code. Fèvre acknowledged that "everyone is allowed to lead the sexual life they wish so long as that remains within the boundaries of the law."[6] So within months, predictably, legislators and prosecutors took steps to criminalize the actions of which Strauss-Kahn had been accused. As this book goes to press, the French state now outlaws brothels and paying for sex, but these laws did not take effect until 2016.[7] Charges of pimping, rape, and sexual assault—all of which were illegal and had occurred in the regular sex parties attended by Strauss-Kahn—could not be substantiated against the defendant. In the end the French magistrates convicted only one individual: René Kojifer, head of public relations at the Carlton Hotel in Lille, who served one year in prison on the charge of pimping for his role coordinating the evenings. Despite multiple accusations, chains of corroborating text messages, and explicit witness testimony, enough doubt remained regarding Strauss-Kahn's own role in organizing or commissioning these gatherings that he evaded criminal sentencing and ultimately eluded civil fines.

Strauss-Kahn's characterization of his behavior as libertine struck some contemporary observers as anachronistic. It is, after all, a term that we more typically associate with the vanished world of the eighteenth-century European aristocracy than today's jet set.[8] Why the fascination with the libertine as a character? Whether we imagine the diamond-draped heaving bosoms of *Dangerous Liaisons*, apply the name of "Casanova" to a sexual adventurer, or invoke the Marquis de Sade to commingle one's torturous pain with another's sexual pleasure, visions of vanished decadence dominate our understanding of the term today. Libertines were sex crazed. Pornographers. Deviants. And, in a world of strict social hierarchy, only members of the nobility could indulge in such perverse fantasies without fear of punishment from church or royal authorities. However, something pathetic lurks in the figure as well. Thomas Wynn explains that it was because elite Frenchmen had been "reduced by royal absolutism to a parody of the warrior, the aristocratic libertine achieves renown through the conquest of women."[9] A man whose social purpose had evaporated, the libertine drifted aimless and impotent vis-à-vis the French Crown, seeking consolation in more intimate combat against a reliably weaker foe. This formula presumes that sexual conquest compensated for aristocrats' eroding political and social power under absolutism. The challenge of seduction and the thrill of physical pleasure motivated the avowed libertine, who required no higher purpose from life than self-satisfaction.[10]

The libertine's excesses also made a profound impact on the society around him, one that has not always been construed as a negative force. Scholars have documented the political and cultural significance of libertine literature, connecting the ethos communicated in these works to core ideals—including the rise of individualism and the separation of church and state—that shaped the contours of democratic politics and the modern state.[11] In eighteenth-century France, the libertine novel represented both a symptom of and the potential cure for the disease of royal absolutism.[12] Those characters who claimed the freedom to engage in sexual behavior outside of the narrow confines of monogamous reproductive relations paved the way to contemporary civil rights for all.

This book demonstrates that the portrait sketched above represents a partisan caricature that has obscured the contours of the libertine as a category in early modern legal, literary, and social registers. We mistake the libertine if we think it concerns only sex, and we err if we presume that the term describes only social elites, or only men. We lose the force that the term marshaled centuries ago and neglect how its meanings have changed over time.[13] Strauss-Kahn's trials have the potential to restore one of the central features of the libertine category because he used it to assert the fundamental legality of his actions. Perhaps, he acknowledged, his was a "rude sexuality, rougher than most men."[14] Scrambling to salvage his career, his reputation, and his fortune, the defendant testified frankly to participation in behavior deemed immoral by the mainstream of his society, but, he insisted, all the sex acts described in the Carlton Case were lawful, between consenting adults. Strauss-Kahn claimed an identity as a libertine precisely because it signaled the fundamental legality of his actions. Libertines admitted to being a "bad subject" of royal, church, or parental authority, but leaned heavily on defenses that their actions did not constitute crimes.[15]

In discussions of libertine behavior, whose liberty was at stake? To do what? And at whose expense? Modern legal codes enshrine individual liberties, but nearly three centuries of case law demonstrate that individuals' rights exist in dynamic tension with the rights of other individuals and require consideration of the collective rights of our communities at local, state, and transnational levels. In Strauss-Kahn's portrayal all individuals who attended the *soirées libertines* were equally free to express their sexuality within the bounds of the law. However, feminist legal theories from the past century that highlight the gender and wealth hierarchies that structure social and legal systems provide methods to interrogate that claim.[16] How did economic, social, and cultural forces unite to legitimate Strauss-Kahn's sexual liberty?[17] How did those same forces strip individual liberty from the women who accused him of sexual violence and solicitation? In their testimony they made clear that Strauss-Kahn's "liberty" in fact constituted abuse of their bodies and violations of their wills. Do these women cede their rights to health and safety standards simply by engaging in sex work, which was itself legal? This case reveals why any analysis of the libertine must ask, first, who can claim liberty and, second, at whose expense that liberty is claimed.

Finally, Strauss-Kahn's cases emphasize the importance of adopting an international frame to assess prosecutorial tactics. Throughout the Strauss-Kahn trials, jurists and journalists shuttled between French and American laws, cultural norms, and prosecutorial strategies in defining and charging assault, attempted rape, and pimping. In his Carlton Case testimony, Strauss-Kahn gestured to the deep roots of libertine masculinity among France's ruling elite, positioning himself and his countrymen against the puritanical Anglo-Americans whose legal pincers he had escaped months earlier.[18] The Atlantic context lent enduring consequence to the Strauss-Kahn trials in both nations, as journalists, politicians, and lawyers published exposés to explain critical discrepancies in the legal and media cultures between the two nations.

In early modern France and its Atlantic colonies, as in this twenty-first-century example, the libertine life was not merely a subject for fiction, nor a topos against which to play out potential revolutions. It was an available concept deployed around the Francophone world to navigate the system of legal pluralism resulting in cultural and legal gaps between ecclesiastical, metropolitan, and colonial jurisdictions.[19] The term identified a category proximate to crime and infused with profound social weight, analogous to present-day applications of "deadbeat," "rabble," or "thug."[20] A quasi-criminal accusation that took shape over centuries and across oceans, this shorthand signaled an individual had as yet broken no laws, but engaged in behavior that threatened families, communities, and the realm. In the French language, the term is gendered: *libertin* in the masculine, and *libertine* in the feminine. These gendered forms connoted different shades of scarcely tolerated wrongdoing that did not always reference sexual conduct. Parents decried their *libertin* sons who left the family home without permission, secretly married against parental wishes, gambled, engaged in extramarital sexual behavior, or spent family funds profligately. When used against daughters, *libertine* almost always condemned individuals' sexual conduct. But an important element complicated the feminine form: a young woman need not have engaged in extramarital sex to be tagged as a libertine. Slanderous talk sufficed.

When families and prosecutors resorted to the libertine accusation, they mobilized gendered strategies of prosecution and punishment.[21] The term typically indicated that an individual's autonomy menaced the collective of family, neighborhood, city, or state. But, because it was not a criminal charge, it proved nearly impossible for the accused to contest such characterizations. One did not need to have committed an identifiable crime to be perceived as disregarding authority and thereby endangering families and social institutions. Relying on the French Crown's power of arbitrary detention, strengthened by a set of laws passed in 1684 and 1700, state and parental authorities agreed that when an individual subverted social hierarchy, he or she could be detained on the charge of engaging in libertine behavior. But, time and again, defendants acknowledged that, while they may have engaged in actions that could qualify as unsocial or immoral, their accusers' reliance on the libertine category confirmed that no crime had been committed, and therefore no lasting damage had been done to the social order.

The libertine category, although deployed in starkly different ways around the French Atlantic, served to bridge shifting jurisdictions between Church and Crown, and between metropolitan and colonial judicial systems.[22] Over three centuries France forged an overseas empire rooted in the fiction of a common faith, law, and language. Legal personnel and institutions proved central to the project of expansion; the colonial *conseils supérieurs* "formed a global network of legal entrepôts, sites for legal services, that allowed subjects around the world to access French law and judicial processes."[23] It was in the space between royal directives, colonial judges' proposals, church authorities' practices, and imperial subjects' petitions that the early modern empire took shape. Following the insights of a generation of historians, this study considers law to be a negotiated set of social and political practices rather than a static list of prohibitions and punishments.[24] Over decades, in extensive correspondence and ministerial directives, royal, church, and colonial officials could agree that a libertine was a "bad subject." But everything else they disputed.

What actions made someone a bad subject? That depended on the time and the place. Under this heading authorities identified a startling array of behaviors, including religious skepticism, gambling, selling alcohol to Native Americans, interracial sex, or salt smuggling. The different definitions, standards, and punishments assigned to male and female libertines revealed key challenges to extend French laws across the seas that remained attuned to local customs, was flexible in application, and swiftly delivered the king's justice. In the contemporary imagination, the French Atlantic empire emerged as the ideal destination for France's libertines, if only such individuals could be trusted to advance the kingdom's goals. The tales of these men and women illuminate the cracks in authority that plagued the French monarchy as it cultivated imperial ambitions through the extension of legal regimes and the Catholic faith.

In casting the French Atlantic as the frame for this inquiry, I bring the insights of decades of scholarship emphasizing the economic, personal, and legal ties that bound together peoples in France, West Africa, North America, the Caribbean and South America. R. R. Palmer and Jacques

Godechot theorize a French Atlantic context that facilitated the exchange of political ideals and military aid throughout the revolutionary era.[25] Sylvia Marzagalli, James Pritchard, Lorelle Semley, and Jessica Marie Johnson have each emphasized the economic, military, commercial, and family ties that spanned France, Africa, and the Americas from the seventeenth through the nineteenth centuries.[26] Research by Sue Peabody, Malick Ghachem, Fréderic Régent, Marcel Dorginy, and Yves Benot, among many others, examines the ways the laws of slavery and racial policing bound the French state to its imperial subjects.[27] Overwhelming evidence documents how legal personnel and practices bound together Francophone communities across the Atlantic Ocean, transforming laws and legal ideals.[28] I argue that libertines reveal the gaps and challenges in that process of forging a coherent royal and imperial legal system.

DEFINING THE LIBERTINE

The word "libertine" as used across Europe derives from the Latin *libertus* (masc. sing.; *liberta*, fem. sing.; *liberti*, masc. pl.), a word that signified the legal category of freed slaves and indicated that even after an individual left the condition of slavery, a measure of social stigma and dependence remained.[29] A freed slave in ancient Rome belonged to the legal class of the *libertinus*.[30] A radical shift in meaning occurred in the sixteenth century, when a libertine came to be defined as an individual who exhibited excessive freedom of thought by failing to conform to religious teachings or divine laws. "Libertine" emerged as a keyword of the European reformations and counterreformations that delineated the boundaries of orthodoxy.[31]

In 1525 the first French-language edition of the New Testament was published in Paris. Several scholars identify the following passage from Acts 6:9–10 as formative in the transition of libertine from freedman to freethinker.[32] In the Acts of the Apostles, the disciples of Jesus recognized that they needed to identify the movement's next generation of leaders to resolve disputes within the community of believers. The community identified seven new leaders, including the Apostle Stephen, who "was filled with grace and power and began to work miracles and great signs among the people. Certain members of the so-called Synagogue of Libertines

(Freedmen), Cyrenians and Alexandrians, and people from Cilicia and Asia, came forward and debated with Stephen, [10] but they could not withstand the wisdom and the spirit with which he spoke."[33] These lines refer to a quarrel that arose between members of the wider Greek-speaking Jewish diaspora community from which the Apostle Stephen likely came, and the followers of Jesus of Nazareth from the province of Judea. Members of the Libertines' synagogue—indicating the members were freed slaves—charged Stephen with blasphemy against God, the Temple, and Moses. The quarrel was brought before the rabbinical high court of the Sanhedrin for judgment, where Stephen made a lengthy speech in which he contended that the life and teachings of Jesus fulfilled the Jewish scriptures rather than subverted them. This passage seems to have lent the term a connotation of theological disputation and associated it with opposition to the message of Jesus and his disciples. Religious reformers fruitfully deployed it against their rivals, and it was eventually adopted by Catholics to impugn all varieties of religious dissenters.[34] As a term of polemic and invective, libertines animated the culture wars of the Reformation.[35]

In 1545 John Calvin denounced as libertine a sect of reformers in Geneva who called themselves the "spirituals."[36] In Calvin's estimation this group ranked worse than the despised Anabaptists, who rejected both the authority of religious leaders and the Bible, entrusting instead the Holy Spirit as a guide to future revelation.[37] One of many indictments he leveled against this sect, "libertine" conveyed Calvin's derision for a group unmoored from authority that spouted heretical theology as opposed to the discipline and order that would be provided by following his own rigorous strictures of faith. Calvin charged that they confused Christian liberty with physical license, even preaching a community of goods and women.[38] But the term was not always clearly tied to specific sects or identifiable liberties; across Europe individuals used it to delineate doctrinal disputes and to identify their opponents in the debates surrounding reformed religions.[39]

In 1573 Geoffrey Vallée circulated *The Beatitude of Christians*, offering a tongue-in-cheek guide to the flavors of Christianities that one might encounter in France. After introducing his reader to the papist, the

Huguenot, and the Anabaptist, Vallée distinguished the libertine from those coherent confessional identities, explaining that "the Libertine neither believes nor denies, neither has faith nor doubts entirely, which renders him always skeptical."[40] But by 1598 such forms of religious heterodoxy were also newly legal, at least within the narrow confines established by the Edict of Nantes. According to some members of the clergy, libertines posed a threat because they sought liberty from the institutional hierarchy and the dogma of both the Catholic and the Reformed Churches.[41] Over the following century, the French Crown painstakingly negotiated the parameters of licit faith; the category of the libertine registered these struggles. Throughout the seventeenth century, the term indicated impiety when used by either Protestants or Catholics and was at times conflated with Epicureanism, connoting a resolutely materialist prioritization of pleasure and a self-conscious sympathy with ancient paganism.[42]

However, "libertine" also signaled freedoms other than the theological. Renowned correspondent, devoted mother, and keen observer of the French court Madame de Sévigné, writing to the Count de Bussy in 1679, refers to her free-wheeling style as "libertine."[43] The 1694 dictionary of the Academie Française sheds some light on the elasticity of the term, clarifying that both the masculine *libertin* and the feminine *libertine* describe an individual "who takes too much liberty and does not assiduously do his duty."[44] Therefore, it could seem to serve as a general term for excessive freedom, but as the entry progresses, it becomes clear that religious liberties constitute its central object. The dictionary identifies a libertine as an individual who is "licentious in matters of Religion, either in professing to not believe what must be believed, or in condemning pious customs, or in not observing the commandments of God, the Church, or superiors. In this sense it is only used in the substantive form: *He is a libertine, he mocks holy things. He is a libertine, he eats meat during Lent.*"[45] While ridicule or resistance to religious orthodoxy might occur for a number of reasons in seventeenth-century France, the libertine category flattened that variety to render suspect all forms of religious dissent, regardless of intent or circumstances.

After 1714 dictionary definitions of "libertine" increasingly connected the term with moral laxity, particularly with sexual licentiousness. The

1762 dictionary of the Académie Française identified the adjective as describing anyone "who loved their liberty and independence too much."[46] What constituted an excessive love of liberty, however, varied a great deal across time and space. To this the editors added that it was said "of a person with disordered conduct. *She leads a libertine life.*"[47] Here is an important hint that the word might take on different connotations in the masculine or feminine forms. Artfully vague, the definition obliquely indicates sexual behavior by adopting a feminine subject. Earlier examples of the substantive form in which libertine signified a religious skeptic remained. By 1787 the dictionary editors again revised the entry, noting that use of the term to indicate a general spirit of independence and refusal to submit to authority were only appropriate for children, as in "This student [masc.] has become very *libertin.*" When used in the substantive form, it referred to an individual who "led a disordered life." And the conclusion confirmed a continued link to religious skeptics: "Strong spirits, incredulous. The impious and the libertines."[48] In these entries French grammarians provide some clues to track how quickly connotations of the category morphed over these decades. Throughout the seventeenth and eighteenth centuries, the word "libertine" might be used as an adjective or a noun, each signifying different kinds of subversive behavior, identifying an individual who seized excessive freedoms in religious thought, speech, or sexual behavior. But, of course, the dictionaries provide only the first step of our transatlantic journey.

Scholars of libertine literature have emphasized the period after Louis XIV's death as formative in moving taboo forms of skepticism and sexuality into the public forum, highlighting the term's connection to the Regency's notable forms of license.[49] By the era of the French Revolution, both masculine and feminine forms of *libertin/e* became synonymous with sexual promiscuity, particularly those forms of errant sexuality associated with noble privilege and power.[50] But attention to these two moments has obscured the transition that took place in the multiple meanings and applications of the term between 1619 and 1814. Although French authorities would have agreed that they had a libertine problem throughout these two centuries, it was not conceived of as a dilemma peculiar to the Second Estate until the outbreak of the French Revolution. Insufficient obedience plagued authorities throughout the French kingdom and colonies; whether they concluded that this widespread waywardness should be reformed primarily through the Church, the family, or the state depended on the time and place. In period literature, police records, family petitions, and judicial documents—all of which deployed the term—"libertine" marked shifting edges of the law in personal faith, family order, and sexuality, alerting us to enduring disputes over legal reforms. This book recovers the cosmopolitan and capacious nature of the term as employed by authorities in France, Canada, Louisiana, and the Caribbean in the seventeenth and eighteenth centuries. The libertine category in law emerges as particularly central to efforts to forge a multiethnic empire across the Americas.

In an array of policies, the Crown and royal ministers provided powerful statements about which liberties were productive and which were destructive, and how these might differ in France versus the colonies. Churchmen often contested royal statements with their own arguments regarding imminent threats to authority in France and its empire, and their assertions were met with equally robust claims from colonial administrators, governors, military officers, and judges, sometimes extending but often challenging metropolitan ideals. As French colonial administrations moved from policies of alliance and adaptation to policies of assimilation or segregation from indigenous populations, the parameters delimiting libertine behavior changed.[51] What had once been asserted as a necessary colonial liberty officials redefined as illegitimate and libertine. Occasionally the accused speak from the judicial record to point out the shortcomings in royal, colonial, or Church conceptions of liberty and obedience. The variety of uses employed by the people who resided in and governed France and its Atlantic colonies enable us to chart perceptions of what were the most significant liberties taken by residents and which posed the greatest threats to political and social order. In this manner the French empire operated as a laboratory of liberties.

Jean-Pierre Cavaillé reminds us that, since historians tend to find libertines in the words of their opponents, we risk falling "victim to the propagandas of the past."[52] There can be no question about it: the libertine life was a subject of obsessive concern for French men and women in the early modern era. But previous studies have missed the crux of what made these individuals significant to their societies. It was not specifically religious dissent, nor sexual deviance, but an individual's relationship to the law that characterized the libertine. In the early modern era, the category of the libertine identified the gray area between the legal and illegal.[53] This zone was extensive, and it might change substantially from one community to another, as we learn from historians of law and society in early modern France and its colonies.[54] Authorities used the term to indicate behavior that should be more systematically surveilled, laying the groundwork for more formal legislation. Or an action might be libertine if it ranked as a minor crime (*crime léger*) that was no longer subject to vigorous prosecution.[55] But whether it indicated a former or future transgression, the libertine had engaged in behavior that was emphatically not criminal.[56]

The legal systems that organized France and its early modern empire underwent dramatic reforms that splintered the foundations of the social and political order.[57] Over the seventeenth and eighteenth centuries, ecclesiastical courts ceded tremendous powers to municipal and provincial courts in France, while the provincial parlements wrestled the Crown for autonomy.[58] Simultaneously, certain actions crossed the boundary between licit and illicit, especially those that revealed heterodox religious beliefs or challenged Catholic orthodoxy in sexual conduct, family order, or social hierarchy. For example, the legal historian Benoît Garnot documents that those sexual activities long condemned by the Catholic Church—including masturbation, adultery, clerical sexuality, extramarital intercourse, and sodomy—remained illegal offenses condemned by the French state throughout this period. Garnot points to the steady decline in the prosecution of these types of offenses during the eighteenth century, even as authors including Jean-Jacques Rousseau publicly admitted in their memoirs or correspondence to engaging in these activities.[59] We know with the greatest possible certainty that masturbation and adultery did not decline as practices in the eighteenth century.[60] In France, Garnot argues, "a relative amorous liberty (young people hoping to marry, adulterers, concubines, but also homosexuals) though partially limited by convention, remained a constant throughout the Old Regime, even if it was a little more obvious in the eighteenth century than in the seventeenth century."[61] However, Garnot ignores the fact that those same activities in Québec remained subject to charges in ecclesiastical or city courts, resulting in fines, corporal punishment, or even exile from the colony.[62] As a result of these shifting jurisdictions and wide variations in regional and colonial law codes, it would have been hard in 1700 for a French subject to know if an amorous liaison with a neighbor was an illegal or immoral act, or a private matter of little consequence to the state. What is more, legal reforms proceeded at very different paces in different places and among the diverse populations under French law. In many regions of France, the Church ceded the authority to police canon law on sexual activities to an increasingly muscular state, while in Québec Church authorities and ecclesiastical courts retained substantial powers to surveil morality.[63] The early modern fiction of "one king, one faith, one law" fractured along these fault lines. Rather than supporting Garnot's secularization thesis, which traces a steady decline in the prosecution of sexual behavior, the evidence from across the French Atlantic world leans toward an oscillation principle of law in which periods of targeted repression followed periods of relative permissiveness on the part of state authorities.[64]

Across France and those Atlantic colonies subject to French law, authorities strove to reconcile existing civil codes with new ideals of human nature and the natural order of the universe.[65] One might write a law requiring water to run uphill, but that code would not make it happen. Just so, legal theorists advised against civil and criminal laws that contradicted human nature.[66] Natural law theory emerged over the eighteenth century as a powerful alternative to the theories of law dependent on monarchical and Church authority. Intellectuals within the judiciary advocated measures to rationalize laws in accordance with these Enlightenment ideals.[67] The resulting reforms meant that last year's criminal act might rank as this year's minor transgression; alternatively, a condoned activity might now draw harsh criminal penalties. Contemporaries in France perceived a strong state with increasing police powers.[68] This era was defined not by a general slackening of laws regulating religion, sexual conduct, or economic transactions, but a remarkable instability of the law in those arenas as deployed by competing authorities. Libertine literature performed important cultural work, staking out this ground and voicing opposition to laws that criminalized core elements of human nature, particularly those laws focused on regulating sexual behavior. Authors placed contemporary legal inconsistencies and reversals of criminal sexuality at the center of literary plotlines in novels that often relied on exotic settings or characters to highlight the culturally constructed nature of law codes and to call out legal discrepancies between the metropole and colonies.[69] For this reason scholars will continue to misunderstand the libertine category if analysis remains located in metropolitan France alone. Imperial rivals—Spain, Britain, and the Netherlands—induced French authorities to reconsider social ideals and revise laws. Non-Catholic subjects—particularly Protestants, Jews, Indigenous Americans, and Muslims and Hindus from Africa and South Asia—posed unique challenges to a French state premised on the principle of one king, one faith, one law. For that reason this book examines the transnational context of the laws and literature constructing the meaning of libertine in the French Atlantic, defined here as the French colonies in North America, South America, the Caribbean, and Africa, from 1619 to 1814.

The Cosmopolitan Libertine

For the most part, studies of libertine literature have adopted national frames that ignore the insistent cosmopolitanism of the genre across Europe.[70] But modern French literature and law took shape in a global context, defined against powerful rivals and in communication with imperial subjects.[71] As a result the legal foundations for family order and sexual relations transformed. By the eighteenth century, those authorities who sought to contain individuals' sexuality within the bounds of Roman Catholic canon law, which required clerical celibacy, sexual abstinence outside of marriage, monogamy within marriage, and prohibited homosexual relations or masturbation, faced a public aware of broad cultural differences. They knew that their Protestant neighbors approved of clerical marriage, and that some Muslim merchants in the Ottoman Empire practiced polygamy. Informed participants in the Republic of Letters were aware that certain South Asian military allies practiced polyandry,

and that select Native American nations welcomed homosexual relationships within specific circumstances.[72] Travelers and missionaries conveyed
this human diversity to French readers in their reports, communicating
with each volume that sexual mores resulted from cultural constructs
rather than immutable divine laws. Travel literature played a central
role displacing European standards of morality and sexuality.[73] Many
of the philosophes postulated sexual desire to be a universal feature of
all humans, understanding the sex drive as among nature's most insistent "laws."[74] Leading intellectuals harnessed this theory to argue that
the kingdom's leaders must acknowledge a certain amount of religious,
cultural, and even sexual diversity if the state hoped to solidify France
as a global power.[75]

In Francophone settlements across France, Africa, and the Americas,
administrators, writers, and subjects relied on the term "libertine" to
connote overlapping religious, moral, and economic transgressions. This
book restores that cultural diversity and geographic breadth to historical
libertines. As the term was applied to individuals engaged in liquor sales
in Québec or interracial sex in Louisiana, or was used to characterize the
children of European and African parents in the French Caribbean, these
mutations reverberated back to France, transforming social, sexual, and
political ideals in surprising ways. As a result libertine literature of the
eighteenth century became a key forum in which authors gave voice to
anxieties regarding the world that might emerge from France's imperial
ambitions.[76]

ORGANIZATION

The following chapters trace libertines in law and literature across the
French Atlantic in the seventeenth and eighteenth centuries. But what I
have assembled is far from a comprehensive catalog of the term's usage.
Instead this text provides a series of snapshots capturing key elements of
the quasi-criminal category of the libertine as it ricocheted between France
and the Americas over two hundred years. Chapters 1, 4, 5, and 7 examine
the impact of particularly potent court cases in defining the libertine,
while chapters 2, 3, 6, and 8 survey ministerial correspondence, edicts,
sermons, memoirs, travel literature, and novels to clarify the meanings

and consequences of libertine actions from France to Canada, Louisiana to the Caribbean. Taken together these documents offer fragile bridges to connect a scattered empire. The narrative proceeds chronologically, identifying important moments when the libertine category centered debates about jurisdiction and legal reform in expansionist France and its colonies. The final chapter considers the significance of the libertine as waves of revolutions roiled societies on all sides of the Atlantic, as the term became firmly hitched to denunciations of aristocratic social and economic privileges on the one hand, and revolutionary excesses on the other.

Attentive readers will note that I locate no chapter within Africa. The small French settlement in Saint-Louis (present-day Senegal), served as the seat of a colonial sovereign council like those that dispensed French law in Québec, Louisiana, colonial Haiti, Guadeloupe, and Martinique. But this book focuses on those sites where French settlers and colonial officials made claims of political and economic hegemony over European-, American-, and African-descent subjects through systems of law. The French sovereign council in Senegal made no such claims until the nineteenth century; it adjudicated trade disputes or military infractions among the small population of French soldiers, traders, and their families, but the French officials in Saint-Louis recognized that indigenous legal systems governed most inhabitants within neighboring West African kingdoms. The story of French colonial legal regimes that I trace here relates only part of a broader global history of imperial law and should be read alongside the scholarship documenting the autonomy of African states and leaders from French imperial legal regimes throughout the seventeenth and eighteenth centuries.[77]

This peripatetic approach relies on decades of scholarship documenting distinctive regional developments of French law and society in each of the provinces of France and Québec, the Louisiana territory, and pockets of the Caribbean subject to French law, especially Guadeloupe, colonial Haiti (Saint-Domingue), Martinique, and Désirade. Assessing the libertine as a quasi-criminal category across France and its colonies makes three contributions to the history of early modern France. First, this inquiry establishes the French Atlantic as a unit in which the actions of one part affected other parts.[78] People and products churned ceaselessly through regions that have been assessed in isolation of each other, but hurricanes in Guadeloupe ruined families based in Africa and France. Laws passed in France moved people and property across oceans. Soldiers and merchants in Bordeaux and Loango played roles in enslaving men and women who built Saint-Domingue's plantation wealth, which enriched France at a staggering cost in human lives and potential.[79] Scholars of Old Regime France have largely ignored the relationships that the kingdom forged through colonial commerce.[80] Decades of research based in the Americas, the Caribbean, and Africa document the centrality of Atlantic exchanges to the development of capitalism in the French economy after the sixteenth century.[81] But this was a trade that plumbed the edges of existing law, and the French state found itself reactively crafting regulations to govern its far-flung territories. For this reason the category of the libertine in law and literature offers crucial insight into the sinews of this empire. Both genres gave voice to the ambitions and frustrations of individuals as they built societies that bound together people and properties across the Atlantic Ocean.

Second, this inquiry restores colonial cosmopolitanism as a central concern of French libertine literature.[82] Here I follow the insights of Joan Dayan and Doris Garraway, both specialists in Francophone Caribbean literature who have advanced compelling analyses of libertine novels as responses to contemporary debates over the violence and sexual terror at the heart of chattel slavery, which played a central role organizing relationships in the French Atlantic.[83] My research demonstrates that such conversations about colonial commerce and slavery did not remain cordoned off in the French Caribbean. Violence, sexual terror, and preferential applications of the law were factors constitutive of settler colonialism throughout the French Atlantic, and libertine authors found parallels from Québec to Quimper, Guadeloupe to Gorée. Many novels that constitute the libertine genre adopted an exotic setting or characters from the Americas or Africa, India, Japan, or the South Pacific.[84] But even novels set within an aristocratic household in Paris articulated the perspective that, although human sexual desire might be universal, human societies varied widely in the most basic customs and mores regarding sexual activity.

Finally, my study concludes that libertines—better understood as transgressors whose acts confronted the flux of law codes than as criminals—provide a critical perspective from which to reassess the relationship between the French and Haitian revolutions.[85] In response to a series of military reversals, colonial officials and then revolutionary legislators identified libertines as among the central threats to French ambitions of Atlantic empire. Authorities in both France and the colonies revised and even reversed laws on race, sex, family, commerce, and slavery dramatically in the period from 1763 to 1804. Seeking to stabilize combustible colonial communities, newly enfranchised citizens ultimately upended traditional hierarchies. One unified law code with clear and stable jurisdictions became the central promise made by the legislators of the French and Haitian revolutions across the Atlantic, in repudiation of the judicial inequities built into Old Regime systems.[86] Along the way France gained a continental empire, and the Caribbean colony of Saint-Domingue became the Kingdom of Ayiti when its inhabitants proclaimed themselves to be free and independent of colonial rule. By 1814 legislators, magistrates, and Francophone populations across the Atlantic had challenged the legal basis for aristocracy, monarchy, patriarchy, monopoly, slavery, and the place of the Catholic Church in the French and colonial states. This book explains how France's Atlantic libertines set the stage to imagine revolutionary liberties and framed the debates over who could claim such freedoms.

I

Among the S*v*ges

The Viau Affair, 1619–1626

Aujourd'huy parmy les Sauvages
Où je ne trouve à qui parler,
Ma triste voix se perd en l'air,
Et dedans l'echo des rivages

Today among the S*v*ges
Where I find none with whom I may speak,
My sad voice disappears in the air
Amid the echo along the shores.

—THÉOPHILE DE VIAU, "To the King from Exile," 1619

Exiled from the French court in 1619, the poet and dramatist Théophile de Viau portrayed his narrator as a civilized man "among the s*v*ges," but whether he imagined himself to be surrounded by American warriors, Catholic fanatics, Dutch burghers, or rural Gascon peasants remains anyone's guess.[1] Such slippage seemed to be the point—after all, what mattered superficial differences in climate, customs, theology, or geography? In the eyes of this loyal courtier, all was wilderness beyond the king's person, his court, and his good city of Paris.

Any account of French libertines must begin with the formative case of Théophile de Viau. A celebrity poet of the age, he won acclaim from both contemporaries and successive generations for his witty and ribald verses. His trial from 1623 to 1625 stands as one of the most important judicial events in early modern French literary and political history. However, scholars have ignored the way Théophile's work and trial referenced the relationship between religious evangelism and the laws regulating colonial expansion in the French Atlantic, although this dimension clearly mobilized Théophile as well as his critics; both sides contended that the consequences of this trial predicted France's fate as an imperial power. Both in the court of public opinion and in the court of law, his accusers agreed that the poet was a libertine, although the term corresponded to no specific crime.[2] The king's prosecutor initially charged Théophile and several of his coauthors with the crime of *lèse-majesté-divine*, or treason against God's authority, for publishing verses in a collection of profane poetry, *Le Parnasse satyrique* (1622).[3] But when it became clear that Théophile's authorship of the offending verses could not be substantiated, the prosecution resorted to presenting character witnesses who relied on hearsay to defame Théophile's personal piety and sexual conduct. In response Théophile and his lawyers mounted a successful defense of both the poet's theological beliefs and sexual behavior, refuting tangential allegations that the author engaged in sodomy, heresy, or corruption of youth, and securing his release from prison.

Théophile's acquittal constituted a watershed moment in which the jurists of the Parlement of Paris established important standards for reliable witness testimony, freedom of expression, and the criminal limits of heterodoxy as France groped toward its new status as a multiconfessional state.[4] But this is no tale of triumph. Although Théophile won the judgment, he died within a year of his release, his health having been so compromised by the rigors of prison and interrogation. Friends mourned his passing, but quietly and in private. Fellow poets preferred to censor themselves rather than risk similar treatment from Théophile's still-active enemies in the Church and the royal court.[5] Despite the acquittal the world of French literature sustained a powerful blow to the liberty of personal expression in the wake of the Théophile de Viau trial. Recognized as the standard-setter for a "modern style" of French literature in the centuries after his death, Théophile's work continues to be standard examination fare on the French *baccalauréat* examination.[6] But the impact of his example extends far beyond the realm of letters.

In this chapter I contend that the trial of Théophile de Viau constituted the first public debate over the libertine category in both literature and law, setting the terms for future contestations between individual liberties and the social good. Moreover, Théophile's trial provides a thoroughly documented case study that traces mutual influences across literature and legal briefs. In poems and novellas, Théophile championed the liberty of thought that could be preserved by a strong monarch, and he argued forcefully that royal edicts transcended theological inconsistencies and contested points of Catholic teaching. In protecting individuals' religious liberties, Théophile suggested, the king's law rose above petty confessional squabbles to unite all subjects.[7] In a flurry of publications, both Théophile and his antagonists made clear the global consequences of charting the space between law and liberty to their readers. This was no small affair. All sides agreed that the Théophile de Viau case would determine the limits of religious tolerance and the nature of kingship within France and beyond.

In voluminous published attacks on the poet and his friends in the French court, Théophile's enemies, particularly the Jesuit priest François Garasse, imagined that libertines posed a diabolical challenge to established authorities.[8] Garasse's collaboration and correspondence with the state's lead prosecutor, Mathieu Molé, brought these accusations into the law courts. In characterizations of Théophile—nearly always referred to by his first rather than family name in contemporary publications—Garasse used the word "libertine" not to identify a coherent group of individuals as John Calvin had in 1525, nor to condemn a particular theological argument.[9] Instead, he employed it to indicate an ill-defined religious deviance that rejected all forms of orthodoxy, either Catholic or Protestant. Incoherence was the point, asserted Garasse when he published the following definition in 1622: "By the word libertine I mean not a Huguenot, nor an Atheist, nor a Catholic, nor a heretic, nor a *Politique*, but an individual comprising all of these qualities."[10] In a Europe riven by confessional conflict, the libertines were those who refused to take a side. The following year, in a work that explicitly denounced Théophile as the ringleader of a dangerous circle of libertine courtiers, Garasse clarified what he meant.[11] There were two types of artistic skeptics that went by the name of the "beautiful souls" (*beaux esprits*), he advised his readers:

the Libertines and the Impious. "The first," he wrote, "are just taking shape, the second are perfected. The first are caterpillars, the second are butterflies. The first are apprentices, the second are masters of malice."[12] Through these naturalistic metaphors, Garasse depicted a spectrum of irreligiosity, but deemed all stages as equally threatening to civil and moral order. Libertines were drunks and gourmands, "with no other god than their stomach."[13] But, because they were not yet committed atheists, hope remained for their souls if they could find their way back to the Church and orthodox Catholic practice. By making an example of Théophile, Garasse contended, the monarch acted as the moral protector of his subjects, rooting out both the fully fledged and the emergent skeptics.[14]

However, Garasse did not have a monopoly on defining and applying the libertine label. In fact, even as the Jesuit published his polemical indictments, Théophile had recognized the power in the term and sought to reclaim it from the religious zealots by placing it in the mouths of his poetic narrators and prose characters. These characters were men of the world, proud participants in building a global France engaged in long-distance trade, colonies, learning, and art. When Théophile's characters spoke of libertine conduct, they transformed the charge of the term, invoking broader liberties of thought, speech, and action for some people in limited times and places. The poet's narrators valorized individual liberties as fundamental rights that could only be guaranteed by a powerful and capable monarch. In return for the Crown's protection, artists and scholars, explorers and courtiers, Catholics and Calvinists would freely choose to promote and praise the ruler.

Théophile's poems and prose alongside his trial demonstrate how the libertine became a quasi-criminal category attuned to the gray areas in French law governing individual liberties in thought and public expression. This chapter documents how men of letters and the law adopted tactics to challenge this characterization of libertine behavior, here primarily defined as questioning Catholic teachings and engaging in sodomy. Second, I demonstrate that the case had global consequences according to both Théophile and his antagonists. The debate over religious liberty in thought and speech proved critical to those who risked lives and fortunes—particularly Huguenot merchants, sailors, or soldiers—to establish settlements across the Atlantic that might position France as a global imperial power or favor coreligionists in Holland or Britain.[15]

The end of France's religious wars left important Atlantic ports, especially La Rochelle and Dieppe, and trade in the hands of an expansioinist Huguenot minority.[16] Indeed, Huguenot authors penned some of the most important French-language accounts from colonies established in the Americas, including Jean de Léry's *Histoire d'un voyage faict en la terre de Bresil* (1578), Marc Lescarbot's *Histoire de la nouvelle France* (1609–11) and Antoine de Montchrestien's *Traicté de l'oeconomie politique* (1615). Marcel Bataillon terms this a "Huguenot corpus on America," while Frank Lestringant further identifies its common features: these texts denounced the violence of the sixteenth-century Spanish conquest of the Americas and defended the right of indigenous peoples to be undisturbed by European settlers.[17] Some, like Léry, drew anticolonial lessons from their experiences, while others, like Lescarbot, championed French Christianity—transcending confessional divisions—as the ideological foundation for a durable empire equally dedicated to commerce and conversion.[18] Montchrétien imagined that the indigenous residents of the Americas would prove to be stauncher allies than were hostile European neighbors, Protestants and Catholics alike, who had manipulated French politics and commerce to their own benefit.[19] But all three agreed that unity for the purpose of colonial expansion should result from the French religious settlement of 1598.

ESTABLISHING RELIGIOUS TOLERATION

In the decades following the Edict of Nantes (1598) by which the French Crown agreed to tolerate France's Protestant population, the terms and limits of religious toleration constituted the most important gray area of law. France had spent the last half of the sixteenth century in the throes of a civil war. Catholic and Protestant nobles vied for influence in the royal court, cultivated foreign sponsors, and funded armies to seize territory claimed by "heretics." The Edict of Nantes charted a path of coexistence for the majority Catholic population with a minority population that adhered to the "so-called Reformed religion."[20]

The first requirement of all French subjects? Forget. Article 1 ordered that "the memory of everything which has occurred between one side and the other . . . shall remain extinct and dormant as though they had never happened."[21] According to the edict, Catholicism remained the state religion, but royal officials would no longer coerce conversion.[22] The French state agreed to tolerate the presence of Huguenots within the kingdom, but outlawed public worship or acts that failed to conform with Catholic doctrine.[23] According to the letter of the French law, Théophile de Viau's identity as either a Huguenot or a Catholic, a skeptic or a satirist, did not matter to the state. The question was, could he lawfully publish skeptical opinions, either under his own name or anonymously? The answer came after two years of confinement and interrogation: he could. But the king and his prosecutors simultaneously reserved the power to make it too uncomfortable to engage in such legal expressions of religious dissent. Signaling a transition, the French state was moving from limited tolerance of religious pluralism to a stricter enforcement of Catholic orthodoxy.[24]

In these early decades of the seventeenth century, what was the character of France? Who belonged and who did not? In a few outspoken works composed prior to and during his trial, Théophile proposed answers to these questions. He suggested that French identity could no longer be defined by the Catholic and Calvinist poles that had animated the prior century's wars of religion; in his framing, France was a cultural mosaic most actively threatened by the ultramontane Catholic advisers then gaining ascendancy in the French court.[25] The poet compared France to the ancient empire of Rome.[26] He applauded the French monarch's global ambitions to rival the wealth of the Spanish American empire and to emulate the luxury of the Chinese empire. Simultaneously he equated Catholicism—particularly that of the Jesuit strain—with a globalist zealotry irreconcilable with the diversity of beliefs evident both in the kingdom and across its nascent American colonies. Théophile highlighted the cosmopolitan nature of the French capital city, where visitors spoke a babel of different languages to engage in commerce, scholarship, and sociability. Théophile's narrators were men of the world who could live anywhere, but they chose France. Why? They articulated rationales that likely surrounded the poet and suggest why millions of quiet religious dissenters might have decided to remain in France or to build small corners loyal to the French Crown across the Atlantic in the early seventeenth century, even as the French monarchy ended civil war by enforcing limited religious toleration while waging war against specific dissenting communities. Rich and fertile lands, gracious traditions, and renowned patronage of the arts made France a beacon even amid troubled times. In this portrait, Théophile echoed Montchrétien's characterization of Louis XIII's France, that all the virtues "honor, courtesy, industry, artifice, make their home among us. They are pleased here, and they will stay forever so long as we don't chase them away."[27] The key factor that invited these virtues to remain? Liberty.

Throughout his work Théophile reappropriated the term "libertine" that had been mobilized against him; he made it synonymous with a man freed from a narrow religious upbringing to respect the diversity of languages and customs within France and its empire. Under those circumstances, the poet proclaimed, he would proudly accept the label. In contrast to Garasse, Théophile contended that the libertine who valued freedoms of speech and religion would actually strengthen the monarch he served and the kingdom in which he resided. By using the limited freedoms afforded to religious minorities, libertines demonstrated that the king's law was more powerful even than the Catholic Church. Respect for religious diversity was an essential liberty first provided and always protected by the French king, Théophile reminded his readers, one of whom he certainly hoped would be the monarch himself.

BECOMING SIEUR THÉOPHILE

Along the banks of the Garonne River rested the village of Clairac, where Théophile de Viau grew up. Halfway between the bustling urban centers of Bordeaux and Toulouse, Clairac had provided a refuge to the Viau family during the religious wars that rocked France in the sixteenth century. Born in 1590 to a large Huguenot family that valued education and military discipline, Théophile entered the Protestant university in Saumur in 1611.[28] But rather than studying the law as had his father, or taking up arms to defend the Huguenot cause like his brother, Théophile pursued more diverting occupations.[29] He entered a company of actors, writing and performing for elite entertainment. With this troupe he traveled throughout France before landing in Holland by 1615, where he briefly enrolled in the university at Leiden.[30] The acting life brought him into the orbit of France's leading noble families as they navigated the shifting political and religious shoals that underlay the early years of young King Louis XIII's reign. Théophile entered service as a butler for the Count of Candale, then enjoyed the protection of Roger du Plessis, Duke of Liancourt, at which point he was introduced at the royal court. Within a year or two, he left Candale's household for the protection of the Duke of Montmorency and then the Count of Béthune, where he likely exchanged household service for more artistic employment.[31]

Henri II, Duke of Montmorency, was five years younger than Théophile, but the teenage peer already commanded attention as one of the kingdom's brightest military and political leaders.[32] From a Protestant family—he claimed the late King Henri IV as his godfather—the duke had amassed powerful titles before he turned twenty: admiral of France and Brittany, and governor of Languedoc. In 1620 he purchased the viceroyalty of New France, which granted him extensive authority over the development of colonies along the St. Lawrence River. In this capacity the Duke of Montmorency financed Samuel de Champlain's efforts to chart Canada and establish the legal and commercial foundations of New France.[33] The French cartographer Pierre de Vaulx imagined these *terres nouveaus* to be verdant countryside that could be peacefully claimed under the French Crown's coat of arms (see fig. 1). Under the young duke's protection, Protestant merchants and sailors enjoyed a period of preferment and took the lead settling territories in Canada and besieging Spanish ships in the Caribbean. At the Montmorency estate in Chantilly, Théophile would have found the model for a new kind of French noble: activist, imperialist, and ideologically pragmatic. The duke entered his adulthood committed to the premise that a robust monarchy rooted in religious toleration could integrate the multiple languages and regions of France and build a powerful empire to compete with European rivals.[34] This was the principle to which the poet devoted his artistic voice with the duke's committed support. Throughout Théophile's legal and public struggles, the Duke of Montmorency remained a staunch ally, vouching for his character and literary merit.[35]

In 1619 came the first blow to Théophile's liberty and literary reputation: the king ordered him to leave the French kingdom for having

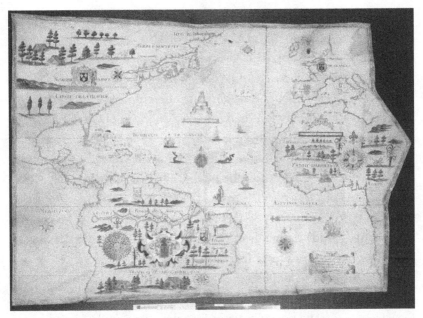

FIG 1. Pierre de Vaulx, *Map of the Atlantic Ocean*, 1613. n.p. Gallica: Bibliothèque Nationale de France, http://catalogue.bnf.fr/ark:/12148/cb43591772n.

composed verses "unworthy of a Christian."[36] He seems to have sought refuge in England or Holland for some months, and he certainly spent time at the family estate in Clairac. What had inspired this order? Did the king and his advisers object to the themes of sexual seduction, nature and reason, or ribald masculine camaraderie woven throughout the poet's work?[37] Or were royal officials testing out the newly developed powers of censorship forged in the 1618 Rule?[38] It is difficult to say. The kingdom's authorities clearly exercised vigilance in the wake of the trial and public execution of Lucilio Vanini by the Parlement of Toulouse in 1619, and it may be that some of Théophile's verses praising nature's laws struck too familiar a chord with that disgraced theologian's assertions.[39] Théophile likely also found himself on the wrong side of the intensifying political struggle between the young king and his family, the final religious wars to rock the kingdom from 1617 to 1632.[40]

Seeking to return to his homeland and political favor, Théophile appealed to the king directly. In the ode "To the King from Exile," he emphasized Louis XIII's far-reaching power and articulated a compelling theory of absolute monarchy. The narrator acknowledged that an all-powerful God placed the scepter in the king's hands, but retained the capacity to take that power tomorrow.[41] These were hardly the words of an inveterate skeptic, but his phrasing also emphasized the common theological ground between the Protestant and Catholic subjects of the French king. Louis XIII, slow of speech, prone to stuttering, menaced by Catholic fanatics on one side and Reformist zealots on the other, fearful of manipulation by powerful nobles and his own mother, struggled to extend royal authority over the extent of his domains in these early years of his reign.[42] But the pen of Théophile depicted the young king as the fulfillment of God's design, heir to a powerful family lineage destined to dominate Europe and, from there, the globe.

According to Théophile's verses, the court, that sociable center surrounding the king, represented the best of France. To be cast out from that haven flung the poetic narrator into despair, as he lamented in the lines below:

AU ROY, SUR SON EXIL

Esloigné des bords de la Seine,
Et du doux climat de la Cour,
Il me semble que l'œil du jour,
Ne me luit plus qu'avecque peine

Aujourd'huy parmy les Sauvages
Où je ne trouve à qui parler,
Ma triste voix se perd en l'air,
Et dedans l'echo des rivages :
Au lieu des pompes de Paris,
Où le peuple avecques des cris
Benit le Roy parmy les rués,
Icy les accens des corbeaux
Et les foudres dedans les nues
Ne me parlent que de tombeaux.[43]

Far from the banks of the Seine
And the gentle climate of the Court
It seems to me that the sunrise
Provides only pain with its light

Today among the S*v*ges
Where I find none with whom I may speak,
My sad voice disappears in the air
Amid the echo along the shores:
Rather than the pomp of Paris
Where people with cries
Bless the King among the streets
Here the accents of crows
And thunder in the clouds
Speak to me only of tombs.

Tombs. Storms. Croaking crows. Life is desolate indeed, banished from the capital and the king's presence, and whether the narrator has imagined himself to be in a foreign land across the seas inhabited only by taciturn humans and crows, or in a rural province peopled by uncurious rustics, is of little consequence. Even before Michel de Montaigne's essay "On Cannibals," published in 1580, the concept of the "savage" performed important work in early modern letters.[44] In French the term approximates "wild" and is applied to mushrooms and horses as well as people and was invoked by Europeans to identify individuals from the Arctic Circle to the Straits of Magellan. Jacques Cartier deployed it throughout his account of exploring the coastline and interior of "New France" in 1534.[45] Jean de Léry used it repeatedly in his *Histoire d'un voyage faict en la terre de Bresil*, an account of a Calvinist colonial experiment in South America published in 1578.[46] In this account Léry spoke with admiration of how leaders of the Tupinambá people harmonized social order with the environment and natural laws.[47] In the years following the Wars of Religion, Montaigne suggested the term was better applied to those

French men and women who massacred their neighbors over points of theology, or the Portuguese who had slaughtered the Tupinambá.[48] They were the real s*v*ges, unrestrained by laws divine or human. In his travel account from Canada, *Of Savages, or the Voyage of Samuel Champlain of Brouages in New France 1603*, Samuel Champlain attended with some detail to the people who inhabited this land across the ocean claimed by the French crown. Likewise, both Claude d'Abbéville and Père Yves d'Evreux favored the term in their accounts of France's Capucin mission to Brazil published in 1614 and 1615, respectively.[49] Théophile's poetic use echoes Montaigne's critique of internecine violence alongside these picaresque travels of Champlain and Evreux.[50] When Théophile wrote of "s*v*ges," he simultaneously condemned the violent bigotry of Christians in Europe even as he recalled an exotic characterization of Americans.[51] If unpredictability and violence characterized the s*v*ge, populations on both sides of the Atlantic had equal claim to that behavior.

Exiled from the court, death and pain are the narrator's only certain companions. Reading these extremist lines, the king's heart must have melted a little. In 1620 Théophile secured a royal order ending his exile, and the Duke of Luynes extended an invitation for him to join Louis XIII in Paris and serve as court poet. Upon receiving this missive, Théophile likely felt some relief at the prospect of rejoining friends, favor, and the pleasing rhythm of the court's calendar of spectacles. But, given his recent experiences, he may have paused for a moment. By returning to court, Théophile proved that he was no hardened dissident, no ideological warrior intent on defying authority. He must have believed himself capable of mediating between the liberties demanded of his art and the obedience required of a courtier. He sought patronage and fame, and, for two short years, he won both.[52]

It is tempting to imagine this brief era when Théophile served the French king as royal poet and dramatist as never-ending rounds of card games, drinking sprees in Parisian cabarets, and revelries with a cohort of breathtakingly talented artists similarly arrayed in lace ruffs and jewel-toned satin doublets.[53] Certainly there must have been some indulgent evenings. Théophile's circle included many friends, some of them powerful like the Duke of Montmorency, others scrappy scribblers who emulated the poet's erudition and connections.[54] These associates would remember him as a gentle and generous man, strikingly handsome, a skilled actor and one of the most playful, innovative authors of his day.[55]

Théophile seems to have excused himself occasionally from the social whirl, however, because he wrote an astonishing corpus of poems, prose, and dramatic works during these few years. His name sold books; in both 1620 and 1621, volumes attributed to Théophile appeared for sale in the bookstalls in Paris.[56] Banishment and the subsequent return to favor seemed to have only heightened his popularity, putting this obscure southerner on a first-name basis with the kingdom's most discriminating readers.[57] They may have appreciated the themes found in Théophile's graceful verses: nature, pastoral love, and the myths of antiquity revisited for a new age. "We must write in the modern style," insisted his character in the novella "First Day," a sentiment that the author seemed inclined to echo.[58]

What characterized the "modern style" in the 1620s? For many authors of this generation, it meant valorizing the beauty of familiar landscapes and inquiring more deeply into local characters. It also meant attending to the breadth of cultural productions around the globe, not just vaunted figures of Antiquity. The modern author showcased the world's geography, religions, and arts but in language of everyday speech that might forge a kind of colloquial cosmopolitanism. The local and the global ennobled each other in this modern style, positioning the people of this time as equally valid subjects of art and literature as were biblical or Greco-Roman mythological characters.

For example, in the elegy "To Cloris," the narrator recounts his recovery from amorous obsession, situating himself squarely in France to observe the Garonne River as it leads into the ocean.[59] In the homey surroundings of southwestern France, along the banks of the Garonne, walking the sun-dappled plains renowned for their robust vintages, the narrator finds solace in simple daily pleasures. Throughout Théophile's work readers encountered intimate sketches of the offbeat corners of France, but his native region of the southwest and his adopted home of Paris particularly drew his attention. He mentioned the Garonne multiple times in his verse and prose, as well as the Seine and the Loire rivers, the

Pyrenees mountains, and the region of Navarre. Alongside the ancient centers of Rome and Delphi, the poet cited the more proximate cities of Angoulême, Marseilles, Toulouse, and his own hometown of Clairac. But he positioned these domestic urban centers within a wider world; London, Rome, Peru, Spain, Holland, Lebanon, the Arctic, and the Ganges River were all referenced in Théophile's globe-spanning verses. Meanwhile the elites of the French royal court jostled with the gods and heroes of antiquity as worthy subjects of his elegies and odes.

Théophile's name made money for publishers, and he capitalized on this after his arrest, publishing poems and letters to declare his innocence, identify his patrons and persecutors, chastise fair-weather friends, and elevate his profile in the public sphere.[60] He pleaded publicly for the king's favor in poetry and prose in both French and Latin.[61] He identified Garasse specifically, and the Jesuit order more generally, as his persecutors. Although he praised the founder of the Order, Ignatius Loyola, and the Mother Church, he depicted his accusers as bad apples who distorted Church doctrine for their own personal gain. Emphasizing his own limited influence, the poet scoffed at charges "that I teach magic / In the honorary cabarets."[62] He was no threat, he insisted, but a simple entertainer who sought only to pay homage to his patrons and his king.

It was the Jesuits who wielded real power in French government and education, he reminded his readers, and their influence stretched across the globe. All of Europe's

> resources have been bound
> By the black and strong machine
> Whose supple, vast body
>   Stretches its arms all the way to China.[63]

In Théophile's estimation it was this militant clerical order and not a few bawdy poets who posed a direct threat to the French monarch's imperial ambitions. The Jesuits' power had been limited of late by European kings who struggled to assert royal power within their domains.[64] In recent years some monarchs might have been lulled into thinking the struggle had been won and the Jesuits subdued. If that were the case, Théophile recalled to mind the allegations made against the Jesuits in the 1605 Gunpowder Plot against James I in Britain, a conspiracy to blow up Parliament with the king inside it.

Théophile compared the direct attack on the British state with his own persecution by Garasse, noting:

> In France and abroad,
> They have cause to avenge themselves
> And to forge a bolt
> Whose strike would kill me
> Though it might cost more powder
> Than they lost in Whitehall.[65]

Théophile warned the French king and court that the forces orchestrating his own trial represented a threat to the French state's independence from the Catholic Church and its activist agents. The Jesuits would succeed in hijacking the king's own judicial system to serve their community's interests of imposing theological orthodoxy across Europe.

The poet's warning would have come as no shock to the young French monarch. Louis XIII's reign experienced periods of intense civil upheaval, so, in addition to crafting court entertainments, Théophile served in a series of military campaigns upon his return to royal favor. The poet was present—even briefly imprisoned—during the brief battle between the king's troops and the queen mother's forces at the Ponts de Cé outside of Nantes on the Loire River in 1620.[66] Théophile heralded the king's triumph and the kingdom's return to order in an ode entitled "On the Peace of Year MDCXX." He accompanied the Duke of Luynes's brother on a diplomatic mission to England in 1621, where he made the acquaintance of the Duke of Buckingham.[67]

From 1620 to 1621, the king directed troop movements against Protestant rebels throughout the southwest, from Bordeaux to La Rochelle. It is possible that Théophile and his brother Paul even faced each other across the battle lines as the king's armies laid siege to the village of Clairac first in 1621 and again in 1622.[68] Later that year Théophile lamented the destruction wrought on his hometown in a powerful sonnet:

Deep ditches filled with rubble,
Spectacles of fright, of shouts, of funerals,
River where blood runs without end
Graves where Crows and wolves will devour all,
Clairac, for the one time you gave me birth,
Alas! How many times you have killed me.[69]

Devastation resulted from the king's continued wars and from the ongoing resistance mounted by the kingdom's Huguenot towns.

That same year Théophile publicly converted to Catholicism. He provided no explanation of his decision to leave the faith of his family, to whom he remained devoted in loving correspondence and powerful verses, and we might conclude that the young king's aggressive actions against Protestant subjects left ambitious courtiers little choice but to renounce reform.[70] But if Théophile considered his conversion to be sufficient cover for his art, he was mistaken. He clearly understood the inherently political act of declaring oneself to be apolitical. This is essential context for the positioning of the author and many of his poetic narrators. When Théophile used the term *libertin* to refer to himself, it was always in an ironic manner that subverted any grander theological significance and so deflated alarmist cries of atheism. In an elegy to Théophile's noble patron, the Count of Candale, the narrator invokes the term to observe that he has difficulty displaying the obedience required of a household servant:

ELEGIE

Je ne puis etre esclave & vivre en te servant
Comme un Maistre d'hostel, Secretaire, ou suivant.
Telle condition veut une humeur servile,
Et pour me captiver elle es un peu trop vile,
Mais puis que le destin a trahy mon esprit,
Et que loin de Perou la fortune me prit,
Je crois aimer mon joug, m'y rendre volontaire,
Et dedans la contrainte obeyr & me taire,

C'est d'un juste devoir surmonter la raison,
Et trouver la franchise au fond d'une prison.[71]

I cannot be a slave and live to serve you
Like a butler, a secretary, or follower.
Such a post requires a servile humor
And is a little too common to appeal to me,
But since destiny has betrayed my spirit
And far from Peru fate found me,
I must love my burden, submit willingly,
And within constraints, obey and keep quiet.
It is a proper duty to conquer reason,
And find freedom at the depths of a prison.

Ambivalence characterized the speaker's relationship with a position of service. But circumstances demanded the narrator's submission to the largesse of the nobleman's sponsorship, and, happily, the patron's character made such obedience tolerable. Portraying his soul as one destined for fame, fortune, and exotic travels to the fabled realms of American empires, he acknowledges that, at least for the moment, these gifts have eluded him. Ah, well, the narrator shrugged:

Or je suis bien-heureux sous ton obeïssance,
En ma captivité j'ay beaucoup de licence,
Et tout autre que toy se laisseroit en fin,
D'avoir si librement un serf si libertin,
Le soin de te servir est ce qui moins m'aflige,
Et l'honneur de te voir est-ce qui plus m'oblige.[72]

Still I'm happy under your command,
In my captivity I maintain great freedom,
And anyone else but you would tire
Of freely keeping such a libertine serf,
The duty of serving you is what afflicts me least
And the honor of seeing you most gratifies me.

Freedom here is the opposite of the servant's position of dependence on a master. And, in those terms, the narrator recognizes his own situation as an existential enigma: he is both materially dependent and intellectually free to compose verse and pursue art. In the paradoxical pairing of the "libertine serf," Théophile encapsulated the predicament of the elite artist, the versifier for hire. In this passage the libertine poses no diabolical threat, as claimed by Father Garasse. Instead he embodies a quotidian concern: How might freedom of thought and speech flourish within the bonds of dependence and obligation that defined society in early modern France? As Théophile sketches him, the libertine is a sort of fool, the figure who may ridicule elites and speak truth to power, but in so doing identifies and enhances that source of power.[73] The poet reminds his readers that the free servant is a paradox, but one that reflects well on the nobleman who maintains such men in his employ. A freethinking servant showcases his patron's largesse, communicating the lord's power to a broader public. In the end it is a calculation that benefits both parties, according to this and other similar patronage poems. Praising his protector's demeanor, conversation, servants and houses, the narrator concludes by keeping it all in perspective:

> J'estime ton merite,
> il vaut mieux que le Gange,
>
> Tes richesses au prix
> sont de terre & de fange.[74]
>
> I admire your merit, it is worth
> more than the Ganges,
>
> Your riches are nothing
> but earth and blood.

In later poetic and dramatic compositions, the poet further explores how intellectual freedom squares with political duties. Taken together Théophile's narrators trace the social bonds—between lovers, friends, servants and masters, subjects and rulers—that were to bring French society back together after civil war. From these intimate duties shared between individuals, a common political good becomes imaginable. In these passages Théophile highlights the libertine's lack of criminal behavior, emphasizing instead that enduring bonds of obedience and service bound servants and masters, subjects and monarchs, despite theological differences.

In a direct address to the French king, composed in 1620, Théophile again used the polemical term "libertine" to communicate a general freedom, not criminal disorder nor politico-religious challenge. The best guarantor of freedom was a strong virtuous monarch, contended Théophile in verses that articulated, first, the necessity of monarchy within European politics and religion, and, second, the preeminence of the French monarch over all others. But what was the king's greatest accomplishment? It wasn't enforcing orthodoxy, but assuring the gentle application of the law, which, after all, continued to assure the Protestant population in France and in a few scattered American colonies that they were guaranteed some key protections by the king.[75]

Even the most libertine are happily governed by a king who rules with kindness. Théophile's representation of docile libertines undermines Garasse's alarmist posture. It seems likely that, in employing this keyword of religious reformations, Théophile sought deliberately to challenge the political dialectic taking shape in the French kingdom. Catholic advocates like Garasse strove to convince the king that political order depended on religious unity, and that the king must eradicate all forms of heterodoxy.[76] Protestant political leaders demanded that the king protect their religious liberties secured in the Edict of Nantes against ultramontane Catholics. In contrast to these factions, Théophile imagines a king who transcends religious divisions and unites diverse populations in loyalty to his person and to his law. Théophile's poetic portrayals depict the libertine not as an individual opposed to the law, but as the very embodiment of the law's efficacy. To hail the king as the effective protector of the law declines royal authority to simply make law or to equate personal whims with state policy. Even in this effusive hymn to monarchical power, we recognize a political theory critical of despotism.[77]

Later in the composition, this poem's narrator identifies the Louvre Palace, the Loire River Valley, and the city of Troyes as the centers of the

French court, the center of civilization. The selections merit reflection, for in these lines Théophile connected royal power not to a political theory—an institution apart—but to its disparate and concrete seats across the kingdom. Monarchy exists in space and relationships, enhanced by aristocratic alliances seated in the Loire and sacralized through Church councils held in medieval Troyes.[78] But Théophile simultaneously eschewed an orthodox symbology by including references to mythological gods and the figure of the sun rather than the one god-in-three central to Catholic theology. Moreover, key lines emphasize the vast scope of the French monarch's ambitions. When the narrator observes that libertines and s*v*ges willingly submit to the king's authority, the poem celebrates the religious and geographic diversity of France's empire, implying that political obedience and legal unity need not rest on a common theological foundation. Empire required tolerance, not orthodoxy.

In contrast to the king's ode, those poems written after Théophile's imprisonment largely abandoned the screen provided by classical mythology. Instead he articulated a more recognizable Catholic theology, referencing Rome as the Church's center and acknowledging the martyrdom of Christ as essential for inclusion in French society. No longer did he emphasize diversity as a defining characteristic of the French monarchy and its empire. If the French king had resolved to insist on "one law and one faith" across the kingdom, Théophile's speakers would pragmatically align with this doctrine. In a poem that blurs the lines between art and life, the poetic narrator takes a friend to task for abandoning him during his trial and the burning of his portrait at the place de Grève.[79] The narrator laments the false accusations made against him, attributing them to ignorance and impertinence, and reminds the cherished reader that they know better than to believe such calumny. He runs down the checklist of Catholic articles of faith, refusing to cede to the injurious characterizations of his personal piety to his accusers. Men like Garasse and Molé are "imposters of blind faith" who claim to represent the Church, but actually act against the "liberties of France." He has been accused of all manner of things, including excessive drinking and lovemaking, but his only crime is to be too well known: "Tout le crime que j'ay, c'est d'estre troup cogneu."[80]

In this moment the narrator highlights his own high regard for the law, be it divinely inspired or royally imposed. He simultaneously considers the space between the letter of the law and human behavior while he identifies social relationships as the site from which to rebuild fractured public order. Friends and friendship are the places where France might undertake that work. The narrator appeals to his friends, those people who know him, sit with him, break bread with him, to ask themselves if they recognize the scandalous character portrayed by his accusers. From the foundations of such friendships, the reader may conclude, begins the work of repairing the social fabric of France.

THE COSMOPOLITAN COURTIER

Men's friendships animate Théophile's novella *The First Day* (*Première journée*), which was likely penned after 1619 but prior to Théophile's arrest in 1623. The plot centers on three characters: the narrator, his friend and traveling companion Clitiphon, and an older tutor, Sydias, who takes the role of the Pedant in this brief travel account.[81] The title refers to the narrator's first day after his banishment from the royal court. In explaining to his friends why he is not devastated by his current exile, the narrator offers a quintessentially cosmopolitan attitude: "This disgrace is just words made up of wind. I was chased from the Court where I did nothing; if they force me to leave France, whatever part of Europe that I might go to, my name will make my acquaintances. I know how to accommodate all sorts of customs and dress, differences in Climate or men matter little to me."[82] On this first day of exile, the friends tell stories and visit a tavern frequented by Germans and Italians. The bellicose Sydias is challenged to a duel by a young man on his way to join the army in Holland, but the friends force them to embrace and drink together instead.

In this novella Théophile provides a powerful testimony of the multilingual character of life in early modern Paris. He observes stereotypical national characters, contrasting the Germans of "cold and nonchalant Gravity," with the extravagant civility of Italians.[83] But all men of every nation were better able to appreciate each other's merits after a few drinks, the narrator concluded; differences of language, religion, and custom faded in this fraternal communion of the tavern. But, as later sections of the story make clear, these friends dwelt in a global France open to trade and influences far beyond their European neighbors.

Departing the tavern the narrator sets off for the port, where a ship had "newly arrived from the Topinambours, where I wished to acquire news of one of my friends who was supposed to arrive around that time."[84] By referencing the Tupinambá people of South America in the area of present-day Brazil, Théophile gestured to the wider world that now arrived in France's Atlantic ports, and the heightened investments in France's global imperial ambitions. Continued internecine struggles between Catholics and Protestants or between the representatives of rival Catholic empires imperiled extensive trade networks.

French Huguenot attempts to forge a colony in South America between 1555 and 1567 had been memorialized in Jean de Léry's account. French Catholics and Huguenots joined together in efforts to establish a French fort in Guyana in 1612 and again in 1626.[85] In 1613 six Tupinambá individuals traveled to France in the company of Capuchin monks, part of a publicity campaign designed to drum up popular and royal support for the colony.[86] But a vigorous Portuguese military offensive wiped out the settlement in 1615, and Louis XIII's marriage to a Hapsburg princess further undermined royal support for the colony. Théophile may have mentioned the Tupinambá to remind the French king and Church officials that they ignored the role of France's Protestant population and their contributions to colonial expansion at the monarchy's peril. Who were the more reliable allies? The Jesuits and the Hapsburgs? Or loyal French subjects who happened to follow different forms of worship?

LE PARNASSE SATYRIQUE (1620)

By tracing the contested uses of "libertine" in the prelude to Théophile's arrest and trial, evidence mounts demonstrating how purposefully unstable and ill defined the term remained throughout the early seventeenth century. According to Garasse it was the preferred label for inchoate, unconfirmed skeptics; Théophile himself reclaimed it to signify general liberties of thought, religion, and association. Everyone agreed that it was not against the law to be Protestant or to convert to Catholicism, as the poet had done. He broke no law in being well educated and conversant

FIG 2. Pierre Firens, *S*v*ges in France* (1613). The caption reads, "These are true portraits of s*v*ges from the isle of Maragnon called Topinambous brought to the Very-Christian King of France and Navarre by Sr. Razilly in the present year 1613. These are the postures they take while dancing."

in multiple languages. What, then, had motivated the French king to order his court poet's imprisonment? And what spurred Théophile's abrupt reversal, when in verse and prose he ceased championing heterodoxy to embrace orthodoxy of religious opinion?

The first clue lies in the pages of a collection of scurrilous poems at the heart of the French prosecutors' questions for Théophile. A volume composed by many poets, *Le Parnasse des poètes satyriques*, was published anonymously in 1620, but showcased Théophile's name on the title page. This collection of short witty epigrams and sonnets centered on themes of love and marriage, but in verses that gave humorous voice to both male and female protagonists, frankly discussing sexually transmitted disease, marital discord, and the limits of seduction. A sonnet attributed to "le sieur Théophile" addresses his mistress Phyllis. But, rather than celebrating the pastoral innocence and chaste love associated with the genre, the narrator of this verse laments contracting syphilis from his not-so-fair lady. "I've sweat thirty days, I've vomited muck / Never have such great ills lasted so long," the speaker describes in visceral terms.[87]

His misery, illness, and isolation are Phyllis's fault, the narrator concludes. Simmering misogyny animates these lines of verse, focused specifically on the failings of the no-longer-beloved. In the final stanza, the narrator "repents for having lived so badly." If he survives this illness, he vows, "to only –uck in the ass."[88] Garasse read this line as a vow "to become a sodomite all the rest of his days," preferring male to female sexual partners, with no evidence beyond that offered by poetic tercet.[89] Prior to publication he circulated copies of his critique to influential jurists and courtiers. The royal prosecutor Mathieu Molé corresponded with Garasse and followed the priest's directives regarding the charges to bring against Théophile.[90] Such coordination between the authorities reveals that the purportedly autonomous French judiciary depended on clerical informants to identify and prosecute religious heterodoxy.[91]

Answering Molé's charges Théophile simply insisted that he had not written the offending verses. Moreover, he asserted in court testimony that when he read the lines in a book stall in front of the palace and saw that such content had been attributed to him, he ripped the page from the volume and quarreled with the bookseller.[92] He ultimately

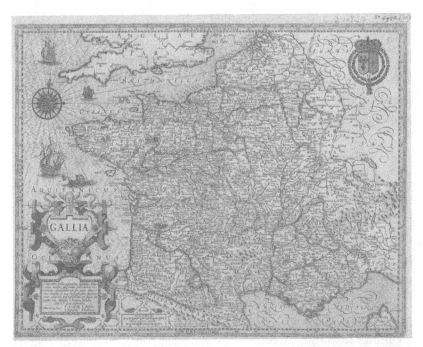

FIG 3. Jodocus Hondius, map of France, 1622. "Gallia: Nova totius Galliae georaphica." Bibliothèque Nationale de France, https://gallica.bnf.fr/ark:/12148/btv1b8492886f.r =hondius%20gallia?rk=42918;4.

agreed to leave Paris but remained in France, perhaps hoping that the affair would blow over, as it had a few years earlier. If anything he was more famous now, with even more powerful friends than had been the case in 1619. But this time his fame and influential patrons could not shield Théophile from punishment. On August 19, 1622, the Parlement of Paris issued an order that identified "Théophile, Berthelot, Colletet, & Frenide" who, as "authors of sonnets of verses containing impieties, blasphemies and abominations mentioned in the very pernicious book titled *le Parnasse Satyrique* will be arrested and taken as prisoners in the Conciergerie of the Palace."[93] The same order prohibited ownership or sale of *Le Parnasse satyrique*, or any other of Théophile's works, "on pain of being declared accessories to a crime, & punished alongside the accused." Initially Théophile took refuge at Chantilly, at the home of the Duke of Montmorency. When the police failed to locate the poet, the

Parisian crowd burned him in effigy at the place de Grève on August 19, 1623.[94] But this public proclamation increased the stakes, and the Duke of Montmorency urged Théophile to leave the French kingdom with all haste in late August 1623.[95] The poet then slowly made his way north to the Picardy region bordering the Spanish Netherlands where he was arrested on September 15, 1623, to stand trial on October 4 of that year.

THE TRIAL, 1623–1625

As Théophile's trial for lèse-majesté-divine opened, the prosecution charged that Théophile was an unrepentant "libertine," using the term as a broad brush to paint both his writings and actions as deviant and destabilizing to the French monarchy. But that accusation identified no crime. For specific criminal charges, the prosecutor adopted a two-pronged strategy: first, to demonstrate that Théophile's poetry deviated from Catholic doctrine into documented heresy, and, second, that the poet pursued and celebrated sexual acts for pleasure outside of marriage, including sodomy.[96] According to Matthieu Molé, prosecutor general in the Parlement of Paris, Théophile was guilty of publishing religious heresy and of cultivating these ideas in a circle of young noblemen who surrounded him at court.[97] Moreover, Théophile's enemies in oppositional pamphlets asserted that his deviance was more than just literary; he was said to encourage young men to join him in drunkenness, debauchery, sodomy, and perversions of all kinds.[98] Thanks to this trial and the public debate surrounding it, Théophile de Viau became the paradigmatic libertine of his own century, and his memory inspired freethinkers and artists of later centuries.[99]

But the prosecution failed on a number of fronts to make the charges of heresy and sodomy stick. In the trial Prosecutor Molé introduced seventy-five of the poet's published texts as evidence, but neglected some of Théophile's most skeptical and materialist works, relying instead on the prose texts that indirectly questioned Catholic doctrine regarding resurrection or demonic possession.[100] Molé confused Théophile's poetic narrators with the author himself, leaving the poet free to deny that any attributed written expressions represented his own personal sentiments.[101] Additionally, the prosecutor failed to collect testimony of immoral behavior from reliable witnesses, depending instead on the poet's court rivals or sworn enemies who quickly admitted to falsifying their accounts. Entering these interrogations with baseless accusations of ill-defined libertine behavior doomed the ambitious prosecutor's endeavor.

One of the most important legal coordinations between Garasse and Molé focused on a scene in the novella *Première journée* published between 1619 and 1622. In his published denunciation, Garasse decried passages in which Théophile made light of demon possession, because, the Jesuit insisted, "to say there are no Demons in the world is a proposition that has its passport among the Libertins."[102] There had been a young woman in the southwest of France who reportedly hosted a demon, and Théophile may have visited her during his first exile from court in 1619. In a prose treatment of the episode, Théophile created characters who recalled a visit to an "obsessed girl," in which the narrator observed that he had spoken to the Devil in several languages: French, Latin, Greek. But the Devil clearly had not traveled, observed the narrator, for it could only respond in Gascon.[103]

In contrast to the provincial Devil, Théophile's characters boasted of wide travels and broad knowledge of multiple languages throughout this episode—indeed, across the entirety of the novella. Is it really plausible, the narrator asks, that an otherworldly demon only speaks Gascon, the dialect of Occitan spoken in southwestern France? That it seemingly comprehends the halting bad Latin of the local priest, but not the fluid educated Latin of a young man trained in classical languages and philosophy? Through these worldly characters, and in humorous form, Théophile rehearses critical, if familiar, theological questions. If demons are universal and transcendent, surely a demon would know either all earthly languages, or none? In posing questions and proffering no settled answers, Théophile perhaps assumed that his art operated within the licit bounds of French religious tolerance. The narrator never asserts that the demon was a fake, nor that the girl was paid or that the attending priest has trained her responses, although such conclusions likely occurred to generations of attentive readers.

With this passage the narrator invites readers to consider the observable fact of linguistic diversity as entry to an ethical stance of cultural relativism that leads to theological skepticism. In the interview with the obsessed girl, Théophile's narrator explicitly positions linguistic education as a tool to critically examine Catholic theology, in much the same way that humanist insights had challenged Church doctrine for centuries.[104] How could a priest demand the public believe in demons, when those demons spoke only in the most uneducated patois regarding matters of the most banal significance? Surely this was not a defining matter of faith for the educated elite? Within a religiously tolerant France there must be space for individuals to both follow Church teachings and question dubious instances of demon possession. From this assertion, obliquely articulated by Théophile's *Première journée*, emerged a more fundamental query: How could the Catholic Church in France claim there existed only one religious truth when neighbors within, and peoples to the north, south, west, and east adhered to divergent religious creeds professed in a diversity of tongues?[105]

Under interrogation Molé asked Théophile if he had visited this girl, and if he had said publicly that it was ridiculous to believe in demons. The poet refused to fall into the trap. He parried the prosecution's charges of heresy, denying authorship of this most controversial of texts, rejecting the prosecution's assumption that his personal theological opinions coincided with those of his poetic or prose characters, and emphasizing his role in simply translating certain ancient texts without providing interpretation.[106]

Upon reviewing the evidence of Théophile's trial, given the uncertain nature of authorship and the grave blunders made in witness testimonies, literary scholar Adam Horsley concludes that the prosecution "committed a crucial error in shifting their focus from Théophile's impiety to his sexuality, thereby neglecting the majority of the poems selected (in part by Garasse, as demonstrated by his correspondence with Molé), to condemn him."[107] This calculation cost the prosecutor a victory and established important precedents for the methods by which evidence was introduced and examined in French courts of law.[108]

In September 1625 the Parlement acquitted the poet of divine treason (*lèze-majesté-divine*). Théophile regretted the limits of his victory in a letter to the Duke of Montmorency: "Having made my innocence clear to the world, still it was necessary to appease the public furor with an order of exile against me."[109] Not a criminal but not exactly free, Théophile keenly felt the injustice of a system that might acquit him of wrongdoing but still refuse to proclaim his innocence. Freed from his prison cell in the Conciergerie, he died within the year, likely from health complications dating back to this insalubrious detention. He remained a rebellious spirit to the end. He declined to comply with the king's order to leave France; under the protection of Montmorency, he remained close to the court and died in Paris in September 1626.

CONCLUSION

At his trial Théophile abandoned his vision of an expansionist, diverse France rooted in tolerance and accepted Molé's assertion that French law required religious conformity—at least in public forums—from all subjects. Adopting Catholic identity and articulating the reliability of his conversion formed the core of Théophile's defense. He insisted repeatedly that he had converted to Catholicism months earlier and accepted the Church's teachings. He identified the priests who had overseen his conversion, pointing to their spiritual authority to buttress his own professions of faith. He denied authorship of the most heretical verses attributed to him and undermined the credibility of the state's witnesses.[110] These proved to be effective tactics. But, in his poetry and prose, Théophile had long contested Catholic orthodoxy as a requirement of French subjects. He drew on allusions from antiquity and Atlantic travelogues to position France at the center of a growing, multilingual, religiously diverse empire. Considering the Viau trial alongside his literary work, this chapter documents how the poet consistently reframed the libertine category as essential for imagining an imperial France capable of embracing people of multiple faiths in contrast to the dogmatic globalism he attributed to the Jesuit order, and how he ultimately abandoned this principle under interrogation.

Imperial cosmopolitanism constituted a central theme of Théophile de Viau's literary output, although this global perspective has been ignored in the scholarship dedicated to better understanding his literary work and trial. The poet valued the capacious liberties promised in a French empire that embraced multiple religious identities. Men like Montmorency and Montaigne had hoped that a strong monarch could knit together his Protestant, Catholic, and Jewish subjects through one transcendent law.[111] Théophile's poetry testifies to the despair of those individuals as the monarch and royal authorities abandoned ideals of religious tolerance, linguistic diversity, and global engagement in the early decades of the seventeenth century. He rooted his art in a broader perspective than that afforded by French Protestantism, and his scope exceeded Christian humanism. At key moments throughout his poetry, his prose, and his trial, the poet articulated his sense that, in a vast world, only France could unite diverse peoples of many faiths and languages who shared common sensibilities: devotion to their monarch, a grace in conversation and the arts, an appreciation of the absurd that lent observations of fact the sharp edge of satire. Don't believe those who would have you believe that Protestants or libertines will destroy society, Théophile counseled; for France to assume its rightful place among the powers of the Earth, its people must cultivate a love of king and country that transcends theological debates. Théophile's familiarity with London and Amsterdam paid homage to those emergent imperial centers of the seventeenth century and testified to his comfort within established Protestant circles of influence.[112] But this was an artist who also wrote love of country in almost every line he penned. Until his death he insisted, despite the troubles he had faced, that all other kingdoms paled in comparison to France for those who claimed freedom as a birthright.

2

Locating the Libertines of New France, 1632–1765

Théophile de Viau's vision of an expansive, cosmopolitan France united by loyalty to a powerful monarch rather than by confessional conformity shimmered just beyond reach, a mirage conjured by political theorists, jurists, and courtiers. But that vision led to the emigration of thousands of settlers—both Protestant and Catholic—who established residences along the St. Lawrence River valley in North America.[1] These communities acquired a reputation of sheltering libertines—committed Huguenots as well as religious skeptics.[2] But the term quickly expanded to locate a unique set of perils in the cross-cultural exchanges that characterized settler societies.

This chapter juxtaposes literary and legal records to investigate the significance of the libertine life in New France and to chart the varied uses of the term by those priests and travelers, judges and defendants, who employed it. I root my analysis in three distinct source bodies that each explicitly considered the libertine as a subversive figure to colonial law and order and circulated those conversations back to metropolitan France: the correspondence and fundraising missives from Catholic missionaries collectively referred to as the Jesuit *Relations*, the Baron of Lahontan's *Dialogues* (1704), and a sampling of laws and court cases generated by the Sovereign Council of Québec. This chapter charts how the idea of the libertine flexed with the extension of state authority across the seas. Royal officers in Versailles depended on alternate institutional authorities than those that came to structure political order in Canada; relationships

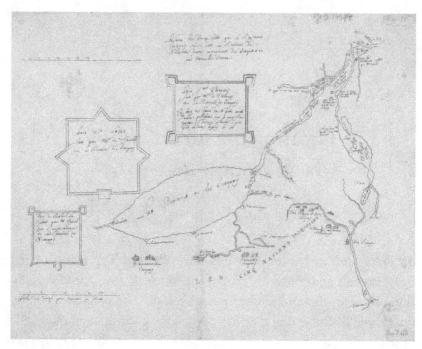

FIG 4. Map of the Saint Lawrence River Valley, Colonial New France, 1660. Bibliothèque Nationale de France, http://catalogue.bnf.fr/ark:/12148/cb405939263.

between civil and Church leaders developed along independent lines in the metropole and colonies, with ecclesiastical officials exercising greater control over family law and morals in New France than in France.[3] These divergent paths expanded quasi-criminal categories in the application of French law. I first orient readers to the libertine category as it acquired novel attributes in New France and then reflect on how aspects echoed back in France. Literary and legal sources reveal that in Québec, as in France, both religious and state authorities came to rely on the category of the libertine to condemn behavior that posed a singular threat to social and political order but did not rise to the level of a technical crime.

What constituted the greatest quasi-criminal threats to social order in New France? First, religious heterodoxy continued to dominate the term "libertine" as it had in France, but in the American context this category included both European and Indigenous theologies. Second, a libertine was any individual engaged in cross-cultural commerce that asserted independence from French regulations, highlighting the colonial state's simultaneous dependence on and anxiety about those exchanges. These conversations proved consequential in weaving theological dissent and cultural hybridity into the warp of libertinism as it took hold across the French Atlantic. Third, a few infractions regularly earned the opprobrium of municipal authorities, requiring both civil punishment and moral correction of offenders including servants who left their masters' service without permission, Europeans who sold alcohol to Indigenous peoples despite repeated prohibitions, and colonists who engaged in sexual activity outside of marriage. Such disparate actions scarcely seem to bear any relation to each other, but, in each case, the actions of individuals flouted established social hierarchies and transgressed the boundaries that colonial authorities believed kept at bay chaos, tumult, and poverty.

LIBERTINES OF NEW FRANCE

Diversity of religious opinion defined the first French colonists in North America. The earliest efforts to colonize New France relied heavily on joint-stock trading companies notably led by Huguenot merchants active in the economies of French Atlantic port towns during the late sixteenth and early seventeenth centuries. Protestants figured prominently among the first settlers and governors of New France, including Jean-François de la Roque de Roberval, Samuel de Champlain, Pierre Chauvin de Rouen, Pierre de Gua, Sieur de Monts, and Guillaume de Caen. As the French monarchy departed from its policy of tolerance of Protestants, formalized in the Edict of Nantes (1598), many Huguenot families took advantage of their extensive and overlapping religious and mercantile networks to take refuge in the Atlantic world. It is estimated that some eighty thousand French Huguenots left France for the Americas, while about one hundred thousand remained on the European continent.[4]

European settlers who professed an array of Protestant faiths posed direct spiritual and political challenges to the proclaimed Catholicity of early French American colonies, as did Indigenous people uninterested in or repelled by the teachings of French missionaries.[5] Ensuring that Europeans, Canadians, and Indigenous people living within colonial communities abided by French law remained an enduring concern.[6] Religious differences resulted in violence between French settlers as well as with their neighbors.[7] Indigenous people quickly learned that they could use these ideological divisions among their new neighbors to their own advantage, and rivalries animated relations among the many missionizing orders as well. Friars from the Récollet order first arrived in Québec City in 1615, the first Jesuit missionaries in 1625. The Récollets, a reform branch of the Franciscan order, announced their spiritual bona fides through evangelical poverty and adopted a strategy dependent on child baptisms in Canada.[8] Both choices contributed to the Récollets' failures to make lasting inroads in Indigenous societies.[9] Militant poverty made the fundraising necessary to support nascent missions more difficult, and converted children failed to convert their communities upon return. Todd Kerstetter notes that the Jesuits "gradually adopted a very different strategy from that of the Récollets."[10] Fundraising was central to their mandate, which gave them a financial advantage over the Récollet friars, who had taken vows of poverty. Moreover, the Jesuits stressed education both for their missionaries and their converts, which fueled the language and cultural exchanges required by missionary work. Initially missionaries targeted the people they presumed to be the most influential members of Indigenous societies: male adult leaders and their adolescent children.[11] Around the Jesuit missions of Québec arose "praying villages" of Indigenous people who professed the faith of the Roman Catholic Church. Many converts remained in close contact with their non-Christian relations and proved to be essential links in the French fur trade, the commerce that defined the colonial economy in these decades.[12]

Early missionaries recognized that theological competition defined the North American milieu.[13] The Récollet friar Gabriel Sagard published his *Histoire du Canada* in 1636 based on his time in Québec in the 1620s. In it he recalls a story from an early French settlement in Acadia when a priest and a minister died at nearly the same time. Sagard relates that the sailors buried them in a common grave to see if they could reside together peacefully in death, since they could never agree during their lives. Entombing a Catholic priest alongside a Protestant minister—unthinkable in France—was presented as a humorous necessity in Québec. Sagard's disapproval is palpable in this passage, which strives to demonstrate that the proximity of religious rivals threatened the piety and conduct of the faithful. For the sailors everything became a joke, including (perhaps especially) points of theology. Sagard muses on how such an objectionable burial could have come to pass among a majority Catholic population and observes that "the lax Catholics adjust easily to the humor of the Huguenots, & these malicious heretics maintain their libertine life, finding no obstacle nor brake to their tyranny even forcing Catholics to attend their prayers and hymns, or they won't be received on Protestant boats nor employed in their workshops, on which point I have often complained but in vain, because God is not respected out here, although His Church is everywhere."[14] Here Sagard wrestles with the responsibility of the faithful amid the economic and social realities of the new colony.

In his *Relation* of 1632, the Jesuit missionary Paul Le Jeune similarly uses the term "libertine" to refer to Protestant colonists in Québec. He relates a story told to him by an English clergyman, "who was not of the same Faith as his people—for he was a Protestant or Lutheran, and the Kers are Calvinists or of some other more libertine Religion (they held this poor Minister a prisoner in our house for six months)."[15] The doctrinal disputes among the many Protestant sects seem to have simultaneously amused and infuriated Catholic missionaries. While it heightened their confidence in the solidity of Catholic doctrine, they were afraid that exposure to such theological disputes—on the nature of the divine, on transubstantiation, or on observation of fast days—would confuse their Indigenous audience.

The religious diversity that had defined the colony at its outset constricted in 1627 when the Cardinal de Richelieu chartered the Company of One Hundred Associates to wield more direct control over the American colonies and proclaimed Catholicism the sole religion of New France. Historian Leslie Choquette observes that, by 1627, "French law explicitly forbade Protestants to settle permanently in Canada."[16] Huguenots who had settled in the territory and started families found themselves required to attend Catholic Mass, marry, and baptize their children in the Catholic Church in order to be permitted to remain in the colony.

By 1663 the French king sought to exert direct rule over New France by establishing a regional court and a law code. As historian Laurie Wood notes, in this respect the French overseas colonies followed an established model designed to absorb new principalities within the French kingdom.[17] The Sovereign Council in Québec City consisted of nine men: the colonial governor-general, the bishop of Québec, the attorney general, five council members, and a clerk.[18] This court presided over a network of lower courts in the colonial communities at Trois-Rivières, Québec, and Montréal. But the council also exercised broad powers to regulate the colonial economy, organize troops and militias, and mediate local disputes. Wood characterizes the colonial sovereign councils as integral to the French global empire's economic and political imperatives, providing legal entrepôts that "catered to those subjects who colonized new territories and sought new trading opportunities beyond Europe."[19] Civil and criminal disputes that came before the Sovereign Council received timely and efficient judgments that constituted the most visible aspect of French monarchical power in Canada.

The Sovereign Council of Québec City, following the king's orders, registered a wide-ranging set of rules for the police of the colony in 1675, addressing especially the establishment of markets, common weights and measures, and building practices. Article 37 concerned the treatment of Protestants within the colony and proclaimed that "it is prohibited to persons professing the so-called reformed religion to gather to exercise their religion throughout this country under threat of punishment."[20] This constituted a colonial experiment in ending the limited religious tolerance promised by the French state that was then applied to the metropole. A decade later Louis XIV ended the fiction of tolerance for French Protestants in France as well, resulting in the mass migration of Huguenots out of the kingdom. Some of those in New France emigrated to nearby Protestant colonies or beyond the reach of Church authorities, but most stayed put, and colonial officials continued a tacit policy of tolerance toward them.[21] The regular publication of royal orders enforcing religious orthodoxy across the colony indicate that it was difficult to enforce an effective ban on Protestant residents.[22]

If Théophile de Viau's case in the 1620s had connected the religio-political charge of libertinism to the realm of prosecutable crimes including freethinking, heresy, and sodomy, then the Jesuit *Relations* and travelers' accounts from Canada united Protestantism with Indigenous theologies and sexual practices. This ideological double helix proposed autonomous female sexuality as the central threat of the libertine ethos. Readers back in France were primed to receive colonial reports penned by missionaries, soldiers, or elite travelers as testimonies from a libertine playground. French readers imagined New France as a topsy-turvy world where Indigenous men and women enjoyed natural liberties and ignored social hierarchies , leaving all people free to pursue their own desires without the intervention of the ever-present Church and state authorities that policed early modern France so effectively.[23]

The religious rivalries of Europe followed colonists and missionaries even as they sought to establish stable communities along the river valleys of New France. Those conflicts informed their encounters with the people of many different Indigenous nations. The elasticity of the term "libertine" served the purposes of the Catholic missionaries in several ways. For one thing, it highlighted the relationship between Catholic theology and political authority. One might assume that rejection of the former resulted in rejection of the latter. Gabriel Sagard recalls that his order undertook the instruction of young boys in French letters, "but as they are libertines and seek only to play and have a good time, they forget in three days what we taught them in four."[24] Here, the term highlights Sagard's concern over the Récollet friars' lack of influence over Indigenous boys. However, when Sagard uses the term in relation to Indigenous girls, it conveys an overtone of sexual morality. Sagard asserts that he finds Indigenous girls to be "wise and honnête," although he admits that, not speaking their language, he is forced to interpret their morality through gestures: "I still doubt that they are libertines, having seen them so modest, without impertinence either in speech or action."[25] It is also possible, he acknowledges, that these girls might behave differently in private than they had in the limited public encounters he had with them.

The Jesuit missionary Paul LeJeune also describes Indigenous individuals, particularly those who questioned Church teachings, as libertine. In his account of a Wendat-Huron woman who had embraced Catholicism, LeJeune acknowledges the resistance that she encountered within her community. But, he observes,

> she knew how to respond—it was the response of solid virtue—to certain libertines who reproached her that all her behavior was only hypocrisy, and that she wished to win the esteem of men by these fair appearances. "That might well have been the case," said she, "when first I began to be instructed; but now that I know what my practice of devotion will be worth to me in Heaven, I do not care to take for sole reward a vain applause which is only smoke, or words which are lost in the air."[26]

The slippage between these various uses of the term "libertine" to indicate Protestants, largely compliant but fun-loving children, sexually expressive women, or skeptical non-Christians reveals that authorities perceived threats to social order from vigorous dissenters as from self-interested pleasure seekers, and that the experience of Reformation-era religious wars framed missionaries' interpretation of Indigenous skepticism.

Following its close connections with leading Catholic missionaries, the colonial state proclaimed the right to oversee the religious observance of all European residents of Québec City and surrounding towns, striving through this surveillance to bring neighboring Indigenous nations into the Catholic Church and under colonial supervision. This was occasionally at odds with the ambitions of the expanding military-commercial state of France. In 1694 the bishop of Québec ordered that he be informed of all "impure speech against the honor of God, the Virgin, and the Saints spoken by Jacques du Mareuil, the lieutenant of the *détachement des troupes de la Marine*."[27] Since his arrival in the colony a year prior, this man had been warned multiple times, but he continued to blaspheme. Guarding against impious speech ensured royal power, asserted the bishop. The council concurred.

Over time Huguenot religious practice took refuge within family dwellings, as Catholic authorities either proscribed Huguenot churches from city centers or razed them entirely.[28] In some ways these new sites suited the theological mandates of the reformed religion, stressing a more personal relationship with God and eschewing the worldly goods and temporal power clearly articulated within any Roman Catholic house of worship. Despite policies that disenfranchised Protestant colonists, many remained in Québec, quietly observing their faith in the shelter of their own homes or alongside coreligionist neighbors. After the British conquest of 1759, some Huguenots "resurfaced next to the British participants."[29] French colonists who made themselves known to the British authorities as coreligionists likely perceived some social and political gain from this identity, and they became prominent in both overseas and maritime trade in the period directly following the Conquest.[30]

LAHONTAN'S *DIALOGUES* (1704)

Alternatives to the French Catholic missions were never far away for those who took up residence at the mouth of the St. Lawrence. The Inuit, Haudenosaunee, Wabanakis, Huron-Wendats, Mi'kmaqs, Naskapis, Algonquins, Atikamekw, Crees, British, Dutch, and even Swedes regularly crossed paths with the residents of New France.[31] It was this context of the vast American marketplace of theological ideas that the Baron of Lahontan and his editor, Nicolas de Guedeville, positioned the publication of the officer's *Memoirs* and the *Dialogues* between "Lahontan" and the Huron chief "Adario." This early "best-seller" was reprinted over a dozen times and "translated into multiple European languages."[32] It must be noted that the following discussion reveals little about Indigenous theology or historical Wendat social practices.[33] But Lahontan comments directly on current events of Québec circa 1700. This critical year for the future of the French colony witnessed colonial officials negotiate a lasting peace with the neighboring Iroquois nation by signing the historic Peace of Montréal, signed by over one thousand Indigenous and French colonial leaders.[34] In a prefatory note, the author observes that the character of Adario was loosely based on the Huron leader, nicknamed "The Rat," or "Muskrat," with whom the author had the opportunity to speak on several occasions.[35] This would have been Kondiaronk, a charismatic and respected man in his forties at the turn of the eighteenth century.[36] An intimate of the governor-general Louis de Buade de Frontenac and the Jesuit Etienne de Carheil, Kondiaronk played an important role navigating the interests of Huron communities between rival Iroquois nations and French and English settlers until his death in the midst of the peace negotiations that took place in Montréal during the winter of 1700–1701. Although he passed away before the great peace treaty was signed, so crucial was his support of the plan to his own nation and to the success of the French that his aides signed his name "Le Rat" and added his icon to the treaty several days later.[37]

The *Dialogues* provide no record of Kondiaronk's theology, nor does the text offer an accurate portrayal of Huron social systems. However, the conversation between Lahontan and Adario reveals historically grounded insights when read alongside the judicial and administrative records of colonial Canada. The ecclesiastical court of Québec and royal directives regularly clashed over questions of religious observance and instruction, alcohol sale and distribution, and sex and marriage in the communities of New France. It was precisely these practical matters that concerned the French and Huron characters in Lahontan's brief text.

Reading the *Dialogues* against the evidence provided by the colony's court cases renders the document less an abstract statement of political ideals of liberty, and more a timely comment on the promise and perils of cultural negotiation and accommodation in the woodlands of New France. Libertine behavior was defined, prosecuted, and tolerated beyond France, and colonial authorities recognized multiple forms of antiauthoritarianism. French experiences of overseas empire shaped this concept, incorporating powerful Indigenous theological resistance to European religious truth claims, and registering contested jurisdiction between leaders of the Church and the colonial state. Furthermore, the text comments directly on the problems that French military men and colonists perceived with universal truth claims made by the Catholic Church in the face of widespread theological disagreements.

The author opens the *Dialogues* with a proclamation by his European character that he would like to discuss "the most important thing in the world . . . the great truths of Christianity."[38] The Huron character responds that he has many questions on the things preached by the Jesuits that strike him as unbelievable. Adario reminds his interlocutor of his extensive experience with Europeans, noting that "you know that I have been to France, New York and Québec where I studied the morals and doctrine of the English and the French. The Jesuits say that among five or six hundred types of religions on the earth, there is only one that is good and true, which is theirs, and without which no man will escape a fire that will burn his soul for all eternity, and nevertheless they don't know how to prove it."[39] Lahontan scripts in Adario a cosmopolitan North American counterpart to Théophile de Viau's narrators: the man who has traveled, mastered multiple languages, and developed the expertise from which to question religious dogma.

When Lahontan points to Scripture as providing proof of Catholic doctrine, Adario responds that people can publish all sorts of lies in books and advises his companion to just look at all the falsehoods that have been said about Canada in the Jesuit *Relations*. He then adopts a humanist criticism of the Bible, asking, "How can you ask me to believe the truth of these Bibles written so long ago, translated from several languages by people ignorant of its true meaning, or by liars who changed, augmented and diminished the words that we see today?"[40] These sacred books are full of contradictions, Adario continues, and he points to the rival sects of Christianity as evidence. The French and the English say that they read the same Bible, but "there are more differences between their Religion and yours than between night and day."[41] At this Lahontan attempts to explain that Europeans might all read the same book but interpret passages differently. The central difference between the French and the English, he asserts, is "that the French believe the son of God having said that his body is a piece of bread, we must believe that is true, because he couldn't lie," while the English believe Jesus "is only spiritually in the bread."[42]

Adario is incredulous that a seemingly minor interpretive difference in the nature of the Communion Host could really be at the root of "such heat and animosity and this is the principal motive of hate between your two Nations."[43] Other contradictions abound, Adario observes, including why an all-powerful God did not know immediately that Adam and Eve had eaten the apple from the Garden, and why successive generations must be punished for that action? Why would He "so abase himself to remain a prisoner for nine months in the entrails of a Woman"?[44] Adario concludes that, for his own people, proof that the Jesuits' God is the one and only God would be easily established if that deity simply descended "in triumph to be seen by many people, revive people, give sight to the blind, make the lame walk and heal the sick: speak and command, go from Nation to Nation doing great miracles to give the same Law to the world, that way we would have one Religion, and this uniformity would prove to our Descendants the truth of this religion known in four corners of the world."[45] Until that time, however, Adario perceives no reason to abandon the ways of his elders.

Adario's criticism of the Catholic Church does not stop at Scripture, either, but continues to indict its priests and missionaries for behavior that he deems criminal. Those that follow laws of abstinence are thieves, he contends, for they eat and drink but, in failing to reproduce, return nothing to the land for the future. They take abominable precautions to prevent pregnancy and disrupt Indigenous households. Among women who excite their passions, they present a very different explanation in private than the one they sell in public, "without which they could not authorize their libertinage, which the rest of you see as a crime."[46] Priests who break vows of celibacy and seduce and impregnate Indigenous women posed problems in the networks within and between the French colonial state and the Huron nation. But was the problem sex, as perceived by the Catholic Church? Or was it the hypocrisy and failure to take responsibility for the results of sexual relations, as perceived by Adario?

In examining the Huguenot network that facilitated the publication and translation of Lahontan's work throughout Europe, France Boisvert notes the important role played by Nicolas Guedeville in editing Lahontan's *Memoires* and *Dialogues*, often infusing raw observations with political and theological import.[47] She concludes that "it is time to recognize that the Dialogues of Lahontan and those edited by Guedeville perpetuate the symbolic pact linking Indigenous Americans to the Calvinists oppressed under Louis XIV."[48] In the context of this expansive community, criticism of the Jesuit missions necessarily entwined with Protestant theology and the French colonial state. Boisvert laments that Lahontan's categorization as a libertine author has precluded serious study of his work for opinions of religious dissent. Alongside theological critiques the *Dialogues* explicitly address sexual mores in North America, which likely contributed to the text's contemporary popularity.[49]

In seventeenth-century Québec "libertine" was the preferred term to characterize the behavior of servants who had left their master's home without permission. In this usage "libertine" signified a religious crime only so far as the Catholic Church upheld traditional forms of social hierarchy. The Sovereign Council passed ordinances in 1663, 1667, and 1673 affirming that servants who abandoned their posts would meet public punishment for their crimes.[50] On January 24, 1664, Charles LeGardeur, Sieur de Tilly and a councillor in the Sovereign Council, put these laws into effect within his own household. When his servant Louis Lepage abandoned his post, LeGardeur demanded that he be arrested and held in the royal prisons. Nine years later, on June 2, 1673, LeGardeur, still fighting to keep domestic servants in their places, both in his own household and throughout the French colony, requested that his valet Gaudriolles be punished for having abandoned his post nearly six months prior, on the 12th or 13th of January of that year. The valet, Marin Varin, nicknamed Gaudriolles, who had been located and imprisoned in Québec City, was brought before the Sovereign Council. He acknowledged that he had worked for the Sieur de Tilly for nearly three months and had agreed upon the wages of twenty-four livres per year. He then indicated that he had not left service altogether; he named some of the other residents with whom he had stayed for two or three weeks at a time: "He served Sieur Crevier and only left his service because he did not provide any clothing."[51] The council sentenced Varin to return to Tilly's service and to pay his master fifty sols for each day of his absence, working for him until the debt had been paid off. Moreover, Varin was ordered to spend two hours in the stocks, with a sign over his stomach that read "Servant Who Left the Service of His Master," and to pay a fine of one hundred sols. Those people who had harbored Varin were also fined one hundred sols each. The case concluded with the Sovereign Council's observation that the council, "seeking to remedy the abuses that increase daily through the desertion of servants from their masters' service despite the punishments ordered by the above laws, and to the great detriment of the colony, prohibit all servants from abandoning the service of their masters on pain of being placed in the stocks for the first time, and for the second time to be beaten with thorns and mark them with the brand of the fleur de lys."[52] Such public disciplinary actions announced colonial officials and the monarchy's shared interest in shoring up the patriarchal authority of masters and fathers.

Several other runaway servants received similar punishments in 1673 as the colonial state sought to make an example of those who flouted accepted social hierarchy.[53] On August 14, 1673, Jacques Renaud was sentenced to two hours in the stocks with the sign "Servant Who Left His Master's Service for the First Time," after abandoning the home of his master, Mathurin Moreau.[54] Renault Chollet, appealingly nicknamed "Liberty," fled his master, Sieur Saintour, a week or so after the Feast of St. John the Baptist in late June. The colonial state caught up with him on October 30, 1673, and Chollet "acknowledged having erred through his libertinage."[55] He was sentenced to two hours in the stocks, bearing the odious sign that publicly identified him as a runaway servant, and the court warned him that, should he repeat his error, he would be whipped and branded with a fleur de lys, representing the royal rule that masters could call upon even in the snow-drifted streets of Québec City.

Charles Bellon deserted his master, the merchant Jean Quenet, in December 1715. Quenet insisted that the Sovereign Council arrest and detain Bellon until he agreed to return to Quenet's service, and then outlined his investment in this servant. He had paid Bellon's passage to the colony from La Rochelle and given him an advance on his wages amounting to two hundred livres worth of clothing and domestic items.[56] Indentured servants throughout the American colonies found that their masters' initial investment in their passage meant that colonial officials tolerated masters who paid no wages, provided poor living conditions, and meted out regular abuse for the term of a servant's contract.[57]

Jean-Baptiste Hervieux had been apprenticed to the arquebusier Jacques Thibierge by his older brother and guardian. When young Hervieux fled his master's household, this older brother and his family were held responsible for the young man's lost days of work and expected to compensate Thibierge for the inconvenience. The elder Hervieux petitioned the city officials of Montréal for help in correcting his errant brother, who had been raised and fed at his table and honorably supported as his own child, "despite this and all the care and attention paid him by the supplicant, he has given himself to libertinage such that he has been found in disorder."[58] In a personal letter dated August 24, 1715, one of very few preserved in the archives of the Sovereign Council, Hervieux's stepmother addressed the young man directly, insisting that "what today gives me the greatest chagrin is that you are a debauch by profession given to all sorts of vice gambling drinking and indecency. These are lovely qualities in a young man. They said it was two or three days before they even knew where you were."[59] She warns him that his brother will suffer professional consequences if Jean-Baptiste does not return to his assigned post and abandon his "criminal debaucheries," signing the letter with her own name, Genevieve Gariépy.

A servant or apprentice who abandoned their post affected not just their master's household; their actions reflected on their family and friends as well. Broad networks mobilized to recover individuals who had fled their professional obligations, and colonial administrators strived to communicate the severity of the punishments that awaited such derelictions of duties. More than strict social order, however, the colonial economy required a flexible labor force to travel long distances by river or sea. Entrepreneurs hired men willing to engage in the privations of the fur trade or military expeditions upon which the colonies depended, and did not inquire too deeply into their background or qualities. Nicknames abounded in this land, adopted or dropped as the situation required men to be anonymous or identifiable.

Not only errant servants risked being called libertine; sons and a few daughters who defied their family also found themselves arrested by the king's orders at their parents' request. In 1684 the French Crown decreed that the sons and daughters of Parisian artisans and poor "who mistreat their fathers and mothers and who do not want to work due to libertinage" would be detained by the French state: boys at Bicêtre and girls at Salpetrière Hospital.[60] Some of these individuals might be detained indefinitely on the king's orders.[61] Some found themselves exiled to the American colonies as punishment for their disobedience. Even after the French state technically prohibited the migration of Huguenots to Canada, the king and his ministers periodically adopted policies that sent vagrants, outcasts, and criminals to the colonies of New France. Historian of Québec Josiane Paul notes that while the "kings of France, particularly Louis XIV opposed emigration as judicial punishment," because, from their perspective, "penal deportation contradicted the fundamental laws of the kingdom," this did not mean prohibition of such transportation.[62] Under the regency forced emigration began with the transportation of those accused of vagrancy from 1720 to 1726 and continued throughout the French colonial period, formally ending only in 1763 with the Treaty of Paris transferring dominion over the inhabitants and institutions of New France to Great Britain.

The archives of Québec reveal the traces of such French transportation policies, such as the 1752 criminal trial of Louis Bonin, a corporal in the Lanaudière company garrisoned in Québec, and Denis Lemoine "Parisian," a fourteen-year-old soldier in the same company, lodged at the Dauphine caserne. Of Denis Lemoine the records observed that he had been sent to Canada nearly a year prior on the ship *Le Catin* "due to his libertinage."[63] Under the expansive powers afforded by the royal *lettres de cachet*, sons and daughters who dishonored their families by committing a wide array of offenses might be imprisoned or exiled, and New France became one of the chief destinations for these libertines. Paul documents the royal policy advanced between 1723 to 1749, using those detained by lettres de cachet by familial request and for salt smugglers (*faux-sauniers*) to populate New France. As secretary of state of the navy, the Count of Maurepas sought to extend the colonial endeavors initiated under his predecessors.[64] He advanced policies aimed to develop populations in New France and to extend agricultural production. Paul notes that although theoretically the French state supported colonial settlement, in practice royal officials opposed any measures designed to spur large-scale emigration from France.[65]

During these decades it was briefly French colonial policy to send some errant *fils de famille* to New France. Officially it was hoped that they could start anew without the distractions of life in France, prove themselves to be worthy subjects, and enrich the colony through their labor. However, Maurepas soon determined that this experiment had been a debacle. Most of these young men came from elite families—although some may have received military training, none were suited to the physical demands of agricultural labor or continental trading that made fortunes in New France.

For example, Gilles François de Ganneau de Senneville arrived in Québec in 1736 aboard the merchant vessel *Saint Joseph de Québec*, accused by his mother of libertine behavior.[66] She presented a timeline of her son's conduct with her request for a lettre de cachet in 1736. Beginning in 1721, after the death of his father, Gilles had completed his studies at the College de Chartres and rejoined his mother in Paris where he "gave himself to debauchery of all kinds."[67] This behavior seems to have persisted until 1727, when he joined the musketeers while continuing to drink, gamble, and carouse, until he was involved in a fight in the streets of Paris and asked to leave the company. In 1728 his mother sent him to live with an uncle, then had him detained for several months in a monastery in 1730. Unfortunately, she related, he could not remain there due to the disorder of his lifestyle—a vague description that hints at more serious troubles. His mother then had him sent to the Isle Sainte-Marguerite, a small island known for its prison fortress, located off the coast of Provence, where he remained for three years. While there, however, he "continued to live in libertinage and contracted many debts and was about to enter a bad marriage."[68] His mother opposed the marriage and called him back to Paris. This time she decided to confine her son to a monastery in Brie, where he remained for three months, but the "monks no longer wanted to keep him due to his continual debaucheries, insulting and hitting everyone when he had wine, and contracting debts just like everywhere else he had been."[69] His mother then sought king's orders to have him imprisoned at St-Lazare, where he was detained for eighteen months. She consented to free him at last when he promised to change and leave France for Québec. Upon his arrival there, though, she learned that he continued to drink and gamble just as before. As a result his mother corresponded with Maurepas, requesting that her son be forbidden to return to France without her permission. In 1740 Maurepas observed that the family still did not want Gilles to return to France, and that they remained willing to pay an annual pension of eight hundred livres to ensure that he remained in New France.[70]

Claude Le Beau arrived in New France in 1729 after a conflict with his father. Lacking employment or friends, he fled the French colony, ultimately making his way to Amsterdam, where he wrote his memoirs, which were published in 1738.[71] This work, quickly condemned upon its publication as derivative of Lahontan, Lafitau, and Hennepin, in fact offers a few rare insights into the experiences of those young men transported to Canada under lettres de cachet. Le Beau conceals from his audience that he had been detained at his father's request: in the *Avantures* the narrator seeks a position as a secretary to the intendant of Québec but is mistakenly taken for one of the eighteen young men transported to New France at their parents' request.

The lieutenant of the ship articulates a sardonic assessment of the familial uses of lettres de cachet. According to Le Beau the lieutenant states that he had met many others akin to the narrator,

> those young men like you who, to honor their Parents, have never done anything but what is good and true, and always tried to make them happy. But those mean Parents, who are already in an age when they no longer like the pleasures of life, don't want to see in their Children's behavior the tableau that daily provides a sad reminder of their own past. That's why they would rather send them far away to Canada, so that if the kids are going to have fun, it won't be under their eyes or at their expense.[72]

The character of the lieutenant in this narrative gives voice to a growing segment of society that perceived libertinage to be a stage of life, indicative of a generational dispute over right conduct rather than a sign of any particular population's inherent and enduring lawlessness. Le Beau was astonished to see that among the prisoners were two old classmates, Pierre Charles Narbonne and Guindal; in fact Narbonne appeared on the register for the *Elephant*, the ship that transported Le Beau from La Rochelle to Québec. The son of a *commissaire* in Versailles, Narbonne had held trusted positions within the royal administration until 1726. Charged with the delivery of some important papers to Fontainebleau, the young man had stopped instead in Paris, spending over nine days and five hundred livres in "debauchery with Libertins and Libertines."[73] In a petition to the authorities, Narbonne's father lamented that his son was "a child of lies filled with all sorts of vice, rebel to God's commandments who lives without faith, without law, without religion and without respect for anything."[74] He agreed to provide a modest pension for his son in Canada, one hundred livres per year, which he asked be disbursed in small increments so as to discourage his son from plunging again into libertinage. About Guindal we know nothing—no such name exists on the hospital or prison registers, nor on the ships' manifests from these years.

At best we can arrive at anecdotal outcomes for the errant young men who arrived in New France under king's orders who had been identified as libertines. Once transported they lacked family support, often made friends with each other, joined the military, or found other work including colonial administration, law, or medicine. Many fled south to the British or Dutch colonies, or else made their way back to Europe. Some did this through the accepted channels, by requesting permission to return to France from the king or their families, while many more simply found passage back to France.[75] By 1730 Maurepas had acknowledged the failure of the policy that used lettres de cachet to transport errant sons to the French colonies in New France. The governor-general of Québec requested that the French Crown cease the transportation of these fils de famille, who were not accustomed to the physical labor required of all settlers in New France.[76]

Royal directives pursued a new tactic from 1730 until Maurepas's fall from power in 1748. During this period the French government sent over six hundred salt-and tobacco-smugglers to the Québec colony. These forced migrants comprised over 50 percent of all French subjects to cross the Atlantic during this period.[77] Many stood accused of behavior that, though classified as a crime in France, was not illegal in Québec. The salt tax had become despised throughout France; the tax varied a great deal by region, a variety that seems to have encouraged illegal interprovince sales of salt.[78] Salt could sell for six livres per *minot* in some areas, and over fifty livres in other areas.[79] Smugglers were men, and a few women sent with their husbands or for their own crimes, who had the skills to survive in the communities of New France. Many were from more agricultural backgrounds than were the largely urban population of libertine young men. They had proven themselves in commerce, and a number of them seem to have found in New France a society in which their initiative could thrive.[80]

DRINKS AND TREATIES

By far the most common invocation of the term "libertine" in the archives of colonial Québec concerned those people guilty of breaking the colonial state's treaties with neighboring Indigenous communities that agreed to limit the sale of alcoholic beverages. Perceived as a problem from the early days of the Québec colony, alcohol had the power to transform the drinker's personality, lower inhibitions against violence and warfare, and remove a sense of responsibility for one's actions. These qualities proved particularly problematic in the context of cross-cultural commodity exchange between European and Indigenous communities.[81]

In 1632 the Jesuit Paul Lejeune observed that, "upon our arrival in Kebec, we heard of the death of six prisoners held by the S*v*ges, the result of the drunkenness which has been introduced here by the Europeans."[82] He explained further that the Montagnais tribe had sought a peace treaty with the Iroquois of that area. The guard in charge of the Iroquois prisoners got drunk on English brandy and incited one of his fellows to kill one of the prisoners. An English minister who witnessed the slaying berated the guard, saying that, in allowing this prisoner to be killed, the guard had failed to keep his word. "It is thou," answered the S*v*ge, "and thine, who killed him; for, if thou hadst not given us brandy or wine, we would not have done it."[83] This exchange illuminates the relationship between liquor and warfare signaling alcohol as an enduring for French and British critiques of imperial trade in North America.[84]

Le Jeune renewed his critique of European sales of alcohol to Indigenous people in 1636. On January 22 of that year, "one of our residents was condemned to a fifty livres fine for having made some S*v*ges drunk. The best laws in the world are of no value, if they are not observed."[85] At first, these laws seem to have figured prominently in French-Indigenous alliance treaties, the prohibitions made at the request of Indigenous leaders who did not appreciate the disorders alcohol bred within their communities. Such laws attempting to restrict the sale of alcohol to certain places, times, days, and populations were continually renewed and just as continually broken. The Sovereign Council of Québec passed laws prohibiting the sale of alcohol to Indigenous people in 1657, 1663, 1664, 1667, 1669, 1676, 1679, 1683, 1699, 1700, 1703, 1707, 1709, 1721, 1745, and these laws were maintained under the English regime in an order dated 1764.[86] The 1663 law specified the dangers that colonial authorities perceived in the sale of alcohol to Indigenous communities; it prohibited all people to "trade or give, directly or indirectly, any inebriating drinks to the S*v*ges, under penalty of a 300 livres fine for the first offense, and whipping or banishment in the case of repeated offenses."[87] The law itself observed that, despite civil and Church laws prohibiting the sale or exchange of alcohol between Indigenous people and French colonists, "this unhappy commerce continues" and had even increased in the past two years, such that "seeing more and more disorders result, and that the S*v*ges inclined to drunkenness hold the laws of Christianity in contempt, surrender to all sorts of vices, and abandon the hunt, which is this colony's only means of surviving day to day," the authorities determined to stiffen the penalties for the sale of alcoholic beverages to three hundred livres.[88] This law articulates the profound dependence of French colonists on their Indigenous neighbors, and the degree to which the pecuniary interests of a few threatened collective survival in Québec.

The terms of French colonial alliances similarly demanded that French inhabitants curb the sale and trade of distilled liquor to Indigenous people. The law promulgated in 1667 made clear the perceived tension between alcohol and Christianity in French-Indigenous relations. The exchange of alcoholic beverages with neighbors from these communities was prohibited, the administrators observed, "due to the disorders that result and that can greatly retard the advance of Christianity among these people either infidels or recently converted."[89] The law made further provisions to have the tenor of the law and its proposed punishments explained by the Jesuit fathers. It is not clear how the missionaries would explain the prohibition of alcoholic beverages on the one hand and rationalize the central role that wine played in the Eucharist on the other.

Between January and June 1667, over twenty-six individuals were questioned and ultimately punished for having given or sold alcohol to

Indigenous people. These depositions provide rare insight into the social networks forged between French and Indigenous residents of colonial cities, forts, villages, and territories. Sieur Villeray served as the head of this commission to prosecute Jean Serreau Saint-Aubin for having traded alcoholic beverages with Indigenous residents, but the investigation soon encompassed French colonists rich and poor in Québec City, Trois-Rivières, and beyond. Jeanne Bouchard, the wife of a farmer, swore that she had never sold liquor. She had exchanged some alcohol with an Indigenous individual the previous fall, she admitted, for some moccasins and four or five pounds of fat, because her husband had been away fighting. Officials responded that she was lying, that they knew she had traded liquor for pelts and silver, which she denied.[90] The resulting sentence identified twelve Frenchmen guilty of organizing an extensive trade in alcohol and pelts. The colonial government fined them each fifty livres and identified the most important Indigenous trading partners as well.

In 1668 the Crown reversed tactics, according permission to "all French inhabitants of New France to trade drinks with the s*v*ges, and requesting them to use it soberly, in light of His Majesty's desire that the s*v*ges will live with his natural subjects in a spirit of gentleness and union to build the promised alliance between them and to best cement it through their continual commerce and visits."[91] The Sovereign Council strived to make sense of this order in terms of their mandate to maintain peace in the colony. The order had the benefit of bringing alcohol sales out of the woods and the realm of the "shiftless, do-nothing libertine people who abandon their cabins and farming to corrupt them [Indigenous people] and take the best part of their hunt." To address this muddled state of affairs, the municipal authorities would take steps to ensure that alcohol was made available only in the colonial cities under government surveillance. This would enable the "better inhabitants to benefit from the profits to be had in providing necessary goods."[92] However, the council also took the king's admonition that Indigenous individuals should use alcohol in moderation as an invitation to punish drunkenness with the sentence of two hours in the pillory and two fat beavers as a fine.

On May 2, 1681, correspondence between the colonial administrators made clear that the liquor trade played a prominent role in the ongoing struggles for influence in the French colony. King Louis XIV had limited the fur trade to specific forts in 1676, and, in this battle against the *coureurs de bois* (woodland traders), colonial administrators also sought to limit alcohol exchange. The Sovereign Council's records reflected an ongoing conversation between the French king and ministers, the governor of Québec, the intendant, and the councillors on the question of the coureurs de bois: "It is undeniable that only the destruction of the *coureurs de bois* can notably augment it (the taxes received from the fur trade), halt the ruin of the colony which is their goal in banning libertinage."[93] The coureurs de bois forged durable alliances with their trading partners, often marrying Indigenous women and seeking adoption by Indigenous nations.[94] They assumed Indigenous methods of transportation, foodways, and dress. However, to their Indigenous trading partners, the coureurs provided access to European material goods, and liquor proved to be one of the most popular items of exchange.[95]

By August 1681 it was clear that the colonial administrators' concerns about the liquor purveyed by coureurs de bois had only increased. The laws prohibiting the transport of alcoholic beverages, threatening punishments of one hundred livres fines for the first offense, three hundred livres fines for the second offense, and corporal punishment for the third had made no impact, "due to the great libertinage of the coureurs de bois who only look after their own interests," in the estimation of the colonial officials.[96] Rumor mills engineered by these independent traders and other "young people" spread fears that the royally sanctioned trading posts sold only poisoned goods, and "that the plague was in these parts, which prevented the Outaouais from coming this year, and thus placed the colony in a state of peril."[97] Colonial officials understood that French inhabitants depended on seasonal trade with allied Indigenous nations and quickly grasped such rumors could endanger the entire colony.

In 1726 Savary de Bruslons's *Dictionnaire de commerce* included an entry for coureurs de bois, commenting on the nature of this short-term trade engagement to make a man's fortune: "This is what they call those Settlers in Canada, who engage in the trade of beaver and other furs, and who seek out the S*v*ges who are friends of the French in their far-flung villages, where they bring them European merchandise to exchange for those of this Country."[98] With twenty *quintaux* of goods including "pots, hatchets, knives, even guns, some contraband, not always with the Governors' permission, although usually with their knowledge, that these traders undertake their journey." Two or three men paddled together at the most and brought back an equal weight of pelts on their return journey. The editor of the *Dictionnaire* observed in judgment that "if these traders were wise, they would make great fortunes; but for the most part, while they make profits, they spend it in feasting, gambling, and debauches of all sorts, only risking a new journey when the money from the first is spent."[99] This stereotype of the hard-working, hard-playing coureur de bois persisted throughout the decades that French trade depended on these independent entrepreneurs.

The Baron of Lahonton observed that the widespread illegal sale of distilled liquor had profoundly destabilized Indigenous communities and routinely threatened French-Indigenous alliances. In his *Memoires* he wrote that "liquor has ravaged the Peoples of Canada, because the number that drink is incomparably greater than the number with the strength to abstain. This drink which is murderous on its own, and which is only brought mixed into this Country, they drink so heavily that one must see its lamentable effects to believe it. It extinguishes their natural warmth and makes almost all fall into that languor we call consumption."[100]

In 1713 the city of Québec gave permission to certain individuals to sell alcoholic beverages, so long as they identified their establishment publicly with a cabaret sign and abided by colonial laws, including the prohibition of alcohol sales to Indigenous people.[101] Such measures would enable the colonial administration to keep closer watch on licit establishments and to threaten punishment for those operating beyond state control. By 1720 the city of Montréal had nineteen cabarets: ten for the French, three for Indigenous people with permission to lodge the French, two for the Iroquois of Sault, two for the Nepissingres, and two for the Ottawas and others who had come to Montréal for the treaty. As over one thousand Indigenous leaders descended on Montréal in 1700 for the great peace treaty that was concluded in early 1701 between France and its Indigenous allies, such provisions for segregated cross-cultural diversion must have struck some compromise between a renewed attempt of commercial exchange between Indigenous and French and the potentially disruptive consequences of integrated drinking.[102]

But in 1721 the colonial intendant returned to blanket prohibitions against any sale or trade of alcohol between French colonists and Indigenous residents and mobilized the colony's guard to the enforcement of this proclamation.[103] The following year Jacques Héry was convicted of having sold inebriating beverages to Indigenous people and sentenced to pay a fine of five hundred livres, received by the central hospital and prison in Montréal.[104] Claude Le Beau, the son of a Swiss guard who had been exiled to Canada for his libertine behavior back in France, articulated a profound fear of those Indigenous people who, despite prohibitions, found access to distilled liquor and drank so much as to be "dead-drunk, others are half-drunk when they kill an Adversary with hatchet blows, still others enraged because they failed to catch enough game kill themselves by their own knife; which rarely happens to tell the truth, but has occasionally, so crazy and furious are they when drinking."[105] By 1745 the intendant had determined to increase the potential punishment, ordering that, even for the first offense, any innkeeper or individual found guilty of having given "eau-de-vie, guildive, or other inebriating beverages" to Indigenous people would face corporal punishment.[106]

Jacques Adam, a day laborer in Montréal, stood trial in 1756 for having distributed alcohol among several Indigenous residents. He admitted to having purchased a bottle of eau-de-vie for a man but insisted that this did not constitute commerce. Among the witnesses figured a priest, an innkeeper, a shoemaker, and a domestic servant, all of whom had interests in limiting the widespread black market in liquor among colonists and Indigenous people.[107] The sale of liquor across cultural boundaries was subject to dramatic legal oscillation and constituted an important zone of libertine conduct in early modern French Canada for the challenges that these sales posed to cross-cultural diplomacy.

In the Indigenous communities neighboring French colonies, access to distilled liquor and, consequently, drunkenness had acquired cultural value. Some individuals may have believed that imbibing distilled liquor might open the spirit to visions.[108] Drunkenness also served as a valid excuse for murderous or vengeful behavior, resulting in scant disciplinary action from either Indigenous leaders or the colonial state.[109] Clearly there was also value in the terror that drinking seemed to inspire among Europeans. On the other hand, distilled liquors were a key commodity in the French-Indigenous commerce of the colonial period; with guns and ammunition, alcohol was among the few European goods that members of Indigenous communities genuinely sought. Canada became an important market for French and British distillers, and in the eighteenth century it was a primary destination for Caribbean liquors.[110] Questions regarding who could sell liquor, to whom, and under what circumstances remained paramount modes of social control and French-Indigenous relations throughout the colonial period.

SEX AND MARRIAGE

If libertinism retained a polysemous character throughout the seventeenth century, comprising religious heterodoxy, subversion of patriarchal order, deserting domestic service positions, and flouting alcohol laws, it also had acquired a connotation of sexual deviance by the early eighteenth century, especially when used in the feminine form. In legal cases filed in the Québec and Montréal colonial courts, the terms *libertine* and *libertinage* did not refer to sex crimes including rape, seduction, sodomy, bigamy, or prostitution. In those cases the court clerks employed terminology that identified the specific crime or moral offense: *maquerellage* was typical for prostitution, *viol* signified violent rape, and *rapt* or *rapt de seduction* connoted consensual sex between two partners on the promise of marriage but lacking parental permission. Many of these sex crimes remained the province of the ecclesiastical courts. The Catholic Church in New France maintained judicial powers lost to the monarch and regional courts during the same century in France particularly regarding the police and discipline of family law, even after the French king took direct control of the colony and established the Conseil Supérieur of Québec in 1663.[111]

A notable case from 1691, in which colonial prosecutors brought charges of sodomy against an army lieutenant and two soldiers stationed with the colonial navy of Montréal, provides important information about military and social hierarchy, and the threats posed to ideal order by acts deemed sexually deviant. Extensive interrogations of the young men involved revealed that Nicolas Daussi de Saint-Michel, the company's lieutenant, had abused his power and compelled two subordinates to engage in sexual relations with him. Saint-Michel, as the instigator, was found guilty of "having wanted to debauch several men, and even of having succumbed to notorious and shameful actions to arrive at this terrible goal," exiled from the colony for life, and required to pay a fine of two hundred livres, half of which went to the central hospital and the other half to the Poor Bureau.[112] The two soldiers, Jean Forgeron "Larose" and Jean Filiau "Dubois" were reprimanded and threatened with more severe punishment for any future sodomy charges. They could have called for help and failed to do so, observed the court, indicating the authorities' sense of the victims' complicity. In this case, and many others that concern sexual deviance, authorities employ terms such as "debauchery" or "shame," but not "libertinage."

To accuse someone of being a libertine did not indicate criminal behavior, but low-grade defiance. It was August 8, 1716, when the gunsmith Olivier Quesnel brought suit against several women whom he accused of "daily debauching Raymond Quesnel, his son, age 18 or 19 years, to have him marry their sister."[113] The father could not direct his son's actions due to the women's bad influence; they were the "reason that his son was a libertine." The women accused were identified as Filiatreau the wife of Deniau, the Widow Desruisseaux, and the wife of Chamaillard. All were either sisters or sisters-in-law of young Raymond Quesnel's girlfriend, Jeanne Hautecoeur. According to the father, these women had sought out Raymond and brought him back to the Chamaillard home, where he had been living with Jeanne, "which is such libertinage that it cannot be tolerated." Quesnel sought a court injunction against the women, prohibiting them from approaching or debauching his son in the future, and requiring Raymond return to work for his father.[114]

Several days later Jeanne herself appeared before the lieutenant. The young woman, aged twenty-five or twenty-six, presented the slip of paper, dated May 14, 1716, attesting to a promise of marriage between herself and Raymond Quesnel.[115] Though Jeanne herself was unable to write or sign her name, she knew how important this piece of paper was for her claim to a durable relationship with Raymond. This was no illicit affair concocted by a clutch of degenerates, as Quesnel intimated, but a marriage duly concluded and fully supported by her family. At this point Olivier Quesnel and his wife, Catherine Prudhomme, changed tactics; on February 19, 1717, they brought suit against Jeanne rather than targeting her female relatives. The lieutenant general of Montréal, François-Marie Bouat, found in favor of the Quesnel family. He declared the "so-called marriage" between Raymond and Jeanne to be "nul, abusive, done against the laws and good morals."[116] The marriage was annulled, the couple separated, and Jeanne condemned to pay court fees. In this case Olivier Quesnel communicated his despair at losing both paternal authority and his son's labor, leaning on the libertine category to convey his fury at filial insubordination.

CONCLUSION

"Libertine" operated as a transitional category as authorities in France, and the French American colonies sought secular grounds for evolving law codes. The term signaled first and foremost excessive individual liberty that defied social superiors, and only secondarily did it indicate the nature of this defiance. The French state's experiments with exiling libertines revealed a hope that such individuals would fare better away from the strict patriarchal hierarchy enforced by both family and monarchy. The colonies might promise them greater opportunities, or an environment that rewarded hard work and military service. However, without orientation to this new environment, funds to establish themselves, or trusted networks of friends and family to support them, most of the libertines sent to Québec quickly ran afoul of the colonial authorities. For the errant fils de famille, the colonies proved no more free than France.

But in other ways, the colonies provided far greater freedoms than the mother country. Certain laws, such as the those imposing a hefty tax on salt, did not apply in Canada as in France, and the salt smugglers quickly established themselves as a desirable exile population, according to colonial administrators. Clever businessmen and women could flourish in the bustling villages, woods, and marshlands of New France. They represented an enduring vision of the colonial libertine: the imagined possibilities of a life unfettered by the layered social obligations, hierarchies, and taxes of Old Regime France.

3

A Colonial Liberty?

Sex and Race in the Louisiana Colony, 1698–1768

France's claim to the interior of the North American continent remained largely a cartographic fantasy throughout the eighteenth century.[1] But it was a fantasy that wove together the lives of thousands of people of European, African, and American descent; spurred one of the major economic collapses of the eighteenth century; and laid the groundwork for a war that spanned three continents.[2] As royal, Church, and local officials struggled to extend authority in this region, the concept of the libertine again became an important tool of the imperial project. As in Québec the definition of the libertine life highlights shifting boundaries in both legal and social standards. But in Louisiana territory, officials rarely applied the term to religious heterodoxy and only occasionally used it to refer to illicit commercial exchanges between European settlers and Indigenous people. Among the many and varied freedoms claimed by the residents of the colony—the economic liberties seized by Gulf Coast pirates, the religious tolerance accorded to Protestant German settlers, or the social license taken by wealthy settlers to adopt honorific titles or material marks of distinction—most did not rank as libertine acts. Instead officials consistently used the term to identify those relations that they perceived as a threat to social order in the first degree: sex between European men and Indigenous American or African women. What had been considered a "colonial liberty" in the early days of settlement began to attract regulatory ire.[3]

By 1700 French and Canadian officials had gained nearly a century of settler experience and built extensive relationships across North America.

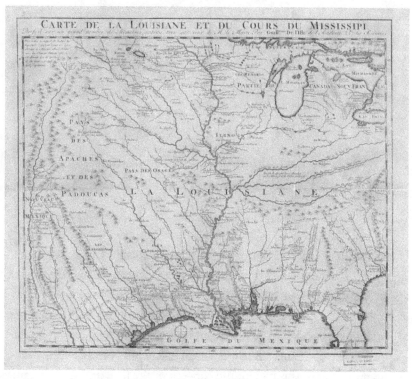

FIG 5. Map of Louisiana and the Mississippi River. Guillaume de l'Isle, 1717. Library of Congress Geography and Map Division, G4042.M5 1717.L5. https://www.loc.gov/item/gm71002183/.

But ideals guiding the mission of empire had shifted over that century. From the founding of the Louisiana colony in 1712, the law of slavery took a more central role in shaping the ideals that guided royal ministers and colonial administrators in the policies they formulated for this territory, discouraging then ultimately prohibiting sex across color lines.[4] Of course, racial prejudice was not simply a switch that flipped at the turn of the eighteenth century. Concepts about race responded to specific events, marking measurable changes in European settlement patterns, French-Indigenous military alliances and conflicts, the intensification of the Indigenous American slave trade, and the expansion of French involvement in the Atlantic slave trade after 1702.[5] The harvest of empire arrived daily in French ports not only in the form of goods but also in new practices, ideas, networks, and people.[6] Resulting anxieties spurred efforts to limit a foundational "colonial liberty" by prohibiting sex across emergent racial lines. I concur with Ann Stoler, who argues that "Europe's eighteenth-century discourses on sexuality can—indeed must—be traced along a more *circuitous imperial* route" engaging with categories of race and ethnicity as these took shape.[7]

INVENTING RACE

As the Louisiana colony grew, the category of "whites" (*les blancs*) slowly developed to rhetorically unite recent European migrants with those of European descent born in the Americas. The category gained currency in official correspondence and law after 1715 as the French Crown tactically shifted from a strategy to populate its empire only with committed French Catholic subjects to authorizing the forced migration of French criminals, vagrants, and foreigners. The category of "white" promised to erase social and economic divisions within these populations, imagining a common culture and identity. Whiteness papered over religious, regional, or linguistic distinctions among the French Catholics, the Canadian Huguenots, and even the German Protestants invited to settle in Louisiana after 1722.[8] As the historian Nancy Shoemaker observes, whiteness emerged first as a critical tool in stabilizing social divisions that intertwined with enslaved labor systems.[9] Simultaneously, the category of "Black" brought into one legal unit the plethora of nations, languages, religious traditions, and social ranks of Africans and their descendants in the Americas.[10] Over the next century, settler colonial policies attributed to Blackness moral and cultural inferiority that served to rationalize the perpetual enslavement of those individuals transported from African states to labor in European colonies throughout the Americas and the Caribbean.[11]

In colonial Louisiana a third color entered the emergent racial lexicon to identify Indigenous Americans. Residents of the southeastern region of North America described themselves as "red" and emphasized a common culture that made them distinct from both whites and Blacks who had settled in colonial settlements by the 1720s.[12] The historian George Milne traces this impulse to the anticolonial political rhetoric developed during and after the Natchez revolt against French colonial expansion in

1729.[13] Milne notes that although the Natchez political discourse "cannot be identified with absolute certainty as the source of the ideology of redness in Indigenous America, they were the first to use it in front of European observers."[14] Racial categories were not just imposed by whites, but shaped by all peoples residing in the Louisiana colony for distinct and competing purposes.[15] Men and women imagined alliances that might transcend histories of rivalry and warfare and developed vocabulary to predict potential partnerships.

Emerging theories of race collided with the committed assimilationist ideals maintained by some French missionaries who ministered to Catholics of European, American, and African descent alike.[16] Furthermore, by every measure, segregationist policies failed to achieve their stated objective—sex continued across these newly articulated color lines. "Mixed-race" families flourished and sank deep roots into the Louisiana and Illinois territories. The men and women who forged French-language societies among the cypress swamps of the Mississippi Delta and the temperate plains of the Illinois and Mississippi river valleys skirted colonial law when useful, embraced it when pragmatic, resisted it when necessary.[17] This chapter documents how sex across color lines moved from colonial liberty to crime, and how the libertine indicated those individuals—both men and women—who flouted a segregationist system.

Notwithstanding French claims, the North American heartland remained Indigenous territory throughout this period. During the eighteenth century, French policies lacked the administrative or military resources to realize colonial officials' ambitions of suzerainty.[18] Thus, I do not spend much time here assessing the impact of French colonial laws and policies on Louisiana and its people.[19] Instead I examine how the unique trajectory of the libertine category in the Louisiana colony transformed the significance of the term across the French Atlantic. It was here that the term first came to identify those individuals who transgressed emergent ideologies of racial segregation, particularly in sexual and family relationships, with broad implications for all French slave colonies.

In observing the overwhelming preoccupation of Louisiana's colonial authorities with criminalizing interracial unions after 1720, I follow the consensus of the past decade of scholarship in French America. Guillaume

Aubert provides a careful history of French colonial race law in Louisiana, while Jennifer Spear, Robert Michael Morrissey, Sophie White, Brett Rushforth, Jessica Marie Johnson, Cécile Vidal, and Emily Clark have documented the social and cultural tensions woven into the Euro-Afro-American societies that emerged during this period in the Louisiana territory.[20] This chapter brings that scholarship into the broader frame of the French empire to document how shifting terms and jurisdictions of colonial law shaped the meaning of "libertine." What once had been legal, sacramentalized, and even celebrated became first discouraged, then forbidden. Just as in Québec, where legislation governing the cross-cultural alcohol trade underwent continual revision, Louisiana's laws prohibiting interracial sex proved remarkably unstable over the course of the eighteenth century. Contested between authorities, advanced then retracted, discriminatory laws were largely ignored by residents until their own property rights or succession plans were threatened. The significance of laws regulating interracial sex rested not in their efficacy but in their failures, which laid bare the inadequacy of the colonial state to fulfill its directives and showcased the limited reach of the so-called absolutist monarch.[21]

COLONIAL EXPLORATION AND SEXUAL ALLIANCES, 1698–1714

The first French explorers along the Mississippi river valleys took it for granted that sexual alliances with Indigenous women served their personal and professional objectives. In 1698, royal officers back in the French Atlantic port town of Brest interviewed two Canadian brothers who had traveled with René-Robert Cavalier, Sieur de LaSalle on his final voyage up the Mississippi from the Gulf of Mexico in 1685. Pierre and Jean-Baptiste Talon had been born in Québec but returned to France with their parents while still young. LaSalle then brought the entire family, including six young children, on the expedition departing from La Rochelle. Pierre was eleven years old when LaSalle took him to reside with the Cénis (Hasinais or Tejas) people, where he remained for five years, while Jean-Baptiste, from the age of six, lived with the nomadic Karankawa people in territory that is part of present-day Texas. Both boys integrated into these adoptive communities, gained fluency in the Caddo language, and forgot French. Captured by the Spanish in 1690 and 1691, the boys lived for several years in Mexico City before they were ultimately transported back to France. From these young men, the French Crown sought unvarnished reports on the territory, inhabitants, and potential profits that might result from future expeditions.

The Talon brothers testified to the goods and produce they had seen in the Spanish colony of Mexico, as well as the racial categories that organized Mexican society along color lines. The Spanish of Mexico were "gentle and civil," they reported, and the Indigenous people of the region were "Christian, civilized, and hard-working."[22] They observed that the hard labor of mining or soldiering was done by Blacks and mixed-race peoples. Here the report paused to delineate between different categories of racial descent for French officials, identifying a "mulatto" as the offspring of a Black parent and a white parent, while a "métis" child resulted from a Spaniard and an Indigenous woman.[23] The explanation is notable for its attempt to orient its audiences to the factors organizing racial categories in New Spain. Both skin color and geographic origins operated as markers of early modern racial categories. When sex occurred across these lines, European colonial officials found the resulting offspring to be different enough from either parent's category to warrant another category between white and Black, Spanish and Indigenous. The racial taxonomy of Spanish America grew complex, tracking degrees of European, African or American ancestry several generations; of mulattos and métis, the clerk who recorded the Talons' testimony asserted that "there are a great number of both in Mexico."[24]

The Talons' report simultaneously named operational racial categories and observed with little judgment that centuries of European and African migrations to Mexico had resulted in multiracial populations, although the report concluded with the note that the Spaniards in Mexico lived in great softness and laziness, without great stores of arms. Perhaps this observation was meant to emphasize the stable nature of the Spanish empire. Perhaps royal officials calculated that a shock force of battle-hardened Canadian soldiers would suffice to take over an abundant and pacific territory. The assessment rings false to the modern reader, given that the Talon brothers had in fact been captured by Spanish soldiers;

their captivity bore witness to the active defenses maintained by the forces of New Spain. But this tale must have found some credulous readers at Versailles, for, within the following decades, the French Crown laid the financial foundations for a vast settler colony in Louisiana territory with persistent ambitions of westward and southward expansion. French colonial administrators increasingly staked the future on establishing a European state in the Americas that would challenge the Spain's "mestizo empire."

In the mythologies that organized French colonial expansion in Louisiana, such tales of an indolent Spanish elite presiding over a mixed-race society to the south proved formative. Both French and British authors inflated a Black Legend that represented the Spanish Empire in the Americas as simultaneously powerful and on the point of collapse.[25] According to this myth, the Spanish ruled through rapacious conquistadors dedicated to looting the region's gold and silver on the one hand and coercive warrior monks practicing forms of spiritual terror on the other. But, these imperial rivals asserted, New Spain was also fragile, for it was spread too thin across a vast territory, reliant on Indigenous elites and dependent on enslaved laborers who showcased the incomplete Christianizing effort. Moreover, by the early eighteenth century, rival Europeans perceived Spain's American empire as sheltering a population with unreliable affinity to the Spanish kingdom. Several French observers in this era attributed Spanish imperial weakness to centuries of "interracial" sex, based on the assertion that only Spanish men voyaged to the Americas, where they fathered a new race of mestizos with Indigenous women.[26] This specter of a multiracial empire, combined with French experiences of French–Indigenous American marriages and families over decades in Canada, would result in a dramatic overhaul of the French colonial legal apparatus prohibiting interracial sex and marriage in the first decades of the eighteenth century. Avoiding the Spanish fate became a primary concern for the jurists, monks, and officials charged with evaluating the stability of the French colony in Louisiana.

The Talon brothers reported that, during their travels through North America, they had encountered at least nine Indigenous American nations and learned a few words from each of these communities, providing a rudimentary glossary to their supervisors. Moreover, they noted frankly the important role played by sexual relationships between French and Indigenous people, highlighting a divergent sexual standard to which European men quickly adapted. They contended that since within Indigenous societies men did not possess women's sexuality, European men had no reason to fear war resulting from beginning or breaking off intimate relationships with Indigenous women. The Talon brothers reported that "several of the people in M. de La Salle's party even took a wife from them, among others the sailor François named Rutre, spoken of above, changed wives seven or eight times, leaving two children with one of his wives, following in this as in all else, the custom of the s*v*ges who truthfully have only one wife at a time, but who change whenever they like, which is to say, often."[27] These men communicated that sexual relations solidified American-French alliances; ensured the French explorers' survival through the shelter, food, and protection provided by entry into a community through intimate relations; and produced children with the potential for fluency in two languages and two cultures.[28] Many French men adjusted quickly to the customs they found among Indigenous Americans, and such unions could have been hailed as the foundation for French Louisiana, as had been the case in seventeenth-century Québec.[29]

But relying on individual initiative to advance cross-cultural commerce made French colonial authorities uneasy. By 1699 the French colonial state had benefited from generations of interaction with Indigenous allies, cultivating and investing in these relationships.[30] Many French colonists had learned multiple Indigenous languages, and missionaries had won and lost converts. Both Indigenous and French communities had raised children valued for their abilities to navigate between cultures. From this wealth of experience, colonial authorities increasingly realized that one of the organizing assumptions of seventeenth-century theories of assimilation—namely, that French Catholicism would prevail over any other language or religious system—had been false. In these final decades of the seventeenth century, French explorers ventured into unmapped territory, crossing paths with some of the French fur traders who had disappeared from colonial sight and taken up residence deep in the continent.

Henri Joutel's journal from La Salle's expedition from 1684 to 1687 records the company's discovery of two Provençal sailors, who had lived among the Cénis (Hasinai) since La Salle's first expedition.[31] Were these men still actually French? Joutel wondered. Naked, tattooed, married to Indigenous women, and veterans of indigenous wars, these men symbolized the greatest fears of this representative of the Crown and Gallican Church: that French subjects would become American.[32] Such examples threatened to upend a powerful European mythology of historical development that positioned French Catholicism as superior to Indigenous American cosmologies, and absolutism à la française as more advanced than the diversity of political systems encountered throughout the Americas.[33]

When Frenchmen abandoned their faith, language, and traditions, it became all too apparent that cultural influences moved in both directions, overturning Europeans' sense of inherent civilizational superiority. For every pious American convert that the Jesuits might report, there were seemingly just as many French settlers who abandoned European towns and traditions for the appeal of Indigenous American communities. These renegades might even adopt a self-consciously American skepticism toward Catholicism, the explorers reported. "As for religion," Joutel observed, the French sailors "were not troubled with much of it, and that libertine life they led was pleasing to them."[34] These were not men who had languished for lack of a mass. They had not longed for the Eucharist, as some priests claimed to be the case, justifying journeys among scattered settlers, delivering Christ's body and blood in specially appointed travel boxes.[35] And if their countrymen were shocked by a lack of structured Catholic piety, for some Frenchmen the personal autonomy and sexual liberties of life in the American interior more than compensated.

DEBATING FRENCH-INDIGENOUS MARRIAGE IN LOUISIANA, 1706–1724

The advantages of French-Indigenous sexual alliances to survival and colonial commerce remained evident into the eighteenth century, and Louis XIV's ministers continued to promote marriage between French and Indigenous American Christians as a means of securing French colonial ambitions. The first governor of the territory, Antoine Laumet de la Mothe, Sieur de Cadillac agreed with the tactic.[36] But, by 1706, the governor of Louisiana, Jean-Baptiste Le Moyne, Sieur de Bienville, objected. He fumed that Henri Roulleaux de la Vente, a priest who presided over interracial marriages at the parish at Mobile, "was authorizing the *coureurs de bois* to live as libertines and under no authority, dispersed among the s*v*ge villages, under the pretext that they have married among the s*v*ges."[37] For Le Moyne intimate alliances merely served as a tactic to evade colonial governance.

During the first years of the Louisiana colony, French authorities embarked on a decade-long debate over which women, Indigenous or French, made the better partners for male French settlers. Saliha Belmessous asserts that this debate hinged on a developing racism among French officials.[38] But it also signals a profound transformation in colonial officials' assumptions regarding gender and racial ideals. After 1706 most secular authorities called for more European women to be transported to the colony with the stated purpose of expanding the white population of landholders and artisans. As curate of Louisiana, Henri Roulleaux de la Vente continued to advocate unions between French men and Illinois women. He pushed back against the racial and cultural prejudice of colonial officials while still adopting racialized terms, insisting that Catholic Indigenous women of northern nations continued to advance the goals of French empire: Catholicization, expansion, and French primacy in Indigenous trade networks. Why? The women of the "Kaskaskias, Tamaroas, Illinois and all those of the Missouri" were "whiter, more laborious, cleverer, neater in the household work and more docile than those of the South."[39] Like Roulleaux de la Vente, the bishop of Québec disputed segregation along racial lines as the key to social order, however. It was not interracial sex, he asserted, but concubinage that posed the true threat to colonial social order. In a *pastoralin* circulated in 1721, he contended that the limited advance of Christian institutions and faith—and not interracial sex—had hindered the imperial project. If the sons and daughters of French migrants and Indigenous Americans were not the reliable agents of empire anticipated by prior generations, he blamed the informality of the parents' union. The products of illegitimate relationships, the bishop warned, "can only become bad subjects."[40] He and many other clerics promised that the path to American dominance required colonial authorities to recognize interracial marriages, baptize the children born of these unions, and strengthen the hand of the Church throughout the territory.

Many Catholic priests and missionaries rejected administrative injunctions against interracial marriage, preferring that devout practitioners marry and raise children within the Church regardless of race. In the missionaries' correspondence, "libertinage" referred to concubinage and short-term sexual relations, not interracial marriage.[41] Although such usages appear to be diametrically opposed, these reveal colonial authorities' anxiousness to distinguish between licit and illicit relations for reproduction and property succession. This context proved powerful in linking the libertine with the connotation of transgressive sex in the French Atlantic. Such discussions intersected with emerging concerns of mixed-race populations in French Caribbean colonies, and with French histories of the abuses of Spanish colonialism in the Americas.

But the clerics found themselves drowned out by a newly influential population in the colonial administration: the American-born settlers, called "Canadians" in contemporary documents. This propertied, often titled, colonial aristocracy consistently proffered racial segregation as the solution to social disorder. In 1709 the governor of New France, Philippe Rigaud de la Vaudreuil, insisted that "bad blood shouldn't mix with good, our experience in this country is that all the Frenchmen who have married Indigenous women became do-nothing libertines, and of an intolerable independence, and their children are also as worthless as the natives themselves, and should keep us from permitting these types of marriages . . . it seems that all children born of these unions seek to give the greatest possible pains to the French."[42] Vaudreuil articulated racial prejudice defined by good or bad "blood" that drew heavily on aristocratic ideologies of social distinction.[43] But his rationale against interracial marriages also highlighted the economic consequences of these unions from the perspective of the colonial state. French men who married Indigenous women, resided in Indigenous communities, and raised children fluent in both European and Indigenous languages and cultures had the skills to slip the bonds of the colonial state. They no longer depended on the colony's protection and could no longer be counted on to equate their personal ambitions with collective settler interests. In response to Vaudreuil's invective, royal ministers undertook extensive discussions in France, considering the merits of encouraging European women to emigrate to the colony; in a striking reversal of previous policies, some even considered German or Swiss Protestants as preferable to Indigenous American women.[44]

By 1715 the finance officer charged with supervising the Louisiana colony, commissaire-ordonnateur Jean-Baptiste du Bois Duclos, Sieur de Montigny, objected to the appointment of a seminarian who advocated interracial marriage. Duclos enumerated four reasons to oppose mixed-race marriages between French men and Indigenous women.[45] Eventually, he said, these women would return to their communities, taking their French husbands with them. The governor-general of Louisiana pleaded with royal officials at Versailles, repeatedly entreating authorities to send him more French women, so that the population of male settlers could find spouses among these recent transports.[46] In his estimation a European population was key to stabilizing the French settlement and strengthening colonial authority.[47] Within this context, as deployed by colonial officials, the term "libertine" referred primarily to those men and women who transgressed emerging racial boundaries by forging interracial relationships and raising children whose existence undermined colonial assertions of European supremacy.

Duclos gestured to the past century of French colonial experience as evidence that interracial unions had failed to transform the Indigenous populations of Canada, but instead resulted in French men who "became almost Indian."[48] He advanced a theory of racial difference, equating skin color with adherence to shared ethical standards and social codes. Moreover, he contended that these qualities were heritable; his central objective in prohibiting intermarriage was to preserve the "whiteness and purity of blood in the children."[49] He lamented that interracial sex, if it went unchecked, would ensure that Louisiana became "a colony of mulattoes who are naturally idlers, libertines and even more rascals as those of Peru, Mexico and the other Spanish colonies give evidence."[50] The Spanish colonies to the south served as a negative example for French officials, as did the perceived failures of the assimilationist policies of seventeenth-century New France. Whiteness took shape—paradoxically—in assessments of European imperial rivalries, as the French weighted their own kingdom's advantages and liabilities vis-à-vis those of the Spanish, British, and Dutch who were similarly grasping for allies and territory in North America.

But in these debates between assimilation and segregation, royal directives remained noncommittal. Establish stability and economic productivity, the Crown insisted, while leaving the methods for achieving these broad goals to those on the ground. In commissioning Sieur de l'Epinay as governor of the Province of Louisiana in 1716, the instructions from the French king established the central objective of ensuring alliances between France and all Indigenous American nations, particularly against the English. The governor must ensure that the troops of Louisiana live in good discipline and encourage the cultivation of tobacco. Finally, "His Majesty is informed that most of the officers and settlers of Louisiana have in their homes enslaved Native women with whom they live in libertinage and debauchery, as noted in this extract written by S. Lamotte Cadilhac on the subject, His Majesty recommends that Sieur de l'Epinay remedy these disorders to the best of his ability as soon as he is on the ground and makes inquiries."[51] Did the directive mean that the governor should encourage French men to marry their Indigenous partners, or break off sexual relations entirely? The interpretations varied, but colonial officials increasingly resolved upon the latter proposition. Prohibitions of interracial sex stood in distinct contrast to the founding assumptions of the Québec colony and the actions of the priests and missionaries that stressed association with Indigenous American allies and encouraged intermarriage. From the inception of the Louisiana colony, interracial sex and its resulting offspring constituted both the central attraction and overarching anxiety for French settlers.

By 1717, with Antoine Crozat's cession of the Louisiana territory to John Law's Company of the West, the rapid settlement of the colony took priority in French imperial ambitions. Transatlantic discussions of libertinage shifted in response to these new concerns. Whether for the intrinsic value of the territory and its resources, or for its geopolitical value in blocking English or Spanish expansion in North America, the myth of the Louisiana colony loomed large in colonial policy discussions throughout the regency.[52] Louisiana was to be France's Peru, a source of vast wealth after a relatively peaceful conquest, hoped the royal officials who pored over maps and testimonies from their offices in Versailles.[53]

From the coastal village of New Orleans, a skeletal French colonial administration presumed to govern a multiethnic society directly engaged in trade with Africa, the Caribbean, and neighboring Indigenous American nations. The increased access to African and Caribbean trade appealed to those French settlers who lamented the geographic isolation of the Québec colony.[54] The population of New Orleans grew from four hundred French colonists in 1717 to over five thousand by 1723.[55] Many of these settlers were forced migrants—salt smugglers, prostitutes, thieves, and vagrants who were transported to the colony as punishment.[56] Young men arrested by king's order might also be exiled to the colony, despite the tactic's manifest failure in Québec.[57] French officials estimated the costs of initial settlement at 400,000 livres in 1717.[58]

The colonial investment was to be financed by the sale of thousands of joint-stock certificates, each valued at 500 livres, and sold by John Law's Company of the West (later, Company of the Indies), which promised its shareholders a return on their investment premised on a trade monopoly of American products—timber, tobacco, even precious metals—for twenty-five years.[59] But within five years Law's bank had imploded, and the financial foundation for the colony disintegrated.[60] Thanks to the collapse of John Law's System, the twinned features of modern venture capitalism—paper money and a state bank—suffered a devastating blow in the French Atlantic.[61] Gordon Sayre reminds us that, in these years, in distinct contrast to the "hyperbolic promotional tracts extolling the bountiful climate and resources of the colony (primarily in the periodical *Le Nouveau Mercure*), 'Louisiana' now aroused images of fraud, criminality, or, at best, false promises."[62] From this point the Louisiana colony provided a cautionary tale of the disorder that resulted when liberties ran amok.[63]

In 1719 both the colonial and French governments issued a series of proclamations indicating that those advocating a segregationist racial regime had prevailed. First, colonial administrators moved to separate the commerce and movement between the French and Indigenous villages at Kaskaskia.[64] Second, the Crown approved plans to forcibly transport French vagabonds, salt-smugglers, and prostitutes to the Louisiana colony. This represented a royal commitment to subsidize European immigration. The text of the law read: "Our predecessors have always paid considerable attention to vagabonds, who had no occupation other than that which libertinage provided, and who often found their living in crime and debauch."[65] It seemed French libertines were to be preferred to those Canadian libertines whose Indigenous wives and children pulled them away from imperial networks. The state hoped that European men and women could traverse the Atlantic, find gainful work, and build enduring societies in Louisiana, and marriage was to provide the social glue that kept men from wandering and women from prostitution. On September 18, 1720, the priest of the St-Martin-des-Champs church in Paris blessed 184 marriages between men and women bound for deportation to New Orleans.[66] Those women transported to the colony without partners were married to European settlers within days of their arrival.

As a result of aggressive enticements to emigrate, French women came to Louisiana in ever greater numbers. Over seven thousand European immigrants disembarked in the ports of Mobile and New Orleans during this period, and Daniel Usner estimates that women comprised roughly 30 percent of that total.[67] The Superior Council Archives conserve the wills and marriage certificates of the French, Swiss, and German women who migrated to this territory, communicating a fair sense of the goods exchanged and family connections forged among the members of these immigrant communities. A small coterie of Ursuline nuns arrived in 1727 and found a community of European girls eager for their instruction. By 1728 the sisters had included religious instruction of Indigenous and Black women.[68] Marc-Antoine Caillot's unpublished journal provides rare comment on the European women he met en route to assuming a position as a clerk in the New Orleans office of the Company of the Indies in 1729, including a wealthy but plain young woman with whom Caillot flirted aggressively and mocked mercilessly.[69] We learn from these sources that some European women arrived with money and goods, and many with skills in nursing, midwifery, baking, and brewing.[70] But the decision to exile several hundred men and women detained as vagabonds or prostitutes resulted in many observers depicting the colony's thousands of other female inhabitants as criminals and sexual deviants.

Many and merciless were the witnesses who castigated Louisiana's European women settlers as mercenary, lustful, and diseased. Jacques La Chaise lamented in 1723 to the directors of the Company of the Indies that he was forced to provide company rations to passengers including "a number of women . . . who are useless and do nothing but cause disorder."[71] A ship's captain, M. Valette de Laudun, wrote, "I think that most of the women sent here are so unhealthy and used up by past relations that they are sterile before they even leave [France]."[72] Upon arrival in Louisiana, colonial and Church officials attempted to communicate strict moral standards to the new arrivals.[73] Many within the government argued that the colonial experiment depended on white women, but then they despaired when faced with the divergent interests and sexual autonomy of actual women who made the journey.

DEVELOPING THE SEGREGATION SOLUTION, 1715–1724

How did racial segregation come to be seen as the answer to French struggles in Louisiana? The answer is simultaneously local and transatlantic. Implementing the solution demonstrates in microcosm how laws written in Versailles shifted and recalibrated in Québec, New Orleans, or the French Caribbean. Three important factors contributed to the "segregation solution" as it developed in Louisiana. First, as Guillaume Aubert has documented, racialized discourse grew out of the French nobility's critique of "*mésalliance* (the marriage of people from different social ranks), which emphasized the perils attached to the mixing of 'unequal bloods.'"[74] In the colonial context, however, this logic proposed that all white Europeans had "good blood," regardless of social station. A mésalliance resulted from sexual relationships with Indigenous Americans or Africans, as colonial administrators attempted to code enslaved status with skin color. Second, successive waves of military conflicts between Indigenous communities and the colonial state from 1715 to 1723 embroiled French officers and their families, posing existential threats to the French effort to establish sustainable communities at Detroit and in Louisiana. These wars amplified French rivalry with British and Spanish colonists and undermined colonial administrators' confidence in how well they understood their Indigenous American allies. Third, the arrival of enslaved Africans into Louisiana provoked a thorough overhaul of the existing law of slavery and of existing American practices of enslavement.

We must ask, how much did the laws that forged a racial regime even matter in French Louisiana? Weren't these precisely the individuals who would be inclined to break whatever regulations an imperial state devised? Inquiring into the features that built colonial New Orleans, Shannon Lee Dawdy reminds us that "colonialism was as much a creation of rogues and independent agents as it was the project of imperial states."[75] Indeed, it is difficult to identify an instance of early modern or modern colonialism that was not more the product of "rogues" than officials.[76] For this reason Dawdy cautions against overly investing in close readings of colonial policies and laws drafted in Versailles; such plans were implemented (or not) and resisted on the ground by men and women employing what Dawdy terms a "rogue colonialism" that advanced self-interest over the good of the empire. What was more, back in France, metropolitan officials recognized the utility of this rogue logic. They tolerated, even encouraged, the entrepreneurial predations of those settlers who undertook projects that promised to extend colonial institutions and commerce. Many of these individuals perceived interracial sex as a necessary part of building reliable alliances with neighboring Indigenous nations, but with an innate hierarchy that assumed indigenous subordination to Europeans. Sexuality was a liberty to be seized, but it was also a tool of intimidation and social control.[77] The will and desires of women played little part in this project by which men used sex to lay claim to peoples and territory. In this way the sexual liberties seized by French settlers constituted the patriarchal warp of colonial societies. But within a generation of settlement, Louisiana's colonial administrators condemned interracial sexual alliances as libertine.

Indigenous leaders had been requesting greater separation between their communities and French settlements for decades. In 1724 representatives from the Illinois, Missouria, Osages, and Otos traveled from New

Orleans to Paris to speak directly with the French king. In their speeches these leaders demanded that the French king recognize his responsibility for the settlers' actions. In an address to the board of the Company of the Indies, Chicagou, a representative from the Illinois nation, pointed to the long relationship between his people and French missionaries to demand imperial oversight: "The French are with us, we have ceded them the land that we occupied at the Kaskaskias; we are comfortable with that; but it is not good that they come mix with us and set up in the middle of our village. . . . My thought is that you who are the great chiefs, you left us masters of the land where we placed our fire."[78] In this speech, and over the course of the extended negotiation, Chicagou appealed to the company and the king to hold settlers to treaty termsand to segregate French settlers from his community.

By 1731 some 7500 souls comprised the population of the vast Louisiana territory purportedly subject to the French Crown. These individuals lived in rudimentary forts along the Mississippi and Illinois rivers, largely dependent on their neighbors for food, trade, and protection.[79] Enslaved Indigenous and African people outnumbered European settlers by a wide margin. Of course, the French census did not include the vast majority of the territory's occupants: tens of thousands of Indigenous Americans who lived in concentrated urban agglomerations or scattered settlements throughout this area which remained "native ground."[80] According to the Indigenous Americans and Africans enslaved in the territory; the criminals and prostitutes forcibly transported across the Atlantic; and the French, Canadian and German colonists struggling to eke out a living in the margins between empires, the Louisiana Colony was no landscape of liberty.[81]

RACE AND SEX IN THE LAW OF SLAVERY

In patchwork fashion, colonial officials in North America strove to limit sex between Europeans and Indigenous Americans by the second decade of the eighteenth century. These policies changed as laws designed to regulate slavery across France's Atlantic colonies moved from conditional acceptance of sex between masters and slaves to strict prohibition.[82] Promulgated in March 1685 for the French Caribbean islands of Martinique,

Guadeloupe, and Saint-Domingue, the Code Noir is best understood as an attempt to promote a distinctly French Catholic form of slavery, reforming the worst abuses associated with more than a century of Iberian hegemony over the Atlantic slave trade, as cataloged in critiques penned from 1677 to 1685.[83]

The Code Noir of 1685 explicitly regulated sexual relations between free men and enslaved women. It made no mention of "race" in explaining the mechanisms by which such unions were to be discouraged by the colonial state, nor did it identify geographic origins or epidermal pigment, for the simple reason that enslaved people in the French colonies were not easily defined by physical characteristics, locale, or parentage in 1685. According to Roman precedent, the legal status of a child followed its mother. But, recognizing the rape of enslaved women as a predictable result from that provision, article 9 proposed that any free man who had children with an enslaved woman would be condemned to a fine of two thousand pounds of sugar. If he owned the woman, both she and the children would be confiscated by the state, and they would be permanently enslaved to the colonial hospital.[84] However, if a French man should free his concubine and marry her in the Church, their children would be free and recognized as legitimate by the Crown. In practice, however, "male colonists considered sex with female slaves a perquisite of their status."[85] These men may also have found in the code a patriarchal ideal that encouraged them to manumit the enslaved women who had borne their children, the better to retain control of their labor through family bonds.[86] This ideal contributed to the substantial and growing population of free people of color in the French Caribbean, the descendants of European male planters and enslaved African women.[87] As a result, in Saint-Domingue by 1789, twenty-eight thousand people of color and emancipated slaves accounted for 46 percent of the free population of the colony. They owned one-quarter of the colony's land, and one-third of the slaves.[88]

The Code Noir of 1685, which legitimated slavery in the French Caribbean, also promised equal treatment under the law to all free-born and freed persons, without reference to race or rank. It is for this reason that the legal historian Malick Ghachem sees in the law of slavery an "important source of human rights law and ideology."[89] By article 59 manumitted slaves were acknowledged as "natural subjects" of the king, following Roman legal precedent. Freed people figured prominently in the extensive policy discussions that considered their status in the French empire. According to the law, freed or free people could own property, seek education, hold public office, and marry, subject only to their family's interests.

By the 1720s colonial administrators and royal officials concluded that provisions of the Code Noir risked the collapse of the slaveocracy by providing too many paths out of slavery. They sought to remedy perceived problems in the governance of both New France and the Caribbean by radically changing the laws governing slavery, and they did so by inventing a legal category of race.[90] Officials applied these insights to the new Louisiana colony, and to the law code forged to regulate the institution of slavery as applied to both Africans and Indigenous Americans.[91]

The Code Noir of Louisiana, enacted in 1724, identified people by color rather than by their status as free or enslaved. As noted above, the category of "white" erased powerful national and confessional divisions, promising that recent German-speaking Protestant migrants would be considered equal to French-speaking Catholic settlers, and the category of "Black" conflated all enslaved people, regardless of their skin color or geographic origin. Brett Rushforth explains that "census records that once recorded 'mulatto, Negro, and Indian slaves' by 1719 collapsed those categories into a single group, sometimes labeled 'negro' or 'negress,' other times merely 'slaves.'"[92] This code prohibited marriages between the white and Black residents of the colony, irrespective of their legal status, and outlawed interracial sex by defining concubinage in terms that profoundly discriminated against the offspring of these informal unions.[93] As a result, Guillaume Aubert concludes, "the 1724 *Code Noir* thus constituted the most racially exclusive colonial law of the French Empire."[94] Race and gender emerged as the essential categories to perpetuate slavery in the colony and announced that the "sexual exploitation of enslaved women . . . underwrote the logic of racial dominance."[95] However, resistance to these policies was widespread, and sex across the emergent color lines continued. Parish priests often declined to report race in marriage and birth registries, effectively whitening populations in the historical record.[96]

Manumission was made much more difficult to secure than it had been in the earlier code, the more effectively to create a population of perpetually enslaved people. In this manner the French colonial state sought to make race—informed by skin color and geographic origin—a category in family law and the law of slavery. By prohibiting sex or marriages between people across racial lines, the French state risked invalidating existing unions in the eyes of the law. The consequences were profound for those who found themselves defined as "mixed-race" in France and in the American colonies. Threats to property, inheritance, and social status resulted. At precisely the moment that historians of the Enlightenment see evidence of the first "sexual revolution," characterized by the withering of laws regulating Catholic sexual morality, new laws constructed racial categories to segregate French imperial subjects, prohibit marriage or sex across those categories, and lay a secular, racialist foundation for sexual unions in the colonies, with disastrous implications for multiracial families throughout the French empire.

MANON LESCAUT AND THE LIMITS ON LIBERTINES

It was no accident that the novel now considered to be the forerunner of the libertine genre of literature showcased the transgressive setting of the French colony of Louisiana and highlighted sentiments of disillusion with that colony. The *Histoire du Chevalier des Grieux et de Manon Lescaut* by the Abbé Prévot was first published in 1731 and provides a remarkable measure of how Louisiana reverberated in French cultural expression. It relates the tale of a young aristocrat, the Chevalier des Grieux, who is blinded by his love and desire for a beautiful, manipulative young woman of common birth, Manon Lescaut. Found guilty of prostitution, Manon is condemned to transportation from France to the colony of Louisiana. The story opens as the narrator enters the Norman village of Pacy and encounters two lines of twelve women chained together around their waists, awaiting transportation to Louisiana. One woman, he notes, is "beautiful and modest" and appears entirely out of place in the scene. Inquiring about her, he learns that all the girls had been at the central hospital in Paris and were being deported on the order of the lieutenant-general of police—and probably not for good behavior, sneers the guard in charge of their transport. But even this guard recognizes that the beautiful Manon "is worth a little more than her companions."[97] At that moment he points out an "unhappy educated young man" who had trailed the party from Paris, "crying the whole time."[98] A glance suffices to convince the narrator of this young man's "quality," his bearing and demeanor revealing him to be a man of "the first rank," in both education and social status.[99] As the narrator questions him, we learn about the young man's love for a "modest" young woman, his attempts and failures to secure her liberty through legal channels, which forced him to seek aid from a band of brigands who promised to attack the guard and free his love, but actually just stole his money. Now he followed the convoy, paying the guards each time he sought to speak with his mistress, until he had exhausted his funds. He resolved to embark with her for America, where "at least I will be free with the one I love."[100] Moved by the young man's constancy and emotion, our narrator presses money for the remainder of his voyage into the Chevalier des Grieux's hand and bids him take it. Two years later the young man returns, and, upon encountering him on the streets of Calais, the narrator begs for the full story of the circumstances that had led him to travel halfway around the world and back again.

Recent literary analysis of *Manon Lescaut* has focused on gender relations within the novel, its discursive deceptions, or its representations of money and value, but scant attention has been paid to the colonial setting that provides the emotional motive and disciplinary moral for the tale, and that occupies the final section of the novel.[101] As with Théophile de Viau's poetry and Lahontan's *Dialogues*, Prévost roots a critique of French society in a flight of fancy that imagines extensive liberties available to European settlers and Indigenous residents within a colonial setting. However, Prévost's novel portrays a maturing mentality, for, in his vision, such imagined liberties evaporate as the characters plunge deeper into colonial territory and face the arbitrary self-interest of "rogue" colonial officials.

The Chevalier des Grieux tells the story of how he fell in love with Manon Lescaut at first sight, turned his world upside down to stay close to her, disobeying his father's advice time and again, despite the evidence that she took many other lovers and accepted cash and gifts in exchange for her favors. Finally, the chevalier's father catches up with the couple, chastising his son: "Thanks to the scandal caused by your libertinage and spending, I discovered your residence."[102] Disobedience leaves its traces in promissory notes and rumors that lead the cunning patriarch to the lovers' abode. Des Grieux's father ensures that Manon is arrested, charged with prostitution, and transported immediately to the Louisiana colony. The chevalier follows her, overwhelmed with regret and grief but determined to stay with his love despite his father's punitive measures. The chevalier does not lament this threatened transportation; on the contrary, he welcomes their exile to a foreign land. He proclaims himself certain that in New Orleans he would be free to live alongside his love without fear from vengeful fathers or interloping rivals, such as the ever-present G . . . M . . . , Manon's wealthy and elderly lover. He does not fear Indigenous Americans, despite their reputation as "irreligious s*v*ges," because they could not be any crueler than his father. The travel narratives from the territory that poured from European printing presses since La Salle's 1684–87 expedition regularly depicted the inhabitants of the North American interior as lacking both religion and the sentimental qualities to cultivate a spiritual life.[103] But, far from frightening des Grieux, these accounts of Indigenous Americans console him. In fact, the chevalier considers the residents of the American colony as potential allies, for "if the accounts of them are truthful, they follow the laws of nature. They know neither the furors of avarice that possessed G . . . M . . . nor the fantastic notions of honor that made an enemy of my father. They would not trouble two lovers that they would see live with as much simplicity as themselves."[104] In des Grieux's assertion, we see the long-lasting impact of Lahontan's *Dialogues* and related travel narratives that emphasize Indigenous Americans' accord with nature. Departing the old world meant a break with wealth, rank, and the social hierarchies that continually threatened to drive the couple apart. In the colony Manon and des Grieux hope to start over, forget the betrayals and duplicity that had characterized their relationship up to that point, and enjoy their love in a state of nature.

Arriving in New Orleans after two months at sea, the chevalier observes that "the country offered nothing agreeable at first sight. It was a sterile and desolate countryside, with only some cattails and some trees stripped by the wind. No trace of men or animals."[105] Here is the first clue that the promise of the colony might not live up to the chevalier's expectations. The ship's captain announces their arrival to the city's inhabitants by firing several cannons. Then, from behind the hill, arrive some "citizens of New Orleans," who receive them with joy as angels, peppering the new arrivals with questions about France and their hometowns: "They embraced us as brothers and dear companions arrived to share their misery and solitude."[106] The first order of business for the governor of the colony is to match the thirty girls who had been transported to the colony with male residents for imminent marriages. Initially this official respects the relationship between the chevalier and Manon, providing them with their own modest lodging and a few chairs. Love makes the cabin a palace, both asserted in moving declarations of love and liberty. The chevalier recalls, "America seemed a place of delights after that. We had to come to New Orleans, I often said to Manon, to taste the true sweetness of love. Here one can love without interest, without jealousy, without inconstancy. Our neighbors came here to search for gold, they cannot imagine that we have found far more valuable treasures."[107] In these few lines the central characters and the reader finally win a brief respite in which their love for each other triumphs over all impediments.

Everything goes well for the couple until they decide to get married officially, motivated by a sense of duty to God and their faith. The chevalier observes, "Manon was not an impious girl. I was not one of those blatant *libertins* who gloried in adding irreligion to moral depravity. Love and youth had caused all our disorders."[108] For des Grieux a *libertin* engaged in both religious and sexual deviance, and, despite all appearances, such a label applied neither to him nor Manon. They had no considered opposition to social institutions; a perverse society had made them oppositional simply for following their natural love. Of course, des Grieux acknowledges, while in France "it was equally impossible for us to stop loving each other or to fulfill our love by a legitimate path; but in America, where we were self-sufficient, where the arbitrary laws of rank or expectation no longer menaced us, where we were presumed married, who would prevent us from actually marrying and ennobling our love by the oaths of authorized religion?"[109] Presenting their unusual case to the colonial officials, the lovers feel certain their plight will be quickly resolved, and their love will be recognized in both the eyes of the law and the Church. After all, the governor of the colony regularly invites them to dine with him, having immediately perceived their elite social qualities. The governor hears of des Grieux's plans, agrees to attend the ceremony, even to pay for a party commemorating the happy event. But within an hour, the chaplain for the colony arrives at des Grieux's residence, this man of God having been charged with observing to the couple that, in this territory, the Governor was the master: "Manon had been sent from France for the colony, and it was up to the Governor to dispose of her."[110] Believing she was already married, he had done nothing to interfere. But, absent a marriage certificate uniting the pair, the Governor had determined to marry Manon to his nephew, Monsieur Synnelet, a young man that des Grieux characterizes as "brave but headstrong and violent."[111] Once again the letter of the law and officials' cupidity threatens to tear apart true love. The chevalier orders the chaplain out of his house and challenges Monsieur Synnelet to a duel, striking a fatal blow, or so he thinks.

In the topsy-turvy world of French America, former prostitutes appear to be ladies, lovers resemble spouses, and libertine young men, cast off by their families, are hailed as the ruling elite. Disaster strikes this New World paradise finally because of des Grieux's attempt to publicly correct the couple's situation, to make the natural law of their love square with religious and civil law. The couple cannot marry. Religious and colonial authorities unite in this account, noteworthy given the rarity of this accord in the historical record, and refuse to approve the marriage of two individuals despite professions of love and evidence of cohabitation.[112]

What can the lovers do? They flee New Orleans, striking out into the wilds in search of an English settlement, where they hoped they would no longer be subject to French social rules and religious strictures. They learn "a few words in native languages" as they make the difficult journey, during which they are subject to inclement weather and hostile inhabitants.

Manon dies en route, much to the chevalier's despair, and with her death evaporates all his reasons for forging a residence in this foreign land. Moreover, the chevalier soon learns that Synnelet has not actually died. The rival is alive and still searching for the couple to exact his vengeance. At this point, then, the chevalier decides to return to France, "to repair, with a wise and ordered life, the scandal of my conduct."[113] After an uneventful voyage, he returns home to find that his father had died during his voyage and his older brother anxiously awaits his arrival. In a sense this tale as narrated by the Chevalier des Grieux constitutes a recovery from the colonial adventure of Louisiana, an endeavor undertaken in haste, lacking crucial information, and encumbered with the weight of France's social systems, all liberties dispelled by the arbitrary despotism wielded by colonial authorities. As the character of the Governor makes clear, a distant king's ideals matter very little when the word of colonial officials is law and carries the threat of force.

By the end of the tale, readers realize that Louisiana's settlers suffered not from too much liberty, but not enough. Rather, many French observers contended that their society had much to learn from Indigenous Americans. In the 1730s Marc-Antoine Caillot compiled his memories of a brief residence in the Louisiana colony.[114] Although he was sensitive to the many differences among Indigenous American nations, he generalized about marriage customs across nations, while gesturing to the impact of Christian churches and traditions in some communities:

> Concerning their marriages, the ceremony is performed early and the banns are published quickly, for when an Indian man and woman like each other, they take each other and get together without any more information. Likewise, when one of the two is not happy, they leave each other and go elsewhere to marry. Nevertheless, it is very rare for them to leave each other, because when they take one another, they truly love each other with a love that lasts a long time, without any vow or pretension of getting goods like three-fourths of the marriages in France.[115]

Like many travelers before him, Caillot interpreted aspects of Indigenous American gender relations as resulting in more genuine attachments, and in love freely given. Still, in state correspondence and judicial cases emanating from Louisiana, the term "libertine" overwhelmingly referred to those settlers who engaged in sex across the color lines. Occasionally officials took pains to explain why this behavior—newly illegal and still widespread—posed a social or political threat to colonial order. The bishop of Isle-Dieu, Pierre de la Rue, served as vicar-general for the colonies in Québec and Louisiana. On April 20, 1750, he wrote to the governor-general of Louisiana, Pierre de Rigaud, Marquis de Vaudreuil-Cavagnial expressing his pleasure that both Jesuit and Capuchin monks had finally arrived in Louisiana.[116] The bishop conceded that the Capuchin superior "has complained a little of the moral libertinage in their missions, I exhorted him to take it in hand, but above all to confer with you on the measures he can take to remedy this by means of persuasion and instruction."[117] The regular and secular orders of the Church here vow to work with the state administration to redress poorly defined ills undermining social order. Together they can root out the moral rot that threatens the French colony. For, the bishop reminds his powerful audience, "only religion is capable not only of forming men and Christians, but subjects for the prince."[118]

The following year Vaudreuil sent military and diplomatic instructions to Chevalier Macarty, as the latter assumed command of the French fort at Chartres in the Illinois country. Vaudreuil reminded Macarty that he was entrusted with bringing good government to Illinois, reforming the abuses that had developed in religion, police, military discipline, and government. Macarty's first task would be to ensure that all officers and soldiers, all settlers and *voyageurs* (licensed fur traders) "live as good Christians" and support the zeal of French missionaries. The military commander was to do his part to make these monks as respected by the French as by the Indigenous Americans.[119] As head of the French military force, Macarty enjoyed police and judicial powers in the colony. Vaudreuil clarified, "An essential point of the police that directly regards only M. de Macarty is to impede marriages that the French have heretofore concluded with the *sauvagesses*. This alliance is shameful and has the dangerous consequence due to the familiarity that results between the s*v*ges and the French and the bad race that it produces."[120] Next

Macarty was to reorganize the Kaskaskia and Chartres forces, lodging soldiers with settlers until a garrison had been built. He was also to publish the following order: "The French were not to build close to the S*v*ges. Presents for the S*v*ges had been set at 3000 livres by M. de Bienville, 6000 livres to the Illinois." He was to encourage communities to become self-sufficient, by milling their own flour and weaving their own fabrics. Those settlers who seek to trade with neighboring Indigenous nations must have permission to leave the fort. Moreover, Macarty "must refuse to those he knows to be libertines and capable of alienating the [Indigenous] nations from us."[121] This directive targeted those settlers who might strike independent bargains with their Indigenous trade partners, and, from Vaudreuil's experience, the only men who had the networks and knowledge to strike such bargains were those who had wives, concubines, or children to provide access outside of the colonial state's circuit. It is remarkable that Vaudreuil addressed so much of his governance memo to delegitimizing such a widespread phenomenon. These directions provide important insight into the overlapping meanings of the term "libertine." Vaudreuil's insistent discouragement of relationships between French men and Indigenous women highlights, first, the moral threat; second, the threat to honor and blood, and, finally, the commercial threat that he perceived these unions posed to the colonial government. Vaudreuil goes on to demand that Macarty ensure that French settlers not hunt along the Illinois River that would "damage our fragile accord with the Cherakis" and warn the fur traders not to hunt on the Mississippi, which France recognized as Sioux territory. The Peoria nation had also demanded that the French colonial government keep the *voyageurs* out of their territory.[122] The French in 1751 surveyed a precarious colonial order, altogether more dependent on their Indigenous allies than they would have liked, and all too aware that the work of empire was in the hands of men they had deemed unreliably loyal and insufficiently French.

CONCLUSION

Did French race laws matter in Louisiana? Cécile Vidal contends that with the prohibition of interracial marriages in Louisiana, such unions declined drastically. But interracial sex did not end in 1724 with the promulgation of the colony's Code Noir, and it did not end in 1751 with Vaudreuil's directives to Chevalier Macarty. Instead the Church officials responsible for recording the race of all individuals born, married, or deceased in their parish collaborated in obfuscating white men's paternity of multiracial children born of Indigenous or African mothers.[123] As French colonial officials strove to erect a durable commercial base in Louisiana, they inserted themselves into indigenous circuits of enslavement and the Atlantic slave trade, resulting in a hybrid slave system subjugating peoples throughout New France.[124] By the end of French rule in Louisiana in 1763, the census identified 4,600 enslaved peoples alongside 3,600 freed slaves, many of whom had French fathers.[125] Families throughout the French Atlantic deployed the legal and social tools at their disposal to consolidate property and strengthen family bonds between France and the Americas. Emergent racial categories were among these tools that could be invoked or ignored as suited families and communities.

4

Libertines and S*v*ges

Explaining France's Defeat in the Seven Years' War, 1754–1773

Writing from his spacious Genevan townhouse, Les Délices, in 1755, the celebrated French author Voltaire saluted his younger Swiss colleague, Jean-Jacques Rousseau, on the publication of *The Discourse on the Origin and Basis of Inequality among Men*. This volume, Voltaire teased, constituted the younger author's "new book against the human race."[1] That the text was compelling in its analysis of social hierarchy among humans, Voltaire acknowledged; that scientific or artistic advances historically coincided with increased political oppression, he granted. Yes, Voltaire concluded dryly, the essay was so persuasive, it might have had the effect of making him "want to go around on all fours, but I've lost the habit," blaming his own advanced age and established habits.[2] Rousseau relied on logical inversions to contend that the luxuries and innovations that Enlightenment-era Europeans so valued in their own societies were better perceived as burdens and chains. The arts and sciences corrupted human spirits rather than uplifting and refining them. Knowledge was poison and ignorance the cure. Civilization degraded the human heart, but the s*v*ge heart remained noble and true.[3] For all these reasons, Rousseau postulated that the inhabitants of the Americas—whom he perceived as representatives of a more "natural" world—were to be envied rather than pitied. Many readers succumbed to these tempting dialectics, seeking a simpler life as their means or fancy allowed.[4] But Voltaire resisted.

Part of the problem with embracing the "natural life" as Rousseau depicted it, Voltaire allowed, was his own age and poor health. He had become set in his ways: beyond walking on two legs, he mentioned medical care and coffee in particular among those trappings of "civilization" that made life worth living.[5] With characteristic equanimity he shrugged, "I can no longer depart to live among the s*v*ges of Canada, first, because the illnesses that I endure make a European doctor necessary, second, because war has broken out in that country, and the examples of our nations have made the s*v*ges almost as mean as ourselves."[6] Proxy wars fueled by the European arms trade had pitted Indigenous Americans allied with French militias against those allied with British militias, reaching a boiling point in 1754 and drawing the agents of these empires ever closer to war.[7] Conflicts prompted renewed scrutiny of empire's costs in blood, character, and treasure from ministerial offices to drawing rooms across Europe. Many, including Voltaire, blamed Europeans for escalating hostilities in North America through coercive trade and bad moral examples. Voltaire consoled himself that, since he could not travel to America, he would have to make do "with being a peaceful s*v*ge in my chosen solitude," residing quietly in Rousseau's own homeland of Geneva.[8]

Throughout the eighteenth century, imperial rivalries between the French and the British sparked conflict across Europe, America, and Asia. The stakes? Hegemony in global markets and trade systems. But it was the American theater that provided the first global test of the union forged between Indigenous Americans and Canadians allied with France against the British empire. In this moment, Voltaire asserted, Indigenous people were not outside the flow of "civilization" as Rousseau imagined, but participants who actively transformed those forces.

FLOUTING THE LAW OF NATIONS

In the context of imperial global war, the quasi-criminal category of the libertine shifted once again. The anxieties of officials in seventeenth-century Québec had taken a term associated with religious deviance and invested it with cross-cultural commercial significance, while the concerns of eighteenth-century Louisianans addressed sex across emerging racial boundaries. During the Seven Years' War, the libertine category morphed yet again to signal transgressions of the law of nations, particularly regarding the conduct of warfare formatively theorized by Hugo

Grotius (1625) and further developed by Emer de Vattel (1758) in direct contemplation of the Seven Years' War.[9] Departure from these standards became particularly important in assessing the conduct of French and Canadian officers during and after the war, as promotions or dismissals followed directly from these evaluations, which penetrated to the heart of what it meant to be French in the world, evaluating the significance and costs of France's overseas empire.[10]

During and after the Seven Years' War, French officers and ministers of state blamed libertines and s*v*ges for military losses. In this context "libertines" typically referred to Canadians of French ancestry who failed to abide by emergent European rules of commerce and warfare, while "s*v*ges" referred to Indigenous fighters (both allies and foes) who did the same. The Canadians' birth and upbringing outside of France led European-born officers to fear that this population had drifted from French authority and identity. Simultaneously, French officers referred to the rank-and-file soldiers drawn from the urban poor of France as "libertines" and inveighed with vigor against this errant population's penchant for drunken disorder.[11]

For over a century, Europeans had termed the Indigenous peoples of the Americas as "s*v*ges." But not until this armed contest did French military officers blame their allies' divergence from European standards of war for strategic military deficiencies, mutiny, treason, and, ultimately, the loss of French North America. Populations of both European and American descent evaded the direction of French officers and the colonial state; their unpredictability, egalitarianism, and diffuse command structure had cost France the war, or so went the story.[12] Moreover, if the French empire sheltered libertines and s*v*ges, the imperial project itself threatened to infect all of France with subjects of dubious mores and dismal industry. France would be consigned to a distant third place in the contest for global power against Britain and Spain, who had better managed their extensive imperial alliances. In contemporary assessments of the war, cultural assimilation and interracial alliances went from being the French empire's superpower to its kryptonite. Officials who in 1752 had confidently assessed the French king to be the best-loved monarch by colonial settlers and Indigenous allies now found cause to doubt that devotion.[13] As a result, in the wake of the Seven Years' War, French officials determined that imperial policy should focus on segregating s*v*ges and rehabilitating libertines to advance the interests of global France.[14]

It is regrettable that the French presence in colonial America has acquired the character of a quaint historical footnote according to both nations. It cannot remain there, for this period was too consequential in determining the course of imperial rivalries and indigenous treaty negotiations, laying the foundations for the early American republic and predicting the political ideals of the first French republic. Most histories of the French Atlantic empire end in 1763 or 1783, despite overwhelming evidence that French-descended settlers remained and maintained cultural and economic ties to France, supporting French migrants to North America long after the Treaties of Paris.[15] What is more, France's republican and royalist ministers nursed ambitions of continental American reconquest deep into the nineteenth century.[16]

Historians have leaned heavily on Voltaire's flippant dismissal of New France as a "few acres of snow" as evidence that the French state effectively abandoned its American territories prior to the war, and that leading intellectuals agreed the colony would never merit the wealth France had spent in colonizing it.[17] This formulation neglects Voltaire's grasp of the financial and geopolitical incentives that had woven French settlers and law into Canadian territories for over a century.[18] It also ignores the vigorous contemporary debate about global trade and power that emerged in the aftermath of this military contest. Against the absolute monarchy, Voltaire sided with those who opposed further colonial expansion on the principle that it grew the king's power in France even as it directed resources across the sea.[19] In contrast to this oppositional wing, most members of the French administrative state, alongside much of the French reading public, regarded French colonies in Canada to be a necessary check against both Spanish and British claims to global hegemony.[20]

To access this debate over empire, this chapter surveys the ministerial and military correspondence, judicial records, novels, and poems composed in the 1750s and 1760s that cast Canadians and Indigenous American allies as libertines. It was a portrayal that built on decades of representations of French settlers, their offspring, and their Indigenous neighbors as prone to excessive economic and sexual liberties. Within the French military command structure, French officers depicted Canadian officers and soldiers as peculiarly transgressive and inclined to subordination. This amplified the rivalry between the French *troupes de terre* against the French-American *troupes franches de la marine*, carefully documented by Christian Ayne Crouch's history of how the Seven Years' War transformed French and French American cultures of nobility and military valor.[21] French officers prided themselves on obedience to a strict military hierarchy, adherence to social systems of titled nobility reliant on performances of personal honor, and European rules of warfare.[22]

Canadian marine officers, in contrast, had trained in the methods of continental proxy wars alongside Indigenous American allies and against imperial rivals. These men prized ingenuity and hardiness, employing surprise and disguise as necessary weapons of warfare. Canadian officers, such as Daniel Liénard de Beaujeu and Charles-Michel Mouet de Langlade, knew that military success depended on diplomacy, deliberation, and their knowledge of Indigenous languages.[23] They recognized the importance of following American treaty procedures and gift-exchange practices to sustain alliances.[24] Perhaps different methods of warfare signaled levels of civilization, reasoned the Canadian colonial officials. Or maybe these methods represented appropriate adaptations to the environment and resources of each region.[25] The martial culture clash made a profound impact on French ideals of empire, infusing the libertine category with distinct strains of military insubordination in the latter half of the eighteenth century.[26]

While French-born officers active in the American theater secured promotions and preferment, many Canadians faced disciplinary action in the postwar period.[27] Several officers were arrested and tried, and a few were convicted for deeds that all agreed had been the norm in Canada: guerilla tactics in war, and enrichment tactics in commerce.[28] Canadian officers were less likely to be promoted to elite posts or to be nominated for military honors. Military historian Julia Osman suggests that these actions hamstrung the French colonial state as it began to reform military and administrative offices to better compete with the British in the ensuing decades.[29]

Conversely, Americans of both Indigenous and French descent held French officers responsible for the sequence of military failures that resulted in the loss of New France to the English. They characterized French commanders' efforts as ill conceived, mismanaged, and half hearted, as flawed defenses of the territories they considered home, where they perceived their families to be in genuine continuing danger at the hands of local threats and imperial rivals.[30] In the postwar peace treaty that ceded much of the territory where French settlers held property to the English or the Spanish, French American settlers and Indigenous American allies perceived a failure of the French state to fulfill its commitments to its dependents.[31] This failure prompted an ongoing conversation across the Atlantic about the obligations of a monarch to subject populations, transformed principles of popular sovereignty, and proved formative to the series of revolutions that roiled the Atlantic from 1776 to 1825.[32]

INDIGENOUS ALLIES IN THE FRENCH IMAGINATION, 1752–1754

By laying the blame for military defeat on the "unlawful" conduct of both settlers and Indigenous allies in French American colonies, French military officers decisively abandoned earlier justifications for empire that had praised the rogue valor and resourcefulness of these populations. Detailed information about the peoples inhabiting New France circulated widely in France. Weekly newspapers including the *Mercure de France* and the *Gazette de France* educated their readers to the many different names, languages, and customs of the Indigenous communities allied with the French. Editors cheered peace treaties concluded between French governors and Indigenous leaders from the banks of the Mississippi to the fort of Detroit.[33]

In 1756 the editor of the *Journal étranger* celebrated the advantages enjoyed by France's American troops, enhanced by Canadians and Indigenous allies. This patriotic observer imagined that although libertines were to be found among the ranks of the dissolute and doomed English, there were none among the stout-hearted confederates of France. "The bad luck of the English military in America," he wrote, "and the superiority in courage shown by the natural Americans over the ordered troops of

England, prove well enough that corruption has caused the English nation to degenerate. This reflection leads one to believe that it is better to muster soldiers from laborers and peasants, than among the libertines, the unemployed and the immoral."[34] The unreliability of British colonists, many of whom were religious dissidents or criminals in the metropole, constituted a recurring theme in French accounts about their imperial rivals.

In the years preceding the war, some of the most influential depictions of the Americas included the natural histories of north America by the count de Buffon, and the imaginative novels penned by Europeans that adopted an Indigenous narrator. The baron of Lahontan's novel *Dialogues avec un sauvage* was still published regularly.[35] But in 1752 European readers delighted in the observations of a new "American" interlocutor, Igli the "Iroquois" at the center of Jean-Henri Maubert de Gouvest's epistolary novel, *Lettres iroquoises*.[36] Maubert de Gouvest was no traveler, and his novel reveals nothing about actual Indigenous Americans. The farthest he journeyed was to the Kingdom of Poland, where he was denounced as a runaway priest and a freethinker and imprisoned in the Koenigstein fortress. There he clearly had access to quills, paper, and ink, for *Lettres iroquoises* was published the same year that he won his release upon promising to take up monastic orders once again. Nonetheless, Maubert de Gouvest's imaginary Iroquois proved to be highly influential: both Voltaire and Rousseau reveal familiarity with the novel, even taking some of Maubert de Gouvest's characterizations of Iroquois life and values as truth in their respective works.[37]

This first edition of *Lettres iroquoises* depicts an educated Frenchman's vision of life in America, noting key Indigenous alliances and enemies and organizing social mores. It demonstrates that the French reading public had access to detailed information regarding the shifting political terrain of Indigenous America. Europeans did not depict all Indigenous Americans as the same but distinguished between members of different Indigenous nations, divergent customs and traditions, and rival alliances with European settlers. By making his narrator a member of the Iroquois nation, Maubert de Gouvest built on his readers' awareness of the long history of contentious relations between French settlers and the Iroquois, and the recent cessation of those enmities. By 1752 several leaders of the

Haudenosaunee Confederacy had concluded peace treaties with the French and deployed French arms and alliances against British settlers who made devastating incursions onto their territories in this decade.[38] From Maubert de Gouvest's perspective, the Iroquois were a powerful ally in the Americas who conceivably could take the opportunity to learn more about the French and France by sending an emissary to live in the kingdom's capital city.[39] The character of Igli invited French readers to occupy his perspective as they considered the pressing questions of the 1750s: Could France count on Indigenous allies and Canadian settlers to defend the French American empire? Or was the Atlantic simply too great a distance to effectively govern? The imperial war of the 1750s became the proving ground in which officials of the French and colonial administrations determined the answers.

INDIGENOUS ALLIES IN THE AMERICAN CONFLICT, 1754–1760

The peace of Aix-la-Chapelle had brought no peace to North America. This treaty concluding the War of Austrian Succession in 1748 resulted in a European truce but did little to soothe the ongoing armed incursions between the imperial rivals in India, the Caribbean, or the Americas. Throughout the 1740s and 1750s, the first objective of the governors-general of New France and Louisiana was to drive creeping British settlers out from French territories.[40]

This simmering hostility explains why the governor-general of New France, Michel-Ange Duquesne ordered Ensign Joseph Coulon de Jumonville to take a small detachment of troops to the far eastern reaches of the Ohio territory. In 1745 then governor-general of Louisiana Pierre de Rigaud de Vaudreuil had recommended establishing a fort at the junction of the Ohio and Wabash Rivers to secure dominion over the continental river trade. Should the British beat them to it, he warned, the rivals would become "masters of the navigation of the whole Upper Country."[41] This was unacceptable to the officers on the ground in the heart of the American continent, urgently surveying maps of French forts and settlements that stretched along the Great Lakes, down the Mississippi, and into the Ohio River valley.[42] But then disaster struck.

Jumonville was dead. That much was clear on the morning of May 28, 1754. But when was he killed? By whom? And what exactly had he been doing there, camped in the shaded glen nestled into a rocky outcropping?[43] The details remain murky, even after 250 years. From the beginning the French and the British attempted to frame the account to suit their own national objectives. Typically omitted from narratives of the conflict composed prior to the 1980s were the perspectives of Indigenous Americans who had allied with the troops commanded by Ens. Joseph Coulon de Jumonville on the French side, and Maj. George Washington on the British side.[44] But these allies were crucial, according to contemporary accounts—neither the French nor the British would engage the other in combat without the approval and support of these Indigenous leaders, painstakingly cultivated through face-to-face negotiations, treaties, and commercial exchange.[45] Furthermore, the conduct of these allies proved to be consequential.

In 1754 the French and British were technically not at war, but, in the Americas, officials on both sides maintained low-level hostilities by funding proxy wars against their imperial rivals. The French stepped up efforts to defend a string of forts in the Ohio River valley against incursions by British traders and their Mingo and Iroquois allies. Jumonville, a French Canadian officer from a family of colonial administrators, arrived in the Ohio territory with some thirty individuals, on Contrecoeur's orders. According to the French, Jumonville had been sent as an ambassador to meet with the British commander in the area and negotiate the terms for a peaceful coexistence in this contested territory. Sighted by hostile Indigenous spies, the French camp was attacked by Washington's forces a few hours after sunrise on the morning of May 28 without warning or mercy. At least eight men were killed, including Jumonville. One man, Monceau, a French Canadian soldier, escaped the massacre and returned to Fort Duquesne to inform his commanders. He told Contrecoeur everything he had seen, and, based on his report, the French commander accused the British and their allies of surrounding the French camp, "English on one side and Indians on the other. They received two volleys from the English, and not from the Indians."[46] Others had heard of the assault as well; the commander at Chiningué had information from the

"Indians who were present at the attack say that M. de Jumonville was killed while he was hearing the summons read; that he received a rifle shot in the head, after which they struck to wipe out our whole force. The Indians who were present rushed forward and stopped the English, otherwise all our men would have been routed."[47] According to multiple accounts (all relayed by Contrecoeur), the French asserted that French officers on contested territory bore summons for negotiation; the British met a peace delegation with arms and slaughtered France's ambassador and troops, to the shock and horror of Indigenous witnesses.

French colonial officials had long claimed that they, and not the English or the Spanish, were the best-loved empire in the Americas. We cannot know whether the killing of Jumonville truly shocked Britain's Indigenous allies—it seems doubtful. For decades leaders of Indigenous nations had played these imperial representatives against each other, accompanied them on raids to harass forts or individuals, and informed each of the other's movements.[48] But the allies' outrage was increasingly central to French colonial officials' rationale for expanded French territory. This discourse made Indigenous people into fictive "constituents" of distant rulers, as early modern monarchies began to consider the political uses of popular sovereignty within an imperial context.[49]

The French response to Jumonville's death was immediate and unequivocal. Here was a clear violation of the standards of war and peace. To kill an ambassador was dishonorable and cowardly. It constituted an assassination and symbolized the underhanded, perfidious, and savage tactics typical of the British. Swiss legal theorist Emer de Vattel obliquely references the incident when he asserts that nations were united in identifying "the independence and the inviolability of an Ambassador among the Natural and Necessary Principles in the Law of Nations."[50] The Spanish reported that this law of ambassadors was recognized and respected in Mexico. "It is the same among the s*v*ge peoples of the Americas," Vattel insisted, as it was in China, India, and among the Arabs.[51] Here was a searing indictment against the British empire, then, to charge the British colonial militia with failure to respect Jumonville in his capacity as an ambassador. In publications that ranged from the official state newspapers to the penny press that circulated in France and across Europe, critics pilloried the young lieutenant colonel George Washington, who was deemed responsible for the slaughter as commander of the British Virginia Regiment. On July 4, 1754, after engaging Jumonville's brother in battle and losing handily, Washington reluctantly signed an "unusual document of surrender," in which he accepted responsibility for the murder of Jumonville, demanded of him by the dead man's brother, Capt. Louis Coulon de Villiers in exchange for a peaceful retreat.[52] The text also required the British to cease activities in the area for the span of one year.

Within the year a professor at the University of Paris, Antoine-Léonard Thomas, deemed the death of Jumonville to be a worthy topic for an epic poem. In this tribute Jumonville fulfilled the sacred mission of the French nobility in military leadership, serving as an august representative of king and nation. His death, warned the Abbé de la Porte, was no "obscure or vulgar crime, it is a crime that must excite the indignation of all people, that attacks the primitive Laws of the Nations, that overturns all the foundations of Political Law established between men."[53] Historian David Bell has addressed the political purpose to which this poem was put, forging French national identity as honorable and well-loved by Indigenous Americans against the British who were characterized as Europe's barbarians.[54] As part of a broader effort of "royal patriotism," Bell contends, the memorialization of Jumonville was designed to build popular support for the French king, navy, and empire.[55]

Thomas's poem has four sections. The first outlines the present conflicts of Europe, holding the English responsible for these. Their jealousy for French "possessions in America, our victories in Europe, the extent of our commerce in all corners of the world" has driven them to attack French ships on the open sea, and French forts on the American plains.[56] The poet celebrates the nobility and the brotherhood exhibited by Jumonville and Villiers and lauds their quest for glory under new skies, along distant riverbanks. In the poem Jumonville wins the honor to confront the trespassing English by popular acclaim, "nominated by one common voice" and, in his farewell address, unites the intellectual favors of Minerva with the military prowess of Mars.[57] In the woods Jumonville's company is surrounded, and all are killed or made prisoners, except for "one lone Canadian who escaped, and brought the news back to the Commander."[58]

Receiving this news Villiers vows to avenge his brother's death and departs immediately to the task. In fact, as the editor of the *Observateur littéraire* notes, it took months before the assassination was avenged, and, even then, the French officers followed the conduct of war. Despite the poetic license taken by Thomas, which would make it appear that vengeance for a brother slain overrode the French officers' standards, in fact Villiers and his men engaged General Washington following the rules of war and secured their honor. This brief review of Thomas's poem concludes by observing that, despite the elegant style and compelling subject matter, the poem has sold only a modest number of copies, from the bookstores of chez Herissant on the rues St. Jacques, St. Paul, and St. Hilaire.

In a satirical diatribe against the English, *Les sauvages de l'Europe* (1760), Robert-Martin Lesuire fulminated that the British even lacked appropriate regard for ambassadors. After all, "didn't they very recently assassinate M. de Jumonville, who came to negotiate with them?"[59] The author contrasts British savageness with Indigenous rules of conduct: "The law of nature, which speaks to S*v*ges, is no longer maintained among them [the British]. They no longer distinguish between the just and unjust, between the regrettable and the crime."[60] Such expressions in the court of public opinion fanned the flames of imperial rivalries and communicated France's reliance on its robust network of Indigenous alliances.

In contrast the British cast Jumonville's errand as suspicious and deemed Washington's attack an imperial necessity. Washington's diary recorded the event, in which he describes approaching the French camp in single file, silent advance. He recalled that only when discovered by the French, and under imminent threat of attack, did Washington order his troops to fire, supported by soldiers commanded by Waggoner. The French returned fire. In only fifteen minutes of battle, "the Enemy was routed. We killed M. de Jumonville, the commander of that Party, as also nine others; we wounded one and made Twenty-one prisoners, whom were M. la Force, M. Drouillon, and two Cadets. The Indians scalped the Dead, and took away the most part of their Arms."[61] Shaw, witness to the battle, asserted that the Mingo warrior accompanying Washington, Tanacharison (Half King), dealt the fatal blow to Jumonville.

The historian Fred Anderson postulates that only by foregrounding the Indigenous political and territorial interests that motivated the attack on French troops can historians begin to make sense of this event.[62]

The events of 1754 remained central to France's national story for decades. In 1785 a weekly newspaper provided a summary of events in French history from the week of May 20, including among several summaries of famous battles "May 24, 1754, the unworthy and cowardly assassination of M. de Jumonville by the English which determined America's fate. This Officer had been appointed by M. de Contrecoeur, Commander of Canada for the King of France. Everyone knows the poem that this perfidious act inspired M. Thomas from the Academy Française to write."[63] Telling the tale nurtured the hope that France might one day return to govern those people who—they told themselves—so ardently desired French rule across the Atlantic.

In his campaign journal, Louis-Joseph de Montcalm, the commanding officer of French troops in New France, provided thorough commentary of the challenges of American combat. Throughout this text he rhetorically conflated Indigenous Americans and Canadians, identifying their shared military practices, social customs, even alimentary tastes. Regarding a local fruit that grew on a particular island, he wrote on May 7, 1756, "in the springtime, this fruit ripens and has a delicious taste much esteemed by the s*v*ges and the Canadians. They make a good liqueur with it."[64] Taste was not universal, it seemed, but local and determined by experience. Montcalm himself might have savored the berries upon distillation, but he gives no indication that French transplants appreciated these American delicacies.

When smallpox made terrible inroads in Canada, resident physicians and savants debated the best course of action. Vaccine technology made rapid advances in Europe during the eighteenth century, and, although inoculations had saved many lives in France and Switzerland, Montcalm observed general resistance to such methods in Canada, explaining that "the s*v*ges don't like innovations, and the Canadians sometimes unite their admirable religious faith to precautions that make them reject a method that I believe useful to the conservation of the human species, under the pretext that it is not permitted to do certain harm, regardless of how small, in order to do good."[65] In other words, here was a population resistant to enlightenment and progress. Montcalm characterized both populations as simple and naive, fundamentally undereducated and out of step with European innovations. More important, both groups resisted extended military service of the type to which French soldiers had grown accustomed. Canadian troops expected to return home to aid their families with the harvest, and Indigenous warriors left military campaigns for weeks at a time. Soldiering was a seasonal duty defined by short-term objectives, rather than a professional identity and multiyear commitment. This difference would prove to be a decisive factor as the conflict in America deepened.

THE FORT WILLIAM HENRY MASSACRE

By 1757 France and Britain had resumed open warfare on the European continent, in the Americas and the Caribbean, and across India. This did not change the landscape of hostilities much in the Americas, where proxy wars and raids had defined the previous decades. But it increased the number of men and arms in each conflict and escalated the potential consequences. Throughout the war's early years, the French and their Indigenous allies maintained the upper hand. The French army led by Louis-Joseph de Montcalm relied heavily on the geographical knowledge and guerilla practices of Indigenous American allies and French American officers and soldiers. However, the conditions by which Montcalm secured military success seem to have caused him to reevaluate the price of that dependence.[66]

Fort William Henry, located on the southern coast of Lake George in present-day upstate New York, had been built only two years prior in 1755. Montcalm commanded a force of 8,000 men, of whom over 2,000 were Indigenous warriors representing nearly 20 different nations.[67] On July 26 a small party of Indigenous Americans attacked a 350-person strong squadron led by Col. John Parker, reducing their numbers by 75 percent.[68] On July 29 forces led by the Chevalier de Lévis took a land route from Ticonderoga, some 120 miles due south of Montréal, along Lake George's eastern shoreline to Fort William Henry. Montcalm led the remaining troops in canoes over the lake. Five days later the French and allied forces reunited and launched a siege on the British fort. The Marquis de Montcalm issued a warning to Munro, noting that the fort was surrounded by "numerous Army and superior Artillery, and all the s*v*ges from the higher parts of the Country." Montcalm assured the British commander that "I have it yet in my Power to restrain the S*v*ges, and oblige them to observe a Capitulation, as hitherto none of them have been killed, which will not be in my Power in other Circumstances."[69] Despite failure of reinforcements to arrive, and devastating news from Fort Edward, this account emphasizes the valor with which British troops defended Fort William Henry to the last hour, and again the great effect of British artillery.

With 2100 troops the British were woefully outnumbered. They lacked the resources to sustain a long-term siege and had little chance of receiving supplies or reinforcements from neighboring forts. After a week the British commander of the fort, Lt. Col. George Munro, surrendered to the French. Montcalm and Munro concluded a surrender in terms that recalled the continental theater: British troops agreed not to serve in the military for eighteen months, and in return they would receive safe passage to Fort Edward, some sixteen miles to the south on the Hudson River.

A British witness, James Furnis, had only recently arrived at the fort to take stock of supplies and implement a system to better account for use and resupply. He highlighted the overwhelming numbers of the French forces and made particular note of the conduct of Montcalm's Indigenous American allies: "During the Time the Capitulation was transacting, the S*v*ges came into the Camp, and began to plunder, but some Companys [sic] of French Grenadiers being ordered in, prevented their carrying off any Thing considerable, and in a short Time disposed them."[70] Of this period the official report read that "Indians came about the Fort, and with great Tranquility in their countenances; took all the Horses they could find and Led them off without taking any manner of notice of us."[71] Nevertheless, Montcalm promised to provide an escort of 450 men to protect the British troops in their removal to Fort Edward.

But as the articles of capitulation were read, France's Indigenous allies voiced vehement disapproval and menaced the British troops physically.

According to the established practices of this continent's warfare, seizing the goods of the loser—particularly arms and ammunition—was all but a guaranteed right of combat. Additionally, Indigenous American combatants knew that they would only receive payment from French commanders upon providing the continent's accepted proof of engagement: scalps.[72] As the British withdrew from the fort, a witness insisted that "the S*v*ges scaled the Walls and came in, Running about, searching every Nook and Corner of the Fort; where we left them to pursue what methods they thought proper: and what afforded them much satisfaction, was, the Murther of the Sick and Wounded in the Hospital."[73] In the breach between the French commander's promises and his allies' conduct opened a yawning gulf in the law of nations governing warfare. Furnis continued his testimony:

> On the 10th early in the Morning when we were preparing to march, the S*v*ges surrounded us, took my Horses which I had given to carry off the Gun, got over the Breast Work, and began to plunder. At all Events the French Troops who we thought were sent to protect us, were of no Assistance, and advised giving up our Effects rather than dispute with the S*v*ges who would not be satisfied until they had got all the Baggage, this tho contrary to the Capitulation (to prevent worse Consequences) was complied with, as the Officers and Soldiers immediately delivered every Thing up to them, except their Arms and the Clouths on our Backs, which we hoped they would suffer us to carry off. Instead of which they took our Hats, and Swords from us, and began to strip us, on which it was thought proper to march out as soon as possible, the S*v*ges [having] taken the Drums, Halberds, and even the Firelocks from the Soldiers.[74]

British troops responded with panic and sought to escape the fort by any means possible. In response Indigenous American combatants attacked many, scalped some, and imprisoned others. The body count may have ranged anywhere from twenty to three hundred individuals.[75] The actions posed a clear threat to the British troops as they surrendered and marched to shelter at Fort Edwards. But it similarly posed a problem for Montcalm, whose word had been broken by his allies' actions. A French officer's honor was forged on the battlefield and at the negotiation table. The members of the officer corps prided themselves on their facility negotiating between cultures and on France's reputation as the "best-loved" empire in the Americas. But here was evidence that they could not make themselves understood by their allies, and that the word of a French officer held little sway over his coalition of supporting nations.[76]

Furnis himself was captured and taken back to the fort, before he was "luckily retaken by a French Guard, who sent an Officer and Twenty Men with me into the Fort."[77] During this time the French seized the fort's "Artillery, Ammunition, and Provisions" before burning the entire structure to the ground. Furnis strove to provide useful information to his commanders and noted hopefully, even in the midst of this military catastrophe for the British, that the officer in charge of artillery, Lt. Thomas Collins, had acted with distinction, and that the "French Artillery Officers acknowledged our Artillery to have much better served than their own."[78] This account, drafted the same day that Furnis arrived at safety in the Office of Ordnance of New York, concluded by observing that he regretted he could not enumerate those slain, wounded, or taken prisoner by those forces allied with the French, but that it "is said the S*v*ges have carried many Prisoners to Montréal, which the French General promises to return."[79]

In total, the British report concluded, no less than 80 men had died during the French siege, for nearly 30 cadavers had been spotted along the road, and many more were assumed to be hidden in the woods, given the stench that extended all the way to Fort Edward, with more than 250 reported missing. These deaths took place after the surrender and could be traced directly to "Montcalm's willful neglect, of sending a sufficient Guard," the British witness argued.[80] The actions at Fort William Henry made victory very bitter indeed for General Montcalm. He had made the protection of the remaining British troops his top priority, and refused to attack Fort Edward, despite the insistence of Governor-General Rigaud de Vaudreuil.[81]

A vigorous public relations battle proceeded directly from this incident, but it remained largely a Francophone affair. Partisans of the French officer General Montcalm claimed a clean military victory over the British and emphasized the honorable service of a nobleman. French American representatives lobbied forcefully to press their advantage; they decried Montcalm as an ineffective leader in the American theater. The few British accounts remained unpublished and forgotten—for their military and political leaders, Fort William Henry was an episode to be learned from, not publicized to the advantage of other nations.[82]

This might have remained the last word on the events of Fort William Henry, had a novelist not seized upon the incident in 1823 as the motivating plotline to a romantic American tale. James Fenimore Cooper penned *The Last of the Mohicans* as an homage to a culture perceived as disappearing in the face of Anglo-American policies of Indian segregation and removal. Cooper returned his audience to a time of imperial contest and struggle, when the Dutch, French, and English rivals all vied for outposts in the North American continent, and Indigenous American leaders determined the winners and losers among European empires. Emphasizing the shared interests and tactics of settlers with Indigenous Americans, Cooper rewrote the history of America as one independent of empires. The events at Fort William Henry took place, he wrote, "during the third year of the war which England and France last waged for the possession of a country that neither was destined to retain."[83]

This novel, which proved immediately popular, rejected the European imperial rivalries that had positioned England against France. Instead English settlers, French settlers, and Indigenous allies worked together or fought each other to achieve local goals, deaf to the overreaching mandates from distant kings and generals. What did the Seven Years' War look like from Michigan, Illinois, or Ohio territories? Cooper's novel provides important insights into the settlers' objectives and values, and their shared opposition to distant metropolitan directives.

Cooper's hero, Natty Bumpo, embodies the colonist positioned between Europe and America, between his European military comrades and his Indigenous American allies. In Cooper's prose, we see how Americans in the nineteenth century drew very different military and political lessons from the Seven Years' War than those drawn some forty years earlier in the courts of Versailles and London. The author and his audience prized the cultural mediator. Natty Bumpo, also called Leatherstocking,

Deerslayer, and Hawkeye, bore multiple appellations bestowed by the many communities in which he moved. He wore moccasins and a fur cap and carried a trusty long rifle. This amalgam of Indigenous and European attire suited his employment as a scout for the British military. English by birth, partially raised within the Delaware tribe and educated by Moravian Christians, this fictional character recalled a time when the world met in the woodlands of North America and articulated a hybrid ethic: "He who wishes to prosper in Indian warfare must not be too proud to learn from the wit of a native."[84] Following this pronouncement Natty launches into a full-throated condemnation of the "white man's courage" that results in face-to-face battles among opposing troops on fields and clearings. It was not the European that won America, Cooper instructs his readers, who were busily distancing themselves from that hybrid past. American independence resulted from those men and women who melded Indigenous American practices of warfare, travel, commerce, and social order with European arms and technical ingenuity.

Cooper's narrator blames the Marquis de Montcalm for the massacre at Fort William Henry. The French general is pictured "in the flower of his age," and at the "zenith of his fortunes."[85] In dialogue with the British officers, Cooper's Montcalm clearly communicates his preference for European enemies over his purported allies among the Indigenous Americans. The nobility of the French general and his obedience to a European code of conduct in warfare are made manifest in his gallantry to women and in his faith in the word of enemy officers. But in the rough-and-tumble backwoods of the Americas, such manners seem quaint, even foolish. Montcalm proved incapable of communicating the end of conflict to his Indigenous American allies, according to Cooper's characters. The massacre at Fort William Henry was a stain on the French commander's reputation and served as a reminder of "how easy it is for generous sentiments, high courtesy, and chivalrous courage to lose their influence beneath their chilling blight of selfishness."[86] Montcalm had given his word, the English had trusted that word, but European-born imperial representatives did not have the final say over either the people or the events in this conflict that had been kindled in the Americas.

The consequences of the Treaty of Paris's devastating peace took years to measure, but already by 1761 the French administration sought explanations for its military losses in the conduct of the British, the Canadians, or Indigenous allies who flouted the "law of nations" regarding rules of warfare. But the trope of the Canadian libertines who threatened French empire nowhere found more resonant expression than in the characterizations that emerged from one of the great scandals of the eighteenth century, the Affaire du Canada.[87] The final years of the American war had been particularly traumatic in Canada, as military losses combined with food shortages to threaten the population with imminent physical danger, either from famine or enemy fire.[88] Canadian officials were never directly charged with losing the war. Instead prosecutors for the Crown focused on measurable charges of corruption, price-fixing, and fraud among the men who administered the colony of New France. On these charges François Bigot and Pierre de Rigaud, Marquis de Vaudreuil-Cavagnail, along with many other colonial merchants and officers, were recalled to France and imprisoned in the Bastille in 1761. During a lengthy trial, these men stood accused of myriad financial abuses. François Bigot, the only Frenchman to stand trial, had served as the intendant of the colony from 1748 until his arrest and trial in 1760. He was accused of running the colony of New France as his own personal fiefdom, and the parallels drawn between his behavior and Louis XV's behavior in France were nowhere starker than in the popular perception of their mistresses. Both Madame de Pompadour in France and Angélique Renaud d'Avène des Méloizes in Canada were reputed for their beauty and pleasant conversation, and both were referred to with disdain as "la grande Sultane" by rival officials and the popular press, who imagined them to be the illegitimate female powers behind despotic thrones.[89]

The French government found plausible scapegoats in the men charged with the governance of New France, including the governor-general, the Marquis de Vaudreuil-Cavagnial, the intendant François Bigot, and fifty-three other officials, clerks and secretaries, merchants, fort commanders, guards, and scouts who worked for the colonial government in Canada. According to the charges brought in the Châtelet court of Paris, Bigot, Vaudreuil, and their accomplices had engaged in "monopolies, abuses, vexations and prevarications" including the misdirection of military resources and defrauding His Majesty's government.[90] By creating a society for trade, these men had enriched themselves and impoverished their fellow Canadians. Their actions injured the king's interests, the accusation contended, and in this way Canadians themselves had doomed the future of New France.

The court's inquiry took three years, during which scores of testimonies were heard and thousands of judicial records created. The legal briefs published by all sides constituted an education in the geography, populations, and administration of the American colonies for those interested members of the French reading public. The memoir that undertook the defense of Michel Jean-Hugues Péan, a captain in the colonial troops accused of enriching himself through monopolistic trade practices, opened with an eight-page glossary to define important colonial terms for French readers, including the names of relevant Indigenous American nations, articles of dress, and American rivers and villages. Throughout the trial Péan insisted on his innocence, pointing to the excellent recommendations he had received from his military superiors. He responded directly to charges that he fostered monopolies by explaining how trade with Indigenous Americans operated through established military forts. Certainly he had made money from the trade, the brief acknowledged, like many officers before him, as the system of commerce had long intended.[91] Péan's wife, Angélique Renaud d'Avène des Méloizes, had been born in Québec City in 1722; married in 1746, the couple occupied the center of Francophone society in the colony. When François Bigot arrived in 1748, it was widely rumored that Angélique became his mistress, presumably with her husband's approval. For the trial Angélique accompanied her husband to France in 1760, visiting him in the Bastille prison fifty-eight times, until he was finally acquitted and released in June 1764.[92] Others were not so fortunate. The trial resulted in the perpetual exile of the intendant François Bigot and the commissaire Jean-Victor Varin de la Marre. Their goods were seized by the Crown, and substantial fines imposed of 1,500,000 livres for Bigot, and 800,000 livres for Varin.[93]

The final verdict of the court found four men guilty, singling out those merchants who had most profited from wartime inflation. They were banished from Paris for nine years and sentenced to additional fines. Furthermore, seven officers were found guilty of embezzlement and misappropriation of funds, for which they were banned from Paris for several years and condemned to pay fines ranging between 20,000 to 100,000 livres.[94] The king's prosecutor ultimately dropped all charges against the governor-general Pierre de Rigaud, Marquis de Vaudreuil-Cavagnail, and the officers Charles Deschamps de Boishebert, Nicolas Desmeloizes, Paul Perrault and Claude-Nicolas Fayolle. The trial and the punishing sentences were the talk of all Europe and America. On December 20, 1763, Voltaire wrote in a letter to Genevan mathematician, Gabriel Cramer, "Since you want news of our country, Bigot the intendant of Canada and three consorts were condemned to perpetual exile, confiscation and restitution, the others to short-term exile, and France is condemned to lose Canada."[95] The philosophe perceived a degree of misplaced retribution at work in this trial and knew that these men's small fortunes would not compensate for France's damaged global prestige and retracting geopolitical power.

In an unusual coda to the case, the judges further vindicated Montcalm's mother and widow in their assertions that Bigot had injured the memory of the fallen general when Bigot called him an informant. This accusation was deemed calumnious, and honor was restored to the military leader's name.[96] It is worth asking, would any of these charges have come to light had France prevailed in the Seven Years' War? Over the course of the trial, French colonial officials were incidentally charged with daily abuses of power. In presiding over a colonial government that distributed aristocratic indulgences and preferments, it was whispered that they had inculcated a libertine environment in which men swapped their wives' sexual favors for pecuniary rewards. Most of the accused were Canadian-born officers, and, in both the legal briefs and popular press, they were depicted as operating by a corrupt ethics coupled with libertine sexual conduct. Historian John Bosher asserts that the officials of Canada did not receive a fair trial—not to claim that they were innocent of charges. But, like the 1766 execution of Gen. Lally Tollendal for the loss of Pondichery, the trial was less about rooting out treason and more about finding a "scapegoat for French mismanagement and

French losses," as Peter Gay has argued.[97] This was also the assessment of Barthélémy François Joseph Moufle d'Angerville, employed as a clerk in the French navy, who wrote an account in 1781 of Louis XV's private life and political choices.[98]

Prior to 1760 there had been warnings that widespread corruption in the administration of New France threatened the colony's ruin.[99] The Marquis de Montcalm's family fanned the flames of these accusations, with the obvious intent of rescuing their relative's posthumous honor. As the military leader in the American fight, Montcalm bore some responsibility for French losses. But, with the Affaire du Canada trial, the family placed blame squarely on the shoulders of the civil administrators.

Charges of corruption might strike modern readers as strange, because the profiteering and preferential economic associations of which colonial officers were accused appeared to be business as usual across Atlantic empires and within European kingdoms throughout the early modern era. Officials used their positions to make fortunes, to advance their families, and to pursue private interests. However, by the mid-eighteenth century, there can be no doubt that "business as usual" struck the reading public in Europe and the Americas as rotten to the core.

One contemporary observed that the lot of Canadian officers had been "judged by the public two weeks ago," a month prior to the court's judgment, and that their deliberations were not generous. According to public opinion, proper punishment would have had "Monsieur Bigot's head cut off and Péan and Cadet hanged, but that is false and we think they will get off."[100] The tremendous costs of the war were blamed on these officers' mismanagement of funds, rather than on some of the financial factors over which the Crown had control: inflation due to payment for troops, rapid troops' increase and demand on goods, increased shipping costs, and the depreciation of paper currencies.[101] Due to the trials, the Crown confiscated Canadian bills, and through fines passed some costs of war on to those officers. Bosher concludes that the trial and convictions "served to justify suspending the entire Canadian war debt and then repudiating more than half of it."[102] Clearly, an important motivation for this trial was to recoup the Crown's expenses by imposing them on the private individuals who had supported and organized the French empire in America. The verdict did not solve France's ongoing debt problem, of course, and it exacerbated many of the government's other challenges in military, administrative, and economic organization.

CONCLUSION

What were the long-term consequences of France's military losses and judicial scandals in North America? In 1763 the French jurist Guillaume François Le Trosne contended that the corruption evident in the Affaire du Canada struck at the heart of the colonial endeavor and therefore undermined the institutions of the French state itself. In this analysis Le Trosne directly followed Emer de Vattel's insights that "corruption is a means contrary to all the rules of virtue and honesty, and clearly wounds the law of nature."[103] Le Trosne observed that the judiciary faced terrible challenges in this generation due to decaying morals and the flimsy education of youths who entered society too soon. He argued that all venal officers—not only colonial administrators—sought to profit from their position, rather than to serve the state to the best of their ability. This was to be expected, and officials should recognize that the state's own structures in fact cultivated the corruption they ostensibly sought to curtail. Le Trosne observed that the decision handed down by the court in the Affaire du Canada, against Bigot, Varin, Cadet, and others, "only proves too well that greed is deadly to the State when it goes unpunished."[104]

But what French elites learned from the Affaire du Canada was perhaps not what the Crown anticipated. This episode drove home three lessons: first, the trials highlighted the seemingly arbitrary nature of justice in the French empire; second, they revealed social hierarchy as a substitute for law; and, third, for subjects in Canada and France, the aftermath of the Seven Years' War highlighted both the fragility of royal authority and the speed with which monarchs renounced obligations to colonial subjects.[105] If the libertine transgressed the law of nations in military conduct or governance, many muttered that the king of France himself seemed to be the worst offender.[106]

5

A Race of Libertines

Gender, Family, and the Law in France, 1684–1789

> Get rid of pride, and you would no longer see that
> spirit of independence and revolt that progresses day by
> day. The fatal germ of the most awful revolutions that
> threatens us with the worst unhappiness, that sustains
> and maintains in the heart of Christianity that impious
> race that blasphemes all, that race of heretics that
> overthrows all, that race of libertines that mocks all.
>
> —ABBÉ REGUIS, Sermon for 13th Sunday after Pentacost,
> "On Pride," 1766

Try as they might, France's royal ministers could not effectively argue that libertines constituted a uniquely colonial phenomenon. Evidence to the contrary surrounded them. Indeed, for every libertine produced in the colonies, two more seemed to take root in France. The phenomenon constituted an epidemic; the plague of the age struck cities, ports, even the most remote mountain villages under the dominion of Europe's Most Christian King. Everyone agreed that France was rife with libertines, and that the inhabitants of the kingdom's capital city pursued pleasure to the exclusion of all else.[1] But why? And what was to be done with them? These questions sparked vigorous debates on the relative merits and dangers posed by religious, economic, social, and political liberties. Resulting conversations took stock of how profound reforms in France's

FIG 6. Map of France, 1762: provinces and main cities. Louis Brion de La Tour. [La France analysée par Gouvernemens, Parlemens, Généralités et Archevechés / par le Sr. Brion ; gravé par Droüet]. Bibliothèque Nationale de France, http://catalogue .bnf.fr/ark:/12148/cb40593927f.

legal systems had already reorganized the kingdom and the empire, and deliberated the potential impacts of future change.

What to do with the libertine sons and daughters of France? In 1684 Louis XIV issued a rule against vagrancy that targeted Parisian youth under the age of twenty-five. Those who would not work, engaged in libertine activities, or were accused of prostitution could be imprisoned—in the Bicêtre (boys) and La Salpetrière (girls) prisons.[2] Sixteen years later the king renewed the edict, applying it to the entire kingdom.[3] Later that year the lieutenant-general of police in Paris, Marc-René de Voyer, Marquis d'Argenson, attempted to address the problem of idleness among the kingdom's youth beyond the capital with a "general order requiring fathers to denounce their libertine and vagabond children" or face fines and punishment themselves.[4] According to the royal ministers and officials charged with policing the kingdom, France's plague of libertines resulted either from the negligence of permissive parents or the increased audacity of rebellious children. Significantly, the text of d'Argenson's order made no reference to sexual behavior; instead it singled out idleness resulting from the failures of children—both minors and adults—to conform to parental authority.[5] Throughout his reports the kingdom's chief police officer employed the term "libertine" to characterize individuals who engaged in gambling, excessive expenditures, concubinage, extramarital sexuality, marriage without parental approval, public harassment of women, irreverent speech outside of a church, and sodomy. The term might also identify disobedient domestic servants, and priests who entered common-law marriages.[6] A handful of these actions constituted crimes, while most were deemed immoral, and all had been subject to contested jurisdictions and recent legal reforms. But for the remainder of the century, the policy seems to have perversely stimulated accusations and detentions rather than curbing libertine behavior. This order, designed to remedy perceived breakdowns in family order, instead laid bare the seams that strained to bind together this fractious society.[7] In every province family-requested detentions increased steadily over the eighteenth century.[8]

Some observers lay the blame for France's libertine problem at the feet of the Jesuits, long suspected of corrupting the kingdom's youth in schools and convents. The 1731 cause célèbre of the novitiate Marie-Catherine Cadière seduced by a Jesuit priest bundled together these anxieties.[9] Others blamed anticlerical authors and strove to reawaken Catholic piety.[10] By the 1760s many conservative commentators found fault with the sweeping reforms of law, prisons, education, families, social order, and political order proposed by the philosophes.[11] Perhaps libertines resulted from the influx of luxuries from around the globe? Or from the disintegration of French military hierarchy following the Seven Years' War, or the example of corrupt colonial officers, exemplified by the Affaire du Canada? Or had the impious examples of Philippe d'Orléans

(r. 1715–23) or King Louis XV (r. 1723–74) played some role, inspiring France's subjects to engage in behavior that challenged social norms?[12]

But none of these targets satisfied the popular moralist Abbé Réguis.[13] No, he asserted in a widely circulated sermon: it was pride that had made the French a "race of libertines."[14] As a people, inhabitants of the kingdom were better known for their pride in scientific innovation, burgeoning commerce, or the worldly arts of pleasure than for their piety. He lamented that luxury, ambition, and greed threatened to fray the moral fiber of a population no longer united behind one king, one faith, and one law.[15] Réguis did not identify the French overseas empire as the source of eighteenth-century libertinage. But, in singling out pride as the root problem of modern society, he echoed arguments made by those members of the parlements, the judges and advocates associated with the provincial law courts who sought to restrain colonial spending following France's devastating losses in the Seven Years' War.[16] In their analysis the French monarch's pride had overextended the legal and economic institutions of the state.[17]

A libertine, according to Réguis, relied on ridicule and mockery, rather than a philosophically grounded atheism, to undermine religious authorities. He proposed that libertines were more committed to a "modern" spirit of reason and knowledge than to pious reflection and charitable acts.[18] As a result the libertine was distinct from the committed heretic, but through needling and relentless inquiry brought society to a similar place, in the estimation of the bishop and his pious readers in every corner of France. This category identified individuals who persisted in religious dissent and theological skepticism. After the Edict of Fontainebleau in 1685 reestablished Catholicism as the sole religion tolerated in France, religious dissent was, of course, technically a crime. But enforcement of religious orthodoxy varied widely throughout the kingdom, waxing and waning with the inclinations of local authorities. Although perceptibly informed by imperial inflections, the libertine category maintained a connotation of religious skepticism resulting in general antiauthoritarianism that shaped contemporary usage in families and communities across the French kingdom.

Denis Diderot sidestepped the ideological connotations of the libertine in his art criticism regarding the Salon of 1765. He relied on the term to

FIG 7. Jean-Baptiste Greuze, *The Father's Curse: The Ungrateful Son*, 1778. J. Paul Getty Museum. http://www.getty.edu/art/collection/objects/28/jean-baptiste-greuze-the-father's-curse-the-ungrateful-son-french-about-1778/.

communicate straightforward filial disobedience, identifying the central figure in a painting by Jean-Baptiste Greuze as a "young libertine."[19] Diderot refers to this image as *The Ingrate Son*, although it was later exhibited under the title *The Father's Curse* (1778). The artist depicts a humble domestic scene, with a young man standing in the foreground, raising his arm in farewell despite the entreaties of his grieving siblings and mother. In the doorway stands an older army recruiter, waiting for this new soldier to extricate himself from family obligations. On the far left of the image, the family's patriarch half-stands, arms outstretched, as if he would physically restrain his grown son from leaving home. According to Diderot, this composition provides a lesson in morality.[20] But his sympathy lay with the aging father, "who loved his children but had never endured that any of them should leave him," rather than with the younger man seeking to break free from patriarchal prescriptions. In his brief essay on the painting, Diderot channels familial irritation with this errant son, imagining that the eldest sister addresses her brother, "Wretch, what are you doing? You push away your mother, you menace your father, get on your knees and demand forgiveness."[21] On this point of filial piety as a keystone of social order, Abbé Réguis, the Catholic moralist, and Diderot, the materialist, agreed that parents had the right to detain and discipline disobedient offspring.

This chapter synthesizes local and regional studies on familial detention requests alongside original research in the Paris, national, and departmental archives. I introduce some of those individuals identified as libertines by their families or neighbors and situate authorities' responses within that broader context of the French empire. Families were sensitive to shifts in the legal and geographical definitions of the libertine and eager to make use of new opportunities to serve their families' interests. In response to the growing volume of requests alongside widespread reforms in criminal justice, royal ministers pushed back, asking their representatives to provide more evidence of specific wrongdoing and periodically reviewing cases for release.

LOCATING A "RACE OF LIBERTINES"

Abbé Réguis and Diderot were not alone in their estimation that France sheltered a "race of libertines"; French police investigators and provincial intendants regularly deployed the term in official reports and informal correspondence to describe a host of disparate actions. In a foundational examination of eighteenth-century prostitution, historian Erica Benabou notes the remarkable nature of such reliance, for we might "search jurists' writings in vain for the term 'libertinage' to designate a specific crime."[22]

However, *libertine* was not applied indiscriminately to all indiscretions. Individuals regularly complained to the Parisian police commissaires and to the provincial intendants of their neighbors' or family members' moral infractions using the types of insults commonly hurled in street accusations, but *libertine* was rarely the term they chose in those circumstances. Common insults against men tended to level accusations of poverty or financial fraud, including *coquin* (mischief-maker), *gueux* (beggar), and *escroqueur* (cheater). Sexuality defined women's reputations in public, and most insults directed at women deployed some variant of selling sex for money, including *maquerelle, fille publique, putain, garce, salope, poisson, poissarde,* and *coquina* (mischief-maker).[23] In public men's honor hinged on perceptions of economic honesty or financial independence, while attacks on women's honor highlighted sexual behavior.

However, when officials and the public did invoke it, the term "libertine" refracted gender ideals and assumptions. When applied to men, the category more reliably signaled a social breach and antiauthoritarian behavior than it connoted illicit sexuality.[24] When applied to women, "libertine" indicated sexual promiscuity, even serving as a synonym for regular sex work.[25] In general, by calling a family member a "libertine," the petitioner warned about a threat to family order with implications for the royal state: vagabondage, apprenticeship contracts, parental authority, or marital relations. Such charges revealed a fraying in familial power relations, as parents and spouses acknowledged to state authorities their own incapacity to require expected behavior from their family members.[26] At least four issues concerned the municipal and provincial officials across France in cases of libertinage: familial insubordination, adultery, prostitution, and clerical sexuality. All had been strictly prohibited by canon law and surveilled by religious and state authorities working in tandem.[27] As the state expanded to enforce canon law, its officers found surveillance of these norms to be among the most challenging facets of their new powers. France never had an inquisition, but the widespread detention of libertines served similar purposes, enforcing religious orthodoxy and family order.

The term "libertine" figured prominently in the thousands of petitions that the king received from those who sought to detain an errant family member after three royal orders promulgated in 1684 linked three distinct types of social disorder—first, that caused by "women of debauch and public, scandalous prostitution," who were to be imprisoned in the Salpêtrière Hospital and treated for venereal diseases. Second, it addressed the turmoil resulting from the children of the poor who were libertine or lazy, sending the boys (under age twenty-five) to Bicêtre, and the girls to Salpêtrière. Third, it intervened on behalf of more financially capable families, enfranchising parents, close relatives, even parish priests, to make accusations of bad behavior against an errant individual. The law promised that these libertines would be evaluated by those in charge of the General Hospital (Hôpital général de Paris), kept as long as deemed necessary, put to "the rudest work that their strength permits, dressed in union cloth and shod in wooden shoes like the poor; their laziness and their other faults will be punished by withholding supper, increased work, prison, and other penalties, such as the directors deem reasonable."[28] In a bid to strengthen the kingdom's morality, the king placed an extensive detention system at the disposal of his subjects to enforce family hierarchies and religious orthodoxy.

On July 27, 1713, by royal declaration, the French Crown outlawed prostitution. But it went further to make illegal the "scandalous life of girls or women," rendering women's reputations legally vulnerable to rumor and innuendo, rather than requiring evidence in flagrante delicto.[29] This law initiated a distinct and gendered divergence in the standard of proof required to prosecute men and women with charges of extramarital sexuality. Eyewitness testimony would be required to convict a man of such a crime, but it sufficed for women to be suspected of living a scandalous life.[30] As many women discovered, living independently and with economic autonomy often sufficed to cast a shadow on a woman's reputation.[31] Pregnant single women took pains to reassure magistrates that their situation resulted not from libertinage—by which they meant intentional sin pursuing casual sex outside of marriage—but from their faith in a steady partner who had promised marriage and then abandoned them.[32]

The term "libertine" signaled a handful of types of insubordinate behavior in French police and intendants' records by the 1760s, as family requests for detention reached their zenith.[33] Most often these petitions documented quasi-crimes—that is, behavior that, though it did not rise to the level of prosecutable crimes, families deemed threatening to their financial and social stability. In these cases, as in the colonial contexts, the category alerts us to a gray zone between law codes and practice, signaling that a compelling logic of public order overrode an emergent theory of due process and rule of law.[34]

Police officers and royal officials most often used "libertine" to report defiant behavior of a child toward their parents. It indicated an individual who rejected proper family order and required state intervention to bolster parental authority or a spouse's rights to preserve family reputation and fortune. It might also describe a soldier or apprentice who undermined professional authorities. Throughout the eighteenth century, the category maintained the sense of impiety. In 1764 the historian and man of letters Adrien Richer recounted an anecdote of a French soldier whose penchant for eating meat on Fridays resulted in an unlikely military victory.[35] "This soldier," Richer commented, "brought to Spain the libertinage to which he was accustomed and did not better listen to scruples among the Spanish: he found meat on Friday, he ate it."[36] This tale imagined that France had achieved an ideological middle ground between Catholic southern Europe, where the Catholic Church still wielded tremendous power to police community morals and religious law, and the Protestant north, where secular states had usurped much of that power. By Richer's estimation the French took Catholic dietary laws much less seriously than did their neighbors to the south and expected to be able to eat meat on a Friday wherever they might be. But such contravention of canon law was libertine, warned Richer, and likely revealed an individual's propensity to defy other customs and authorities.[37]

In contrast to Spain and Italy, where the Catholic Church established muscular judicial systems to interrogate and prosecute violations of canon law, in France the state assumed authority for enforcing religious codes consonant with Gallican liberties.[38] The urban police surveilled public meat markets and food commerce for violations of Catholic dietary law.[39] From 1560 to 1747, the police in cities and towns throughout the French kingdom enforced prohibitions on prostitution, adultery, bigamy, and extramarital sexuality rooted in canon law.[40] Then, in response to recommendations by Enlightenment-era reformers, the state made prostitution legal in 1747 within recognized brothels subject to direct surveillance by the urban police.[41] But this reform did not indicate a general loosening of laws regulating sex. Though Parisian police no longer relied on monastic and Church authorities to enforce clerical celibacy, they waged a veritable "priest hunt" between 1756 and 1761, patrolling the city's darkened alleys and quais for sexually active clergy, resulting in 663 arrests.[42] Dramatic shifts in the legal landscape regulating sexuality and family order moved many of these activities considered formal crimes under canon law into the gray zone of the libertine.

Police might observe that an individual was a libertine because he or she had not slept at home, wandered the streets at night, gambled, consorted with other libertines, or generally disrespected parental or apprenticeship authorities. The archives of the Bastille prison recount the detention of young Pasdeloup, who sold banned books on the highways and byways of the kingdom. His mother was devout and regretted his libertinage, the files concluded. Pasdeloup entered the Bastille on June 28, 1767, and was not released until July 3, 1772.[43] The infraction here was not sexual in nature, but a violation of censorship law, a notably nebulous area of law subject to dramatic reforms and reversals throughout the eighteenth century.

When a police commissaire employed the term "libertine," he warned the state that a threat to family order simultaneously challenged the broader community. State authorities progressed logically from a disregard for parental authority to include the threat of vagabondage, broken apprenticeship contracts, theft, and prostitution in a "slippery slope" theory of criminal potential. The punishments proposed included immediate detention in the kingdom's prisons, hospitals, convents, or monasteries, or advocated colonial exile to discipline the miscreants.[44]

DETENTION OF LIBERTINES AND VAGABONDS

Parents across the social spectrum found the prospect of arbitrary detention—particularly colonial exile—to be appealing punishments for problematic progeny. Relatives professed willingness, even enthusiasm, to pay for the individual's transportation or incarceration. Exile of bad subjects within the French kingdom sufficed after the colonial option shut down briefly after 1770.[45] Elite families might request king's orders to detain their offspring as libertines in an effort to keep truly heinous crimes out of the public record, as had occurred in the case of the Marquis de Sade.[46] They might seek to preserve family resources, as in the case of Alexandre-Balthasar-Laurent Grimod de la Reynière, or to punish disobedience of parental orders, as in the case of the Count of Mirabeau.[47] For decades historical analysis of familial detention focused on these high-profile cases that imperiled family fortunes and honor.[48] But middling urban professional families and the working poor also approached state officials to have errant children detained, often to the surprise of authorities. These individuals similarly indicated that they perceived an errant family member to pose a real threat to their families' honor, with ramifications for their household's trade, fortunes, and networks.

Four types of arbitrary detention existed in eighteenth-century France: lettres de cachet for state affairs, lettres de cachet for family affairs, king's orders emanating from requests made by military or monastic disciplines, and detention orders delivered by the lieutenant of police.[49] The cases introduced here all represent families' requests for the second type of lettres de cachet, which constituted the largest proportion of king's orders. Historian Deborah Cohen reminds us that these cases were the ones most removed from the formal systems of justice and even occasionally worked at cross-purposes to those court systems. The lieutenant of police might assign punishment without requiring a trial, intervene in an ongoing case, even assign a harsher punishment in place of a determined judicial sentence. Justice determined individual cases based on the merit of assembled evidence, while police orders reflected the demands of maintaining public order.[50] Eighteenth-century critics emphasized the arbitrary nature of these detentions, whether the result of royal order, lettres de cachet, or police order. But Cohen cautions that historians miss the operating logic of the police if we fall into the critics' argument. She notes that, while justice evaluated facts of crimes committed, the police orders reflect a "radical pragmatism" focused on reducing future social harm. Authorities agreed on the necessity of both approaches, and if the libertine was less likely to be found culpable of criminal action, there was a general acceptance that these detentions were necessary due to the potential damage they might inflict on their families' honor or fortunes. In this project the police benefited from the active cooperation of the population.

DISORDER IN THE PROVINCES, 1737–1790

The departmental archives of the Bouches-du-Rhone department in Aix-en-Provence conserve a rich collection of king's orders within the provincial intendant's correspondence.[51] The intendant represented royal authority in the provinces.[52] Individual families' requests for *ordres du roi* (king's orders) against a family member, and the intendant's examination of the situation and correspondence with royal officials between 1737 and 1790 are preserved in scores of archival boxes.[53] These exchanges demonstrate significant transformations in both royal directives and provincial modes of investigating individuals accused of libertine behavior.

The historian François-Xavier Emmanuelli documents 1,287 requests for king's orders in these provincial archives. Of these 1,052 (81.7 percent) were requested by families, 67 for religious discipline, 9 for local political reasons, 55 in order to exclude a person from municipal councils, and 104 affairs to request the prorogations of municipal officers. Of those requested by families, orders detained 777 males and 263 females. In 642 cases the person requesting king's orders could be identified, and of those the father made the request 44 percent of the time. The mother or parents together requested king's orders in a further 27 percent of the cases. These requests reveal a family logic of parental authority bolstered and deepened by the state. Wives rarely requested the detention of their husband—such petitions account for only thirteen of 642 requests—although husbands did request the detention of their wives in 56 cases, or 8.7 percent of all requests. In-laws, grandparents, the procureur-général, or other individuals made arrest requests in the remaining cases.[54]

Emmanuelli demonstrates a dramatic increase in both family requests for and officials' granting of king's orders in the two later periods, precisely when the royal administration repeatedly sought to limit the extension of extrajudicial detention.[55] Claude Quétel corroborates this trend in the province of Normandy from 850 requests for king's orders.[56] Families made 730 of these requests to have errant individuals detained. Again, the vast majority of those detained were boys or men. Quétel identifies the charges made against family order as including delinquency, libertinage, bad conduct, disobedience, dilapidation (usually excessive expenditures), threat of a bad marriage, and madness.[57] Twenty-three percent of men and fifty percent of women were detained for behavior their family or state authorities deemed libertine. But Quétel does not attend to the transformation of that term over the course of the eighteenth century. In response to the stress on royal officials and institutions posed by family requests for king's orders of arbitrary detention, the secretary of state at Versailles directed profound reform of the lettres de cachet system at two moments: in 1775, when Malesherbes took the post, and again in 1784, when the baron de Breteuil assumed the office. Both men sent out directives requiring provincial intendants to take a census of all prisoners held in their province on king's orders and provide more careful oversight of these prisoners' release.[58] Breteuil went further to define three categories for the legitimate use of king's orders, indicating that he would be far more ready to refuse requests than his predecessors. Despite these pronouncements under both ministers the number of detentions requested and granted increased nearly every year until 1789.[59]

Emmanuelli concludes that a study of the province's archives of king's orders confirms a pattern of Provençal regionalization and predicts both the revolutionary troubles and processes of dechristianization identified by Michel Vovelle. The archival records highlight the provincial intendant's overwhelming interest in the cities of this province, to the exclusion of its small villages and rural stretches. Finally, Emmanuelli asserts that the intendancy provided no new ideas on the question of king's orders, but merely transmitted ideas and information from the Crown to the people of Provence.[60] However, this tale of provincial acceptance of royal authority requires us to overlook the discrepancy between the Crown's repeated directives to decrease the provision of king's orders alongside the steady increase in requests over the course of the eighteenth century. Such was the case all over the French kingdom, in fact. Requests for the detention of libertine sons and daughters, husbands and wives highlight the degree to which royal policy responded to local demands and family strategies. Delving into the specific cases preserved in the police reports and provincial intendants' archives reveals the varieties of families and the complex axes of authority in practice.

DISORDER IN PARIS, 1760–1790

The research of Emmanuelli and Quétel reveals important similarities in the lettres de cachet accorded in Provence and Normandy, where petitioners typically sought aid from the representatives of the royal state.

In Paris families seeking king's orders to detain a relative for libertine behavior appealed directly to the neighborhood police commissaire, who could order an immediate arrest if necessary. These requests fall into four general categories: parents who request the detention of a minor child, parents who request the detention of an adult child, spouses who request the detention of their partner, and neighbors who request the detention of a close resident whose behavior invites trouble and intrigue into the neighborhood.

LIBERTINE MINORS

Antoine L'Ecuyer was a coachman at the service of Mademoiselle de Thil who on August 29, 1764, lodged a complaint with his neighborhood police commissaire against his son, Guillaume, then eighteen years old. The father dwelt in the home of his employer on the rue Varenne, visiting his wife and child across town on the rue de Verbois as his duties permitted. Ever since Guillaume turned fifteen, he had given his parents cause for concern. Over the preceding three years, Antoine had apprenticed the boy with a carpenter, a glazier, a pastrycook, a wigmaker, and a saddler, among others. But Guillaume always left after a brief period, insisting that he would fare better in an alternate profession. Meanwhile, wherever the father "went, he received reproaches for his son's laziness, his libertinage, and his bad inclinations."[61] For the past three months, Guillaume had "given himself entirely to debauchery and no longer returned to his mother's house to sleep." He cruised the boulevards all night and visited "bad places," including the home of Fanchon, identified as a lace bonnet worker on the rue de la Voirie behind the city storehouses, the open-air haunts of area prostitutes, or a room on the rue de Charonne where other libertines took refuge. Antoine insisted that he had no idea what the boy did to earn money. He only knew that Guillaume demonstrated a lack of respect both for himself and for the boy's mother, Louise Hugot, and had even threatened her physically. Antoine asserted that he lodged this complaint so that if his son was arrested, the boy would be imprisoned or even transported to the islands in order to correct him and keep him from doing something to dishonor the family, who had "no other resources than their honor and their work."[62]

Nearly a week went by before Antoine reappeared before the police commissaire with his wife to pursue the case that he had initiated against their son. Since his previous audience, Antoine had quit his job to search "day and night" for his son, fearing that Guillaume's "libertinage and debauchery would lead to undesirable and dishonorable circumstances."[63] Both he and his wife had spent several nights out on the boulevards along with their other children searching for Guillaume. Finally, they located him drinking in a cabaret on the rue St-Antoine, where they immediately seized him and dragged him before the commissaire. At this point both parents signed their statement. As the commissaire turned to the errant youth, Guillaume L'Ecuyer affirmed that he was eighteen years and two months old. He had spent the previous night in the stables of Madame la Dauphine, thanks to a friend who worked as a *postillon* (coach boy) and had brought him food from the caterer LaBeauve. He had spent about two weeks at LaBeauve's place, where he ate, and it had been about three months since he had seen his parents. He had stayed in Compiègne for a long time where he sold wine and beer. Upon returning to Paris, he had gone from one inn to another, but he insisted it had been over three weeks since he had been sleeping out on the boulevards. When his parents found him, he was on his way to recover his clothes from an innkeeper where he had taken a carriage two weeks prior. He had never threatened to hit his mother, he protested, and although he knew Fanchon, he had not seen her for a long time. When asked to sign his statement, Guillaume declared that he did not know how to write or sign his name. Based on this testimony, the commissaire concluded that there was sufficient evidence to establish that Guillaume was a great libertine, and the clerk noted in the margins that he might also be considered a vagabond and a night wanderer (*coureur de nuit*), who demonstrated no fear or respect for his father and mother. He was condemned to imprisonment at Grand Châtelet until further notice.

A similar tale of parental woe was told by Pierre Paillot, a coachman in Dijon who had traveled to Paris in search of his stepson, Jean Petit, age fifteen. For the past seven or eight years this boy had lived the most disordered life, Paillot observed. "He has the worst inclinations, every day visits the worst subjects and libertines in the city of Dijon," and had left the family home at least two times every month, often for five or six nights at a time.[64] Occasionally he had even returned home "completely naked, having sold his clothes down to his shirt, shoes and hat."[65] Paillot had placed the boy in an apprenticeship with a shoemaker in Dijon nearly one year ago. There Jean remained for six months, before fleeing to Châlons sur Saone. Paillot chased Jean down, and the mayor of Dijon sent the boy to the prisons of Dijon for three months. Upon his release a week prior, the boy headed to Paris. Paillot had driven after him but was required to return the carriage the following day in Dijon, and, "as he fears the consequences of the libertinage and disorderly conduct of Jean Petit will lead only to something dishonorable for his family, he brought him before the police commissaire to request his imprisonment." Upon questioning Jean acknowledged that he had sold his clothes several times, but protested that he "did not frequent anyone, and only went two or three times to a cabaret with Jacques Perrot, an apprentice wigmaker."[66] He promised to be wiser in the future and change his conduct. At this point he signed his name carefully in a fine hand. The commissaire ordered that Jean be taken to the prisons of Grand Châtelet immediately and remain there until ordered otherwise.

Of course, not only the parents of rebellious boys sought the support of the royal state in disciplining errant offspring. The day before Christmas 1765, Antoine Pollet, a schoolmaster, and his wife, Marie Catherine Dechaume, filed a complaint against their daughter Catherine, aged twenty-one-and-a-half.[67] Her independent and incorrigible character, they said, forced them to lodge the present complaint. Catherine refused to settle down and learn a trade. She had been placed in the home of Dame Capelain, mistress bag-maker, but left to go work with several other female workers in the same trade. She remained there for three years without learning a thing. Despite her parents' counsel, she wanted to go from boutique to boutique earning nothing, saving nothing, and dependent on her parents for food. Nearly three years ago, she had even left Paris and roamed the countryside for two months. She stopped for a few weeks on the Isle Adam and stayed with a merchant there, Demoiselle Nicolle. But, as she could not pay for lodgings or food and had told some dangerous lies, she was forced to sell some of her belongings and return to Paris having been eaten by vermin and in the most miserable state. To draw her away from an errant life, her parents encouraged her to live with them. But their gentle methods had been exhausted. She did as she pleased and remained out until 9 or 10 p.m., sometimes even all night, despite their reprimands. She decided to leave their household, claiming she could earn ten to twelve sols per day, and therefore she "did not want to be their servant." With this defiant assertion, Catherine had fled again, this time taking up residence with the Widow Huguet, who lodged by the night. Catherine had even had the audacity to lodge a complaint with Commissaire Carlier that her father had kept her things. She had taken a job as a boutique girl with Demoiselle Charonne, but left within a year because of a "thousand quarrels" resulting from her "bad genius."[68] Young men who behaved in this manner were regularly called *libertins* by their parents or by the municipal authorities who seem to have counseled families on its proper application. When applied to women, the term connoted sexual promiscuity. So it is significant that Catherine's parents accused her of bad humor, but not libertinage.

THE RACINET-VALMONT CASE

Fear for their daughter's reputation dominated the complaint filed by Joseph Racinet and Marie Gabrielle Flamant, porters at a house on the rue des Cannettes, on the evening of August 12, 1778. Together the couple made a declaration against Dame Valmont, a painter who had moved into the house where they resided and struck up a friendship with their twenty-two-year old daughter, Jeanne Julie Gabrielle Racinet. When Valmont became ill, they had even agreed that Jeanne might stay overnight in the lady's rooms, "but for nearly a month, they have become convinced that Dame Valmont has debauched their daughter through her bad advice and example." They forbade Jeanne to see Valmont again. In response Valmont insulted the girl's mother and said that Jeanne "would never be anything but a slut [*putain*] and other horrors of this sort," to the parents and to the neighbors.[69] Then, two weeks prior to their visit to the commissaire, Dame Valmont moved out of the neighborhood. The parents hoped at this point that they could return to tranquility with their daughter. However, that very morning, Jeanne had said that she was going to visit one of her aunts. When she failed to return for dinner, they talked to the aunts and realized that no one had seen her. They went to Valmont's new residence, where Flamant heard her daughter cough and spit, but could not get anyone in that house to return her child.

The next day at noon, the Racinet family returned to Commissaire Dupuy's office. They had spent the night outside Valmont's house, watching for their daughter to exit the residence. Valmont had refused to return their daughter or even to open the door when they knocked. Finally, a hired carriage drove up to the house, and the parents saw Valmont and their daughter, dressed in one of Valmont's dresses and wearing a ribbon-bedecked bonnet with her hair expertly styled, exit the house and get into the carriage. The parents approached the carriage, insisting that Valmont should not keep their daughter against their wishes or take her anywhere dressed in clothes that were not her own. Valmont said nothing to them, only ordered the coachman to drive on to the rue des Cordeliers. For this reason, the parents appealed to the police commissaire to guarantee their parental authority, observing that since the "present parties being masters of their daughter, and the conduct of the said Dame Valmont seeming absolutely suspect to them, they told her that they expected their daughter to come with them before the commissaire to be informed of her conduct; the said Dame Valmont consented to come along and as a result the carriage brought them to our hotel to make the present declaration."[70] The whole party thus arrived at the commissaire's office to explain Jeanne's behavior and Dame Valmont's role in this family drama.

Dame Valmont introduced herself as Marie Antoinette Blanchard, the wife of Henri Louis Valmont, an engraver in Paris, residing on the rue des Cordeliers in Paris. Her statement emphasized the friendship she and Jeanne had cultivated, insisting that she had provided no bad example, but took a charitable interest in the girl's education and welfare. She and Jeanne had been on their way to dine with Sieur Dage, an upholsterer of her acquaintance, which was why she had loaned the girl a dress, so Jeanne need not wear the shirt and skirt she had worn the previous days. She acknowledged that she had been wrong to let the girl sleep at her home overnight, but that the girl had come of her own accord and had not been enticed by Valmont. She concluded by observing that she had no way to keep Racinet and Flamant from taking their daughter back.

Jeanne testified that she was a linen worker, twenty-two years old. She admitted that she had gone secretly to Dame Valmont's home the day before and stayed until noon today to keep the lady company. She slept there and acknowledged that she had done wrong to not alert her parents, "promising to no longer disobey them and to not leave the house without their consent."[71] Copies of the statements were made for all parties, and the girl returned home with her parents, who must have felt vindicated in their pursuit of their daughter, while Dame Valmont left as free as she had entered. Jeanne's parents never identified her as a libertine. Indeed, although they identified debauchery and sexual promiscuity as possible threats, they seemed most anxious about their daughter's reputation if she maintained a relationship with Dame Valmont, an independent professional woman with extensive connections in the world of Parisian artists and engravers.

OF LIBERTINE SONS AND DAUGHTERS

Families regularly gestured to the social networks threatened by a child's insubordination, and authorities took these relationships and reputations into account in their appraisals of each situation. Sieur Bailly, a trader in Marseilles, requested king's orders to detain his son in June 1778. The secretary of state Amelot ordered the intendant of Provence Delatour to make the necessary inquiries: "If it seems necessary to deprive this individual of his liberty, tell the father that he must indicate the detention site and agree to pay the pension."[72] Delatour responded three months later. Having made the necessary inquiries, the intendant observed that while it was impossible to know if the young man had really stolen money from his father, "his libertinage is notorious. He only frequents bad company and it frequently occurs that he is away from the paternal household."[73] As he was only seventeen years old, the family feared he would continue down this bad path without some powerful correction. Delatour approved the request for detention, and the family chose to send the boy to the fort on the Ile Sainte Marguerite and agreed to pay his pension there. Within the week Amelot responded with the orders for detention. In December Delatour wrote back. He had received the king's orders, but the father had "requested that the execution of these orders be suspended for some time to test this young man, who had declared that he no longer needed to use them. He had determined to send his son to the islands."[74] If the Crown would not finance colonial exile of bad subjects, or ensure speedy detention in France, some families could afford to make such arrangements on their own.

LIBERTINE ADULTS

Even after children became adults at the age of twenty-four or twenty-five, they continued to owe their parents obedience in the eyes of the law. Claude Barnabé Cardon was a master wigmaker who charged his adult daughter, Marie Marguerite Cardon, with libertinage on August 18, 1763. He stated that she had married Nicolas Simon Nicolas, a fellow master wigmaker, at the tender age of eighteen. Rather than "conducting herself wisely and prudently towards her husband, she succumbed to continual disorder, being assiduous neither in the house nor over the affairs of her household." Her husband found ample cause to complain about young Marie Marguerite's conduct to her father, who advised his colleague to be patient, given the girl's youth; they could work together to gently reform her character. But this "only served to irritate her and she grew more disordered than ever."[75] Finally, Cardon asserted, Marie Marguerite's bad behavior so disturbed her husband that he died on July 5, 1759, leaving a twenty-month-old son, Claude Nicolas.

Marie Marguerite moved back in with her parents for a year, leaving them to take up residence in a series of apartments, where she led a disordered life, at some time even giving birth to a baby girl, whom she took to the orphanage. Cardon had convinced his daughter to return to his house after the baby's birth, but just the day before he discovered that she had made plans to leave again. The following day Marie Marguerite's mother, Marie Louise Piochot, confirmed her husband's account and further added that her concern focused on the impact of her daughter's behavior on little Claude Nicolas, now five years old. Marie Marguerite had taken him from the nurse who had raised him, and, due to her harshness with the little boy, her parents had intervened to bring the child to live with them.

She asserted that Marie Marguerite's recent daughter was the result of a liaison the young woman had formed while living at their home with a man named Rosay, the valet de chamber for M. Demornay. Importantly, in this account, parental supervision had not ensured model behavior. When Piochot reprimanded her daughter for breaking the promise to return to her parent's home, Marie Marguerite replied "that she did not give a damn about her father and mother or anyone."[76] Piochot lamented that her daughter went to "all the bad places" and consorted with *libertins* before relating an encounter Marie Marguerite had just a few days before giving birth to her daughter when Piochot followed her to the home of the widow Blanchard, a privileged wigmaker who lived on the third floor of a wine merchant's establishment on the rue de coutellerie. There Piochot found her daughter in the arms of an apprentice surgeon named Loubadier, both of them in the "greatest disorder."[77] At this confrontation Marie Marguerite screamed at her mother and threatened that she would come get her son as soon as she turned twenty-four, the age of majority. It seems to have been this threat that brought the Cardon family to seek the aid of municipal authorities. The parents' goal was to have Marie Marguerite imprisoned for the foreseeable future, which, they asserted, would conserve their honor, end their daughter's disorder, and preserve the life of their grandson, whom they portrayed as mortally endangered by his mother's lifestyle. They promised to pay fifty ecus in pension for her imprisonment, if necessary.

Men as well as women found their adulthood stalked by filial obligations. It was 10 a.m. when André Fournier lodged a complaint against his adult son, Louis-André, on October 19, 1764. In his presentation he positioned the son's misbehavior within a narrative of family strife and turmoil. André recalled that he had had the misfortune to marry Françoise-Denise Lejoix in 1736, and that this woman's irregular conduct and dissipation of their household goods had forced him to have her confined in the convent of Sainte-Pélagie in 1749 until her death in 1756. Now his son, aged twenty-seven years, "who exhibits all the vices of his mother's family, dishonors his father and decries him to all acquaintances. The plaintiff sees in this son only a monster of nature, his most cruel enemy who forgets the respect owed to a father."[78] The father lamented that he had spared no expense for the son's education, and this despite the expenses he incurred due the long-term imprisonment of his wife. After sending his son to the finest schools for nearly a decade, André secured a position for Louis-André with a lawyer in 1751, and then with M. Gaignant, prosecutor at the Grand Conseil.[79] André soon learned that his son had alienated his employer through his excessively free speech, at which point the father ordered the boy to leave Paris and placed him in the infantry with the Rouergue Regiment. Rather than taking this opportunity to learn from his mistakes, however, Louis-André's behavior worsened in the army. On August 21, 1758, Sieur Decan, the commanding officer of the regiment, wrote to Fournier and recommended that he send his son to the islands as punishment for his bad behavior. Failing this, the regiment's captain dismissed Fournier fils, at which point the boy enlisted in the regiment of la Sarre. Here again the commanding officer wrote to the father to warn of the boy's "bad inclinations" and recommended exile as a suitable punishment. Dismissed from this company, in December 1759 Louis-André sought refuge in Pithiviers with his father's friends, who took the boy in, lent him money, and even found him employment with a notary in the nearby town of Baumont. But within six months the young man lost this job due to "his odious character and the quarrels and fights that he starts."[80] At that point he returned to Paris, where he imposed on his father's friends, sought his mother's dowry, and insulted his father. Events had reached such a state by 1764 that André had been counseled to lodge an exact report of his son's behavior with the police, in case of future conflict.

François Meunier was a journeyman printer who complained to the police about his stepson, Joseph Ralé, late one Saturday evening, on January 10, 1778.[81] The young man was twenty-seven years old and a constant source of chagrin to his mother and the plaintiff ever since their marriage. Meunier stated, "He is given to libertinage and drink, he has had the audacity to hit his mother several times, he has daily disputes with his friends and with the prostitutes he frequents for which he has on multiple occasions been imprisoned at the Bicêtre prison."[82] When drunk Joseph would visit his mother and make a ruckus at their home, swearing the worst oaths against her and threatening to beat her. On at least one occasion, the neighbors had even been forced to call the neighborhood guard to intervene and the parents had asked for the police commissaire to arrest the young man. The commissaire so ordered, and the young man was arrested outside of a cabaret near his mother and stepfather's residence. He was then questioned, testifying that he was a dockworker, twenty-seven years old, native to Paris, and residing in a room of the house where the family lived presently. He denied brawling outside his mother and stepfather's door and asserted that he never threatened to break it down with a large rock or piece of plaster. He acknowledged that he had spent time in the prison of Grand Châtelet and had been sent to Bicêtre after rebelling against the Garde. The commissaire concluded that because Ralé had been arrested while committing bad actions, he would be detained at the Petit Châtelet prisons until otherwise ordered.

LIBERTINE SPOUSES

Spouses, as well as parents, might request each other's detention for libertine behavior. In 1770 the travails of the Bagnoly family in Avignon came to the attention of regional and royal officers. Dame Bagnoly sought king's orders to detain her husband, who had wasted his own fortune on "clandestine debauches, bonne chère and frivolous expenses."[83] He had wooed her by playing the rich man around town, but after their marriage the creditors arrived. Her husband had sold the horses, dismissed the servants, and revealed a debt of 4500 livres. Now he seemed intent on spending her fortune as quickly as he had his own. Dame Bagnoly's protests had resulted in her husband threatening her life on several occasions, including holding a knife to her throat and attempting to poison her tea. She requested this detention for the benefit of their son, because the "ignominy of the father will rebound on the son: the son, if he has no fortune must at least inherit a good reputation. Your Grandeur will repress this crime without attention; by this order you might detain, or at least distance from me an audacious husband."[84] In correspondence the intendant of Provence and the king's secretary of state observed that the couple had also taken each other to court in the Provençal Cour de la Justice, so the lady's argument regarding summary detention as necessary to safeguard the family's reputation seems less compelling. The secretary of state urged the intendant to mediate between the two parties, to which the intendant replied that he was trying, but they were so opposed, it had proved difficult. Plus, he complained, it was difficult to determine if the wife's accusations were true. In August, after a summer of correspondence between royal officials, Sieur Bagnoly wrote to the intendant himself to complain that, although he had agreed to arbitration, his wife's uncle had then arrived with a lettre de cachet in hand, ordering his arrest at the fort on the Isle de Sainte Marguerite. But if the civil case continued, then Bagnoly would not go to prison. "Your Grandeur understands how such proceedings wound Justice," he noted before denying all of his wife's claims regarding his threats to her life.

Guillaume Gruitgens was a master cobbler who had married Catherine Picard in 1772. For the first two years of their marriage she had been "reasonable," he recalled, but for the past two years she had "completely ruined him through her debaucheries, having pawned or sold all their household goods to satisfy her drunkenness and to receive men with whom she undertook bad commerce."[85] Not wishing to see daily this woman who so dishonored him, Guillaume had sent her away from his house nine months ago. She had asked to return home, promising to conduct herself honestly, and he relented and took her back. But, since that time, her conduct became as irregular as before; she even dared to tell him several times that she owed him nothing, mocked him, and declared that "she was the mistress of doing what she wished."[86] This past Christmas she had finally moved out, taking some furniture and belongings with her, into a room on the rue Chartière. A neighbor had reported to Guillaume that, in this new residence, his wife and her female roommate received men every day. On February 2, 1778, having learned that his wife was living with another man, Guillaume went to her residence, but, as it was late, he left without making a scene. The next morning he returned and knocked on his wife's door. After some time the door opened, and Guillaume saw his wife and another woman in one bed, while a man hid under another bed. On this second bed he saw a few items of men's clothing and took a pair of gray breeches with him as he left, to avoid further conflict. The other inhabitants of the house told him that they had seen another man leave that room earlier that morning.

The commissaire's clerk noted, "As his wife's scandalous life is capable of dishonoring him, and as he has interest in imprisoning her, he came to make this declaration and make a statement against his wife and the male and female companions of her debauchery."[87] If Catherine was arrested or charged for either adultery or prostitution, no record remains in these files. Such cases were not common, but the eighteenth-century police files overflow with evidence that men and women often behaved in ways that violated canon and civil laws regulating sexuality.[88]

THE BRANCHU-BOURGEOT CASE

The adultery case that René Jean Branchu brought against his wife, Anne Sophie Bourgeot, stands out as anomalous for several reasons.[89] This case, first initiated on January 8, 1779, pitted the tinsmith against his wife of eight years, then aged twenty-seven. She had requested a separation from him in 1774, when she realized that he did not have the investment income he had claimed when they married. He had also become physically and verbally abusive, even refusing to allow her the independence to do the shopping for their household.[90] Bourgeot's request was finally granted in 1778, separating the couple in both body and goods.[91]

Within that year Branchu struck back by charging Bourgeot with adultery, an accusation of moral and criminal consequence that carried the potential for serious punishment.[92] His wife had attacked the honor of marriage as an institution, he charged. When they married, she was nineteen years old, and he had "no way of imagining her failings of character." He observed that "the libertinage of his wife and the scandal of her life" left him no option but to prosecute her and her accomplices for adultery. Bourgeot had rented rooms in which to have sexual encounters and told a disapproving servant that she could "take my husband, leave me LeDreux," referring to Charles LeDreux, a feather merchant with whom she had an ongoing relationship.[93] She had engaged in debauchery, her husband asserted, with three other men, including one of the journeymen in his own household.

It was several weeks later, on January 24, that Commissaire Dupuy and his clerk took down the testimony of seventeen witnesses who corroborated Branchu's charges of Anne-Sophie's adultery over the previous five years. Nearly all the witnesses came from the household of Abel Dominique Desbois, a confectioner accused of conducting an affair with Anne Sophie Bourgeot for several months in 1774 and 1775. Immediately the tenor of the testimonies strikes the reader as odd—so many of the witnesses came from one household, their testimonies repeated the same stock phrases, and they professed knowledge they could not have had about a master's emotions. On all these fronts, the accusations against Bourgeot diverge from typical police reports of the period. In the frank discussion of sexual overtures and a couple's physical intimacy, too, this report reads more like a pornographic novel than a police account. In the prepared testimony, Desbois's brother André, who also worked as an apprentice in the Desbois household, asserted that "he had reproached the Femme Branchu several times for her libertinage with Sieur Desbois, his brother. To which Femme Branchu responded, *I need to enjoy myself, I'm not of an age to deprive myself.*"[94] Other witnesses also claimed to have witnessed Bourgeot initiate physical intimacy with Desbois both in public areas of the household or in the three different bedrooms.

Based on this testimony, Bourgeot was detained, first at the convent of St Michel, and then at the prison of Grand Châtelet, where she suffered from convulsions and hallucinations. After months of investigation, the royal court determined that Commissaire Dupuy had fabricated the testimonies and colluded with Branchu to have Anne Sophie imprisoned, likely for a substantial bribe.[95] During Commissaire Thierion's inquiry into the case, witnesses asserted that Dupuy's clerk had composed these fictitious testimonies prior to their depositions or during their time in Dupuy's office, relating the fact that no sexual relationship existed between Desbois and Bourgeot. Dupuy sometimes took advantage of the witnesses' inability to read to coerce signatures. On at least one occasion, he required a cook who provided testimony to remain in his household to replace his own household's cook, who had left for the countryside for a few days.[96] The French Parlement identified gross abuse of power on the part of Commissaire Dupuy and set Bourgeot free after five months of arrest and a sustained attack on her reputation.

Historian Arlette Farge relates this unusual case as evidence of the gulf between the sexual codes of the elites and those of the common people, representing Dupuy's fabricated reports as emanating from an elitist libertine literature that sat at odds with the sexual morals and practices of the working people of Paris. She asserts that, in aiding Branchu, the commissaire depicted Bourgeot "with the finery of a marquise" rather than as a depraved wife of a merchant.[97] "He surely thought that this luxurious and licentious figure of a woman would suffice to have her condemned definitively," she writes. "These lies did not condemn her, but she would know in the convent and then in prison plenty of tears and intolerable 'pains of the soul.'"[98]

However, if we take libertinage as a lens, the social worlds of Paris, the French kingdom and the French empire seem less divided between elites and the people than Farge contends. Libertine literary tropes emphasizing sensual accessories: perfumes, silver snuffboxes, flowers, jewels, ribbons, silk, beautiful dresses, oysters, wine consumed in private rooms, and attendance at the opera and organized balls were not the exclusive possessions of aristocrats. They were currency. We know from a wide array of sources that men and women of middling and marginal incomes gained access to these goods and entry to these spectacles through their youth, beauty, wit, talent, or promise of sexual favor.[99] Such proximity to wealth, the wealthy, and the luxury goods that seemingly defined the century constituted one of the more attractive features of urban life for the thousands of men and women who left the countryside every year to seek their fortune in Paris.[100]

THE THREAT OF ADULTERY

Adultery was both a moral infraction and a crime, but the state regarded female adultery as by far the greater threat to social order, meriting heightened disciplinary action. Even though charges of male adultery rarely resulted in strict punishment, some women still brought their marital woes before the municipal and regional authorities for evaluation. The representatives of the state heard these women out and regularly provided them with the means to protect personal assets or separate from these men, if they chose. Libertine husbands who disrupted their households' peace, spent family resources in pursuit of sexual indulgences, drink, or gambling, faced the consequences, as did libertine wives. For example, Constance Alexandrine Dupuis was the wife of Sieur Dutertre, a mathematician whose bad behavior elicited the testimony of multiple witnesses. He regularly asked his wife for money after he had spent all of his own. His neighbor, Joseph Etienne Blezy, a goldsmith, asserted that he knew Dutertre to be a "spendthrift who had completely ruined his business through his bad conduct, his libertinage and his drunkenness; he abandoned his wife and had the shame to go live with a prostitute, although he often visits his wife and makes a fuss to get more money."[101] These cases invite a reconsideration of the perception of a sexual double standard in which men's adultery meets acceptance, even macho celebration, whereas women's adultery results in severe criminal and social condemnation. Male and female witnesses indicated that men's sexual transgressions had the power to shock and even shame.[102]

On January 12, 1778, at 6 p.m., Marie Henriette Legrand Debois Landry lodged a complaint against her husband, Pierre Dartis, a prosecutor at the Parlement of Paris.[103] Earlier that week he had entered into the convent of St. Michel where she was residing and in the presence of several nuns and residents had publicly stated that she had not slept there several times; that she had gone to the theater, opera, and dances; and that she lived the most licentious and scandalous life. He had eight witnesses, he avowed, who would testify to these facts, although Marie Henriette asserted that she had never left the convent except when accompanied by a woman recommended by the Mother Superior. This was the latest stage in his plot to undermine her in the esteem of all her acquaintances, she asserted, and for this reason she had been advised to make a complaint before the police commissaire.

Claude Françoise Gaudet had been married for thirteen years to Michel Aubert, a journeyman carpenter, when she appeared before the Commissaire Dupuy on November 30, 1778. Despite her best efforts to win his friendship, "she had not succeeded in keeping him from the libertinage in which he had plunged, he always saw women of debauchery, he had even had the audacity to bring them into her room to sleep."[104] He was given to drunkenness, returning home in such a state that he did not recognize her, or would curse her terribly and threaten to beat her, often fulfilling these threats. He publicly denounced her in the neighborhood and to all their acquaintances as a slut. He had even communicated a venereal disease to her the previous June. Despite all this Claude Françoise said that she had still hoped to remind her husband of his duty. But in July she learned that he had deposited some three thousand livres with a notary—money, she noted, that had been earned through her own hard work and thrift. On the prior evening, he had returned home at 7 while she was out buying a salad. When he threatened her physically, she fled to her aunt's house with nothing except for several silver items she had managed to grab on her way out the door. When she returned home that day, she told the commissaire, her husband had locked her out. She sought protection from the state so that she could recover her clothes and be assured that he would provide her with a pension, as he had a fortune and she was now pregnant. In cases such as these, the police commissaire exercised a great deal of independence in determining whether to pursue charges, advise marital separations, or simply counsel women to steer clear of angry husbands.[105]

It was December 4, 1778, when Amelot wrote to Intendant Delatour to request more information about the Bajolet couple. The husband had requested king's orders against his wife, who had been living in Marseille without her husband's permission for the past nineteen months. "Is it necessary to deprive this woman of her liberty?" asked the secretary of state in the standard formulation that made clear the degree to which the state weighed the claims of individuals against their families. The intendant responded within the month, noting that Bajolet's wife lived in Marseille with Sieur Paillardel, an actor. The police had already visited this woman and exhorted her to return to her husband, but this was all they could do. Delatour observed that, in his estimation, the husband bore some responsibility for the situation, for, while they were in Spain, Bajolet had confided his wife to the director of an acting troupe, "which could not fail to produce a liaison between her and some actor. However as nothing can excuse her bad behavior, I believe there is cause to provide Sieur Bajolet with the orders that he requests to have her arrested."[106] No further correspondence exists in this dossier, so perhaps the requested orders were not granted to Sieur Bajolet, however.

Marie Jeanne Mezy lodged a declaration against her husband, François Lignier, a gardener, on January 25, 1779. She noted that thirteen years had passed since she had the misfortune to marry him. Since that time he had mistreated her every day for no reason. He drank, and his libertinage had completely ruined their household, due the extraordinary expenses he incurred. He often slept away from home, or more often returned drunk at two or three p.m. She had tried everything to change his behavior, but he ignored her advice and indulged in the most crapulous debauchery. He had infected her with venereal diseases, "the fruit of his libertinage," on four separate occasions, notably in 1774, when they both had been obliged to seek serious remedies for their recovery.[107] For nearly a year he had lived publicly with the daughter of Bricée, a former baker, taking most of their household's furniture for that alternate residence. He only returned home to hit her and threatened that if "any misfortune came to the Bricée girl, he would end Mezy." Marie Jeanne's statement was intended to protect her physically from her husband and to keep him from taking any more of their goods. The commissaire concluded Mézy's declaration by concurring that "Lignier is a bad subject and seems determined to do anything to get money to support his libertinage, since he is in the deepest misery having sold and dissipated everything he possesses."[108] The record provides no further information as to Lignier's fate. But the commissaire's expression of sympathy for Lignier's desperate circumstances indicates that this bad subject was not imprisoned or exiled for his actions, which included extramarital sex, physical abuse of his wife, and theft of household goods held in common.

LIBERTINE NEIGHBORS

Marie-Madelaine Christine Raffron was the twenty-three-year-old wife of a pastrycook, Pierre-Denis Jean. She had been born in Mantes-sur-Seine, where she had been arrested on January 22, 1762. She was first sent to the Salpêtrière Hospital in Paris, then the Bastille prison a month later, on a king's order. Raffron claimed that two people had demanded she give them her baby, who had been born during Epiphany. They said that they needed the infant's brain and marrow to make the king die. She told the commissaire that she had been horrified by this proposal and cried out. After they put white powder in her mouth, she lost consciousness, only recovering in hospital in Mantes. The report of her arrest concluded:

"It was thought that the two individuals identified by this woman were libertines who wanted to enjoy her, because she was rather pretty, and that she adjusted the story to pique interest in her cause and for vengeance ; but when she was questioned on that point, she said there was no question of libertinage, and these people had only touched her on the chin, saying that she was pretty."[109] The record fails to indicate why Raffron, rather than her attackers, was arrested and detained for over a month. State officials, including members of the police and judiciary, treated sexual assaults on poor women as mild infractions rather than crimes and rationalized the assailants' motivations as stemming from a victim's appearance.[110]

It was August 3, 1778, when Pelagie Dubourg appeared with her husband, Pierre Edmé Berthe, a clerk, to lodge a complaint against her neighbor's cook, the Fille Thierry, who "for some time has had the most injurious words on her account designed to attack her honor and reputation, notably in publicizing that she lives in Debauch, that she was never married and that everyone who visits her house obtains her favors without difficulty."[111] Moreover, this woman had attempted to turn neighbors against her by attributing to Dubourg the most notorious speeches. For instance, she told their neighbor, Dame Carré, that Dubourg had announced to all who could hear it that Carré's daughter was a libertine and that she had pox, which resulted in the most disagreeable reproaches from Dame Carré. Because Dubourg wished to end these defamations through the means of the law, she lodged her declaration with the police commissaire. Dubourg signed this declaration alongside her husband, presumably indicating his continued support for his wife's innocence in the face of calumny concerning her sexual conduct, which bore equally on his honor as on her own.

Only by the final decades of the eighteenth century did the term "libertine" in the police reports reliably indicate sexual debauchery for both men and women, as it intersected with the erotic literature that would come to define the century. Several authors took note of the change. Louis Antoine Caraccioli's *Dictionnaire critique, pittoreque et sentencieux* defined a libertine as "a debauched man, not an impious one, as some dictionaries assert."[112] It proved to be one of the more difficult insults to refute, depending primarily on reputation rather than concrete action. Moreover, the category remained profoundly gendered in its deployment. As Rousseau observes in *Emile*, if a man's reputation depends on his actions, a woman's reputation relies on others' perceptions of her.[113] The intersection between law and literature reveals how policy shifts recalibrated the scope of the libertine category. The author of the *Code or New Rule for Sites of Prostitution in the City of Paris* opened with a dedicatory letter, "To Male and Female Libertines," chastising these "vicious people" for the horrors caused by their debauchery. This historical-sociological essay on prostitution relied equally on moral condemnation and sensory titillation to pique readers' interest. In contrast to *The Pornographer*, which had blamed the French government for the lamentable state of brothels and the kingdom's sexual health, the author of the *Code* contended that the government was to be commended for bringing some discipline to places that "tolerance has always recognized as necessary" and instead found fault with the kingdom's "bad subjects."[114] The category of libertine thus had become firmly intertwined with sexual promiscuity, prostitution, and venereal disease. In 1775 a Versailles-based initiative to distribute free medical treatment for venereal disease took shape. Its advocates lamented that "the unfortunate victims of libertinage are rejected by most Hospitals, and in those designed for them, they are obliged to wait their turn, although the malady makes such rapid progress, that it is sometimes impossible to repair the damage."[115] Officials sought to reduce stigma in order to expand medical treatment.

In 1778 the Paris police adopted an ordinance that expressly linked sex work with libertines. The preamble observed, "Libertinage is today pushed to such a point, that girls and public women, rather than hiding their shameful commerce, have the audacity to display it during the day from their windows, where they signal to passers-by to attract them, to pose in the evening at their doors, and even to cruise the streets stopping people of all ages and all stations."[116] The law forbade prostitution "in the streets, on the quais, squares, and public promenades, and on the boulevards of this city of Paris, even in the windows," under penalty of arrest and detention in the hospital of the capital city.[117] The health of the kingdom required treatment of the disease, rather than judgment of the afflicted.

If individual petitions to the Paris commissaires and to departmental intendants reveal French families' efforts to preserve honor amid forces of social disorder, they also reveal popular expectations that the royal state would intervene on behalf of parental authority and in favor of marital accord.[118] In fact, so strong was the assumption that the Crown would side with parental—read patriarchal—authority that even criminal parents who had sold their daughters into prostitution assumed the state would secure their rights.[119] By the end of the century, royal advisors resisted these demands, although their subordinates continued to investigate petitions, file briefs, and imprison individuals on charges of libertine conduct. The king's power of arbitrary detention, solicited by families of all stations from all over the kingdom, continues to be construed as one of the blackest marks against the French monarchy. But perhaps the families that sought the imprisonment of their kin bear some of the responsibility for these extrajudicial practices? For decades royal ministers strove to reform a system that detained young, capable men and women at their parents' pleasure, arguably depriving the state of their labor and productive capacities.

The Swiss jurist Emer de Vattel, whose consideration of legal reform, *The Law of Nations, or Principles of Natural Law* (1758) influenced states-men and jurists across Europe and the Americas, contended that laws should accord with natural law, which was the most accurate gauge of divine will, rather than canon law, which was a flawed product subject to human corruption and vice. He reminded readers that "blind piety only makes superstitious followers, fanatics and persecutors, a thousand times more dangerous, more harmful to society than are the libertines."[120] The reform movements that swept provincial assemblies and parlements in the late eighteenth century prompted authorities throughout France to reconsider the dangers posed by rebellious teenagers, gamblers, illicit publishers, and adulterers.[121]

6

Redeeming Libertines

The Désirade Experiment, 1762–1768

The bells of the St-Antoine-des-Champs abbey church tolled four o'clock on the afternoon of December 7, 1762, when the Parisian pastrycook Pierre Royer and his wife, Margueritte Mambrun, appeared before a police investigator in his office on the rue du roi de Sicile in Paris. The couple explained that their sixteen-year-old son Jean showed the worst inclination toward libertinage. He spoke to them "with much brutality and lack of respect. He doesn't want to learn anything and wanders endlessly from morning until night. He has even left their house without asking permission, without even informing them." The investigator then turned to Jean, who agreed that he was a "bad subject."[1] But, he rationalized, he had only left his parents' home once without permission. He promised to obey his father and mother in the future, pleading for favor from the disapproving familiar and municipal authorities surrounding him. No matter. Despite the boy's protests, the police official ordered that Jean Royer be detained in the prison of Grand Châtelet until further notice.

Bright and early the following day, Jean's parents returned to provide further evidence of their son's errant ways. Since his most tender youth, they narrated, the child had undermined the family business and revealed an incorrigible character. It had been on Ash Wednesday two years prior that a young Jean left the family home in the morning "without saying a word" to his parents, not to return until 2 a.m. They awoke and found him asleep in their basement "in an awful state, his clothes and shoes so soiled and destroyed that they had to be thrown away." At the time Jean had admitted that he had been taken by two men into a cabaret at the edge of the city, but that "he escaped from them because they had put a hand in his pants."[2] Pierre and Margueritte presumably recounted this tale to document patterns in their son's behavior that risked the family's honor, although their testimony provides an important reminder of children's independent mobility in urban spaces, and their vulnerability to physical violence and sexual assault.[3]

From his parent's perspective, Jean had erred in leaving the parental home without permission—an initial act of disobedience that opened the door to uncalculated risks to family reputation. But honor was not all that was at stake. Jean had stolen money from the household on several occasions, notably during a holy day as everyone else was on their knees in prayer to observe the procession of the host through the street outside. Really, it was bad enough that he robbed his family. To do so during a sacred community observance magnified his ignominy. By the end of the Royers' testimony, they had accused their son of filial disobedience, petty larceny, and vagabondage. His impiety was almost an afterthought.

Beyond the impact of Jean's actions within the Royer household, the boy also threatened to imperil the family business, which depended on good relations and trust among the members of the pastrycooks' guild who constituted Pierre and Margueritte's colleagues and Jean's would-be masters.[4] In the past few years, Jean had begun and abandoned apprenticeships with some of the city's leading pastrycooks. He had forged his father's signature to collect payment for pastries that the Royers' shop sent to the provinces. And, just weeks earlier, Jean had slipped out of Paris without his parents' permission, heading for Fontainebleau, where his brother cooked in the household of the Duke of Estissac. He only returned when that brother urged him to reconcile with their parents. After that final escapade, the family had settled into an uneasy truce until the previous morning, when a family friend teased the boy about his journey, and Jean lashed out with vehemence, declaring he would not remain in his parents' home another moment before storming out to take refuge in a nearby cabaret.

The theft, the broken apprenticeships, the forgeries, the lying, the impiety, even the desertion of the family home—none of these actions had driven Jean's parents to seek out the police. It was the public outburst that finally prompted Pierre and Marguerite to declare themselves incapable of managing their son and to seek the aid of state authorities, detaining him in the Grand Châtelet prison for the foreseeable future. The Royer family must have agreed to pay a pension to support Jean in prison and presumably only took these steps after he proved to be an irredeemable threat to the family's reputation and fortune. Several months passed before Jean's parents again contacted the investigator, reminding him of their situation, which had required them to seek the state's resources to discipline an errant son. This time they concluded their tale of woe by observing that, as Jean remained unrepentant and unwilling to reform his behavior, they sought to communicate their preference that Jean be transported to the Isle of Désirade, "or whatever other island you may deem suitable."[5]

Arlette Farge and Michel Foucault argue in their classic analysis of the lettres de cachet conserved in the Bastille prison's records that this tool of arbitrary detention, although occasionally used to arrest high-profile authors critical of the Crown or Church, was in fact much more commonly employed by families—elite, middling, and working class—to detain problematic relatives.[6] The Royers' request demonstrates the degree to which family relations and state police activities intertwined to discipline and punish adolescents in eighteenth-century France. However, the Royer case also indicates this system of detention functioned in a context of colonial expansion and investment to a far greater degree than has been acknowledged.[7] These interlocking circuits of metropolitan and colonial legal systems became a dominant concern during the era, as documented by petitions, court cases, and the publication of volumes such as Emilien Petit's *Droit public ou le gouvernement des colonies françoises* (1771).

FRANCE'S ATLANTIC EMPIRE, 1763

At the precise moment that the Royer family sought the state's aid in disciplining their wayward son, the French crown had secretly ceded extensive American territories comprising the colony of Louisiana to the Spanish. After losing a series of critical battles against the English in Canada, the French government was on the verge of abdicating substantial swaths of American territory to the British as the Seven Years' War came to a close in 1763. As a result many scholars have concluded that, by 1763, the French Crown rolled up and packed away its imperial ambitions.[8] However, careful examination of state policies and programs actually reveals intensified imperial efforts throughout the remaining French colonies in the Western hemisphere, particularly in the Caribbean.[9] Extensive reforms of the military and the navy, and the codes governing slavery and race relations, followed the peace of 1763, as the French state strove to learn from previous mistakes and strengthen their hold on remaining colonial possessions. Moreover, during this era the French empire was much more than a tissue of royal directives. Men and women in France closely followed the news of their kingdom's place in the global war and supported administrative actions to advance an empire in which they invested substantial imaginative and economic energies.[10]

Across the Caribbean French subjects followed the king's actions on their behalf and lobbied hard to convince royal officials to increase colonial spending on military defenses, infrastructure, and trade. The French Crown approved plans to protect Acadian families and relocate them to the islands of St. Pierre and Miquelon in the wake of territorial losses in Canada to the British.[11] Throughout the territories of the former New France, those individuals who considered themselves to be French made concerted efforts to defend their language, faith, legal structures, and society.[12] Emigration increased, and the colonies of Saint-Domingue, Guadeloupe, and Cayenne witnessed remarkable growth during the last half of the eighteenth century.[13] This was a period of imperial retrenchment that witnessed strategic shifts of resources and dramatic reforms in policy, but the evidence makes clear that no one in France or the Americas considered the French Atlantic empire to be doomed.

AN ISLAND OF LIBERTINES

Among the dramatic strategic policy shifts in the French empire, this chapter attends to one that has gone largely ignored. In 1763 the French Crown issued a royal decree that determined to send "young people of bad behavior" to La Désirade, an enticingly named, palm-covered spit of an island some twenty kilometers square to the east of Guadeloupe.[14]

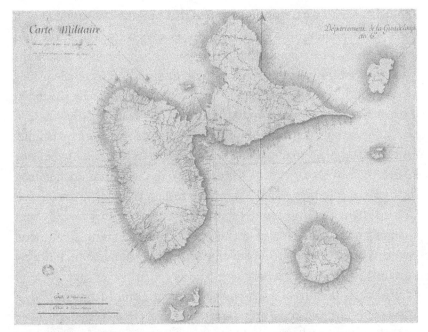

FIG 8. Map of Guadeloupe, Marie Galante, and Désirade, 1797. [Carte militaire dressée pour le site et le tableau général des fortifications et batteries de cotes. Département de la Guadeloupe.] Bibliothèque Nationale de France, http://catalogue.bnf.fr /ark:/12148/cb43861450d.

The text of the law expressly charted a path from shame to redemption, from exile to contributing colonist. Forced emigration was to be a key element of the reformed French empire, by better employing all the human resources of the metropole for settlement. In July 1763, by royal decree, the king of France established a tropical detention center in Désirade for libertine *fils de famille* (sons of wealthy families).

These few bad apples, officials postulated, might profit from the isolation of their island exile, engage in meaningful work, thus learn the value of labor, and return to France having improved the empire and themselves. The law's advocates seem to have imagined that a handful of elite families would have the financial means to take advantage of this opportunity to distance their progeny from the corrupting influences of Paris and Versailles. But, within just a few months, parents rich and poor from across the kingdom demanded that this punishment be applied to their own offspring. So it was that hundreds of young men of every social station, from every region of France, converged in the port of Rochefort, where it soon became apparent that the navy lacked the food, the housing, and the transatlantic transport capacity to adequately provide for this population. Nearly a year into the experiment, the intendant of Caen wrote to the royal minister of the marine, "There is, Sir, such considerable demand regarding bad subjects requested by families for the island of Désirade, that it is impossible for the King to provide all necessary funds for either their detention in the port of Rochefort or their transport to that island and food to sustain them."[15] These officials worried about keeping detainees fed, healthy, and safe; they fretted about arranging transatlantic transport and worried that parents might abandon payment after receiving confirmation that their troublesome kin were safe and secure across the Atlantic.

Within six months of its promulgation, Pierre and Marguerite Royer knew of the law, saw in it a promise for their own family's errant member, and asked that Jean be sent to Désirade, while indicating they remained amenable to alternate island detentions as well. Their request was denied, with the lieutenant general of police observing that the colony was no longer accepting exiles. A lie. In fact the island of Désirade received new residents until 1765. It was largely reserved for libertines of higher social status than Jean Royer, however. And it is worth inquiring more deeply into the qualities that were shared by the colony's accepted prisoner-settlers.

There was some precedent for the new policy. As detailed in chapters 2 and 3, the French state had exiled libertine young men and salt smugglers of both sexes to Louisiana in 1721, and then to Québec between 1726 and 1730.[16] But, in general, the Crown frowned on forced emigration of French subjects. Royal policies limited emigration to voluntary migrants, avowed Catholics of good character and proven reproductive capacity. By the middle of the eighteenth century, a growing chorus of writers and administrators bemoaned these limits on French emigration and trade that had inhibited the growth of French colonies vis-à-vis their continental rivals, Britain and Spain.[17]

Libertines might play an important role in settling the reformed empire, royal administrators suggested, if these young men could start over, entering adult life once again but without the luxuries of life in France distracting them. Of course, in Louisiana and Québec, such experiments had been quickly abandoned due to the unsuitability of the exiles—mostly elite young men trained to the law or the sword—to the manual labor demanded of residents in the colonies. Colonial officials decried such policies, which saddled settlements with obstinate and indulged young men. In 1730 the governor-general Beauharnois wrote to the minister of the marine Maurepas, requesting that the kingdom send more salt smugglers and fewer libertines to Québec. The latter proved unwilling to enlist in the colonial militia and were unaccustomed to work and impossible to punish in "this Country where escape opportunities abound."[18] In the eyes of colonial officials, they were incompetent and entitled individuals lacking the necessary expertise and drive to succeed in Canada. Moreover, the governor-general was forced to spend valuable time and resources tracking down these unwilling migrants, for the young men often fled the French settlements, taking refuge in neighboring Indigneous towns or small British encampments to the south. The salt smugglers, however, were men of rare initiative. The governor-general tried to make the royal officials understand how a salt smuggler's most notable qualities rendered as deception and fraud in France translated into financial acumen, ambition, and commercial ingenuity in Québec.

Given the poor track record of libertine exiles, therefore, what made the minister of the marine think that errant young men could prosper in Désirade? Initially used to quarantine lepers, the island was uniquely positioned in the Atlantic to be accessible to French Caribbean ports, but off the beaten path of international trade routes. In general French administrators perceived the islands of Martinique, Guadeloupe, Désirade, and Saint-Domingue as more secure sites for exiles than the North or South American outposts that neighbored rival European colonies. In 1763 the Duke of Choiseul noted that the condemned prisoner Martin could be released from galley service, so long as he remained "in perpetuity in the colonies." Choiseul advised that Martin be deported to Martinique, Guadeloupe, or Saint-Domingue, "and not to Cayenne where he would find it too easy to escape."[19] Moreover, the Caribbean climate was perceived as more hospitable than was Québec, where the

St. Lawrence River froze and rendered harbors impassable for nearly six months during the winter and early spring. French administrators further indicated a desire to bring Désirade's isolated stretch of sandy beaches closer into the imperial fold, investing population and military personnel to facilitate a more extensive and sustainable settler colony.

Historians of Guadeloupe have recognized the July 1763 decree to be a turning point in French colonial administration of the Caribbean, but the law receives little critical analysis beyond that sphere of local history.[20] However, this story intersects with the history of arbitrary detention within France, particularly those requests for lettres de cachet, and with the history of libertinage in the French empire. Every year, hundreds of families asked the French king or his officials for king's orders to confine an errant individual whose behavior threatened the family's reputation, even if it was not technically criminal. Some families, as the Marquis de Sade's notable case reveals, pursued lettres de cachet to avoid criminal proceedings that might bring notoriety to the family name.[21] Others sought to protect family fortunes, demonstrate paternal authority, or prevent undesirable marriages.[22]

Colonial exile appealed to both families and the state as a means of lightening the burden on France's prisons, monasteries, and convents while simultaneously building French populations throughout the Atlantic. The language of the decree observed that many families preferred colonial exile to prison in France, not only because the errant relative was further away but also because the individual might have a real chance for a fresh start and transform their behavior. The families of those young people who had "exposed the honor and tranquility of their families, or for which they have been detained by the Police, although not necessarily found guilty of crimes for which the law demands punishment," could appeal to the secretary of state for war and the marine (offices united in the person of the Duke of Choiseul at this point). If this minister found evidence of bad conduct, he could order the detention of the libertine in the prisons of the Rochefort port, where the prisoner would be housed and fed at the king's expense until the next ship for Désirade embarked. Throughout their detention at Rochefort, they were to be treated as prisoners, but as passengers on board ship, and provided a modest sailor's ration.

The decree went on to propose that an agrarian utopia awaited exiles upon their arrival in Désirade. The commander of the island would assign prisoners to plots of common land, to be worked with tools and seeds distributed for that purpose. He would also take charge of distributing soldiers' rations and clothes to the prisoners: three shirts, two pairs of culottes, a vest and a jacket, three pairs of shoes, and a hat. Those who became ill would be received and treated at the hospital, just like the soldiers who supervised the detainees.

Finally, the new law charged the commander with supervising the detainees' behavior, maintaining a chart divided into classes of improvement, and identifying those suitable for reentry to society. With his permission they could establish themselves on territory on the nearby islands of Marie-Galante, Guadeloupe, or Saint-Domingue to work for their own profit, or, with their family's permission, even return to France. Fifteen days after the initial decree, the king provided a further directive establishing regular mail ships (six per year) between France and the Caribbean islands.[23]

The naval officer at Rochefort first received official word of this new decree that would channel the kingdom's libertines through his port on August 3, 1763. The Duke of Choiseul explained that the king had decided "to allow the transport of bad subjects who are all too common in families," to Désirade at private expense. However, these exiles would need to be moved through France to Rochefort, housed in the prisons there, and surveilled throughout their detention and transport. The duke reported, "His Majesty wishes for four reliable men from the Sergents and Corporals of the Colonial Troops that are stationed in Rochefort to inspect the bad subjects in Désirade."[24] He proposed wages of 300 to 400 livres per year, plus two rations per day for these officers. As governor-general of the island, Choiseul appointed the Canadian naval officer Gabriel Rousseau de Villejouin, who was to receive 3,000 livres for this office. In addition, Villejouin's sons would join him as military supervisors of the libertine exiles. The oldest was to receive 2000 livres per year and four rations a day in the office of major, while the second would serve as aide-major with 1500 livres and three rations per day. The youngest was also to be accorded the office of aide-major, receiving 1200 livres per year and three rations per day. The appointments for the governor-general, his sons, and attending officers set a minimum annual expense for this detention island at 9,000 livres. This constituted a substantial and continuing expense for the French crown, requiring twenty-five detainees each paying 200 livres per year just to cover the officers' salaries. The island detention center would also require substantial infrastructure investments to provide housing, extend the harbor, promote agriculture, and increase security. The expense would be worthwhile, contended the kingdom's colonial administrators, if exile improved the behavior of these bad subjects, and encouraged the broader settlement of the Caribbean.

REDEEMING LIBERTINES

Social critic Denis-Laurian Turmeau de la Morandière applauded the king's decree in his *Appel aux etrangers dans nos colonies* (Appeal to foreigners in our colonies), published that same year. Aside from his publications, we know remarkably little about this author, a member of the Turmeau family established in Romorantin. Turmeau held the honorific of chevalier and was a member of the Royal Societies for Agriculture in Orléans and Soissons.[25] For France to succeed in empire, Turmeau observed, it required more people. It was that simple. France had the most populous kingdom in western Europe; every other state lagged far behind. But that population paled in comparison to what it might have been under a different monarch. Turmeau identified four major factors that had drained France of inhabitants: first and most important from Turmeau's perspective was the revocation of the Edict of Nantes in 1684, which had spurred the emigration of French Protestants to neighboring states. The following year Turmeau would devote a treatise to laying out the consequences of Louis XIV's decision to turn on his Protestant subjects in 1685. Second, over a century of colonial migration to distant posts in New France, India, and the Caribbean had already dispersed thousands of French subjects all around the globe. Third, excessive taxation inhibited the poor from having more children, and, fourth, excessive luxury constricted French demographic growth.

To this initial list, Turmeau then added five more factors that sapped the French population's potential: libertinage, excessive vagabondage, excessive numbers of servants, the excessive youth of most soldiers, and the law forbidding soldiers or officers to marry without the consent of the court. As he defined it, libertinage was any sexual activity outside of marriage, and it lay at the root of most French social ills. For the past sixty years or so, he asserted, too many men and women of every social station chose to remain single "for show," engaging multiple partners for sexual pleasure rather than marrying one partner to bear and raise children. In this essay and in his 1760 essay denouncing courtesans and kept women, Trumeau declared open war on these "destroyers of the population . . . [and] enemies of the State," who prioritized sexual recreation over procreation.[26] In that earlier essay, Turmeau explained that the French penchant for extramarital sex could be traced to "a certain taste for diversions, and a natural distance, from serious things . . . but these things also have their origins."[27] Too few Frenchmen were involved in political administration—deprived of civic virtues, they became depraved. Vice was the only liberty left to them under the strictures of absolutism. We recognize in this misogynistic caricature some of the features that defined the libertine character of eighteenth-century literature.

Turmeau particularly targeted the elite courtesans for which Parisian society had become famous: "kept women" who relied on stipends provided by aristocratic lovers and engaged in lives of idle luxury. Carriage rides, promenades, intimate suppers, and trips to the theater occupied their daytime hours, while at night, presumably, they were to be available to their lovers.[28] Such women set a bad example to the rest of society, the patriot economist lamented, and gave foreigners the impression that not one woman of upstanding morals resided in France.[29] In the profusion of courtesans in Paris, particularly among the actresses and dancers engaged by the opera and the Théâtres des Foires St. Germain and St. Laurent, Turmeau located a paradox of good government. The king provided privileges and protections for these spectacles, but these sites undermined the very foundations of good government, which held that the sovereign would not corrupt his subjects, that the state would respect a father's authority over his children, and that the state would affirm the incontestable authority of husbands over their wives' conduct. The king's power resided in the general authority of fathers over their children, and husbands over their wives. If the monarch protected entertainment that attacked these very principles, then he sowed the seeds of rebellion.

As Turmeau understood it, the expulsion of the Protestants from France, the policing of prostitutes and courtesans, and the role of foreigners in French colonies all pointed to a root cause. Laziness and libertinage, he asserted, constituted the central problems that limited the expansion of the French population at home and abroad. He charged:

> I attack those many of every station and profession who are single by choice and by debauched refinement, who live with women that they leave or who leave them every day; I attack prostitution and those mercenary girls who have five or six husbands at a time without having one of their own; finally I attack those of one and the other sex who indulge with impunity in the most extreme and scandalous dissolution, under the eyes of the magistrates and the police; I declare open war on them as destroyers of the Population and enemies of the State.[30]

French subjects' failure to marry young and raise many children cost the kingdom thousands of subjects, according to this author, and this more than any other factor limited the French capacity to build a global empire along the lines of the Spanish and the British. "This loss of citizens from all ranks of Society is so immense," he declared, "that it increases daily and is irreparable."[31] Turmeau's breathless diatribe offered a profound critique of sex for pleasure rather than reproduction, not because it constituted a moral failing or because use of contraceptives represented an action against divine law, but from an early concept of the sociological costs of such behavior. Declining birth rates meant declining wealth for the French nation, the physiocrats agreed.[32] Turmeau de la Morandière articulated the most extreme instantiation of this tenet, recognizing no absolute limit on the number of subjects to be maintained by France's territory.[33] The French population crisis was such, he contended, that the only possible mechanism to populate the empire resided in encouraging foreigners to move to the colonies through legal and financial incentives. Of course, we must check these contemporary assessments against the demographic picture that we have of France in the eighteenth century, during which time it remained the most populous kingdom in western Europe, with an increase of at least a half-million souls every decade from 1720 to 1790.[34]

According to Turmeau the French state should even consider appealing to foreigners of different religions, because to embrace religious diversity would enhance the French state economically. In some ways, he argued, it was desirable to use foreign dissenters as a settler population. Spain had made the mistake of populating its empire with its best and brightest, leaving the mother country deserted as a result. Sacrificing its population for gold and silver, the Spanish kingdom entered a long decline. The English, on the other hand, populated their empire with foreigners, and this, Turmeau contended, should serve as the model for France. England had invested in population and agriculture, which produced long-lasting wealth for the kingdom "more precious than all the gold, silver and diamonds in the Universe."[35] More people in the colonies would increase the productive capacity of these territories, which would in turn enrich France. Moreover, the French state should encourage foreigners to settle in French colonies irrespective of their religious beliefs, an argument clearly modeled on the British settlement of North America and the Caribbean by religious dissenters.

Religious diversity was, Turmeau argued, the great secret to ensuring population growth, agricultural productivity, and encouraging industrial development in the colonies, based on the example of how surrounding Protestant states welcomed French Huguenots and benefited from their labor. Turmeau found a sympathetic ear in the French colonial administration for this message, and the settlement of Cayenne in 1763 included nearly five thousand inhabitants of German provinces who had settled in Rochefort until the French state arranged for their passage.[36] Among this population, too, there were concerns about libertinage. On September 16 Choiseul advised that his officers in Rochefort prioritize the transport of migrants to Cayenne, using all ships headed to the Caribbean to move even a few individuals at a time: "M. de Chavalon informs me that there are many colonists among those destined for Cayenne who are already associated with girls who want to get married to avoid the inconveniences that could result from their exchange. I wrote to the Bishops of La Rochelle and de Saintes to permit their marriages to avoid the libertinage that could result if these associations are not promptly authorized."[37] Marriage between settlers promised the imperial state more stable communities, maintenance of European customs and institutions across the seas, and the promise of white offspring in the colonies.

Turmeau recommended a four-point plan to recover French economic strength at this critical moment: first, reduce taxes on agriculture throughout France and the empire to encourage increased production. Second, encourage young, vigorous foreigners of both sexes, regardless of religion to settle in French colonies, so long as they do not trouble the dominant Catholic religion. Third, provide each new settler with work, either at public works or in private engagement. Fourth, give each settler a home, a bed, the necessary household utensils, and some land so that, through hard work, they could become self-sufficient. New settlers to French territories could be given "one cow and three sheep," each, with males evenly distributed to facilitate the continued reproduction of the herds. Such expenses would not exceed the capacities of the "King of France, the first, the richest and the most powerful Monarch in Europe."[38] While, at first glance, these expenses seem like gifts, they are actually investments that will ensure colonists become productive much more quickly and profit France.

Turmeau believed that the king's order to send errant youth to Désirade provided a road map to a brighter future for the kingdom and empire. This was precisely the type of policy that simultaneously populated the French empire by putting to work the kingdom's worst libertines. The administration had thought of everything, he enthused, from promoting agricultural production to providing adequate supervision of these exiles. He applauded "the foresight of the Minister who engages, for the state's profit, subjects who could only be detrimental and even dangerous, providing paternal care to their correction. These *libertins*, thanks to such wise and gentle precautions, will be masters of their own work and actions, so long as they do not abuse their liberty to abandon themselves to laziness or to commit crimes. By enriching the Colony where they live, they will enrich the State and themselves."[39]

The Crown's new law establishing Désirade as a tropical detention center had been published only a few weeks before Jean Royer's parents seized upon the order as a possible solution to their own family problem. It seems likely that the French Crown devised the policy as a mechanism to populate a corner of their empire while placing some distance between France's leading families and their errant youth.[40] Doubtless, royal administrators had not considered that a family of pastrycooks would seek island exile for their wayward son, but that was the effect. Across the kingdom families of great wealth and little means alike appealed for the king's grace to remove objectionable sons or nephews from the family fold. In the province of Normandy, the intendant M. de Fontette addressed his concerns directly to the minister of the marine, M. de Choiseul. He attested that the appeals for the transportation of libertine sons were "innumerable" and requested guidance to prioritize their movements to the port at Rochefort.[41] Choiseul advised Fontette to ensure the family could pay two hundred livres annually to support the bad subject, as well as assume all costs associated with travel to and provisions in Rochefort while they awaited their ship. The families' appeal would not be granted until the intendant had ascertained their financial situation.

Typically, when families requested lettres de cachet from the French king, representatives of the French state undertook to substantiate a family's charges of bad behavior.[42] No such records are preserved in Commissaire Auret de la Grave's files—no interviews seem to have been conducted with Jean Royer's neighbors, other family members, or former employers. However, royal administrators did ultimately respond to the family's request, indicating that island exile was not an option for this particular individual.[43] Within weeks of the promulgation of this decree, demand for island exile overwhelmed the French state. Before Governor-General Villejouin had been able to leave France to make a tour of Désirade's facilities or ensure housing for his own team, let alone for the mounting wave of bad subjects, requests came in from all corners of the kingdom to secure this uniquely appealing option of tropical island exile.

The first challenge to the new policy appeared while the bad subjects were still in France. Transport from their home towns to the naval port of Rochefort on the Atlantic coast provided ample opportunities for the young men to escape, and directives sent from the minister of the marine, the Duke of Choiseul, over the next few months made clear that these evasions had forced administrators to reconsider the wisdom of gathering the exiles together in one place. In December 1763 several of the young men who had entered the Rochefort prison as libertines and then transferred to the hospital due to illness disappeared.[44] They had escaped with the aid of the hospital attendants, reported Michel-Joseph Froger de l'Eguille, naval commander at Rochefort. Unacceptable! thundered the response from Versailles. The minister had to account for these young men's whereabouts to their families—it was essential that the state know their location and status at every moment. And on July 14, 1764, Charles Durozais, Artus de Saveuse, and Sieur Boyer, all bound for Désirade and held for months in the hospital at Rochefort, escaped and were noted in the hospital register as having "deserted."[45] The Duke of Choiseul advised Froger de l'Eguille to establish a hospital within the prison if he could not exercise better surveillance over the port's hospital.[46]

Those subjects who complied with exile found themselves housed alongside runaway soldiers, vagrants, and thieves in the prison at Rochefort until transport to the Caribbean could be arranged. Sixteen bad subjects arrived in Guadeloupe with the first ship, reported Villejouin on August 3, 1763.[47] A seventeenth, Louis Huguenin, had been sent to Cayenne accidentally and would be conveyed to Martinique before he could finally make his way to Désirade. These documents reveal that the French military and governors lacked the basic infrastructure and administrative attention to bring this modest plan to fruition.

As the commander of Désirade, Villejouin promised to faithfully submit his evaluation of the exiles' behavior every month, keeping the royal administrators up to date on the deported men's well-being throughout their island exile. However, he observed at this moment early in the colony's establishment, and repeatedly throughout his tenure there, that the state's pension of 200 livres to be paid by the accused's family was entirely insufficient to provide the necessary food, clothing, transport, and housing for exiles. It was October 11, 1763, when the minister of the marine advised the naval commander at Rochefort to delay the exiles' passage in order to give more time to Villejouin to "put lodgings in place and make all necessary changes to receive them with security in Désirade."[48] While awaiting transportation prisoners ran the risk of contracting illnesses either serious or mild and requiring the insalubrious ministrations of the hospital in Rochefort. The next shipment of bad subjects left Rochefort over two months later, on the ship *Le Bergère*, according to Froger de l'Eguille's letter of December 29, 1763.[49] Of the eight young men identified on this list, two were sick and in the hospital. Others would become ill during the voyage and remain at the hospitals in Guadeloupe. Throughout the winter and spring of 1764, more bad subjects descended upon Rochefort and were to be transported twelve at a time, on the paquebots that the ministry had commissioned to increase communication between France and its Caribbean colonies.[50] Thirty-six men in total were exiled to Désirade in 1763.[51] Throughout the winter and spring of 1764, forty-six more bad subjects descended upon Rochefort to be transported across the Atlantic.[52] These men waited in the prisons at Guadeloupe for their island exile to be made ready, a task not completed until late summer of 1764.

Villejouin wrote on November 10, 1763, to inform the Ministry of the Marine of his arrival in Guadeloupe after a quick and pleasant thirty-seven-day voyage across the Atlantic. This would not be the rule; it could take up to four months to make the voyage. He observed that he was prepared to depart imminently to inspect the island's barracks, lodgings, and arable land. Désirade already had lodgings appropriate to the officers assigned to guard the island, along with a house for the king's clerk, store-houses, a hospital, and a prison. However, he had substantial work to do before prisoners could arrive. This trip, he noted, was simply intended to survey the prospects for the proposed exile community and identify the best site for the exiles' cottages to be built. Furthermore, in confidence to his patron, Villejouin lamented his appointment as Désirade's governor to be a "very sad post."[53] The royal administration's ambitious schedule to begin transporting bad subjects to the island within months would be delayed by the significant time it would take to build lodgings for them all on this island, which had no easily accessible harbor for large ships, no building materials, and scarce laborers in the surrounding area. He made clear later in the letter that his major motive in accepting this post was to advance his own sons' military careers by bringing them along as officers with corresponding promotions in rank and pay.[54]

Once in Désirade these bad subjects were housed in humble cottages and expected to perform daily agricultural labor, proving their industry and value to themselves, their governor, and their king. More commonly they drank heavily and plotted their means of escape. Villejouin lost one prisoner a month, on average, as individuals set off in rickety rafts across the calm waters that separated the island from Guadeloupe.[55] We know of the exiles' behavior thanks to the governor's regular reports back to the naval minister, in which he reported how each prisoner conducted himself and spent his time. This correspondence reveals a man increasingly opposed to the discipline he was enjoined to oversee, for he ate and drank with the young men under his supervision, and he seems to have developed some sympathies for his prisoners.

Already at the end of 1763, British newspapers caught wind of the French scheme to populate Désirade with libertines. A brief article in the *Gentlemen's Magazine* summarized the text of this "remarkable ordonnance," noting that when "young fellows of family shall be guilty of irregularities, capable of wounding the honour, or disturbing the quiet of their families, or which are reprehensible by the Police, without being crimes punishable by law, it shall be lawful for their parents to ask the Secretaries of State in the department of war and of the marine, to transport them to the island of Désirade."[56] The editor reported erroneously that they would be maintained at the prison in Rochefort at the king's expense, transported safely, and rationed alongside the ships' sailors. Upon arriving in the island, the commander undertook to station detainees "in a fruitful, healthy part of the island. They shall be lodged in cabins built on purpose for them."[57] There was a great deal of idealism in this reporting, the editor dwelling on the valuable transport, food, lodging, new clothing, agricultural tools, and seed to be provided to these young men. Finally the editor observed that if families had used the law as a means of dispossessing their sons "that they may enjoy their estates; the young fellows shall be assisted to recover 'em, if they chuse to remain in the colonies, or they shall even be allowed to return to France, to take care of their affairs in person."[58] It is unclear what lesson British gentlemen were to learn from this French example, although clearly the editor communicated France's continued and deepening investment in colonial settlements in this decade.

So long as the island detention center remained open, parents sought transportation of their errant offspring. In 1765 the director of the post at La Rochelle, Claude Baudry, requested that his son be detained in Désirade due to his libertinage. The twenty-two-year-old was currently a sous-lieutenant in the Royal Marine stationed in Martinique, where he had racked up gambling debts and occasioned numerous violent confrontations with his fellow officers. His parents promised "to faithfully pay the two hundred *livres* pension every year" to have him disciplined for this behavior.[59]

But, by July 1765, royal support withered for this colonial detention center that had proved to be incredibly difficult to build, staff, and police. The demand was clear—the kingdom's parents cried out for a destination for their wayward sons. But few were ready to provide their sons' or nephews' pensions in such a manner that could turn a profit for the Crown. The decree of July 1763 had committed a company and a half to surveil the detainees, but the governor of Guadeloupe refused to send that many soldiers from his own island's troops. The governor of Désirade was ordered to prepare the colony to be evacuated. Villejouin complied with his new orders to identify those prisoners of good conduct who could be released, and those who should be imprisoned elsewhere in the colonies or back in France.

THE DETAINED LIBERTINES

For the most part, Villejouin could observe that his prisoners "behaved themselves well."[60] In this first class, he listed twenty-two prisoners by name and recommended they be accorded immediate liberty. Of Antoine-Philippe du Hecquet, the governor noted, he has "always behaved well. His only fault is drink, and that occurs only rarely." Over twenty young men scrounged for sustenance in exile, sacrificed to their families' sense of honor, deprived of useful employment and the means of self-improvement. The second class included sixteen prisoners who had committed light offenses but merited liberty nonetheless, from the perspective of the colony's commander. For instance, of Jean-Felix Paon who was "filthy and libertine," Villejouin remarked, for all that, he "is not among the worst of his class."[61] These men had broken no laws and harmed no one, and they suffered greatly in exile. As for the third class, the governor identified his seven worst offenders—liars, thieves, and deserters. Of Noel D'Argouge he noted that he "unites all the faults and nearly all vices, is dangerous, made several attempts to escape, gives bad counsel, spent three-quarters of his time in prison and in irons."[62] What was this man doing in island exile, threatening the very existence of his fellow exiles and the officers charged with supervising detention? Reading through Villejouin's correspondence, it is hard to escape the governor's frustration with both the state and families that could consign to island exile so many healthy, able-bodied young men due to youthful indiscretions or generational disputes. In Villejouin's estimation only seven of his forty-five prisoners merited detention, and all would have been better imprisoned in fortified centers rather than the eminently escapable Désirade.

One exile, Jean-Baptiste Alliot, won Villejouin's confidence. In August 1765, the young man penned a letter professing deep remorse for past wrongs and testifying to the extreme privations of his living conditions on the island. The head of the Colonial Bureau, Jean Dubucq, prevailed upon Alliot's family to provide a more generous pension for him, observing that it had been over a year since he had received any money or news from them. Alliot suffered from a terrible infection in his leg that had no chance of improvement without the necessary remedies and in "this climate which is completely contrary" to recovery.[63] Villejouin had loaned him money on several occasions, and Alliot bemoaned the fact that "for nine months he [Villejouin] has written to my father in my favor to ask him to send the money which he should have sent; I see with pain that my father has not even responded to him." The prisoner concluded by asking for administrative favor in the absence of paternal recognition: "Am I not punished enough, separated from my wife and my son, without being sent two thousand leagues from my homeland, more miserable than the blacks who inhabit this country?"[64]

In Alliot's appeal he equated his own captivity with that experienced by enslaved Africans in the Antilles. Transported in a passenger ship, provided with lodgings and regular food and access to paper, ink, and political influence, Alliot's circumstances bore no resemblance to the forced labor and inescapable terrors faced by enslaved people. But he was not the only one to draw these faulty comparisons. In equating monarchical, patriarchal, and enslavers' authority over social subordinates, revolutionary discourse would galvanize people of all social stations to challenge absolute monarchy by 1787, patriarchal authority in law by 1789, and the law of slavery throughout the French colonies by 1791.[65] Throwing himself at the mercy of the French administrators to judge his crimes and punishment, Alliot became a case example for both Dubucq and Villejouin of the abuses of this settlement policy. As diplomatically as they could, both men opposed the open-ended detention of young men in a tropical island detention center.

By the end of 1765, the governor of Guadeloupe, Pierre-Gédéon de Nolivos, argued persuasively that the Désirade colony was too expensive to maintain and requested permission to transfer the bad subjects to Guadeloupe, where they were to be imprisoned for fear that they might flee to nearby British colonies or join the maroon communities of runaway slaves.[66] The penal colony was not completely closed until 1767, when thirty remaining prisoners were transported to Guadeloupe. By 1768 Villejouin returned to France with an annual pension of four thousand livres as befitted an officer of his skill and service. The president of the Naval Board wrote to the Duke of Choiseul to request that the Crown consider bestowing the office of brigadier upon Villejouin for his remarkable service. Here was an officer who had "distinguished himself very much at Ile Royal as well as in the naval battle of M. de la Jonquière," only incidentally mentioning his service supervising the island of libertine exiles.[67] Families continued to request colonial exile for their libertine sons, but left the specific destination vague.[68] Alternatively, they might request that the young men be drafted into the colonial troops as punishment for their libertine ways. The royal officials, anxious to ensure the efficacy of the military in both Europe and the American colonies, would require that these individuals meet the physical fitness requirements of all soldiers, and proof that the family would actually provide financial support for their errant youth.[69] With Villejouin's departure, the island once again became Guadeloupe's leper colony and provided a refuge for infected former slaves throughout the 1770s.[70] For most of the Désirade libertines, however, we know very little, beyond the governor's notes recommending that most of them should return to France and their families.

But of Jean-Baptiste Alliot, a robust archival record developed. In 1770 the Parlement of Paris, the French kingdom's premier law court, reviewed the details in a suit filed by Alliot's father against his son. The trial briefs submitted by counsel for both the prosecution and the defendant were published in 1776 in the fifteenth volume of a series dedicated to circulating the causes célèbres of the era.[71] It summarized the case, beginning with the son's birth in 1733. Commissioned in the army at the age of nine, Jean-Baptiste served as a lieutenant in the Prince de Conti's forces that invaded Flanders and retired at fifteen. His father then pensioned him in a series of monasteries, insistent that his son would take up ecclesiastical orders.

Jean-Baptiste refused. He was twenty-five years old when he fell in love with Demoiselle Michault, then twenty-three, and she became pregnant. Forbidden to marry by Alliot's father, the lovers sought refuge in autonomous principalities beyond the kingdom of France—Lorraine, then Sénone, and finally Basel in Switzerland—where the police might not catch up with them. Or so the young man thought. His father called upon his connections with the royal household of Poland and orchestrated the young man's arrest in the tavern of a Swiss innkeeper, M. Imhoff. He was bound, sent across the continent, and imprisoned in the island fortress on Mont-Saint-Michel within months of his thirtieth birthday. The entire time that he sat in prison, his defense attorney attested, his central concern was for his beloved: "Was she alive? Was she dead? Was she free or a prisoner?"[72] He had to find her. The trial brief embroidered romantic impulses into Alliot's actions, noting that "love and duty fueled his new effort; they fooled the guards again and Sieur Alliot was free; he fled Mont Saint-Michel on 29 August 1763."[73]

Young Alliot made his way to Coblentz, located his lover, and married her in a Catholic ceremony on October 31, 1763. Within a year he was back in prison. In letters to his father, he offered to change his name, renounce his right to succession, leave Europe, and move with his new family to the colonies—all to no avail. Alliot's father demanded that he be transferred to Rochefort and exiled to Désirade. The ship, the *Ambition*, sailed out of the harbor on June 5, 1764, with Jean-Baptiste aboard. "He was thrown into a crowd of these corrupt and degraded subjects," his attorney contended, "that the police condemn to the hardest labor to prevent the dishonor of a judicial condemnation."[74] And if he survived these degenerate influences, it was due primarily to his own resolute character, which impressed the leaders of the islands at both Martinique and Désirade. Alliot received certificates of approbation in 1765 and only resided in Désirade for eight months before the colony's governor, Villejouin, authorized his free movement throughout the island.

After three years of exemplary reports, Alliot finally won an order of release from the French king and left the islands on July 29, 1767, arriving in Le Havre only thirteen days later. He soon located his wife, who had delivered a son in his absence; the infant had died due to her lack of resources and misery. The couple sought out Alliot's father, who reluctantly agreed to pay his son's debts and provide them with 1000 écus, on the condition that the young man change his name and leave Paris. Under the name of Duchesne, the couple attempted to start over. But they spent the pension quickly and, lacking any other resources, returned to Alliot's father. He demanded they separate, to which Alliot purportedly replied that he preferred to renounce his father rather than his wife, because "we are inseparable one from the other."[75] An ethic of marital attachment animates Alliot's brief, matched on the father's side by forceful statements of paternal devotion. His son, the father asserted, had been seduced by his lover, falling victim to a plot engineered by her parents. The devoted father's sole thought was to protect Jean-Baptiste and the Alliot family's interests from these rapacious in-laws' predations. The consent of parents was essential for a valid marriage; because his son had failed to secure it, the father considered the union void.

The Parlement struck a compromise. They found with the elder Alliot that the marriage was abusive and prohibited the younger Alliot and Demoiselle Michault from representing themselves as spouses or frequenting each other's company. But the Parlement pronounced that the elder Alliot must pay his son 3000 livres as a pension, in quarterly install-ments. Summarizing the case in 1776, the editors of the monthly news digest, *L'esprit des journaux français et étrangers*, pronounced it "one of the most interesting" both for the "profoundness of the reasoning" and an "uncommon eloquence" exhibited by both sides' lawyers.[76] But it is difficult to consider this verdict as a victory for the younger Alliot. Essen-tially, the judges accepted that marriages could not be contracted by men and women without their parents' permission and reaffirmed the father's duties to financially support his adult son. The court supported a coherent paternalist logic, but it was one that denied the insistent "natural law" of sexual desire so central to Jean-Baptiste Alliot's defensive arguments.

CONCLUSION

In 1779 the intendant of Normandy refused a request for king's orders requiring Caribbean exile, observing that "the king no longer wants to transport rascals."[77] Reform was in the air, and the royal administration labored to ameliorate systems of criminal justice while maintaining social stability and political legitimacy.[78] Within a generation revolutionary legislators would condemn and destroy the mechanisms of arbitrary detention that had consigned a handful of young libertines to island exile. But France's experiment with forced emigration had only begun. From the 1770s into the twentieth century, France deported thousands of criminals to their South American colony of French Guiana, to the North African colony of Algeria, and to the South Pacific colony of New Caledonia, relying on the blueprint of remote, military-supervised exile laid out by the Désirade detention center.[79]

The lessons learned from this brief episode left their mark. In 1781 the editor of the *Gazette de commerce* included choice excerpts from M. Weuves's recent historical-economic inquiry into France's American colonies, particularly those sections reflecting on the policy of deport-ing libertines. Weuves noted that "many serious persons thought and still think that for punishing those for whom family or State politics requires prison, it would be best to send them to the colonies; in this way they are not wholly lost to society."[80] But the policy was ill considered, concluded the author; the result had been to relegate "all vices and bad conduct two thousand leagues from the Metropole."[81] Moreover, both families and royal authorities too often overreacted to youthful indiscretions that would be resolved in time with maturity. The journalist observed that there were those among the exiles who could take the opportunity to transform themselves, and that a "young man who had no other fault than laziness, which is what sensory libertinage is called, could correct himself with emigration. This young man, isolated in a distant country, filled with active and laborious People, could, by good example and the need to survive, acquire a taste for work and virtue: there exist notable proofs of this."[82] Reform could happen, observed de Weuves, but it rarely did.

Exile had been the punishment of choice for such a wide range of bad behavior, from the lazy to the murderous. Decades of indiscriminate detentions, therefore, had contributed to a lawlessness in the colonies compounded by minimal police and justice administrations. After all, de Weuves warned, "a vicious soul, gangrenous and charged with crimes, can only take these with him, and bring them to a country where he will not find the same vigor of the Police, nor the same methods of correction as in the Metropole."[83] Moreover, the example of hardened criminals posed a particular threat in the colonies organized around racial hierarchy. In this theory de Weuves repeats one of the central truisms of colonial administrators from Québec to Kourou: "I am assured, the bad conduct of the Whites is the principal cause of the corruption of Blacks, by the impression it makes on them. It can't be too feared, nor too much avoided, particularly in a new Colony. It is therefore essential that only Subjects of upright conduct and non-suspect morals be sent to the Colonies."[84] In the racial hierarchy that French officials strove to stabilize across the Caribbean, libertine white men and women undermined colonial administrators' claim to exercise moral authority. These prisoners gave proof to the lie of racial hierarchy, their conduct serving only as bad examples and as a site for officials' anxieties. For all these reasons, the policy of transporting libertines, although it may have fulfilled the objectives of parents across France, proved irreconcilable to the king's authority and to the durable extension of colonial communities.

7

Racializing Libertines

Sex and the Law of Slavery in the French Antilles, 1763–1789

By 1763 French administration in Saint-Domingue had clung to the mountainous western bays of the island of Hispaniola for nearly a hundred years.[1] It had been over a century since French settlers had claimed the verdant island of Martinique some 1000 kilometers to the southeast. From the time Europeans stepped onto these rocky coastlines, authors and officials united in describing them as havens for transgressors, cultivating reputations as "libertine islands" beyond the reach of French law.[2] But what they meant by the term shifted markedly while France occupied this territory, inserting its people and produce into the global economies of the Atlantic world.[3] In western Hispaniola in the 1620s, French buccaneers seized pockets of the island, terrorizing the inhabitants and flouting Spanish authority, only to see King Louis XIV lay claim to the western third of the island, comprising some 27,750 square kilometers in 1665. It was over one hundred years later that Spain grudgingly acknowledged France's claim to this stretch of land formalized in the Treaty of Ryswick in 1697.[4]

As a map (fig. 9) from 1722 announces, European imperial powers aimed to consolidate colonial footholds in the Antilles, with French and Spanish settlers warily occupying the island of Hispaniola, the western edge claimed by France, and the eastern portion acknowledged as the "Spanish Quarter." Huguenot, Jewish, and Catholic settlers coexisted uneasily in Martinique, provoking violent confrontations with the Indigenous Carib residents throughout the seventeenth century.[5] From these

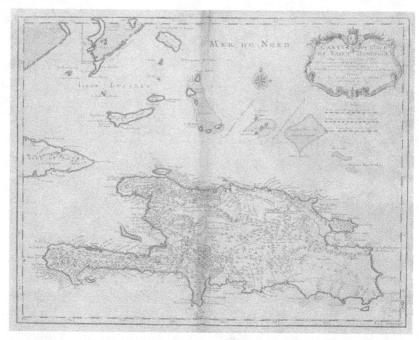

FIG 9. Map of Saint-Domingue, 1722. Guillaume Delisle. [Carte de l'isle de Saint-Domingue dressée en 1722 pour l'usage du Roy sur les mémoires de Mr. Frézier, . . . et autres assujetis aux Observations Astronomiques / par G. Delisle], . . . Echelle de 25 lieues communes de France de 25 au degré [=0m. 085 ; 1 : 1 300 000 environ; Marin sculpsit.] Bibliothèque Nationale de France, http://catalogue.bnf.fr/ark:/12148 /cb40633355z.

corners of the French Atlantic, writers and colonial officials used the term "libertine" to characterize the impieties of early pirates, the spendthrift ways of luxury-loving colonists, and the bid for personal freedom claimed by maroons, formerly enslaved people who developed independent communities beyond the reach of enslavers and colonial officials.[6] Under the circumstances of colonial settlement, "libertine" functioned as an imperial shorthand that described the challenges in exerting royal authority over conflicting populations in distant territories.[7] But in the decades after the Seven Years' War, the meaning of the word took a turn. Officials, travelers, and residents now used it to refer to the entire population of "mixed-race" inhabitants. In distinct contrast to prior applications, the libertine identified not an objectionable action, but an identity, an essence.

Doris Garraway has documented how "discourses of libertinage" in the French Caribbean represented what was "threatening and uncontrollable about the creolizing process as French emigrants reacted and accommodated to the cultural difference of native Caribs and imported Africans while spontaneously fashioning new identities outside the bounds of traditional authority, morality, and social codes."[8] Cultural hybridity characterized the societies that took shape in the Caribbean, and anxieties about mixture informed the social category of the libertine in this context. Garraway's nuanced analysis showcases how Antillean representations of libertinage differed fundamentally from those developed in France. Nonetheless the libertine figure articulated those social and economic ties that bound France with the Antilles. What liberties struck contemporaries as specific to the Caribbean colonies? Could these liberties travel the Atlantic? How might these colonies and their people transform France?

In this chapter I first provide a brief overview of Antillean colonial laws and legal institutions before identifying the quasi-crimes that most troubled royal ministers, Church leaders, and colonial authorities in the islands of Saint-Domingue and Martinique. This summary is not intended to be exhaustive, but to sketch some of the most pressing social anxieties that attended the establishment of these tropical colonies. From 1685 to 1760, officers of both the Crown and Church identified transgressions of the law of slavery—by enslavers but especially by the enslaved—as the most important instances of libertine conduct.[9] But officials gave wide latitude to colonial elites and their managers on these matters, for the most part turning a blind eye to all but the most egregious of violations. The Crown's response changed after the loss of France's extensive North American territories after the Seven Years' War. In a series of laws passed between 1761 and 1789, royal authorities strove to strengthen the mutually constitutive powers that they hoped would undergird societies in France and the Americas: the Catholic Church, the monarchy, and the patriarchal family. Officials in Saint-Domingue contended that the category of "race" (requiring enforcement of a stricter hierarchy privileging those of European descent) composed an essential fourth pillar of society comparable to France's aristocracy.[10] The Crown disagreed. And so, over the following two decades, a series of lawsuits set metropolitan and colonial authorities on a collision course that demonstrated how monarchical authority might undermine paternal authority and vice versa. These causes célèbres also reveal how new concepts of race challenged principles of family, inheritance, and property with unpredictable consequences in France and its colonies. As *mémoires judiciaires* for these cases circulated the Atlantic, the reading public absorbed these paradoxes at the heart of the law that bound France and Saint-Domingue; many in the metropole denounced bondage but accepted racial prejudice. In these decades European authors and readers learned to equate forms of unfreedom, decry vastly divergent limitations on economic or personal liberties as "slavery," and champion the rights claimed by colonial libertines.

THE LAW OF SLAVERY, 1685–1730

According to the letter of the law, the French Crown prohibited slavery on French soil, having abolished unfree labor by royal decree in 1315.[11] In 1583 Jean Bodin famously described slavery as inimical to a "well ordered Commonwealth."[12] Bodin perceived that every enslaver wielded the power of life and death over the humans they held in bondage, which corrupted their hearts and inflated their sense of their own power, making them poor subjects of an absolute monarch. But Atlantic trade required slavery, insisted some contemporaries. Indeed, the merchants and planters from competing European empires placed the slave trade and enslaved labor at the center of the Atlantic economic system by the late seventeenth century.[13] How, then, to reconcile the Crown's paradoxical opposition to and reliance on slavery? In response to widespread revolts, unregulated commerce, and growing populations of runaway slaves, the French Crown worked with colonial governors throughout the Caribbean colonies to develop a legal framework to regulate the institution of enslaved labor, culminating in the Code Noir promulgated in March 1685.[14] The law of slavery touched on every aspect of life in the Antilles, establishing the religious, economic, and social contours of this society. The Sovereign Council of Martinique affirmed the code in 1685, while the Sovereign Council of Saint-Domingue registered the law on May 6, 1687. Theoretically the French Crown extended principles drawn from Roman precedent to regulate slavery in the Antilles, though Louis XIV's advisors reflected more interest in systematizing the ad hoc policies that enslavers had developed to benefit their own interests.[15] But royal officials designed these laws in concert with those members of the colonial elite with an eye to establishing a sustainable and economically productive colony. In those territories the Crown determined that a child born to an enslaved mother remained a slave regardless of the father's status.

The Code Noir introduced critical innovations that aligned systems of enslaved labor with seventeenth-century French social and economic ideals. First, the code placed singular emphasis on enforcing religious orthodoxy in the first eight articles of the law. The first article commanded colonial officials to "evict from our Islands all the Jews who have established their residence there" within three months or these subjects would risk confiscation of "body and property."[16] Article 2 required that enslaved people be educated in Roman Catholicism, although the law failed to articulate if responsibility for this education fell to the enslaver or the colonial government. Article 3 limited the public exercise of religion to Catholics, while article 4 required all overseers to be Catholics, and article 5 forbid Calvinist subjects from interfering with the free exercise of Catholic services. Article 6 required all subjects—"whatever their status or condition"—observe Sundays and Catholic holidays by ceasing labor.[17] Article 7 forbid holding slave markets (and presumably other commerce) on Sundays or Catholic holidays, and article 8 held that only Catholics enjoyed valid marriages. Individuals of any other faith risked having their unions and children declared illegitimate, thus invalidating property claims and inheritance rights.

According to the provisions of the 1685 Code Noir, French law relied first on religious identity and second on legal status of "free" or "slave" to determine an individual's place in the body politic.[18] Sexual relations were not to cross those boundaries. The king held everyone, but especially the enslaving elites of society, subject to these laws. And colonial officials had the means to vigorously enforce several of these provisions; Jewish residents in Martinique and Guadeloupe were driven from these islands based on article 1, although Saint-Domingue again sheltered an important group of Jewish merchants by the eighteenth century.[19]

Article 9 of the Code Noir prohibited sex resulting in children between free men and enslaved women under a penalty of two thousand pounds of sugar. Furthermore, the Crown threatened that for those free men who "are the masters of the slave by whom they have had the said children, we wish that beyond the fine, they be deprived of the slave and the children, and that she and they be confiscated for the profit of the [royal] hospital, without ever being manumitted."[20] With this punishment the monarch announced an ideological commitment to segregate free from enslaved peoples. But the law did provide a loophole to enable an enslaver to retain both an enslaved concubine and the children that she bore: marriage. If an enslaver married an enslaved woman with whom he had children, she would be manumitted and the children "rendered free and legitimate."[21] The woman would have to be a Christian and baptized in the Catholic Church for the marriage to be recognized. But, in this manner, the French king established a legal provision to retroactively legitimate children born out of wedlock, securing personal liberty along with property rights and civil status for formerly enslaved people under French law. It was rarely used, and colonial administrators almost never enforced the prescribed punishments for sex across the freedom line.[22] Nevertheless the law remained an important statement of the French Crown's theory of social organization. After establishing the ideal of a unitary religion and the legal conditions governing relations between free and enslaved people, the code outlined the process for manumission. All freed slaves became subjects of the French Crown upon their liberation. In these articles the Code Noir imagined that a hierarchical aristocracy would take shape in the colonies: planters following the king's law, and slaves following their master's law. This vision of colonial absolutism mirrored the aristocratic system taking shape in France, simultaneously growing the French state and the ranks of ennobled royal officers.[23] But the interests of the ruling elites in the colonies diverged markedly from the king's stated interests, and the Crown lacked the means to compel their cooperation.

The language of the Code Noir made it clear that the French Crown positioned itself as a mediating force between potentially oppositional populations. The king was the protector of the poor and powerless, and the judge of the powerful. Thanks to the global networks that Atlantic commerce opened, the French king would be required to integrate new populations into the empire. With article 57 the French Crown proclaimed that manumitted slaves "enjoy the advantages of our natural subjects in our kingdoms, lands, and countries under our obedience, although they be born in foreign lands."[24] This proved to be a critical innovation that transformed the rights of royal subjects both in the Atlantic colonies and back in France. Malick Ghachem documents how, in this provision and the court trials that invoked the principle, the Code Noir contributed an essential plank to the legal foundation of human rights as theorized by eighteenth-century jurists.[25] Based on the code's provisions that prohibited the torture of slaves, and the routes established to manumission, "the law of slavery was interpreted to signify the role of the king, not as oppressor-in-chief, but as protector of all persons residing within the royal dominion, including slaves."[26] But, alongside this ideal, Ghachem documents how colonists' regular, unapologetic violation of that law systematically fractured the French king's authority.

The Code Noir prohibited sex between free and enslaved people. It outlawed torture. And enslavers routinely ignored it, holding their own personal interests and profits to be the ultimate authorities in this realm, rather than the monarch or his agents. When such behavior was rendered by royal or colonial officials as libertine rather than criminal, it communicated that the French state concurred with the colonial planters and tacitly accepted rape and torture as regrettable but necessary "colonial liberties." The Crown and its officers failed to prosecute violations of religious codes against extramarital sexuality, civil prohibitions of sex between free and enslaved persons, and torturous treatment of enslaved people. If the Antilles provided a refuge for libertines, it was because enslavers positioned themselves beyond the king's law. There the libertines made the law.

IDENTIFYING THE RACE OF LIBERTINES

So it was that for decades the provisions of the Code Noir went largely unenforced. Jewish and Protestant residents owned property, engaged in commerce, and observed their faiths with little interference from colonial officers.[27] Enslavers demanded sex of enslaved people, and these unions regularly resulted in children who were also enslaved. Indeed, this happened with such regularity that it became a defining feature of life in the

Antilles, taken for granted and portrayed as inevitable. The Dominican missionary Jean-Baptiste Labat, writing in 1724, even echoed biblical phrasing when he passively intoned that in "the beginning when Blacks arrived in the islands, libertinage produced Mulattos there."[28] Libertinage, not enslavers who exercised sexual violence, was the problem.

Racial categories, entirely absent from the 1685 Code Noir, acquired legal force in the 1720s. French authors relied heavily on Spanish terms to identify different combinations of peoples and physical characteristics. Race became an essential category in French colonial society in this decade, spurred by conflict between colonists who sought increased autonomy in imperial trade and the Crown that strove to channel colonial profits back into the royal coffers.[29] Moreover, the Catholic Church played a central role in forging these categories and policing these boundaries. In Père Labat's telling, "mulattos"—defined as the offspring of free white and unfree Black people—were a uniquely colonial phenomenon in which color marked a liminal legal status between freedom and slavery. He does hold European colonists responsible for this population of "mixed-race" people who confounded a simple color-coded social and economic system of slavery. Labat bemoans the degree to which French settlers had followed the example set by Spanish settlers throughout the Americas. He observed that "this libertinage of white men with black women is the source of an infinity of crimes."[30] Which crimes? Here the priest remains vague, but abortion, infanticide and jealousy-fueled murder likely topped his mental list.[31]

In a chapter dedicated to explicating the category of "mulatto," Labat introduces his readers to physical characteristics before elaborating on character. He generalizes that people with a European father and an African mother possessed a color that "combines the white and the black and produces a sort of bisque." According to Labat the resulting children were "well-made, of good size, vigorous, strong, nimble, industrious, courageous, and brave beyond imagination; they have great vivacity, but they are given to their pleasures, fickle, proud, suspicious, mean, and capable of the greatest crimes." Such ambivalent assessments were characteristic of the era's race theory, with no clear articulation of hierarchy. Perceiving the existence of mulattos to be a consequence of empire, Labat asserts that "the Spanish who have more of them than do all other Europeans living in America, have no better soldiers and no meaner men" than the multi-racial offspring of Europeans and Africans.[32] But even as Labat testifies to the ubiquitous transgression of article 9, he also insists that the law had been effective in regulating sexuality. The number of "mulatto" children "would be even greater in our Islands, if it weren't for the penalties risked by those who do it . . . but it will be permitted to the Missionaries to say that in seeking to remedy the scandal that this crime caused, a door was opened to another crime even more enormous, that of the frequent abortions that the *Negresses* procure when they feel pregnant, and this very often with the consent or advice of those who abused them."[33] Enslaved women's activism in terminating pregnancy, and European men's actions of sexual violence motivate colonial society, in Labat's account, but these actors remain curiously invisible and anonymous. Asking his reader to consider increased abortions as the result of colonial authorities' vigorous enforcement of the law of slavery rather than enslavers' sexual tyranny, Labat's analysis highlights the consequences of royal policies while ignoring the power structures of the colony.

CARIBBEAN LIBERTINES, 1721–1763

For decades European travelers like Père Labat and colonial officials had described as libertine those European settlers' transgression of the Code Noir's provision for sexual segregation. As in Louisiana this term simultaneously acknowledged the social ills resulting from enslavers' rape and sexual assault of enslaved people, and minimized the illegality of colonists' actions. Sex between free and enslaved people explicitly violated the king's law of slavery. European-descended men who undertook long-term relationships or who raped enslaved people broke religious codes designed to confine sexual behavior within the sacrament of marriage.[34] But these transgressions never constituted the focus of targeted state policing, as libertine clerical sexuality or elite prostitution had in eighteenth-century Paris. Colonial officials introduced several legal and social mechanisms by which they shamed European settlers into sexual segregation from enslaved people, giving rise to racial categories and racialized social distinctions.[35] However, policies consistently excused enslavers who engaged in sexual assault and rape as predictable, even natural, thus dissolving the potential force behind regulatory statements.

Travelers, priests, royal ministers, and colonial officials alike deemed European men's sexual domination regrettable, but largely accepted it as a necessary colonial liberty.[36] In the context of the United States and the Caribbean, scholars have documented how the state benefited materially from enslavers' deployment of rape and sexual assault to terrorize the enslaved population and to produce children.[37] In language that mirrored colonial administrators' critique of interracial sex in Louisiana, the libertine category of the Antilles most reliably indicated those European settlers who engaged in sexual relations proscribed by canon law and the law of slavery during the first half of the eighteenth century.

Among the European settlers of the Antilles, however, invocation of the libertine category more often condemned enslaved people's exercise of personal liberties of movement or dress. Settlers also used the term to describe fugitive ex-slaves who seized their own freedom by escaping to live in communities beyond the colonial state. For example, in 1710, the intendant of Martinique complained to royal officials about the "disorders raised in this Isle by the libertinage of runaway Blacks" to justify the horrific punishments he had dictated against seventeen individuals accused of plotting a rebellion.[38] In 1727 fifty-three slaveowners in Martinique demanded the cancellation of several Catholic holy days. Perhaps those feast days requiring all people to refrain from labor to attend Mass were intended to "honor God in the person of his Saints, thank him and praise him," observed the colonists. But these celebrations originally "destined for the sanctification of souls are for slaves nothing but days of libertinage and drunkenness, it is in these days that they gather and make their conspiracies, either for running away or for escaping the Island."[39] This petition presents an incoherent vision of the dangers posed by enslaved people who had been granted a modicum of leisure time. Simultaneously depicted as lazy and ambitiously plotting, drunken and calculating, enslaved people could be called "libertine" even as they observed a Catholic holiday. And settlers all agreed that long periods of holy days meant that enslaved people might "taste a ray of Liberty that makes them feel more forcefully the unhappiness of their Slavery and animates anew the desire to deliver themselves from it."[40] How far this notion of "excessive liberty" had traveled from signifying heterodoxy, if it could be applied to an enslaved person who rested on Christmas Day. Never mind that article 6 of the 1685 Code Noir mandated that all inhabitants observe Sundays and all Catholic holidays. The law clearly stated, in the voice of the monarch, "We forbid them to work or to make their slaves work on those days from the hour of midnight until the other midnight."[41] In direct contravention of this law, colonial officials agreed with the settlers and wrote to the island's missionary priests, demanding that they cut the Christmas feasts from four days to one, in order to "put in order the libertinage of the Blacks and remove from them the means of assembling and conspiring."[42] Leisure constituted excessive liberty, even when mandated by the calendar and personnel of the Catholic Church.

Pères Lebrun and Mane took charge of the clerics' response to the colonial government's request, informing the governor-general that, after consulting with each other and their fellow priests, they determined that they lacked the authority to suspend the Christmas holidays. However, they agreed to seek approval from the pope. They sidestepped the question of whether the observance of holy days constituted libertine behavior. The governor-general responded forcefully that the priests certainly did have the authority to cancel feast days, and he insisted that for the "good of Religion, the King's service, and the colony" they must permit enslaved people to work on these upcoming holy days. He must have recognized that the pope could never respond in time, given that this exchange occurred only three days before Christmas. The priests responded once more, insisting with regret that they had no power to cancel holy days. But, they consoled the colonial authorities, upon consultation with priests in France, they had decided to authorize their parishioners to work and allow their slaves to work on the third day of Christmas, the Feast of St. John the Evangelist.[43] The governor's palpable frustration registers his recognition of local priests' authority within these communities. Remarkably for all participants in these exchanges, the elasticity of the libertine category had been stretched to apply to enslaved people exercising orthodox religious observance.

After the Treaty of Paris concluded in 1763, a series of events moved royal officials' concern for libertine behavior from European settlers to creoles, those individuals born in the Caribbean. Including both free and enslaved people; those of African descent, European descent, or both; this heterogenous group included some of the colony's wealthiest and some of its most destitute residents.[44] New policies were certainly informed by the colonial politics of the Seven Years' War, particularly the distrust and animosity that developed between French and Canadian officers in the North American theater. According to environmentalist racial theories of the era, creoles' common climate of origin gave them shared characteristics and differentiated them from their migrant parents whether these hailed from Europe or Africa.[45] In the wake of the North American colonial wars, French royal and military officers particularly distrusted the property-owning creoles whose interests—to engage in free trade with neighboring colonies, strengthen the institution of slavery, maximize profits and minimize labor expenses—so dramatically diverged from those of the Crown. The French state sought to strengthen its trade monopolies, guarantee the rule of law and protections to all subjects, and recoup the losses of imperial wars through taxation. After 1761 Saint-Domingue's politics careened from one showdown to the next as colonial and metropolitan authorities disputed basic facets of social order.

What was more, creoles disagreed about how best to accomplish their objectives. After 1763 some creoles identified race as an essential organizing factor of colonial society and sought to reserve privileges to those of European parentage. They imagined a white race with a common identity and shared interests, ignoring the geographic, religious, and economic divisions that so fractured this group. Other creoles instead emphasized wealth and property as the essential elements of the colonial aristocracy and demanded the inclusion of Euro-Africans—termed "people of color" (*gens de couleur*) in colonial parlance—in the privileges accorded the ruling elite: royal office, military commissions, and honorific titles.[46] Both groups hinged their arguments on the nature of relationships between Europeans and Africans in preceding generations, marriage, and the law.

The creoles who advocated stricter racial hierarchy relied on an argument that represented those of Euro-African descent as universally the products of illegitimate unions. Libertine parents birthed libertine children, they asserted. If notable Euro-African people went on to serve king and country honorably, or to demonstrate piety and probity in their conduct, it did not alter the fact that their very existence testified to a former generation's excessive liberties in the estimation of these colonial authors and jurists.[47] This argument aimed to segregate people of African descent and make them distinct in French law and society. Meanwhile, critics of racial hierarchy argued that such laws held free people of color responsible for the sexual transgressions of their European fathers in terms that intersected with metropolitan debates over bastardy, the legal category for children born outside of wedlock until it was abolished in 1793.[48] This debate ultimately resulted in the dramatic circumscription of people of African descent in the French empire that made them subject to prejudicial laws limiting basic rights of mobility, property, and marriage.[49]

FREE PEOPLE OF COLOR

The characterization of Saint-Domingue's creole population as libertine coalesced in the years following 1763.[50] But which creoles posed the largest threat? White, Black, and multiracial creoles each identified the other as embodying the libertine in a fundamentally new manner. The *gens de couleur* composed a population to the libertine manner born, white creole observers inveighed. Meanwhile, Black and multiracial creoles documented decades of systematic transgressions of the law of slavery by European settlers. In these accusations libertinage became a heritable quality; it referred less to an individual's own actions than to a libertine lineage. Such charges recalled French social critics regarding the children of extramarital unions or prostitution.[51] But in Saint-Domingue, skin color was read as a sign of character, and the entire population of Euro-African individuals found themselves subject to these assumptions, regardless of their personal behavior and education or their familial wealth and property.[52]

In contrast to racist invectives, evidence from the archives reveals members of the Afro-European population to be dynamic and ambitious, engaged in all types of commerce, and active in charity and community leadership. Research by Dominique Rogers and Stewart King emphasizes the diversity of occupations practiced and incomes enjoyed by the free women of color in colonial Saint-Domingue, whose work enabled them to "support their families, educate their children, free their family members still in slavery, and assure their own future."[53] In recovering these women's contributions to their communities in economic and social terms, scholars reject the characterizations imposed by the racist assumptions of European and white Saint-Dominguan contemporaries.

Jennifer Palmer explores the tension between structural racism and family intimacy in Saint-Domingue, resulting in some unexpected property and manumission arrangements between free and enslaved members of a family.[54] French planters, as Palmer demonstrates, built racial hierarchy into the fabric of colonial society and their own families, which meant that intimacy "across racial lines was a site of racial production and its profound disruption."[55] Individuals simultaneously challenged and were constrained by French colonial social structures.

Tracing Euro-African French colonial families over generations, Palmer reveals the tensions of intimacy and dependence at the heart of these families, whose existence transgressed the color lines that organized colonial society. For example, the French-born planter Aimé-Benjamin Fleuriau made a fortune in Saint-Domingue and raised eight children with Jeanne Guimbelot, a free woman of color who appears to have been enslaved to Fleuriau for some time. Although he was a Protestant, Fleuriau had their children baptized at the Catholic Church, which "wove children into the community . . . forging links that cut across notions of race and relied on shared experience and place."[56] But Fleuriau never acknowledged the children as his own. Upon his return to France in 1755, Fleuriau married a young French woman. Five of Fleuriau's children with Jeanne accompanied him back to La Rochelle, but French elites' prejudice profoundly restricted their employment and marriage prospects.

During the Seven Years' War, creole soldiers and sailors from Saint-Domingue played a central role in the island's defense against British invasion and took part in battles across the Atlantic.[57] Colonial officials from Spain, Britain and France armed enslaved Blacks, promising freedom to those who joined their cause.[58] A spate of poisonings in 1757 fanned fears of a widespread rebellion led by François Macandal, who was tortured and executed in March 1758. In the closing months of the global conflict, Saint-Domingue planters sought to solidify economic liberties for themselves, while reducing the social liberties afforded to free people of color. They argued that a society dependent on enslaved labor required strict racial hierarchy, and they took steps to dispossess their Euro-African neighbors and relations of their property and civil status. Between 1761 and 1777, colonial officials passed legislation that systematically discriminated against free people of color, segregating public theaters, denying access to key professions, even imposing sumptuary laws designed to distinguish racial groups at a glance.[59] And, increasingly, European colonists demanded that the French government enforce these discriminatory practices in the colony and back in France.

The French state responded with ambivalence, enacting half-hearted measures that oscillated between a continental freedom principle and overt racial prejudice. In 1762 the Admiralty Ordinance required that every person of color resident in France register with the state. This policy established race as an operational legal category, irrespective of free or enslaved status.[60] All French households were enjoined to declare all Blacks (*nègres*) or multiracial (*mulâtres*) individuals resident in the household and identify their places of birth. Furthermore, the ordonnance "mandates . . . that all other *nègres* and *mulâtres* of whatever profession they be, and who are in service to no one, will be obliged to make likewise in person or by an agent, furnished with their declarations of their nicknames, first names, age and profession, place of their birth, date of their arrival in France, and by what ship, and if they have been baptized or not."[61] Many former slaves registered and took the opportunity to have their freedom recognized in this official record made by the French state. Nevertheless, as Palmer observes, "relatively privileged mixed-race people likely found this blanket cataloging galling in the extreme, particularly in comparison to the legal and social distinctions made between slaves and wealthy free people of color in Saint-Domingue."[62] Race superseded family name, wealth, social rank—all of those factors that French society claimed to prize.

According to the Admiralty Ordonnance, naval offices in France's port towns must maintain registers of African-descended people who resided in the kingdom.[63] A generation of historians have fruitfully excavated these records, documenting how race operated in thousands of transatlantic families.[64] Palmer reveals how the patriarch of the Fleuriau family used this register to articulate his rights as a subject of the French king. Benjamin Fleuriau gave lengthy testimony in which he sought to establish his sons and daughters as free people, and as creoles currently resident in France. Facing state authorities who clearly expressed their preference that mixed-race individuals born in the Caribbean remain there, Fleuriau pushed back forcefully. The boys had to be in France, he argued, to learn their trades, while the girls were of delicate health, and family obligations required them to remain together. The father made financial resources available to these children, and the boys ultimately returned to Saint-Domingue, where the existence of a politically and economically powerful class of free people of color gave them peers they lacked in France. The girls remained in France and never married; Palmer notes that these young women remained "simultaneously part of the prominent Fleuriau clan and very much outsiders."[65] When one of the sisters died, her funeral was not attended by her French relations or her father. Only her sister and a friend attended the mass. But in the funerary record, the surviving sister laid claim to both their father's name and their island home. She instructed the priest to identify her sister as "Marie-Charlotte Fleuriau, called Mandron, daughter of Sieur Benjamin Fleuriau, merchant, and of Jeanne called Guimbelot, native of the parish of Notre Dame du Saint Rosaire of Croix des Bouquets, in the canton of Cul-de-Sac, in the jurisdiction of Port-au-Prince, island and coast of Saint-Domingue, in America."[66] In the face of laws designed to segregate white from Black and French from creole, the members of these families refused to take sides. They chose kin. They insisted that the state take seriously familial bonds across emergent color lines. The Mandron family that remained on Saint-Domingue continued to call on the Fleuriau family for aid in hosting and educating successive generations of children in France.

In Saint-Domingue increasingly rigid racial hierarchy resulted from the colonial government's local ordinances and white colonists' daily practices of discrimination and exclusion.[67] But the French state participated in advancing laws aimed at segregation rather than assimilation of its subjects of African descent. In the decades after the Seven Years' War, every colony paid more and received less from the Crown as it struggled to staunch the financial hemorrhaging caused by warfare and disrupted global trade. The admiralty required that all people of color register upon arrival in France in 1762 and recommended against Black or multiracial individuals' long-term residence in the kingdom. But the registers also reveal that, over these years, thousands of individuals of African descent resided in France. They were free members of prominent families, like the Fleuriau girls and their brothers; they were independent sailors and artisans; and they were enslaved individuals like Sally and James Hemings, who accompanied their enslaver and family member, diplomat and future president of the United States Thomas Jefferson.[68]

The French state had first imposed a "freedom tax" on people of Euro-African descent in the 1730s. But in 1761, as Ghachem has explained, "the intendant of Saint-Domingue ordered that all taxes imposed upon the manumission of 'mulattos and other persons of mixed blood' be reported to the controller of the navy."[69] This law set the price of freedom at eight hundred livres. But the colonists resisted this new tax, insisting that taxing the manumission of mixed-race individuals imposed an undue burden on the innocent offspring. One colonist observed, "If one can, one must punish libertinage, because it is dangerous and criminal, one must spare the fruit of this libertinage, because it is innocent. It is forbidden to sell freedom to the slaves or to give it to them conditionally. Will the king practice for his own part that which he prohibits for his subjects?"[70] Why hold children responsible for their parents' actions? Ghachem observes that "the libertinage of certain masters, in other words, was a blatantly insufficient reason to hold hostage the freedom of the colony's mulatto population."[71]

The freedom tax provided critical revenue to the French state. Throughout the 1760s colonial and royal officials debated the ideal amount to charge slaveowners who sought to manumit an enslaved individual. Low rates would result in widespread enfranchisement, they anticipated, while high rates would limit manumission, ensuring only a few slaves were able to secure freedom. This would strengthen the color barrier, Saint-Domingue's white colonists argued. Most important, they sought to reserve the right to manumit slaves to themselves, not to the king.

In 1764 Charles d'Estaing arrived as governor-general of Saint-Domingue. During his short tenure, he consistently contended that the French king's interests lay in growing the population of free people of color, integrating the property-owning elites irrespective of color into the king's service, and protecting enslaved peoples against the worst depredations of the enslavers. Under his leadership the freedom tax was dramatically lowered from one thousand to three hundred livres. Ghachem notes that, "in doing so, the administrators announced their motive of increasing the size of the free population of Saint-Domingue while also preventing the increase from getting out of hand."[72]

During the Seven Years' War, the militia had played a critical role in the island's defense against British invasion and occupation. But colonists hated the obligation, which fell on all inhabitants regardless of social station. Many of the wealthiest colonists offered to pay a substantial tax of four million livres to exempt themselves and their children from service.[73] Choiseul, the naval minister, had abolished the militia in 1763, recognizing this institution as the seat of long-simmering colonial hostility against France. But he kept the annual four million livres tax. Then, in 1765, Governor d'Estaing ordered the creation of a new colonial legion, in which free men of color served alongside their white neighbors. This law was preceded by a notice that reformulated race in the French colony, abandoning the Spanish-inspired categories that tracked percentages of European, African, and American ancestry to group all mixed-race individuals in one mulâtre category. The militia was to rely on mostly white leadership, both European and creole, but the lower ranks of the officer corps, from corporals down, were to be evenly distributed between white and mixed-race young men. The law explicitly stated the military's racial preference: "Whites, of equal merit, will always be preferred to the mulâtres."[74] The bulk of the troops were to be drawn from the free people of color: d'Estaing's new legion required service of all free men of color between the ages of sixteen and nineteen. The French military retained important mechanisms to perpetuate familial preferment and racial privilege while bringing free men of color into this militia. Free women of color were not expected to serve in the militia themselves, but they were required to provide a male slave to serve in their stead, effectively a tax of 1000 livres. John Garrigus points out that the negative reaction of the free people of color on the island was predictable, for they quickly understood the legion to be "an attack on their freedom and social status."[75] Meanwhile white officers resented the racial integration of their troops.

Charles Frostin notes that, in the wake of the Seven Years' War, all the European imperial powers in the Americas faced mounting pressure from their debts on the one hand, and their colonists' resistance to increased taxes and oversight on the other. "A breeze of revolt blew through the New World," he writes, "a phenomenon of notable and vast span which multiplied the trouble spots, here and there, in the same era."[76] Frostin observes that in Saint-Domingue, as in New England and New Spain, European settlers objected to new impositions from metropolitan governments, particularly as regarded the maintenance of colonial troops. In Saint-Domingue this conflict heightened racial tensions between white planters, the *libres*, who were free people of African and European ancestry, and free Blacks. The libres had been essential in the policing of colony, and in tracking marrons. On January 15, 1765, the governor-general of the colony ordered the integration of white militia companies with free men of color.[77] The white colonists rejected this initiative, warning that such a measure threatened the very foundation of colonial society. They insisted that "all distinction of the sort proposed would be the signal for the slaves' disobedience who would soon lose the respect that they have for the White name, the only link that keeps them in order."[78] An intense anti-integration campaign followed—undertaken by both the colonies' whites and free people of color—and by June of that year Choiseul condemned the effort. D'Estaing's dismissal from office in 1766 ended the integrated legion, but his successor adapted several innovations. Returning to racially segregated militias for the island's defense, the Chevalier de Rohan placed white officers in charge of the "colored" troops in an attempt to solve the colony's fractious social order by imposing racial hierarchy in military service.[79]

Recognizing that colonial affairs would continue to vex the global empire that France sought to sustain, Choiseul advised a member of the French diplomatic corps: "We have plenty of trouble governing the States where we live, and even more hardships in governing those in America."[80] Colonial tensions erupted in 1769 with an antimilitia movement that bore remarkable resemblance to anticolonial actions taken around the Atlantic in this decade.[81] The community of libres was extensive. They were men and women of property, including slaveowners. They actively sought to demonstrate virtue and investment in their community through service in the colonial militia.[82] Governor Rohan sent the order for three militias to be reestablished in the island: one white, one mixed-race, and one of free Blacks. The result was one of the largest revolts in the history of Saint-Domingue, led by both white and multiracial men of property and influence.

On March 7, 1769, the merchant François Lamarque and ten of his colleagues on the Sovereign Council in Port-au-Prince were arrested, taken onto the *Fidèle Jean-Baptiste*, and transported back to France for judgment. First held at the Chateau-Trompette in Bordeaux, they were transferred to the Bastille in June of that year. There Lamarque and his companions remained until December, when they were sent first to the prisons in Rochefort, then to the Capucin monastery in Rochefort, before returning to Saint-Domingue to be judged by the new council in Port-au-Prince.[83] The motives for their arrest and imprisonment? The archivist of the Bastille explains that the "root lay in the reestablishment of the militia, that had been suppressed in March 1763, and which the settlers of the colony denounced in the fear that this new formation would not end old abuses of military power and would produce new ones."[84]

The trial in Saint-Domingue lasted two years. Only one member of the original company was condemned by the new colonial council. Of the settlers who had participated in the trouble, eight were hanged, one sent to the galleys, one banished from the colony, eleven admonished, and one acquitted. Upon return to the island, those acquitted lived free without irons in the prison. Nearly all who had endured voyage were absolved.

The chevalier of Rohan provided some who had been condemned with special letters of recommendation. Revolutionary politicians who edited and published the proceedings of the trials in 1789 contended that "you could say that the chevalier of Rohan only persecuted the innocent, and only protected the guilty."[85] The law of slavery had clearly been broken, and the French state proved itself incapable of holding colonial elites to account for those transgressions.

RACE AND INHERITANCE, 1772–1778

Family histories document the stability of many "interracial" unions regardless of marital status, for thousands of these relationships resulted in multiple children and long years of cohabitation. Matthew Gerber demonstrates how two inheritance suits originating in Saint-Domingue demonstrate the development of racist rationales among jurists considering the relationship between the colony and France. He notes that these cases "simultaneously raised questions about bastardy and race, they also entailed clashes between colonial and metropolitan systems of law. Because they were separated by less than a decade, an analysis of the two cases together helps reveal how racial discrimination originated in the colonies and then only gradually infiltrated metropolitan legal discourse."[86]

In both cases the debate hinged on representations of race and inheritance in French law. The French judges who formed the final court of appeal initially showed resistance to including race as a factor in considering inheritance rights. In 1772 the case of *Jamet v. Guerre* pitted the white and mixed-race heirs of Nicolas de la Fargue against each other. Although the court of first instance found for the multiracial children of Jean Guerre, the nephew identified as the preferred heir in Fargue's will, the colony's court to appeal supported a white nephew's claim to the estate. The king's Conseil du Roi found for the original heirs, concluding that when Jean Guerre married Petit-Nanon, an enslaved woman with whom he had five children, that action legitimated their children according to the provisions of the Code Noir. But by 1779 this same body accepted colonial lawyers' arguments that stricter racial boundaries were necessary for both the colonial economy and the metropolitan body politic. In the

Raymond v. Casse case, the white and mixed-race heirs of Antoine Casse disputed how race should factor into inheritance once again. Although the judges on the Conseil du Roi found that Casse was entitled to leave property to Françoise Merida, a mixed-race concubine and their three children, race entered into their deliberations to a far greater extent than in 1772. Asked to consider Casse's soundness of mind, the prosecuting attorney Antoine-Louis Séguier concluded that he was sane because he had chosen to leave exponentially more property to his one white son, also born of an extramarital union in France. Gerber concludes, "Séguier believed that Antoine Casse was sane because he had acted like a racist."[87]

Lawyers found that judges in both the colonies and the metropole considered seriously the argument that sex outside of marriage would be rewarded if bastards could inherit equal to legitimate children. And since Moreau de Saint-Méry and other colonial observers asserted that nine-tenths of all people of color had been born outside of marriage, it became a commonplace that free people of color were all the products of libertinage.[88] In this way color communicated morality. In 1777 the French Crown seemed to accept the racist logic that colonial officials had been spouting for decades. The king signed legislation that required all people of color return to the colonies.[89] Furthermore, the law outlawed marriages between white and Black individuals resident in France. Sue Peabody emphasizes the degree to which the 1777 efforts to police France's population of African descent failed.[90] But clearly these laws reflected the Crown's acknowledgment of profound interdependence between the peoples and economies of France, Africa, and the Caribbean. Efforts to impose racial segregation, both in the Americas and in France, reflected anxiety about this interdependence.

In 1777 Emilien Petit obscured the role of European men and merchants in constructing the Atlantic slave trade, plantation system, and rape of enslaved women when he attributed the existence of mixed-race people in Saint-Domingue to "the concubinage of black women and successive manumissions [that] have given rise to a class of *libres*, different from the white blood, known by the name of *gens de couleur* or mixed blood, blacks, mulâtres, mestis, quarterons, who, although admitted to the privileges of liberty, enjoy it only with the modifications that constitute a middle place between the Whites and the slaves."[91] Petit's comments illustrate the multiplicity of terms regarding mixed-race categories, and the lack of exactitude in their applications.

Petit compared French and Spanish approaches to empire and settlement patterns, consistently underwhelmed by the Spanish. He reflected on Spanish laws that require Church authorities be advised of men traveling without wives. Those individuals who left wives in Spain and who married in colonies would be punished according to the law. "It seems, to the contrary," he wrote, "that if one fears to neglect bad examples in families, to applaud it, by the welcome that the most honest people, the husbands and wives most united, would not blush to make, to the libertine husbands who are seen living publicly with prostitutes, that they support at the expense of their family."[92] Most people go to the colonies to make a fortune on borrowed money, but they intend to return to Europe, Petit insisted. These laws should promote and ensure family stability, rather than encouraging bigamy in zones of license.

REFORM OF SLAVERY, 1784–1785

Marriage remained the preeminent strategy to stabilize family fortunes in both France and in the French colonies.[93] In a pioneering study of the free people of color in colonial Saint-Domingue, Stewart King writes, "Matrimony was central to the free coloreds' social advancement and a state to which many free coloreds aspired. Yet contemporary commentators described free people of color as 'licentious' and the product of 'illicit unions.'"[94] John Garrigus similarly notes that the libertine reputation of Saint-Domingue targeted free people of color, particularly women.[95] Officials and authors engaged in a peculiar sleight of hand in this portrayal. During the 1780s colonial officials subjected free people of color to discriminatory laws designed to degrade and then dispossess some of the island's leading residents. Meanwhile, in poems, songs, plays, and histories detailing the island's society, white observers ignored prejudicial legal structures to portray themselves as helpless and subservient to the sexual powers of Black and multiracial women.[96]

In Saint-Domingue, as in the rest of the French empire, concerns of illicit commerce and interracial sex preoccupied colonial authorities. But

slavery and the lengths to which colonial authorities went to institutional-
ize white supremacy meant that the preeminent peril to social order in
Saint-Domingue resided in perceived assaults to that racial hierarchy. After
the Seven Years' War, colonial officials and residents identified interracial
sex and the children that resulted from such unions as the state's single
greatest threat. However, a dramatic change occurred. White French men
who engaged in interracial sex were now rarely identified as libertine, in
sharp contrast with discussions in colonial Louisiana. Instead, after 1763,
the term was most often applied to the Black women who bore mixed-race
children, and to the offspring themselves. Authors and administrators
alike portrayed African women as sexually promiscuous by culture and by
nature. They depicted creoles—those born in the colony, whether white,
mixed-race, or Black—as climatically predisposed to sexual license. But
these inclinations were supposedly most pronounced among enslaved
African women and their descendants. It is disconcerting to encounter this
trope time and again in the work of colonial authors. Women who had
been deprived of humanity's most basic freedoms were purportedly too
free with their sexuality. White authors and jurists blamed Black women's
physical attractions for the various social ills attributed to creolization.
The colonial apologist Moreau de St. Méry wrote that, among the many
admirable traits of Congolese enslaved people, "the inclination of black
Congolese women for libertinage has increased the [white men's] regard
for them."[97] Sexual desirability and receptivity therefore entered into the
pseudoscientific racial classification that Moreau established, outlining
an enslaver's perception of the religious, ethnic, and cultural differences
among the many different regional and language groups of Africans who
had been sold into slavery and transported to the Caribbean island.[98]

In the Antilles the meaning of "libertine" traveled a great distance
from its Roman origins and Reformation applications. Originally the
term used to designate freed slaves, it now became a crucial tool to
denigrate Black and mixed-race people as innately and excessively sexual.
Sex was a liberty, the first and most insistent of the laws of nature. And
when nonwhites engaged in sex—regardless of the circumstances—the
behavior was categorically libertine. The term was never used to signal
the legal transition from enslaved to free in France's wealthiest colony.

Instead, authors and officials employed the term *esclave affranchi* (or simply *affranchi*) to identify those individuals who had secured liberty for themselves and their descendants.

CONCLUSION

By 1789 free people of color and emancipated slaves owned one-quarter of the colony's land, and one-third of the slaves in Saint-Domingue.[99] Free people of color in Martinique constituted a much smaller percentage of the population but played a similarly important economic role.[100] These individuals were considered libertine simply by virtue of their existence, and this application transformed the term yet again within French law and letters. In Saint-Domingue during the last quarter of the eighteenth century, "libertine" referred not to specific behaviors or actions deemed transgressive, but to a group of people whose births purportedly symbolized the moral transgressions of their parents. As historical observers we might just as readily contend that this population testified to the lie of a racially coded system of slavery, blurring the color lines that many European settlers and colonial officials might have liked to draw in Saint-Domingue in the late eighteenth century. Moreover, when prominent individuals like Julien Raimond and Vincent Ogé challenged the racial hierarchy of Saint-Domingue, they insisted that the French state uphold its promise to themselves and their families to receive all free-born and manumitted persons as equal subjects of the French Crown. This ethic of equality struck a nerve in 1780s France, and free men of color found a French public receptive to challenges against hierarchies of birth, championing those who would lay claim to the inherent rights of all men.

8

Aristocrats and Libertines

Disputing Liberties in the Age of Revolutions, 1784–1804

It was raining that Tuesday evening as hundreds of men, women, and children crowded into the floor of the Odéon Theater in Paris on April 27, 1784. Of course it was raining. But inside the curtains parted to reveal a modest, half-furnished room where a young couple in simple, elegant dress occupied center stage. The man painstakingly measured the floor while the woman pinned a crown of orange blossom flowers to her head before turning to ask, "Well, Figaro, check out my little hat: do you like it better like this?"[1] The crafty Figaro—familiar to audience members as the lead character from the successful *The Barber of Seville*—and his intended, the virtuous Suzanne, prepared in giddy anticipation for their upcoming wedding.[2] Figaro had decided to measure the room to determine if a bed, a gift from their employer, the Count of Almaviva, will fit in the room. But Suzanne is adamant: they will not accept the gift. Why on earth not? inquires her fiancé. She won't say. After a series of verbal volleys, she finally reveals that she suspects the bed is just part of the Count's plot to claim his *droit du seigneur*, a lord's alleged feudal right to sleep with any bride of his domains on her wedding night. The Count is only giving them the bed so that he can do the deed in greater comfort, she warns Figaro in clear terms.

Figaro gasps. Such a generous gift represents Almaviva's sexual dominance over his people? In the 1785 preface to the play, the playwright characterized the Count of Almaviva as a "young lord of those times, prodigal, rather gallant, even a little *libertine*, as other lords were back then."[3] No longer, presumably. In this characterization we might finally recognize the stereotype of the libertine as a sexually aggressive nobleman, with social class and attendant privileges at the center of the definition. By setting the action in the not-so-distant past, and in Spain, Beaumarchais bowed to pressure from royal censors who urged the author to moderate his stinging social criticism. But, for all that, Beaumarchais refused to depict the Count as a villain. In the staging notes, the playwright recommended that the actor portraying this role not stoop to obvious and dastardly stereotypes. Instead he "must be played very nobly, but with grace and liberty. The corruption of his heart takes nothing away from the elegance of his manners."[4] The Count conducted himself with assurance and ease while taking excessive liberties with the women that he desired.

Only in the final two decades of the eighteenth century did the libertine reliably become a synonym for a member of the titled nobility, and more specifically a reference to forms of sexual license associated with social elites. And, in these discussions, colonial shadings on the term clearly shaped metropolitan applications. The shadows of "colonial liberties," including the sexual demands of enslavers, lurked in these diatribes against abusive elites. Denouncing a broad array of privileges claimed by the nobility, the term particularly rebuked those who asserted themselves to be above the law. Writers and legislators alike inveighed with particular animus against the sexual liberties they associated with the kingdom's elites, be they the fabled droits du seigneur, casual acceptance of extramarital affairs, or homosexual relations. This portrait of elite libertinism took particular inspiration in the 1780s from Pierre Choderlos de Laclos's novel, *Dangerous Liaisons* (1782) as well as the real-life exile from court of Pierre-François Paulin, Count of Barral, following the circulation of his wife's *Mémoire* detailing his serial adultery.[5] Moreover, it was during this decade that long-simmering rumors about the sexual conduct of the previous French king, Louis XV, and his consorts, especially Madame de Pompadour and Madame du Barry, reached full public boil.[6] Why were the 1780s such a contentious period?[7] This chapter traces the tempestuous fortunes of the libertine category during the revolutionary era to provide a gauge of how quickly the law governing individual liberties transformed, as journalists and legislators alike deployed the term to attack political enemies, portraying their opponents as transgressors of the laws of nature and the state. Republican legislators conflated those keystones of early modern European social order—nobility and patriarchy—to mount a sustained attack against these social institutions as despotic and unrestrained by law in the age of revolution. Few authors give clearer voice to this critique than did the son of a watchmaker who became a diplomat, spy, and esteemed playwright: Pierre Caron de Beaumarchais.[8]

THE CRAZY DAY

The play follows the events of one day: the plot hatched by Figaro, Suzanne, and the Countess. To prevent the Count from claiming his droit du seigneur, the conspirators trick him into seducing his own wife, who dressed as Suzanne. Then, in a grand finale, Figaro and Suzanne marry, receive an ample dowry from their employers, and everything ends in song.[9] Within a romantic comedy of mistaken identity, Beaumarchais skewers elite entitlement and self-gratification as organizing principles of eighteenth-century society. The play struck such a chord that revolutionaries as diverse as Georges Danton and Napoleon Bonaparte would recall the Odéon Theater performance in April 1784 as a cultural turning point when the dissolute and hierarchical mores of the Old Regime came tumbling down.[10]

The Crazy Day, or The Marriage of Figaro was a smash hit. Performed seventy-two times in 1784, the Comédie-Française theater earned nearly half a million livres for staging the failed seduction of Suzanne night after night.[11] Fashion merchants capitalized on the spectacle's popularity, selling *toques à la Suzanne* and *chapeaux à la Figaro*.[12] But to remember this play as a death knell for the Old Regime requires creative distortion of both Beaumarchais's intention and the play's impact. Commissioned by the prince de Conti, performed for the royal family, *The Marriage of Figaro* enjoyed patronage from the highest echelons of French society.[13] Certainly Beaumarchais had been subject to some censorship in the writing process. He altered a few plot details and lines of dialogue due to official input, but he also knew the value of censorship politics in forging literary reputations and marketing. In the published play's preface, he amplified his struggles for material profit.[14] We err if we take his word at face value regarding the social affront posed by this spectacle.

The Marriage of Figaro was not the first play to depict hierarchies subverted by disguise, nor was it the only performance where elite men revealed themselves to be sexual predators. Such plots hearkened back to Renaissance Italian comedies, informed by ancient Greeks' innovative New Comedy.[15] But Beaumarchais's script and direction are unique in the regular asides that vigorously challenged that presumed right of elites. Out of the Count's earshot, Figaro rails against his master's presumption and greed in laying claim to what Figaro conceives of as his own property. He gives voice to widespread exasperation with elite entitlement during his noted monologue in act 5. Addressing an absent Count, Figaro fulminates, "Just because you are a great lord, you believe yourself a great genius! . . . Nobility, fortune, rank, positions; it all makes you so proud! What did you do to earn it? You took the trouble to be born, nothing more."[16] Figaro contrasts the Count's advantages with his own "science and calculations just to survive."[17] He boasts that he is sharper than the Count, quicker-witted and more successful in advancing his own interests. Indeed, who in the audience would not have sympathized with him? Even those who had begun life with great advantages could still perceive the privileges accorded their superiors while emphasizing their own education and efforts.[18] In this context the droit du seigneur was a shorthand for every illegitimate privilege that France's elites had accrued unto themselves.

LIBERTINE NOBLES?

But the world depicted in *The Marriage of Figaro*—a world of elite sexual domination without limit or consequence—did not exist. It was a literary construct that bore little resemblance to the realities of eighteenth-century France. The droit du seigneur figured in no recognized article of feudal law; sexual predators found little support in elite mores informed by theories of protecting noble blood and fears of mésalliance.[19] The myth took shape due to eighteenth-century dramatists' fixation on this alleged feudal privilege, a theme addressed in 1763 with Voltaire's comedy in verse by the title *Le droit du seigneur*. A flurry of identically titled plays followed in 1764, 1770, 1777, 1784, 1787, and 1788 as other authors sought to profit from the public's interest in the sex lives of elites.[20]

Though no legal droit du seigneur existed, social elites certainly coerced sex from subordinates. But such exploitation was not reserved to the titled classes. Heads of household regularly preyed upon the young people they employed as domestic servants.[21] The rape of unmarried women was a crime and subject to prosecution, but rare were the individuals brave enough to file a complaint against their employer for fear of social retribution and lost wages.[22] Members of the nobility who committed these crimes found themselves subject to the king's law, as did the common people. As preceding chapters have documented, even the term "libertine" functioned to identify an action as out of bounds. Punishments for all crimes varied according to rank, but no nobleman had the right to break canon and civil laws that prohibited extramarital sex.

In fact, at its root, the king's law existed to limit the feudal rights of the nobility, just as it promised to limit the abuses of enslavers in the colonies. The myth of the droit du seigneur took hold of the public imagination at precisely the moment that decades of royal coordination and legal reform had effectively curbed key social and political powers of the nobility.[23] Some titled individuals, like the Marquis de Sade's mother-in-law, took advantage of the lettres de cachet system to voluntarily detain a relative, rather than subject the family to the dishonor of a criminal case publicly tried. But, as Sade's own case reveals, there were limits even on this informal detention system.[24] Violent crimes—rape or murder—demanded public prosecution. Moreover, more modest families regularly petitioned for summary detentions of their relations as well, as demonstrated in chapter 5. So, while French literature is filled with debauched aristocrats who impose their sexual will without consequence, we would be wrong to conclude either that violent rapes, extramarital affairs, or practices of seduction and coercion characterized the behavior of France's noble families, or that such behavior was limited to the aristocracy. Crimes did not go unpunished, nor did literary tropes accurately depict the values of a class.[25]

In fact the character of the aristocratic libertine reveals that, during the revolutionary era, leaders and writers across the political spectrum and around the Francophone world had wrestled into shape a fundamentally new definition of this quasi-criminal category. Informed by the political struggles of the previous two decades, it was a category that reflected how dramatically entwined were French law and global commerce. Demands for economic and civil liberties from the colonies ricocheted back to France, adopting the language of social critique that we find embedded in *The Marriage of Figaro*. After this transition the libertine no longer referred to the errant individual who skirted the king and the Church's law, but to someone who wielded excessive power over their subordinates. Such behavior was the very essence of "despotism," and it violated the law of nature, which insisted upon the inherent equality of all men. Time and again the portrayal of the aristocratic libertine construed sexual domination of women as men's most important right. Substituting the paternal hierarchy of the Old Regime for the individualized egalitarianism of the revolution meant a thorough transformation of the law and, therefore, quasi-crimes. Somewhat paradoxically, alongside the image of the rapacious libertine aristocrat developed a depiction of the nobility in France as feminine. In such discursive gymnastics, the aggressive sexuality associated with aristocratic libertinism acquired a feminine quality, regardless of the accused's sex.[26]

The Old Regime libertine had linked the commercial and cultural liberties of Québec with sexual transgressions from Louisiana, the subversion of paternal authority in France by errant children or of Church authority by sexually active priests and nuns. In using this term, observers called out the despotic and subversive authority wielded by elite planters in Saint-Domingue and Martinique. European settlers applied the term to an entire population in Saint-Domingue, part of a process of racialization that threatened to delegitimate the property claims of people based on their forebears' behavior. In all of these sites, the category of the libertine revealed law to be a flexible set of standards forged in mediation between local concerns and royal objectives. For across communities in France and the French Atlantic, jurists recognized the necessity of extending certain liberties in specific times and places while explaining why not everyone could enjoy equal freedoms across the French kingdom and empire.[27] The category of the libertine bridged these gaps in Old Regime systems of law, unifying a fractured code into the transcendent authority embodied by the king.

For several years muckraker journalists and pornographers had mobilized the libertine category to undermine not only the authority of the nobility but also, ultimately, to attack the royal court and the royal family itself. Charges of libertinage figured prominently in screeds against the illegitimate and excessive power of the French queen.[28] The public slander surrounding Marie-Antoinette's supposed role in the Diamond Necklace Affair of 1785–86 played a central role in this broader phenomenon.[29] Rumors swirled that the queen had engaged in seduction, perhaps even extramarital sex, in exchange for jewels offered by the Cardinal de Rohan.[30] She had not, but the truth mattered little in this climate of calumny.[31] After 1785 the queen was the frequent target of pornographic literature and castigated as a libertine for conducting amorous relations for political advantage with men and women in her social circle. For example, in "Fable," the radical journalist Camille Desmoulins depicts Louis XVI as an ass, "simple, good, and gruff." But "his wife [Marie Antoinette] was a tigress, / Hating her own subjects, / And libertine to excess."[32] Such scandalous quips prepared the public for Marie-Antoinette's trial in 1793, in which she was charged not only with maintaining foreign correspondence with the intent to overthrow the French Republic, but also with baseless accusations of committing incest with her son, the child dauphin.[33]

Marie-Antoinette was not the only member of the royal household subject to such innuendo and rumor.[34] During the fall of 1789, a city press in Caen published a letter supposedly written in code by the Prince de Lambesc, officer in the French military and commander of the Royal-Allemand Dragoons, who was held responsible for injuries sustained by members of a crowd gathered in the Tuileries Gardens in July 1789. The editor asserts that, in this letter, the prince reveals "the most abominable character, arrogant, deceitful, impious, libertin, bloodthirsty."[35] Writing from Vienna the prince addressed the Marquis de Belsunce, commander of a regiment in Caen, to disparage the National Assembly and those members of the nobility who supported profound social and political reform efforts underway in 1789. Lambesc enumerates the French royalty and nobility already at work canvassing the crowned heads of Europe for military and financial aid to crush the revolution.

Another pamphlet published in 1789 castigated the morals of the entire French court and blamed them for the current rebellion. Directly addressing the king's brother, the Count of Artois, "Yes, you, libertine Prince, denatured Brother, it's your fiery spirit, your vicious soul that foments sedition, and that enflames hate."[36] The journalist further accused the princes of Conti and Condé of organizing an aristocratic league that formed a "diabolical Assembly" to determine their methods to best betray their country and king.[37] The queen's closest confidantes, her ladies-in-waiting and the Abbé de Vermond, all were presumed guilty of sexual transgressions that led directly to treason in the eyes of this republican journalist.

In *Le Ministère de Monsieur de Calonne dévoilé* (The ministry of Monsieur Calonne revealed), an essay penned in the voice of Louis XVI's minister of finance, the beleaguered adviser appealed to a tribunal of the people. "My youth was spent divided between a little study and a lot of pleasure. Like all my friends, I was a libertine, but among you, French people, this is no longer shameful. Everyone down to the streetwalkers mocks a novitiate."[38] In the topsy-turvy world of the French court, virtue and piety counted for little, while respect and honor rained down on profligate men and women known for their sexual prowess.

Moreover, in 1793, a scurrilous biography of Louis XVI's cousin, Philippe, Duke of Orléans, esteemed him to be one of the "greatest libertines of the court," referring to the republican royal's series of extramarital affairs.[39] Journalists mobilized sexual rumor and innuendo to undermine political opponents' legitimacy, and popular opinion swayed with these rumor mills. Although Philippe was a committed republican and had voted for the king's execution in 1793, he was executed in November of that same year.

LIBERTINES AND LAW IN REVOLUTIONARY IMAGINATION

During the first years of the French Revolution, legislators and journalists leaned heavily on the category of the libertine to challenge the old social hierarchy entirely and imagine a new legal order rooted in natural law, universalism, and egalitarianism. Some revolutionaries decried absolutism at all levels. They explicitly equated the abuses of patriarchal authority that had consigned men like Jean-Baptiste Alliot to Désirade and a life of misery, the French monarch's executive and legislative authority, the Church's demands of sexual chastity from clergy, and the planters' power of life and death over enslaved peoples.[40] In republican conversations those who wielded excessive authority over social subordinates were libertine, in defiance of the law of nature. Some representatives and journalists emphasized the arbitrary qualities of both the king's law and the father's law. They contended it was an act of justice to break those laws that failed to accord with nature, thus guaranteeing the inalienable rights of men. These activists wove a powerful dissent, braiding together critiques of the power wielded by paternalists, monarchs, and enslavers, mixing these metaphors in a palimpsest of antiauthoritarianism. According to these self-proclaimed visionaries, undoing one institution would unravel the whole authoritarian bulwark. But, as preceding chapters have demonstrated, each of these institutions had developed mechanisms to challenge rival institutions. The power of fathers over their sons had been litigated and contested in the parlements for decades. The Crown ostensibly limited and regulated the power of enslavers over slaves, though local colonial authorities flagrantly violated these statutes. In legal encyclopedias and archival collections from the early revolution, jurists highlighted the injustices of the preceding decades; the arrest of city councillors from Québec and the scandals of Bigot and Vaudreuil's trials after the Seven Years' War, as well as those arrested in the Saint-Domingue militia revolt and the Lejeune case, were all included in texts memorializing the simultaneous inefficacy and despotism of the French Crown.[41]

Meanwhile, from the first revolutionary movements of 1788 and 1789, social conservatives applied the libertine label widely to actions they perceived as lawless upheaval associated with republican legislators and their supporters among the people. In this formulation conservative legislators and journalists maintained traditional logic that identified religious skepticism as the first step on a long and slippery slope toward the erosion of all social order. Certainly, the course of events left ample room to interpret the actions of revolutionaries as overstepping the bounds of their authority. Delegates to the Estates-General had been elected by the people, but only to serve as an advisory body to the king. When they arrived in Versailles in May and June 1789, these representatives had no mandate to make law for the kingdom, nor to override the will of the Crown. But, within a month, they had claimed just such power, promising to provide France with a constitution rather than simply approving a new slate of taxes. By undermining the king's authority, general lawlessness would be the order of the day warned the conservative journalists, legislators, priests, and employers who wrung their hands and tore their vestments identifying all manner of brigands, rape, the dissolution of the Church and the family as the inevitable result of the National Assembly's presumption.[42]

Great changes were underfoot. In fact, within the next two years, Republican legislation fundamentally transformed property rights with profound implications for social order, religion, politics, and the family across France and the Atlantic colonies.[43] The National Assembly reformed family law to abolish the category of bastard, legalize divorce, and regularize inheritance between male and female heirs.[44] Legislators made dramatic changes in the criminal code, declining to criminalize prostitution in 1790, abolishing the lettres de cachet and arbitrary detention in 1791, and by 1792 asserting that the state had no interest in enforcing canon laws on matters of individual sexuality, marriage, or religious observance.[45] In response conservatives denounced the transformed role of the Catholic Church in the new nation, the nationalization of Church property, and the abolition of clerical celibacy, all deemed libertine reforms of the legislature.[46] For social conservatives throughout Europe, these measures were taken as examples of the French Revolution's attack on traditions and morals. Many members of the clergy perceived this as the predictable consequence of philosophical critiques of the Catholic Church, and the French Crown's embrace of policies of religious toleration from 1787.[47] Edmund Burke's extended critique of revolutionary excesses remains the most powerful instantiation of this opinion in English letters.[48]

In response to such broad conservative criticism, revolutionary legislators rejected the very foundations of Old Regime law. The abbé Raynal provided an especially vitriolic response. Writing in 1789 he asserted that in previous centuries, France had been ruled by disorder, hierarchy, oppression, but not law. He emphasized the personal aspect of royal rule and cataloged instances of authorities' abuses of power. The Crown had emboldened Church leaders' abuses, and the Church had repeatedly declined to hold temporal power to account. As a result convents and monasteries had become dens of vice and libertinage, beyond the reach of temporal officials.[49] Revolutionary reforms aimed to correct the failures of the previous order by substituting honesty for hypocrisy. Raynal argued that, contrary to the opinion of his colleagues, who feared the vice that would result from legalizing divorce, the new law would increase the sanctity of marriage, rather than condoning the widespread extramarital sexuality practiced in the Old Regime. Considering the impact of the revolution in France, Raynal acknowledged that some were now saying that they missed the old ways. But what did they miss, he wondered? The past had been nothing but a "disorder of morals, laws, & administration. Eh! What disorder where there is no longer unshakable balance between vice and virtue, crime and law! What brake remains on the passions? Is it religion? Reason took the talismans away from priests; folly made a caricature of it; libertinage rejected it and insulted it, & its ministers debased it."[50] By 1789 those institutions designed to order and regulate society had failed utterly, according to Raynal. But the fault lay with authorities who had abused power and so sapped the legitimacy of the state and Church.

Itemizing the crimes of the French Crown, Raynal contended that, for all the deceased monarch's failings, King Louis XIV at least had possessed the vices of a king. Not so his descendants. "Under his successor," Raynal wrote, "we saw the labyrinth of intrigue, but there was no thread to recognize our path. At each instant, one was lost, because it became a labyrinth of crime, or of the lowest passions. The mire of libertinage infects public morals; luxury and license pass from the bishops and the great benefactors to the priests: in a word, corruption transcends the ranks that surround the throne to the next ranks, from the capital to the entire empire."[51] If French morals were in decay, the rot began at the head. Both conservatives and republicans saw the same behavior in the streets and theaters; both called it immoral. But these writers and legislators, rabble-rousers and journalists, drew very different conclusions about where immorality had originated. Condemning the sexual conduct of political elites became central to the revolutionary claim that they could build a more virtuous society and state.

It should be clear, however, that, in advancing a critique of Old Regime law, revolutionaries never embraced a libertine identity for themselves. In the writings of prominent republican legislators and journalists, no one ever portrayed the libertine as a misunderstood and oppressed victim of authorities. Instead, casting themselves as dedicated defenders of liberty, they conserved the term as derogatory, simply turning it around to castigate those individuals that they themselves accused of exercising excessive liberties. In speeches on street corners and at the legislative rostrum, "libertine" became synonymous with "aristocrat."[52] Drawing inspiration from the fictional characters portrayed in novels or plays including Laclos's *Dangerous Liaisons* and Beaumarchais's *Marriage of Figaro*, republican political discourse imagined an entire class of dissolute aristocratic libertines. This invention became lodged in popular memory of the Old Regime.[53] Stereotypes of elites' sexual debauchery and coercive force became important weapons mobilized to undermine the political influence of that order. The actual sexual behavior of individuals within this group was beside the point.[54]

ABOLISHING THE LETTRES DE CACHET

Inventing the aristocratic libertine required a drastic revision to the category that had taken shape over earlier decades. In newspapers and speeches beginning in 1789, reformist authors identified as one of the worst examples of absolutist despotism the collusion between Crown and household heads to arbitrarily detain libertine sons. These young men were not libertines, they argued, just because they claimed their natural rights to love and inheritance. The eradication of the law of arbitrary detention became one of the central demands during this early phase of the French Revolution, led by men who had been subject to lettres de cachet themselves, but particularly central to the revolutionary identity claimed by Honoré Gabriel Riqueti, Count of Mirabeau.

The stereotype of the dissolute young nobleman could have found no better embodiment than Mirabeau. Born in 1749 into a family of career military officers ennobled in the sixteenth century, young Honoré had a series of scandalous love affairs and gambling debts that motivated his father to have him detained by lettres de cachet not once but thrice, in 1766, 1774, and 1777.[55] He had served time in the French kingdom's most notable prisons on the Ile de Ré, the Château d'If, and the dungeons at Vincennes before he turned thirty. But, during his final forced residence, public opinion was turning against this system of parental detention, based in no small part on the Alliot case and the debacle of the Désirade penal colony experiment chronicled in chapter 6. During his stay at Vincennes, Mirabeau fanned the flames of this sentiment when he penned *Lettres de cachet and the State Prisons*, a forceful condemnation of the French prison system and the king's orders in particular, published "posthumously" in Hamburg in 1782.[56] As a result, in popular imagination, rather than representing aristocratic excess and debauchery, Mirabeau came to embody valiant resistance against tyranny, earning him a seat in the National Assembly and, ultimately, an honored state funeral and eternal resting place in the Republic's Panthéon upon his death in 1791. That is, he remained there until the tides of opinion turned against him in 1794, when his remains were exiled from the secular temple.[57]

In the state prisons of the French king, Mirabeau observed, popular wisdom had concluded that the men enclosed within are "little worthy of our regret or our pity."[58] After all, the subjects of France largely trusted that "*lettres de cachet* are expedited with discernment and justice."[59] Those outside the prisons could reassure themselves, those inside were an unruly lot "whose crimes need not be revealed; a quantity of *scélérats* who wait for liberty only to hang themselves, libertines who learn well under such good masters; the insane who are vegetating, and finally, the elderly who, ruined by debauchery and dissipation, are happy to find a refuge."[60] But Mirabeau aimed to draw his countrymen's attention to these unfortunates. He appealed throughout his account to the law of nature, demanding the end to this collusion between familial, ecclesiastical, and civil authorities which deprived individuals of their liberty on the basis of hearsay and prejudice rather than law and evidence.

Moreover, Mirabeau set this injustice in the context of broader injustices, equating the libertine son's detention with an enslaved individual's captivity. In this he blamed the king less than the Church. After all, was it not the Church that "armed the West against the East?" In the name of a God of peace, Church authorities had sanctioned the crusades against foreigners and Europeans, the massacre of Saint Bartholomew, the Gunpowder Plot, and the Irish massacres, "the assassination of so many kings, the desolation of the new world."[61] What was at stake in France's system of arbitrary detention, therefore, was not merely the fate of several thousand libertine sons of the nobility (and those young men's often forgotten sisters), but an entire world system based on war, imperialism, and slavery.

Mirabeau's essay on lettres de cachet stoked jurists' own critiques of the system and accelerated the Crown's efforts to dismantle arbitrary detention throughout France. Within the year the secretary of state, Louis Auguste Le Tonnelier, the baron de Breteuil, circulated a memorandum to all intendants and the heads of the police, urging them to reform their inquiries into family requests for lettres de cachet. It was an embarrassment in a monarchy governed by laws to rely on this extralegal standard. And it was an expensive proposition, for families rarely paid in full for all the costs associated with arresting and imprisoning their relatives, especially when the detentions lengthened into several years. Despite the Crown's efforts, the number of families requesting that the king issue orders for their relative increased steadily throughout the 1780s.

The Crown issued some two hundred thousand orders for arbitrary detention between 1660 and 1789.[62] In 1789 over seven thousand individuals were detained on king's orders across the kingdom, and 80 percent had been incarcerated at the request of their family.[63] They were not political prisoners, outspoken playwrights, or philosophers committed to scientific inquiry in violation of Church teachings; they were disobedient children like Jean Royer, or adults who had gambled, fallen in love, and spent family funds unwisely. They were no different from their fellows who went free about the streets of France and the French colonies. While the issue had gained public attention in the 1780s with both the Alliot case and Mirabeau's essay, still in 1789 no unified public opposition existed to protest the King's power to detain individuals. Certain petitions within the lists of grievances (cahiers de doléances) solicited by the French Crown in 1789 mentioned the issue, but most sought its reform rather than its outright abolition.[64] However, those legislators who organized themselves into the National Assembly in June 1789 identified the lettres de cachet as a key symbol of royal despotism to be dismantled in a constitutional monarchy. For this minority of men trained in the intricacy of Old Regime law, the king's ability to imprison individuals with no criminal charge or requirement for evidence embodied abusive power, and the storming of the Bastille prison in July 1789 represented the nation's first attack on that power.[65]

In the *Declaration of the Rights of Man and Citizen* promulgated in August 1789, articles 7, 8, and 9 opposed the practice of arbitrary detention as facilitated through the lettres de cachet. Article 7 explicitly insisted that individuals could only be accused and arrested for breaking a law and forbade arbitrary detention.[66] After the declaration's publication, prisoners addressed the legislature directly, demanding their freedom and informing the National Assembly that they had seized liberty as their right guaranteed by the state's new guiding principles. The commanders of Château d'If prison assured the nation's representatives that "in breaking the bonds of the unhappy victims of despotism," they would give "a new existence to the sensitive soul of an old soldier who for seventeen years has had the honor to command the chateau d'Iff [*sic*], groaned at the fate of the unfortunate people that tyrannical orders held there."[67] But Bailly, the mayor of Paris, perceived the threat to general liberty from this proposal. What would the National Assembly do, he inquired forcefully, with those people who were arrested under "illegal orders?" Because "to keep them irrevocably would be an injustice, but to release them immediately would be imprudent."[68]

The concern regarding those imprisoned upon family requests did not die away in 1789. Months of early legislative debates inquired into how to transition away from this method for maintaining public order.[69] Legislators were tempted to simply open the prison doors and release all individuals held on king's orders. But they knew that some people were there for good reason. The question centered on how to reconcile "their rejection of 'the arbitrary' and of 'despotism' with the security of the kingdom and domestic tranquility."[70] On November 24, 1789, the revolutionary legislature decided to create a committee to study the issue of lettres de cachet. Following their recommendations the National Assembly voted to abolish the lettres de cachet on March 13 and 16, 1790, and the king confirmed this abolition as law ten days later.[71] But, as the National Assembly deputies were realizing, formulating and publishing a law was only the first step in a complicated process of making and implementing law.

The committee—composed of the deputies Fréteau de Saint-Just, Mirabeau, Boniface de Castellane, Barère de Vieuzac (president)—now had to prepare a list of the prisoners detained by lettres de cachet, identifying the reason for their detention and the legislature's recommendation regarding their release. The delegates Boniface de Castellane and Barère de Vieuzac undertook most of the work, but they made slow progress in their goal of liberating the thousands detained across France. The committee was accorded a clerk in August 1791, which seemed to speed the process somewhat. Petitions from prisoners decried inhumane conditions. They lamented their abandonment by families who refused to pay their pensions. Many prisons were on the verge of revolt as the kingdom's leadership acknowledged the widespread injustices across the prison system. At the same time, the National Assembly received petitions from families who sought to maintain their relations in prison. Article 16 of the law abolishing detention by king's orders put the power in the hands of prison commanders, local assemblies, and courts to determine those cases that concerned members of their own communities.[72] This constituted a decentralization of the prison system, but it also meant that unelected representatives all across the kingdom of France now determined prison sentences behind closed doors, with little input from families and communities. Envisioning a new penal system and a social order predicted the committee's abolition of king's orders. The state did not abandon families to govern themselves. Instead the state made itself the regulatory arbiter, setting the stage for the detention of political dissidents.[73]

REVOLUTIONARY LIBERTINES

Composed quickly and published in November 1790, Edmund Burke's *Reflections on the Revolution in France* provides an influential outsider's perspective on the first year of the French Revolution, and the risks it posed domestically and abroad. Burke had not traveled in France, nor was he especially familiar with the country or its current political struggles. He frames the letter as a response to a French friend who had asked for Burke's opinion of events in France, but he clearly intended the missive for publication. Throughout the essay Burke considers the French Revolution to be the predictable result of a people unmoored from their past and their ancestors. A lack of filial piety had been the political nation's first mistake, according to him:

> Respecting your forefathers, you would have been taught to respect yourselves. You would not have chosen to consider the French as a people of yesterday, as a nation of lowborn servile wretches until the emancipating year of 1789. In order to furnish, at the expense of your honor, an excuse to your apologists here for several enmities of yours, you would not have been content to be represented as a gang of Maroon slaves suddenly broke loose from the house of bondage, and therefore to be pardoned for your abuse of the liberty to which you were not accustomed and ill-fitted.[74]

Burke sees European men's comparison of themselves to slaves as inept, serving as a rhetorical excuse for bad behavior.

But the conclusive mistake had been made when the king ceded authority to a National Assembly that convened itself in the name of the French people. Burke contends that when France "let loose the reins of regal authority, doubled the license of a ferocious dissoluteness in manners and of an insolent irreligion in opinions and practice, and has extended through all ranks of life, as if she were communicating some privilege or laying open some secluded benefit, all the unhappy corruptions that usually were the disease of wealth and power. This is one of the new principles of equality in France."[75] He almost seems to agree with revolutionaries who condemn the libertine behavior of elites, but, instead of condemning the elites, he notes that these forces have emboldened all—not just elites—to adopt similar laxity in religion and morals.

Whose fault was the upheaval in France? Burke blames political leaders—not the king or the royal family—but the members of the regional Parlements, and those among the king's advisers and ministers of state who struggled against monarchical authority. That they allied against the king is unnatural, Burke warns; turmoil follows from that initial subversion. In contrast to the republican screed against aristocrats and priests as rapacious libertines, Burke credits nobility and clergy with keeping "learning in existence," orchestrating charitable outreach, and spearheading commercial initiatives.[76] Revolutionary legislators criticized Old Regime gambling and the speculation inherent to global commerce. But with the nationalization of Church lands and the creation of the Church Bank (Caisse d'Eglise), those same legislators in France "are the very first who have founded a commonwealth on gaming and infused this spirit into it as its vital breath." Burke likens the great revolutionary financial scheme to other notable investment bubbles. He recalls the limits of previous examples of colonial financial speculation:

> Even when it had its greatest extent, in the Mississippi and South Sea, it affected but few, comparatively; where it extends further, as in lotteries, the spirit has but a single object. But where the law, which in most circumstances forbids, and in none countenances, gaming, is itself debauched so as to reverse its nature and policy and expressly to force the subject to this destructive table by bringing the spirit and symbols of gaming into the minutest matters and engaging everybody in it, and in everything, a more dreadful epidemic distemper of that kind is spread than yet has appeared in the world. With you a man can neither earn nor buy his dinner without a speculation. What he receives in the morning will not have the same value at night.[77]

The revolutionary state erected a financial house of cards that would collapse with the slightest economic breeze.[78] During the first two years of the French Revolution, conservative authors and legislators agreed that the libertine category effectively signaled the lawlessness of their political opponents. Decrying "republican libertines" positioned the speaker on the side of virtue and moderation. Naturally, the term did not remain cordoned off in political rhetoric confined to speeches and pamphlets. In police reports and official correspondence, it became clear that municipal and colonial authorities shared real concerns about the potential breakdown of law and social institutions amid revolution. Would sons obey fathers? Would wives obey husbands? Like Burke these officers feared that libertinism would become ubiquitous as men and women claimed liberties formerly forbidden to them.

LEGAL REFORMS: ENSHRINING LIBERTIES OR LIBERTINES?

For all the high-volume polemic, the libertine category was not just effective invective against political enemies. It remained an essential, though unwritten, quasi-criminal category in French law. In 1791 the *Encyclopédie methodique* on jurisprudence offered the definition of *libertinage* as the "custom of unruly morals," indicating that it posed a moral-ethical offense that could not be contained within a clear criminal classification. The editors observed that "much has been written about morals, and different methods attempted to ameliorate and limit libertinage, but these attempts appear to have been fruitless to this point. Libertinage itself has not been well-defined, although in general, it is easily identified in many cases."[79] As U.S. Supreme Court Justice Potter Stewart observed of pornography in 1964, "I know it when I see it."[80]

The editor observed that when individuals used the term "libertine," it "[was] generally meant by this name the deregulation of morals in their relation, with the enjoyment of women: the man, who displays tastes that are different or course, or too licentious, will be called *libertin*; but with this nuance, that a certain action will seem to be a very reprehensible act of libertinage to some, while in the eyes of another, it is only a sanctioned pleasure, or at least a tolerated one."[81] In terming both men's extramarital heterosexual and homosexual activities as libertine, the editors told their readers that authorities did not agree on the perceived social harm of such acts.

The editor continued by observing that public authorities had few tools to control the libertine who does not break any established civil codes. The police "cannot inquire into individual libertinage, as long as it does no harm to the interests of the soul or trouble public order. Prostitution itself, which results from libertinage and misery, is only punished, under the rod of the police, as the women who engage in it excite scandal and public disorder; so it is not as libertines that they are punished but as disturbers of the public peace."[82] Here the editors of the encyclopedia announce an obvious double standard regarding men's and women's extramarital sexuality, relaxing the codes that had regulated the first group and criminalizing the latter group's behavior.

Even at this point, the libertine referred to more than just sex. The editors acknowledge that "gambling is another genre, but very ill-suited to libertinage. The rights of the police, in this regard, are again restrained within the limits of public order: because it is not permitted to crack down on a gambler as a gambler, but only as a disturber of public tranquility, or for potentially causing the unhappiness of others."[83] They conclude, "Finally we believe that the police have no reason to get involved in domestic libertinage. Too long have they extended their inspection into families, under the pretext of maintaining morals, which can only be the province of the police indirectly and not coercively; that is, the police must never authorize licentious public institutions, but it cannot punish harshly, or in anyway whatsoever, the libertine man who frees them."[84] The revolutionary legal regime promised to prosecute only crimes committed, rather than imminent or potential violations of the law. The libertine category, so indispensable in curtailing undesirable behavior for over a century, should cease to function as a punishable offense.

Throughout the era of the French Revolution, the term "libertine" regularly appeared in plays, comic operas, and vaudevilles performed in France and the Francophone Atlantic.[85] At the Théâtre de la République on rue de la Loi, players performed *The Morals of the Old Regime, or the Results of Libertinage*, a drama in five acts and in verse, a new title for a play first performed in 1776 under the title *The School of Morals*. Neither performance was a success. The plot detailed an attempted seduction by a libertine wealthy young man, and a theater critic found the subject too serious for such a comic treatment—the director was brave to bring this figure before a public in revolution. Such characters "whose conduct, audaciously criminal, reveals the atrocious depravity of their morals and the incapacity of the law, when it acts to punish them."[86] So, was the absolutist government of Old Regime France excessively or insufficiently capable of enforcing the law?

In 1792 the Jacobin journalist Jean-Paul Marat asserted that despotic governments can demonstrate a remarkable tolerance for spectacle and diversion, linking the indulgences of the Persian emperor Cyrus, Roman emperors, and the city fathers of eighteenth-century Venice. This municipal government, "far from controlling the residents' tastes, opens the door to entertainments, games, pleasures, and in that way occupies those who want to attend to matters of State. It is not only the religious who may have an errant life, and who the government favors in their disorders: so that all the libertines hail the gentleness of a government of the seigneurie."[87] Marat concluded: "So this licentious life that people call liberty, is one of the principal sources of their servitude."[88]

More conservative authors agreed that young people were especially prone to mistaking libertinism for liberty. In an essay that called for young men, particularly those who hoped for state office, to travel and acquire knowledge of the political and social situation across Europe, one writer warned, "Experience proves that a young man, abandoned to himself, far from making progress in culture, sees only losses; he forgets the studies he has undertaken, and in believing himself free, he is only a libertine."[89] Individuals required a social education and broad international experience to awaken a virtuous orientation to the collective good.

How were revolutionary legislators to distinguish libertinism from liberty? In 1793 the owner of a bookstall in Montmartre was arrested for displaying "several erotic works, among which was the *Catéchisme libertin*. He declared he could neither read nor write and had displayed these books 'without any evil purpose and that in the future he would not display others.'"[90] The theater critic Grimod de la Reynière warned his readers in a republican vein that the *gens du monde* (worldly people) were avaricious, greedy, and incapable of love, which can't take root in their corrupt hearts. "But," he wrote, "we know them to be libertines without desire, debauched without remorse, and crapulous without shame."[91] Conservatives, on the other hand, used the term to refer to those priests who swore loyalty to the Constitution, those who abandon the pope, or those who are secret Jansenists.[92] The ubiquity of the term communicated that Frenchmen and women traversed a uniquely amoral and lawless age.

The libertine category figured prominently in debates on the revolutionary legalization of divorce. The *Gazette des Tribuneaux* considered the question of unions in which one spouse gave the other a venereal disease. The editor mused, could the injured spouse use this fault to claim the right to divorce? Response: here is how that question was answered in cases of separation requests, by a judge celebrated for his learning.[93] Robert-Joseph Pothier, in "Treatise on the Marriage Contract," contended that venereal disease no longer provided grounds for separation, because such ailments could be cured by most surgeons. The Parlement of Paris had avoided weighing in on the matter, but the Parlement of Metz twice found in favor of the wife and approved separation on grounds of venereal disease transmission. The judges in those cases found that "it is true that the art of healing this terrible illness that seemed to follow the progress of libertinage and succeeded in removing from that vice the powerful fear that it held. However, there remain frequent victims that serve as examples for whom the recovery is only partial."[94]

A law guaranteeing all citizens the right to divorce was desired by all "friends of humanity, especially unhappy spouses, who are most affected by it: if this law is fair for them, who would dare oppose it?"[95] Authors observed that marital unhappiness usually fell hardest on women, for a young girl married at her parents' will, unable to influence the choice. She marched to the altar and found herself linked to a man whose faults were impossible to know. Women had few means to avoid a bad choice, and even fewer methods to correct poor results, since the husband was the master recognized in law and social order. And so "the unhappy woman watches as a violent passion or an unsociable attitude grows in her spouse; a gambler, or a libertine, jealousy or greed, or insanity; sometimes all of these together."[96] She became a slave to the worst kind of tyrant. Old Regime law that did not allow for divorce sacrificed "gentleness to violence, virtue to vice, modesty to libertinage, reason to dementia, innocence to crime, and honor to infamy."[97] The essay concludes by asking what kind of religion would condemn people to life without marital union for having made one wrong choice. "It is an insult to the Divine," Pothier writes, "it profanes the Christian religion, to conclude that a bad union, uniquely founded on the mutual consent of the two spouses, cannot be dissolved."[98] In considering dramatic reforms to family law, the author proposes that readers could reconcile their Christian faith to divorce. Regarding a court case that pitted half-sisters against each other as retroactive "bastards" dispossessed from their family, the editor observes that these laws of a previous era reflect the prejudice of Church teachings. In the name of faith, which was really fanaticism, the people of France had been told to "abhor bastards, as they abhor libertines."[99] The whole point of the legal and political revolution of 1789 was to dismantle these prejudices of birth in favor of equality.

Louis-Abel Beffroy de Reigny, a journalist who wrote under the pen name "Cousin Jacques," composed a lengthy pamphlet in 1793 entitled *The Constitution of the Moon: A Political and Moral Dream*. In it Beffroy imagines a Republic established on the moon, very similar to France. But Christianity there had been spared the Reformation. Liberty, equality and fraternity had reigned for centuries there in the lunar empire. These principles were served more by good "fathers, good sons, good husbands, good friends, good citizens, than by all the lights of modern philosophy."[100] Where previous writers and moralists considered structural or legal changes necessary to improve behavior, Beffroy advocates an individual approach, recalling men to serve their social roles with humility and dedication. The only enemies of order on the Moon's Republic were the egoists, the proud, the vindictive, and the libertines, "who don't want to rule their senses, nor moderate their desires, nor renounce their pleasures."[101] Beffroy's solution to bring revolutionary society closer to his utopian lunar republic is to abolish the old Church and establish a new religion of the majority with salaried clergy and temples ranked as national buildings.[102] In this manner he clearly identifies the libertine as a product of the Reformation and the Catholic Church's failings in moral leadership.

Many republican legislators agreed with Beffroy that the Church was to blame for French subjects' libertine conduct. The deputy Bourdon de l'Oise defended the Revolutionary Tribunals and the juries who judged their fellow citizens' patriotic fervor. Bourdon took seriously the gray area between undesirable and illegal activity and used the term *libertin* to code such behavior as less threatening; in his usage the term maintained an association with selfishness just on this side of legality. In 1794 he wrote of a hypothetical young man, charged with overseeing his family's commerce in Spain, who lost the family's fortune, driving his relations to despair, even death. The jurors would find him responsible, no doubt, "but unless he turned the merchandise to his own profit, they could not say he was a thief, only that he was a scatterbrain or a libertine."[103] Here the term indicates one who has committed a grievous act, with detrimental consequences, as a result of personal limitations or self-interest, not criminal intent. The libertine was not a criminal, but an individual who pursues pleasure regardless of the results.

An anonymous screed against Robespierre, the revolutionary legislator and member of the powerful Committee of Public Safety, depicted him as "weak and vindictive, sober and sensual, chaste by temperament, and libertine by imagination. Women's glances were not the only attractions of his supreme power; he enjoyed attracting them, he mixed *coquettrie* with his ambition; he imprisoned women to have the pleasure of setting them free; he drew tears from them to dry them off."[104] Robespierre would be memorialized as the Incorruptible, but even his opponents attempted to mobilize the slander machine of revolutionary pamphlets to sully him with lascivious aspersions.

This collision of libertine categories communicated a fundamental struggle over the law in revolutionary France. Was the law rooted in nature, and did it reflect eternal principles? Or was it a human institution subject to error and prejudice? Was it universal and absolute, or conditional and contextual? Laws regulating sexuality underwent dramatic reforms during the revolutionary era, decriminalizing prostitution, sodomy, and extramarital sex to reflect many republican legislators' cosmopolitan perspective of the variety of human sexualities. The writings of the Marquis de Sade—freed from prison by revolutionary-era legislation in 1790 and a section leader in Paris by 1793—provided important insights on these questions in the pornographic novel *Histoire de Juliette* (1797–1801).[105] Sade's character Noirceuil affirms that laws grow from a region's specific custom and climate. This resulted in a patchwork of laws across Europe that criminals and libertines might leverage to evade prosecution. As Mladen Kozul observes, according to Sade, the Italian city-states in particular exhibited fluid jurisdictions in which "it is only a matter of changing provinces to evade justice: [the police] of one State cannot pursue you in another; and as governments change every day, and often twice in one day, the crime committed at lunchtime cannot be prosecuted that evening."[106] The revolution as it unfolded in France and across Europe here is imagined as a criminal's ideal. But Sade also reminds us that long-standing traditions in French law took precedent, custom, culture, even climate and character, into account in the development and application of legal codes. Kozul writes, "It is no accident that the most fabulous and perfected of Sade's libertines, such as Minski or Brisa-Testa, set themselves up in Italy after having torched their departed country. For Minski, ideas of the just and the unjust as those of vice and virtue are 'purely local and geographic; and have nothing intrinsically concrete.'"[107] Wide reading in the world-historical literature of the day reinforced this sensibility; in particular travelers to India and China reported laws and legal institutions strikingly different from those established in France. Kozul notes that "Sade was in direct contact with this Oriental vogue; his works are flooded with references to all the history manuals he had read and the kingdoms of China, Japan, Arabia, Turkey are a permanent reference to indicate the relativity of the laws."[108]

Libertines also figured prominently in the legal debates surrounding clerical celibacy during the revolution. The delegate Grégoire-Pierre Herluison opposed the political speeches that attacked clerical vows of celibacy, a common occurrence in the National Assembly, particularly by a priest from the Aube department to the east of Paris. Herluison proudly claimed, "There is, Sir, a Law, immutable in its nature, universal in its breadth, eternal in its duration: here it is: *In man the body would submit to the soul, and the soul would submit to God.*"[109] Herluison gives voice to the long-standing Catholic theological rationale for clerical celibacy. In response many of Herluison's colleagues leaned heavily on a natural law theory to oppose clerical celibacy, channeling generations of critics and travel writers to contend that refraining from sex was unnatural, unhealthful, and perverse.[110]

French men and women found themselves in the midst of nothing less than a remarkable overhaul of the legislation governing society, especially focused on sexual mores. These debates inside the legislature seem to have occasioned debates on the streets and in homes that transformed social actions. Contemporary observers attest that prostitution increased in years of economic hardship brought on by revolution and continental and Atlantic warfare. In surveying over two thousand police records of prostitution, Clyde Plumauzille found dramatic increases in the arrests of prostitutes between 1789 and 1799. From this rich source base, Plumauzille argues that legal changes decriminalized prostitution and cast women who sold sex as doubly victimized, first by men's sexual appetites and second by state stigma.[111]

By 1798 many of the émigrés who had fled France during the height of the Jacobin Terror returned with cosmopolitan tales of the sexual mores encountered in German states, Prussia, Austria, and England.[112] Etienne Dupin, a jurist who had fled France during the revolution, asserted that Parisians loved anything from abroad and despised their own nation's products, and so they would no doubt welcome foreign customs regarding commercial sex trades. He focused on the licensed sex workers of Berlin as an example of the utility of well-policed prostitution. Dupin playfully adopted ecclesiastical terminology to refer to the women who worked in brothels, observing that "for public safety, the nuns of each convent are visited officially, every fifteen days, by a surgeon attached to the police. He charges each of them, for his visit, a tax of two *groschen*, and quarantines those who appear suspect to him. These are de rigueur, and in case of contravention on the part of the entrepreneurs, they are condemned to pay the cost of the illnesses that were contracted at their establishment."[113] Perhaps the Parisian police and surgeons could adopt similar tactics to regulate the capital's sex workers and improve the health of all French citizens as a result, he suggested.

Dupin considered the role that surveillance could play in regulating commercial sex work, querying, "What can a good police do? Above all, contain scandal; admirable severity, no doubt, but too often abusive; for if these creatures can exercise their traffic without worry, they would become libertines; when forced to hide, they steal and assassinate. Add as victims of their ignominy the long list of honest people that they poison, and tell me if the rules of Berlin seem impolitic to you? I will go farther: these laws are of good morals," Dupin concluded.[114] During the Directory legislators and authors struggled to identify the new foundations of social order that had not been thoroughly reviled during the revolutionary process. Imagining a "good police" force that took minor vices in stride while providing some regulation and assurances to the public proved a formative step in reconstituting social authority during the Directory.[115]

CONCLUSION

This chapter has focused on how different factions mobilized the libertine category against political opponents during the French Revolution, casting rivals as a threat to law and moral order. But libertine characters did not simply crowd the pages of newspapers and pamphlets; they spilled onto the streets. We get a sense of the disorienting profusion of libertine spectacle from the following scenes, drawn from the archives of the Paris police. It was the fall of 1790. It had been over a year since the people of Paris overran the Bastille prison, seizing arms, releasing the few remaining prisoners, and lynching the prison commander who attempted to hold back the crowds. In the heart of the revolutionary capital city, police officers made their rounds in the gardens of the Palais-Royal. Of the republican speeches from soapboxes and lanterns, they made little comment. Instead they encountered a spectacle advertised outside of a boutique in the galleries with loud music and barkers who promised that spectators would see a man with one leg who had a second leg growing from his right arm reaching to his waist. A small theater, Chinese Shadows, promised light comedies. A third barker cried, "Here it is, the wild man! Here, you'll see the man without equal."[116] Police officers noted that, upon entering, they saw a man with a long black beard, his nude torso covered in a black net tucked into his belt. A young woman danced on a tightrope to accompanying music. When asked if he had permission from the city to put on this show, the theater manager admitted that he did not but promised to secure it right away. Though the officers deemed it unnecessary at that point to stop the show, they recommended that the city authorities outlaw barkers, the exhibition of disabled people, and music in cafés due to the likelihood of complaints from neighbors.

On Christmas Eve of that same year, the police received an anonymous letter complaining about the indecent spectacle of libertines and debauched women in the Palais-Royal. The head of police addressed a sympathetic letter to the neighborhood's chief inspector, asking him to redouble efforts to control license in that area.[117] The revolution seemed to have unleashed all the kingdom's simmering vices onto the galleries and garden of this center of urban pleasures.[118]

Months went by. April 11, 1791. The police happened upon another illicit spectacle. It had only taken place for a few days, they assured their superiors, although the evidence cited above gives us reason to doubt that assertion.[119] In a boutique under the galleries of the Palais-Royal, barkers collected payment from spectators to see a "wild man and woman," purportedly "s*v*ges" from the Scioto region of North America, nude to their waists.[120] Police officers reported that they had heard that, for a payment of three livres, the audience would see a "natural man" and a "public girl" on display. A naked man apparently connoted the philosophy of Rousseau and Locke, while a naked woman meant a sex worker.[121] For an additional three livres, they could watch the "s*v*ges" engage in the most intimate relations, depicting "debauched scenes."[122]

Nothing about this spectacle was secret, and police had required no special undercover sleuthing to locate the performance. In fact contemporary newspapers included accounts seemingly written up by the spectacle directors themselves. The *Chronique de Paris* newspaper reported that the so-called wild man was a powerful blacksmith, and his companion was a *fille publique*, performing for crowds up to nineteen times per day. The *Courrier des 83 départements* newspaper related news of a similar spectacle that promised debauched scenes but featured an apprentice locksmith who shouted gibberish at his audience while devouring pebble-shaped pastries.[123] Police arrested those involved: three individuals including Constant, an unemployed hairdresser who served both as the wild man and the show's director; his wife, Françoise Chiron, who collected spectators' money; and her sister, Louise Maurice, a sixteen-year-old laundress, who had performed the part of the wild woman. Louise became the main witness in prosecuting her brother-in-law for fraud and counterfeiting.[124]

Constant's decision to adopt an American identity for this performance—and to announce it using the code words of "s*v*ge," "wild," "natural," with specific reference to the Indigenous people who claimed the Scioto river valley in Ohio as their home—lurks beyond the historical record.[125] But the spectacle suggests an enduring audience for entertainment employing literary allusions that recalled the world conjured in the pages of Lahontan's *Dialogues* and Voltaire's *L'Ingénu*. First, this is a clear example of Europeans engaging in cultural appropriation for titillation and for profit. Published over two decades ago, Philip Deloria's foundational work has provided important theoretical insight into the significance of white settlers "playing Indian" in the North American context.[126] He documents how British colonists during the revolutionary war used "Indian costume to claim unconstrained freedom as an essential American quality, a customary right inherent in the land itself."[127] In this context settlers adopted elements of Indigenous dress and identity to momentarily position themselves as locals rooted in the land against the distant British empire. Settlers played Indian to lodge a complaint, to air a grievance, or to highlight a perceived injustice in violation of their natural liberties. But what did it mean for Europeans to play Indian back in France? The record of this spectacle suggests first that there was money to be made in marketing sexual spectator entertainment with literary devices that recalled the world of exoticist license conjured in the pages of promotional pamphlets, travel literature, and political philosophy. Second, it reveals the enduring popular appeal of speculative settler schemes, such as that promoted by the Scioto Company in the 1790s, predicated on a plan of Indigenous dispossession. But a few details of the case might also sustain an interpretation of this performance as a critique of those Parisians gullible enough to pursue such schemes.

Scioto had been in the news and on the lips of Parisians for over a year. The new government of the United States was seeking European settlers and investment, sending the American businessman Joel Barlow to Paris to recruit potential colonists to the Scioto River Valley in Ohio Territory.[128] Suzanne Desan's analysis of Sciotomania emphasizes the global scale of revolutionary politics revealed by this land speculation scheme. A flurry of publications regarding the Scioto Company littered the city's thoroughfares, including at least one lubricious image of a young man preparing to leave his lover to seek his fortune in Scioto. These publications paid scant attention to the residents of this territory.[129] European settlers imagined instead a vast unpeopled wilderness unbounded by treaties or obligations. Crowds of people pressed into the Scioto Company's offices on the rue Neuve des Petits Champs, purchasing modest plots of land across the ocean, usually fifty to three hundred acres, paying three livres per acre as down payment, with a promise to pay an additional three livres upon taking possession.

By adopting similar financial terms for his spectacle—three livres to view, another three to witness copulation—I suggest that Constant both participates in and critiques colonial capitalism. At least with his performance, individuals got what they paid for. The same could not be said for the investors in the Scioto Company. A group of nobles who called themselves the "Society of Twenty-Four" purchased thirty-two thousand acres, planning to establish paternalist, monarchist utopias along the banks of the Scioto River.[130] The first ships carrying prospective colonists departed in February 1790. Upon arrival it became clear that the company had failed to mention a few key matters: the U.S. Congress had not authorized it to sell land in Ohio territory. Settlers had paid for paper promises rather than land. There were no roads to access the proposed territory, large sections of the river were unnavigable, and thriving communities of the Lenape, Shawnee, Miami, and Cherokee nations mobilized forceful resistance to settler encroachment. Desan concludes, "Only after years of struggle did roughly a hundred persistent French emigrés gain the right first to *rebuy* some of the land or apply for full title from the U.S. Congress for a few thousand acres further down the Ohio" founding Gallipolis in present-day Kentucky.[131] Meanwhile the Scioto company quietly shuttered its office, and Barlow threw himself into revolutionary politics.

Within the pages of novels and under the galleries of the Palais-Royal, the French public might consider the liberties of empire without leaving the comforts of Paris. They could imagine a society unconstrained by canon law, royal writ, and hierarchies of rank, wealth, or family. Colonial libertines made revolutionary liberties imaginable.

From 1789 to 1814, men and women across France and the Atlantic colonies challenged every unfreedom protected by law. Across the Atlantic world, it became clear that the expanded freedom of one individual often demanded the submission of others. Sons' and daughters' duties to their parents, spouses' duties to each other, employees' obligations to their employers, and taxpayers' duties to the state all might be rendered as unacceptable oppression by inflammatory journalists and ambitious legislators. If all power was despotic, then all subordinates might interpret their own subservience to be "slavery." The libertine—that quasi-criminal category used by royal and Church officials to defend religious hegemony, royal and paternal authority, and social hierarchy—was now turned on its head to attack those very institutions. In imagining the libertine as a quality inherent to the nobility, revolutionaries picked up the racializing discourse that had been powerfully employed in the Caribbean to challenge the property rights of free people of color. The actions of individuals mattered less than the scurrilous accusations made against an entire population of marked variety.

In the property revolution at the heart of French Atlantic colonialism, the law had proven itself capable of local nuance, cultural relativism, and dynamic transformation over time. All of these qualities would be condemned during the French Revolution by legislators and journalists who prized universality and equality. No longer would the law engage with local concerns and attend to varied interests between residents of different religions, languages, traditions, and races. Rather, one standard set forth from Paris should govern the entirety of France's empire. This was the promise made by Napoleon Bonaparte as he claimed authority over France and all Frenchmen around the globe as First Consul in 1799 and then as Emperor in 1804.

The Civil Code, promulgated in 1804, represented the fulfillment of that promise. Adopted as the law throughout France, the French Atlantic and occupied Europe, the Civil Code enshrined equal property rights of all adult men as its first priority. It reestablished paternal authority over minor children, without the Old Regime's extended control over adult sons' property rights. It asserted husbands' control over their wives' property, undoing the careful steps made during the eighteenth century and revolutionary era to enable married women to hold property in their own names. The provisions of the Civil Code restored hierarchies of age and sex in France and throughout the French empire, subordinating wives to husbands, sons to fathers, and employees to masters. The Napoleonic legal reform movement has long been recognized as a watershed event in recognizing individual civil rights, including freedom of religion, and property rights. But not every individual was equally entitled to civil rights under the Civil Code.[132]

Moreover, by 1802, French military and administrative leaders had restored slavery in every colony except Haiti, where formerly enslaved men and women—libertines in the ancient Roman sense of the term—waged an urgent war for independence rather than submit to the French. Bonaparte ordered the arrest of Toussaint Louverture, the governor of Saint-Domingue, and attempted to force Saint-Domingue's residents back into colonial enslavement. He failed. And the military leaders in the island clearly perceived the existential threat posed by a universalist French legal code. Under the military and political leadership of Jean-Jacques Dessalines and Henri Christophe, Haitians rejected French law and chased all Frenchmen from their shores, enshrining this separation in founding documents that declared the independence of Haiti.[133] These leaders perceived and distrusted the enduring hierarchies embedded in French law and in the colonial institutions used to lay claim to property and peoples around the world.

Epilogue
The Law and the Libertine, 1814

Arguably the most consequential legal reform of the revolution resulted not from events in France, but from those actions taking place across the Atlantic in colonial Haiti. From the first stirrings of revolt in 1789, free men and women of color insisted that equality before the law included them and their children. The uprising of enslaved peoples begun in 1791 ultimately resulted in the abolition of slavery, first in the colony and then across the French Antilles. The oscillation in laws considering the rights of free men of color and the abolition of slavery radicalized military and political leaders both in France and around the Francophone Atlantic world.[1]

The revolutions in the French Caribbean depended on a dramatic expansion in the colonial press, established after 1764. During that time local newspapers and political pamphlets facilitated the circulation of a "flood of proclamations from rival political authorities."[2] In 1789 a colonist from Saint-Domingue responded to Abbé Gregoire, asserting that it was surprising that free people of color had mobilized against concubinage, for the institution had

> procured both their existence and the goods that they enjoy, and that they reproach Whites for abjuring expressions of paternity towards them. This illegitimate commerce that offends morals and Religion, is a necessary evil in the Colonies where white women are in small numbers, and where marriages cannot be numerous, it [concubinage] prevents greater vices. The weaknesses of Masters tames them and

slavery is more gentle. The population gains because it is less libertinage than need that motivates these illicit unions. The heat of the climate that irritates desires and the facility to satisfy them, render useless the precautions of the Legislator to remedy these abuses because the Law is quiet, where nature speaks imperiously.[3]

Julien Raimond, a free man of color and a property owner in colonial Saint-Domingue, observed that the National Assembly's proposal to enfranchise only some people based on the "color of the epidermis" would exacerbate racial tensions in the Caribbean colonies. Such distinctions would perversely discourage marriages, instead pushing "women of color to libertinage; it is more advantageous to enter a concubinage relationship with a white man, & raise children who can pass as white, rather than seeking a marriage with a man of color."[4] In 1791 the National Assembly agreed to extend equal rights to all free men of color, but left the enforcement of this decree up to the local legislature, reinforcing the sense that French law tolerated colonial injustice.

Recognizing the gulf between metropolitan law and colonial practice, the National Convention determined to draw Saint-Domingue more closely into the Republic after 1793. Enslaved people in Saint-Domingue had freed themselves by overthrowing their masters and burning plantations across the island.[5] When the Jacobin legislator, Etienne Polverel, sent to Saint-Domingue to restore the French Republic's authority, issued an emancipation decree in the western province, it was part of a broad initiative to recruit support for the struggling Republic's global war against Spain and Britain. Malick Ghachem writes that "on September 4, 1793, he lectured the ex-slaves in terms that recalled the colonial concern with the libertinage of manumitted slaves. The freed persons, Polverel intoned, would only find happiness in 'property and work,' not 'disorder, idleness, and brigandage.'"[6] Republican virtue in France and Saint-Domingue hinged on work and family stability. Republican legislators hoped that these realms would provide proof of the political revolution's superiority to the tyranny of the past.

Marriage was a critical institution from which to dismantle the colony's reputation for libertine conduct. The revolutionary commissioners issued a proclamation in July 1793 incentivizing formerly enslaved men to marry their partners to ensure the freedom of the women and their children.[7] "At one level," Ghachem notes, "this rhetoric hearkened back to an old colonial tradition of decrying the libertinage and unruliness of freed persons in Saint-Domingue, particularly those residing in the colony's cities and towns."[8] In 1796 the devastation of Saint-Domingue's commerce provided fodder for the politician and colonial intendant François Barbé-Marbois, who considered the future of global trade at this watershed moment after the abolition of slavery throughout the French colonies. Observing that an enormous quantity of fine fabrics had been imported every year by the "colonists both white and of color, and especially by a multitude of free women of color, who, giving themselves up to the libertinage and desires of the whites as few courtesans have been more captivated and pressured, seem to have as their sole purpose to satisfy an unrestrained taste for all of the richest and finest goods that Europe and India sends to this colony."[9] Barbé-Marbois imagined that colonial demand might continue to generate wealth for France, laying his hopes in the aspirational consumption of free women of color. He failed to consider how the abolition of slavery and the collapse of French colonial governments might transform social hierarchies and law across the Antilles.[10]

LIBERTINE POLITICAL SYSTEMS

Republican participants in the French Revolution proudly claimed to have destroyed the libertine institutions of aristocracy, monarchy, and slavery. They had replaced social and sexual disorder with republican virtue. We have largely inherited this frame of the significance of their actions, replicating what is essentially partisan doctrine with every new historical film or video game set in eighteenth-century France.[11] But, soon enough, republican leaders too proved to be susceptible to charges of sexual extravagances and excessive financial liberties, stoking public rumor and innuendo.[12] Moreover, it was difficult to claim that a virtuous republic reigned when gamblers and sex workers overflowed urban public spaces. By 1804 Napoleon's efforts to limit social vices relied on an extensive network of spies and secret police. As emperor he restored both patriarchal authority and the Catholic Church as institutions organizing daily life throughout the kingdom. But when the emperor's fall brought to an end a generation of warfare in 1814, the question of what to do with France's republican laws preoccupied Europe's coalition powers. Conservatives all, they might have thrown out the Civil Code along with the Bonaparte family, and reverted to the prerevolutionary patchwork that had served France for centuries. But they did not. Inviting the executed king's brother to rule as Louis XVIII, the coalition ultimately retained many of the legal and social innovations advanced by the revolution's legislators and by Emperor Napoleon Bonaparte.

Across the Atlantic the Baron Jean-Louis de Vastey, a man of letters of Haitian descent and the leading political theorist for King Henri-Christophe in independent Haiti, attempted to explain to the European coalition how the actions of his own countrymen coordinated with those of the British and the Russian armies. When hundreds of thousands of enslaved men and women had cast off the chains of slavery in 1804, argued Vastey, they had followed the laws of nature.[13] The inhabitants of Haiti successfully rejected libertine enslavers and despotic colonial officials. But, throughout his essay, Vastey linked Old Regime despotism less to monarchy than to the economic system of chattel slavery and to the racist social institutions that scaffolded it. Vastey reminded his readers that the monarchs of France had endeavored to enact laws to protect the weak from the strong, the enslaved from the enslaver. He recalled that "Louis XIV attempted in vain, through his royal ordinances, to place restrictions on the cruel and dissolute conduct of the colonists by ameliorating the lot of the free people of color and the slaves. His good intentions had no effect and the regulations were never enforced; in the beginning they were evaded, and soon thereafter they became a dead letter."[14] Over the course of his book *The Colonial System Unveiled*, Vastey rejected the French revolutionaries' claim that overthrowing the monarchy ended despotism and libertine conduct. Moreover, he charged that, in failing to keep principles of equality and liberty for all at the center of their revolution, the French under Napoleon revealed themselves to be eager heirs of a colonial system rooted in human oppression. If not for the actions of the men and women of colonial Haiti, the revolutionaries in Paris never would have abolished slavery. After all, hadn't Napoleon

FIG 10. Left: King Henri I Haitian coin (1811). Bibliothèque Nationale de France, http://catalogue.bnf.fr/ark:/12148/cb44994840v.

FIG 11. Right: King Henri I Haitian coin, reverse (1811). Bibliothèque Nationale de France, http://catalogue.bnf.fr/ark:/12148/cb44994840v.

reinstated slavery throughout the colonies of the French Atlantic, except Haiti, where the true principles of the revolution lived on?

In the coins circulated by Emperor Napoleon and by King Henri Christophe in the first decade of the nineteenth century, we discern clues about how this ideological war deployed political symbols. Both men are depicted as political leaders who have eschewed monarchical crowns for the republican crown of laurel leaves with its associations to ancient Rome. But where Napoleon's coin evokes the emperor's secular authority alone, Henri Christophe's coin explicitly connects political power with divine favor. The obverse reads "Henri by the Grace of God King of Haiti" and the Christian date of 1811. On the back the designer has united the royal crown above a phoenix amid flames. The motto around this image reads, "Born from the ashes," acknowledging the widespread devastation that a decade of war had wrought in Haiti. Around the outside of the coin, we read the Latin legend "God, the Cause, and my Sword," again heralding the role of faith in uniting this people against their oppressors. This was a savvy political move at a time when Haitian leaders sought recognition from other European countries, especially the Vatican.[15] But alongside

FIG 12. Left: Napoleon I coin (1808). Bibliothèque Nationale de France, http://catalogue.bnf.fr/ark:/12148/cb41963140n.

FIG 13. Right: Napoleon I coin, reverse (1808). Bibliothèque Nationale de France, http://catalogue.bnf.fr/ark:/12148/cb41963140n.

these symbols of monarchy and religion, we note the republican date at the bottom of the coin. King, Church, and republican ideals coexisted in the political ideologies that underpinned the early Haitian republic.

Vastey's analysis requires us to reconsider: What were the accomplishments of the Age of Revolutions in the end? How did the consequences vary across Europe and the Americas, depending on participants' starkly different understandings of liberty and who could claim it? If the gauge of a revolution's efficacy was republican government, then a generation of political turmoil, civil and foreign wars, had been for naught in France as in Haiti. Napoleon ended the republican experiment in 1804 crowning himself emperor of France, while Jean-Jacques Dessalines took the title of emperor of Haiti that same year. But if the gauge was the abolition of slavery, Vastey contended that the era could still redeem itself. Addressing the powers assembled at the Congress of Vienna in 1814, Vastey urged Europe's representatives to abolish slavery and the slave trade worldwide and to recognize an independent Haiti. He asked all, "Englishman, Frenchman, German, Russian, white men, from all the regions of the earth: who is one among you that could be so ungenerous and so bereft of the feelings of justice and humanity, graven by divinity on every heart, as not to shudder when reading the account of what we have been subject to for centuries, the persecutions and the horrors of which we are the unhappy victims?"[16] And, in this effort, Vastey located the gulf between moral action and the letter of the law that had so long been termed libertine but not criminal.

In tracing the peregrinations of the libertine category over two centuries, I aim to recover some submerged features of the term's capacious and mutable meanings. This quasi-criminal category facilitated legal pluralism and smoothed over radical structural changes in Old Regime legal systems, as the royal state assumed jurisdiction from the Church, and as the metropole strove to systematize a dizzying array of provincial and colonial privileges. Revolutionary reforms of the law resulted in vigorous debates that attributed libertine excesses to political opponents. To this day the enduring appeal of the libertine character exceeds the sexual connotation it acquired by the revolutionary era. This figure plumbs the half-hidden layering of rights and privileges reserved for some but deemed off-limits for others. From the individual who claims religious liberty in a state that promises but routinely fails to protect that ideal, to the enslaved individual who celebrates a religious holiday despite his enslaver's orders, libertines illuminate the space between the letter and the spirit of the laws.

NOTES

INTRODUCTION

1. The trials of Dominique Strauss-Kahn, the French Socialist politician and managing director of the International Monetary Fund (2007–11) for sexual assault and attempted rape in *People of the State of New York v. Dominique Strauss-Kahn* (2011) and for aggravated pimping in *L'Affaire du Carlton du Lille* (2011–15) returned the term "libertine" to courtrooms and the front pages of major newspapers. Muriel Rouyer offers crucial insights on the sexual politics of both the trials and journalistic coverage in "Strauss-Kahn Affair and the Culture of Privacy." http://dx.doi .org/10.1016/j.wsif.2013.07.004.

2. Strauss-Kahn referred to group sex parties organized for his benefit as "soirées libertines" in trial testimony. Marie-Amélie Lombard-Latune, "Affaire du Carlton: ce que DSK a dit aux juges," *Le Figaro*, April 29, 2012, http://www.lefigaro.fr/actualite -france/2012/04/29/01016-20120429artfig00213-affaire-du-carlton-ce-que-dsk-a -dit-aux-juges.ph

3. "Procès du Carlton," *Le Monde*, February 10, 2015, https://www.lemonde.fr/societe /article/2015/02/10/dsk-a-la-barre-du-proces-au-carlton_4573130_3224.html.

4. Caroline Politi, "Procès du Carlton : du libertinage pour DSK, de 'la boucherie' pour les prostituées," *L'Express*, February 3 2015, https://www.lexpress.fr/actualite/societe /proces-du-carlton-du-libertinage-pour-dsk-de-la-boucherie-pour-les-prostituees _1643849.html.

5. "Epilogue de l'affaire de Carlton de Lille: la condamnation civile de Strauss-Kahn annulée en cassation," *Le Monde*, March 2, 2018, https://www.lemonde .fr/police-justice/article/2018/03/02/epilogue-de-l-affaire-du-carlton-de-lille-la -condamnation-civile-de-strauss-kahn-annulee-en-cassation_5264764_1653578 .html.

6. Vivienne Walt, "The Former Head of the IMF May Have Been Acquitted but He Has Lost Everything," *Time*, June 12, 2012, http://time.com/3919026/strauss-kahn -acquitted-lost/.

7. Individuals who solicit prostitutes are now subject to a $1500 fine: "Prostitution: la pénalisation des clients définitiement votée au Parlement," *Le Figaro*, April 6, 2016, http://www.lefigaro.fr/flash-actu/2016/04/06/97001-20160406filwww00283 -le-parlement-vote-la-penalisation-de-la-prostitution.ph

8. See for example, the commentary offered by Larry Wolff, "Free to Be a Sexual Predator?," *New York Times*, October 16, 2012, https://www.nytimes.com/2012/10 /17/opinion/dominique-strauss-kahn-and-libertinisms-sordid-history.html.

9. Wynn, "Libertinage," 414.

10. Cusset, *No Tomorrow*.

11. The essential readings on the *libertin* genre of literature include Pintard, *Le libertinage érudit*; Adam, *Les libertins au XVIIe siècle*; Darnton, *Forbidden Best-Sellers of Pre-Revolutionary France*; Dejean, *Reinvention of Obscenity*; Hunt, *Invention of Pornography*; Foucault, *Histoire du libertinage*; and van Damme, *L'épreuve libertine*.

12. Steintrager, *Autonomy of Pleasure*.

13. Evident in many scholarly treatments of the libertine as a defining feature of French elites, most recently in Denton's *Decadence, Radicalism*.

14. Pascale Egré et Victor Fortunato, "Carlton: DSK assume son 'libertinage' parfois 'rude' mais pas la prostitution," *Le Parisien*, February 11, 2015, http://www.leparisien .fr/dsk-la-chute/en-direct-proces-du-carlton-deuxieme-journee-d-audience-pour -dsk-11-02-2015-4524151.ph

15. The title of this monograph borrows the term from hundreds of police and legal records, in which individuals accused of libertine behavior acknowledge themselves to be "bad subjects." The phrase also signals this book's location at the disciplinary intersection between literature, political theory, and law.

16. Summarized in Bartlett and Kennedy, *Feminist Legal Theory*; for a thoughtful consideration of the varieties of gendered violence within a complex matrix of social and economic power relations, see Cahill, "Unjust Sex vs. Rape," 746–61.

17. Addressed by Jurney, "Médias et inégalités," 60–71.

18. On the silence of the French press regarding the sexual conduct of political leaders, see Quatremer, *Sexe, mensonges et médias*.

19. On legal pluralism as an undertheorized reality within most systems of law, see Swenson, "Legal Pluralism," 438–62.

20. Each of these terms have their own associations with extrajudicial accusations. The term "deadbeat dad" originated in the 1980s and entered legal lexicons by the 1990s, including the textbook by Pyle, *Family Law*, 316. Nicolas Sarkozy notably referred to young men of African and Arab descent in the banlieues as "racaille," or "rabble," a term that links an entire population to undesirable behavior of a few individuals prior to legal judgment, as analyzed in Laurent Greilsamer's article "Le chiffre et le mot," *Le Monde*, November 7, 2005, https://www.lemonde.fr/idees /article/2005/11/07/le-chiffre-et-le-mot-par-laurent-greilsamer_707236_3232.html. In 2015, in the wake of widespread violence in Baltimore following the death of Freddie Gray while in police custody, Barack Obama referred to accused looters as

"thugs," as reported by Mike Lillis, "Black Lawmakers Push Back on Obama over 'Thugs,'" The Hill, January 5, 2015, http://thehill.com/homenews/house/240807 -black-lawmakers-push-back-on-obama-over-thugs.

21. Michel Foucault interrogates the 'repression hypothesis' of modern sexual conduct and discourse, identifying a twinned power of transgression accompanying repression, in *History of Sexuality*, 1:5–6.

22. An extensive literature of "Atlantic" history traces the economic, social, and political connections between Europe, Africa, the Americas, and the Caribbean from the sixteenth to eighteenth centuries. The field inherited methodological insights and limits from imperial historiography, with scholars of Anglo-America examining the "British" Atlantic, and scholars of New Spain tracing the "Spanish" Atlantic. Despite the contemporary importance of the Dutch and French in early modern Atlantic exchange, the literature remains thin on the French or Dutch Atlantic. For an entry to the scholarship and research questions of the French Atlantic, see Marzagalli, "French Atlantic World."

23. Wood, *Archipelago of Justice*, 3.

24. Following insights of Little, *Religion, Order, and Law*; Beik, *Social and Cultural History*; Stone, *French Parlements*; Breen, "Law, Society and the State," 346–86; Desan and Merrick, *Family, Gender and Law*; Kessler, *Revolution in Commerce*; and Hardwick, "Women 'Working' the Law," 28–49.

25. In two pathbreaking texts: Palmer, *Age of Democratic Revolutions*; and Godechot, *France and the Atlantic Revolution*.

26. Marzagalli, "French Atlantic and the Dutch," 101–18; Pritchard, *In Search of Empire*; Semley, *To Be Free and French*; Johnson, *Wicked Flesh*.

27. I follow the insights of the following foundational treatments that establish French laws of slavery and racial distinction as constitutive of the French Atlantic: Peabody, *There Are No Slaves*; Ghachem, *Old Regime and the Haitian Revolution*; Régent, *La France et ses ésclaves*; and Benot, *Les Lumières*.

28. Wood, *Archipelago of Justice*, 34–35. Dewar makes an important addition to this scholarship in *Disputing New France*.

29. *Libertine* in French, English, Welsh, Irish, Scots Gaelic, Icelandic, Norwegian; *libertino* in Spanish, Portuguese, and Italian; *libertinoa* in Basque; *libertyn* in Polish; *libertin* in German and Swedish. On Roman *liberti*, see Smith, *Dictionary of Greek and Roman*, 705–6. On the social status of freed slaves, see Mouritsen, *Freedman in the Roman World*. On slavery and freedmen's status, see Harper, *Slavery in the Late Roman World*, chap. 12.

30. Thanks to Rangar Cline, historian of ancient Rome and early Christianity at the University of Oklahoma, for his aid with Latin grammar on this point.

31. Pettegree, *Reformation*, 3:286–96.

32. Woo, "Nicodemism and Libertinism"; van Veen and. Spohnholz, "Calvinists vs. Libertines."

33. This is the modern Catholic English translation of Acts 6:9. From the website maintained by the U.S. Conference of Catholic Bishops, http://www.usccb.org /bible/acts6:54 (accessed August 30, 2022).

34. Kaplan, "Dutch Particularism,'" 286–301.

35. Cavaillé, *Les déniaisés*.

36. Calvin, *Contre la secte phantastique*.

37. Van Den Beit, *Authority of Scripture*, 29–31.

38. On Calvin and the spirituals, see McKim, *Cambridge Companion to Calvin*, 53–54.

39. Wynn, "Libertinage," 413.

40. Vallée, *La Béatitude des Chrétiens*, presented in Lachèvre, *Le libertinage au XVIIe siècle*, 8:25. The manuscript is in the Bibliothèque Nationale de France (BNF), Rés-p-z-1199 (37) and also available in the BNF's digital library: https://gallica.bnf .fr/ark:/12148/bpt6k71722w/f14.image.r=les%20beatitudes%20des%20chretiens (accessed August 30, 2022).

41. Pintard, *Le libertinage érudit;* Bossuet, *Histoire des variations*.

42. Boitano, *Polemics of Libertine Conversion*, 32–33.

43. Marie de Rabutin-Chantal, Marquise de Sévigné, 20 July 1679, in *Lettres de Madame de Sévigné*, 420.

44. *Dictionnaire de l'Académie Française* (1694), vol. 1, https://artflsrv03.uchicago.edu /philologic4/publicdicos/navigate/3/10922/ (accessed August 30, 2022).

45. "Libertin," *Le Dictionnaire de l'Académie Française* (1694), vol. 1, https://artflsrv03 .uchicago.edu/philologic4/publicdicos/navigate/3/10922/ (accessed August 30, 2022).

46. "Libertin," *Le Dictionnaire de l'Académie Française* (1762), vol. 2, https://artflsrv03 .uchicago.edu/philologic4/publicdicos/navigate/9/549/ (accessed August 30, 2022).

47. "Libertin," *Le Dictionnaire de l'Académie Française* (1762), vol. 2, https://artflsrv03 .uchicago.edu/philologic4/publicdicos/navigate/9/549/ (accessed August 30, 2022).

48. Jean-François Féraud, "Libertin," *Le Dictionnaire de l'Académie Française* (1787), vol. 2, https://artflsrv03.uchicago.edu/philologic4/publicdicos/navigate/6/3221/ (accessed August 30, 2022).

49. Nagy, *Libertinage et Révolution*, 24; Foucault, *Histoire du libertinage*, 434–45.

50. A survey of the ARTFL database identified more than three thousand occurrences of the term *libertin/e* in that electronic collection of canonical French literature and documents a perceptible shift in meaning over time from religious to sexual deviance.

51. On this transition in French colonial law, see Gilles Havard, "Les forçer à devenir Cytoyens."

52. Cavaillé, *Les déniaisés*, 26.

53. This category functions as a "quasi-crime" in modern legal theory. Examples might include failure to pay child support or to wear a seatbelt while driving. These are acknowledged offenses against established law, and authorities may impose penalties for them, but they do not rank as technical crimes. Robust scholarship exists for modern European and American law codes and the distinction between real or technical crimes and quasi-crimes. See Martin and Storey, *Unlocking Criminal*

Law, 93; and Norrie, *Crime, Reason and History*, 104–18. The scholarship is not developed regarding post-Tridentine legal codes and systems in France and the Atlantic empire. Berman's *Law and Revolution II* ably assesses the British and German legal traditions but does not engage the impact of Protestantism or confessional divides within France. The standard account of the development of French law is Olivier-Martin, *Histoire du droit français*. See also Garnot, "La législation"; and Traer, "From Reform to Revolution," 73–88.

54. The negotiated nature of Old Regime law in practice is a central thesis of a generation of social historians, especially the work of Farge, *Fragile Lives*; Cohen, *La nature du peuple*; Schneider, *King's Bench*; Desan and Merrick, *Family, Gender, and Law*; Hardwick, *Family Business*; and Lanza, *From Wives to Widows*.

55. On this point, identifying Old Regime distinctions between enormous crimes, serious crimes, and minor crimes (*crimes énormes, crimes graves*, and *crimes légers*), see Garnot, "La législation," 76. An instructive comparison could be made in twenty-first-century law to the decriminalization of marijuana possession across the United States, which has required the recalibration of drug sentencing and current prison sentences for all those incarcerated on charges that no longer rank as crimes.

56. Scholars of libertine literature have largely ignored this critical distinction in the archival record and represent the authors and narrators of this genre as unrepentant criminals or wrongfully charged with crimes. In a study of the Marquis de Sade's work, Alphonse Lingis asserts that "libertinage is defined formally by its relationship with law . . . the singular, and singularizing, will to violate the law for the sake of violating the law" ("Society of the Friends of Crime," 112). My research demonstrates that this misrepresents both the nature of law and the significance of the libertine category in eighteenth-century society. To call someone or something "libertine" typically indicated no serious crime had been committed. Sade, in contrast, committed serious crimes and spent much of his adult life in prison as a result.

57. Summarized by Ruff in *Crime, Justice, and Public Order*; and Desan in *Family on Trial*.

58. On Church officials' resistance to royal authority in France, see Van Kley, *Religious Origins of the French Revolution*; and Maire, *De la cause de dieu*. On the role of the Paris Parlement in these struggles, see Swann, *Politics and the Parlement*.

59. Garnot, *On n'est point pendu*, 106–7.

60. Hardwick, *Sex in an Old Regime City*, 130–31.

61. Garnot, *On n'est point pendu*, 160.

62. Séguin, *La vie libertine*.

63. Bergin, *Crown, Church, and Episcopate*, 45–46; Riddell, *Rise of Ecclesiastical Control*.

64. This oscillation principle is a staple of contemporary legal theory from tax law to drug enforcement to prostitution regulations. See Scoular, "What's Law Got to do with It?"

65. Edelstein, *Terror of Natural Right*, 12–14.

66. Boucher d'Argis, "Law of Nature."

67. Roche, *France in the Enlightenment*, 106. See contributions by Emma Rothschild, John Shovlin, Pernille Røge, and Florian Schui to Gabriel Paquette's edited volume, *Enlightened Reform*.

68. From Rousseau's denouncement of this aspect of "civilization" to Mercier's castigation of the ubiquity of the police in Old Regime France, contemporaries noted the dramatic extension of state power after 1760. The continuity of these processes of state centralization became the central thesis of Alexis de Tocqueville's *Ancien Régime and the French Revolution*.

69. Montesquieu theorized a relationship between law, popular character, climate, and geography in his *Spirit of the Laws* (1748). Callanan, "Liberal Constitutionalism and Political Particularism," 589–602.

70. Turner, *Libertines and Radicals*; DeJean, *Reinvention of Obscenity*; Muir, *Culture Wars*; Barbierato, *Inquisitor in the Hat Shop*; for a rare comparative analysis of libertines across Europe, see Turner's *Schooling Sex*.

71. Agmon, *Colonial Affair*.

72. As Faramerz Dabhoiwala contends, "sexual toleration grew out of religious toleration" (*Origins of Sex*, 80). The diversity of human sexual practices figures prominently in eighteenth-century French letters: Montesquieu's *Les lettres persanes* (1721) considered fantasies of harems and the consequences of polygamy, while Jean-Nicolas Démeunier's digest, *L'Esprit des usages et des coutumes des différens peoples*, introduced woman of the Nairs caste in India who had several husbands, notably analyzed by Verjus, "Non-patriarchal society: James Henry Lawrence (1773–1840) and The Empire of the Nairs," in Cossic-Péricarpin and Jones, *La Représentation et la reinvention des espaces de sociabilité*, 395–421; themes of short-term marriage and autonomous female sexuality figured prominently in Lahontan's *Dialogues*, and interracial sex in *Le Sopha* by Crébillon fils. On the two-spirit customs identified in early French accounts among Indigenous inhabitants of Illinois territory, see Dumont de Montigny, *Mémoires historiques*; Désy, "L'homme-femme"; and Hauser, "Berdache."

73. Requemora, "Voyage et libertinage."

74. Vyverberg, *Human Nature, Cultural Diversity*, 27–29.

75. On religious tolerance as a requirement of empire, see Turmeau de la Morandière, *Principes politiques*. Voltaire, Montesquieu, and Diderot also negatively compared the French kings' exclusion of religious minorities to the relative tolerance of policies that they attributed to British and Dutch policies in the Atlantic colonies. See the discussion in Elliott, *Empires of the Atlantic World*, 72–73. Religious toleration required some acceptance of sexual diversity, notably articulated in Diderot's *Supplément au voyage de Bougainville* (1772) and in the Abbé Raynal's *Histoire philosophique et politique des établissements et du commerce*.

76. Libertine literature dominates an enduring subfield of eighteenth-century literary analysis. Among the best treatments are DeJean, *Libertine Strategies*; Saint-Amand, *Libertine's Progress*; Blanc, *Les libertines*; and Cavaillé, *Les déniaisés*. The colonial

dimension of this genre has been ignored, however, outside of Dayan and Garraway's foundational works (Dayan, *Haiti, History, and the Gods*; Garraway, *Libertine Colony*).

77. On the nascent French colony in West Africa, see Jore, "Les établissements français"; Boulle, "Eighteenth-Century French Policies toward Senegal"; Marie-Knight-Baylac, "Gorée au XVIIIe siècle"; and Johnson, *Wicked Flesh*, chap. 1.

78. On debates regarding the promise and perils of the "French Atlantic" as a geographical-historical concept, see the discussion in Marshall, *French Atlantic*, 1–8.

79. On slave trade in the French Caribbean, see Gisler, *L'esclavage aux Antilles françaises*; Rushforth, *Bonds of Alliance*; Dorigny and Gainot, *Atlas des esclavages*; and Cheney, *Cul de Sac*.

80. The classic account by Pierre Goubert in *Ancien Régime* gives the Atlantic colonies short shrift in their contribution to the French state and economy. Doyle's *Oxford Handbook of the Ancien Regime* includes one chapter on the Atlantic colonies by Silvia Marzagalli, in which she contends that Atlantic trade had very limited impact on the French economy. Clark's *Compass of Society* makes almost no mention of role played by the Atlantic colonies. Ladurie's *Ancien Regime* is an exception, including references to Canada, Louisiana, and Caribbean colonies that enriched the French economy.

81. Recent research in colonial trade promises to dramatically revise this long-standing neglect. Wimmler, *Sun King's Atlantic*; Heath, "Visualizing Colonial Trade." In his recently published *Death of the French Atlantic*, Forrest argues that "slavery and anti-slavery were not just the subject of abstract debate; they were burning issues that redirected their trade, threatened their investments, and left families scattered across the western hemisphere" (xvi).

82. Noted scholars of French libertine literature, including Joan DeJean, Michel Féher, Pierre St. Amand, Olivier Blanc, James Steintrager, and Catherine Cusset have ignored cosmopolitanism as a key theme. In early research of the genre, I relied on the canon of libertine literature edited by Trousson, *Romans libertins du XVIIIe siècle*.

83. Dayan, *Haiti, History, and the Gods*, 212–14; Garraway, *Libertine Colony*, 25.

84. Abbé Prévost, *Histoire du chevalier des Grieux et de Manon Lescaut* (1731); Crébillon fils, *Le Sopha* (1742); La Morlière, *Angola, histoire indienne* (1746); Jean-Henri Maubert de Gouvest, *Lettres iroquoises* (1781); Mirabeau, *Le libertin de qualité* (1783); Diderot, *Supplément au voyage de Bougainville* (1772), among many others. Even those novels that describe the sexual coming of age of individuals in a strictly circumscribed setting in a French convent, or within the city limits of Paris, articulate the sense that their behavior is not so uncommon, given the wide range of sexual customs around the world.

85. Hunt, "Global Financial Origins," 32–43.

86. On these promises and revolutionary reforms in family law, see Desan, *Family on Trial*.

1. Théophile de Viau, "To the King from Exile," 1619, in Saba, Oeuvres poétiques, 1:157. When this term is used to denigrate specific people, I have replaced it with the neologism s*v*ge. French and colonial authorities became attuned to the diverse linguistic, political, and cultural traditions among First Nations, but still employed the derogatory term "savages" ("sauvages" in French) when referring to Indigenous people in the aggregate. The ongoing legacy of colonial dispossession and genocide freights this term with a host of prejudices that legitimated the violence committed by European settlers and colonial states across the Americas. I avoid that term when possible and replace the "a" with an asterisk when essential to a direct quote. Throughout this text, then, readers will encounter the term "s*v*ge" to highlight the mechanisms by which this term has done violence in the history of Indigenous peoples. For more on research practices that disrupt these power dynamics, see Smith, "Decolonizing Methodologies."

2. On the court case and trial documents, see Lachèvre, *Le libertinage*. Lachèvre was partisan and relitigated the Viau case in light of Church-state struggles of the early twentieth century, intent on documenting the threat posed by religious dissent, as Aurélie ably documents in "Frédéric Lachèvre."

3. The Arrêt of Parlement specified the immediate arrest of "Théophile, Berthelot, Colletet, & Frenide, Authors of Sonnets of Verses containing impieties, blasphemies and abominations mentioned in the very pernicious book titled *Le Parnasse Satyrique*" (*Arrest de la Cour de Parlement*).

4. On the Viau trail, see DeJean, *Reinvention of Obscenity*, chap. 1; Saba, *Théophile de Viau*; Cavaillé, "Libérer le libertinage"; and Van Damme, *A l'épreuve libertine*.

5. Whether or not scholars perceive that Viau "won" or "lost" the trial depends a great deal on interpretation. Spink, *French Free Thought*, 44–45.

6. On the impact of the Viau case in French literature see Saba, *Théophile de Viau*, 216–17.

7. For an orientation to the social-political divisions within French Catholicism in this era, see Bergin's *Politics of Religion in Early Modern France*. Ultramontanes sought to increase Rome's direct authority, while Gallicans strived to protect and expand the French monarch's authority over the French Church.

8. Garasse, *La Doctrine curieuse*.

9. Lachèvre attributes more coherence to Garasse's polemical accusations than did the Jesuit himself (*Le libertinage*, 5:275–76).

10. Garasse, *Les Recherches des Recherches*, 681. *Huguenot* referred to a Calvinist, and a *Politique* was the term for a political pragmatist who advocated a strong monarchy guaranteeing religious tolerance and reconciliation as the antidote to civil war. In *Doctrine curieuse* Garasse elaborated his definition of *libertine*, linking it to sexual and gastronomic pleasures eschewed by pious Christians, both Huguenot and Catholic.

11. Garasse, *Doctrine curieuse*, 30–33.

12. Garasse, *Doctrine curieuse*, 36–37.

13. Garasse, *Doctrine curieuse*, 37.

14. On the broader context of early modern skepticism, see Popkin's essential study *History of Skepticism*, especially chap. 5, "The Libertins Érudits," on Théophile's larger intellectual circle. Pintard makes the link with religious skepticism in his classic study, *Le libertinage érudit*. But, from Pintard's perspective, Viau did not rank as an "erudite libertin" since his poetry incorporated themes of sexual license alongside theological skepticism. See Cavaillé's critique of this category, "Le 'libertinage érudit.'"

15. On legal lexicons in early modern France, see Olivier-Martin, *Histoire du droit français*. On the gulf between early modern legal theory and practice regarding Protestant civil status, see Chareyre, "Le roi, les protestants."

16. Stanwood, *Global Refuge*.

17. Bataillon, "L'Amiral"; Lestringant, "Philosopher's Breviary," 201. For context on Lescarbot's humanist colonialism, see Brazeau, *Writing a New France*, especially chap. 3, "Nos Ancêtres Les Américains." On Montchrétien's nationalist colonialism, see Wells, "Loathsome Neighbors and Noble Savages."

18. Zecher, "Marc Lescarbot Reads Jacques Cartier."

19. Wells, "Loathsome Neighbors and Noble Savages."

20. As translated by Jotham Parsons, "The Edict of Nantes, with Its Secret Articles and Brevets," in Goodbar, *Edict of Nantes*. Also available here: http://www.huguenot-museum-germany.com/huguenots/edicts/01-edict-nantes-1598-english.pdf (accessed August 30, 2022).

21. Article 1, Parsons, "Edict of Nantes."

22. Holt, *French Wars of Religion*, 186.

23. In English the best introductions to the limits of religious toleration in seventeenth-century France are provided by Bergin, *Politics of Religion in Early Modern France*; and Forrestal and Nelson, *Politics and Religion in Early Bourbon France*. This limited tolerance did not extend to Jews, who were prohibited residence or shelter in France by royal edict of April 23, 1615. Benbassa, *Jews of France*, 49–50.

24. This transition is ably documented in Parker, *La Rochelle and the French Monarchy*.

25. Moote, *Louis XIII, the Just*, 45–46.

26. Emphasizing overlapping territories and literary traditions between the two. See Alain Lanavère's insightful work on Viau's debt to ancient Roman poets and philosophers in "Théophile de Viau."

27. Wells, "Loathsome Neighbors and Noble Savages," 98.

28. Saba, Eustis, and Gaudiani, *La poésie française*, 216.

29. On Paul de Viau, see Garrison, "Paul de Viau."

30. Adam, *Théophile de Viau*.

31. Shoemaker, *Powerful Connections*, 127.

32. Sandberg's *Warrior Pursuits* provides great insight into the military leadership of the young duc de Montmorency, 82.

33. Fisher, *Champlain's Dream*, 603.

34. Montmorency's military leadership augmented French royal power against both Spanish forces and Huguenot rebels, but in 1632 he joined Louis XIII's brother Gaston d'Orléans in a revolt against Cardinal Richelieu's consolidation of power. Moote, *Louis XIII, the Just*, 224–25.

35. On the Duke of Montmorency's patronage of Théophile de Viau, see Shoemaker, *Powerful Connections*.

36. *Mercure François*, 1619, cited in Lachèvre, *Le Libertinage*, 1:31.

37. Saba, *Théophile de Viau*.

38. Petterson, *Poetry Proscribed*, 38.

39. Vanini had taken up residence in Languedoc and also enjoyed the protection of the Duke of Montmorency by 1616. Cavaillé, *Dis/simulations*.

40. Holt, *French Wars of Religion*, chap. 7. See also Kettering, "Political Pamphlets."

41. Théophile de Viau, "Au Roi sur son exil. Ode," in Saba, *Œuvres complètes*, 1:159–61.

42. Ably illuminated in the account of court politics provided by Kettering, *Power and Reputation*.

43. Viau, in Saba, *Œuvres complètes*, 1:159–61.

44. Wintroub's *Savage Mirror* provides analysis of a 1550 royal entry ceremony in Rouen that reenacted a battle between Tupinamba and Tobajaro for King Henri II's entertainment, emphasizing the commonalities articulated between the French and their American allies, the Tupinamba against the Portuguese allied with the Tobajaro. See also Duggan, "Epicurean Cannibalism"; and Melzer, *Colonizer or Colonized*, 91–121.

45. Berrong, "Nature and Function of the 'Sauvage,'" 213–17.

46. York, "Translating the New World," 293–308.

47. Léry, *Histoire d'un voyage*.

48. Montaigne, "On Cannibals," 228–41.

49. Abbéville, *Discours et congratulations*; Evreux, *Voyage dans le Nord*.

50. Saba suggests Viau's travels may have been more circumscribed (*Théophile de Viau*, 44–45).

51. Wintroub, *Savage Mirror*, 10–11.

52. Shoemaker, *Powerful Connections*, 127–35.

53. Adam Horsley details this convivial milieu in "Le Président libertin."

54. Including Guillaume Colletet and Gabriel Naudé, both Parisians of modest families who rose to great literary influence in the decades following Théophile's trial.

55. Horsley, "Le Président libertin."

56. Théophile de Viau, *Le Parnasse Satyrique*, in *Oeuvres*, 1620, 1621.

57. On the publishing politics in Théophile's court case, see Van Damme, *L'épreuve libertine*, chap. 5; and Rosellini, "La composition des *Oeuvres poétiques*," 231–29.

58. The novella *Première journée* was likely written in 1620, after Viau's return from exile. Riou, "Théophile de Viau et les paradoxes," in Peureux, *Lectures de Théophile de Viau*, 43–62.

59. Théophile de Viau, "Elégie," in Saba, *Œuvres complètes*, 2:33–40, 2:39.

60. Zim, "La nuit trouve enfin la clarté."

61. Shoemaker, *Powerful Connections*, 127–30.

62. "Requête de Théophile au Roi," in *Oeuvres poétiques*, February–March 1624. "Que j'enseignais la magie / Dedans les cabarets d'honneur" (284–94, 288, lines 119–20).

63. "Requête de Théophile au Roi," 288, lines 121–24. "Qu'on avait bandé les ressorts / De la noire et forte machine / Dont le souple et le vaste corps / Etend ses bras jusqu'à la Chine."

64. On Jesuit relations with the French monarchy during this period, see Nelson, *Jesuits and the Monarchy*; and Wright, *Divisions of French Catholicism*, 33–84.

65. "Requête de Théophile au Roi," 288, lines 125–30. "Qu'en France et parmi l'étranger, / Ils avaient de quoi se venger / Et de quoi forger une foudre / Dont le coup me serait fatal / En dût-il coûter plus de poudre / Qu'ils n'en perdirent à Vuital."

66. Rossellini and Caron, *Théophile de Viau*, 28.

67. Rosellini and Caron, *Théophile de Viau*, 28.

68. Cabrol, *Essai*, 75–80

69. Viau, "Sacrez murs du soleil où j'adorai Phillis," in *Oeuvres complétes*, 2:8: "Fossez larges et creux tous combles de murailles, / Spectacles de grayeur, de cris, de funerailles, / Fleuve par où le sang ne cesse de courir, / Charniers où les Corbeaux et loups vont tous repaistre, / Clairac pour une fois que vous m'avez fait naistre, / Hélas ! combien de fois me faictes vous mourir."

70. Kettering, *Power and Reputation*, 102–3.

71. Viau, *Les œuvres de Théophile*, 1:191.

72. Viau, *Les œuvres de Théophile*, 1:191.

73. Otto, *Fools Are Everywhere*.

74. Viau, *Les œuvres de Théophile*, 1:191.

75. Viau, "Au Roy Estreine," in *Les œuvres de Théophile*, 1:124.

76. Garasse's discursus of over one thousand pages targets Huguenots, Lutherans, Jews, and Zoroastrians alongside the indeterminate "libertines" as threats to political order. He inveighs against women reading sacred texts and generally articulates a hyperconservative, crusading Catholicism subordinate to Rome as the sole legitimate foundation for a government.

77. On this point, I extend the insights of Swann on monarchy and the politics of disgrace in *Exile, Imprisonment, or Death*.

78. Troyes, located east of Paris in the rich agricultural Champagne region, hosted several Church Councils from 800 to 1200. However, Troyes was deeply divided during the French Wars of Religion, notably in 1562, when the Bishop Caracciolo appealed to Theodore Beza, John Calvin, and the Evangelical community of Troyes for political support, as discussed by Roberts in *City in Conflict*. On religious-political alliances, see Leroy and Oddos, *La vie a Troyes*.

79. Viau, *Œuvres*, 20.

80. Viau, *Les œuvres de Théophile*, 1:138.

81. Clitiphon's name pays homage to an ancient Greek novel by Achilles Tatius and translated into English in 1597 by William Burton in *The Most Delectable and Pleasant History*.

82. Viau, "Première journée," in Saba, *Œuvres complètes*, 2:20.

83. Viau, "Première journée," 36.

84. Viau, "Première journée," 38.

85. Sadlier, *Brazil Imagined*, 31–36.

86. Abbéville, *Discours et congratulations*.

87. *Le parnasse des poètes satyriques* (1622), 1. "Sonnet de Sieur Théophile" : "J'ai sué trente jours, j'ay vomy de la colle / Jamais de si grands maux n'eurent tant de longueur."

88. "Je fais veu desormais de ne . . . tre qu'en cu" (1).

89. Garasse, *La Doctrine curieuse*, 782.

90. Horsley, "Strategies of Accusation and Self-Defense," 162.

91. Lachèvre, "Un mémoire inédit."

92. "[Théophile a dit qu']il n'a faict fayre ladite composition ny composé ledit sonnet et que au contraire ayant veu ledit livre entre les mains d'un libraire qui tient boutticque devant le Pallays et leu ledit sonnet, il deschira le feuillet où il estoit escript, pour raison de quoy il eut querelle contre le librayre" (22 March 1624). Quoted in Lachèvre, *Le libertinage*, 1:373.

93. *Arrest de la Cour de Parlement*.

94. Adam, *Théophile de Viau*, 159.

95. Viau had sought favor with the duc de Luynes, one of the young king's chief advisers in 1621, even penning pro-Luynes pamphlets in 1620, as Kettering notes in *Power and Reputation* (226–36). With the death of the duc de Luynes in 1621, Viau lost an important supporter in the royal court.

96. Horsley, "Strategies of Accusation and Self-Defence," 165–66.

97. Lachèvre, *Le libertinage*, 1:364–85.

98. For an orientation to the charge of sodomy in this case, and in early modern France more generally, see Dupas, "La sodomie," 4.

99. Memorably in Théophile Gautier's literary history, *Les grotesques* (Paris: Michel Lévy frères, 1873). This text offers an introduction to a dozen worthy poets of the seventeenth century. Gautier takes a possessive, almost familial, interest in avenging the reputation of his namesake.

100. Horsley, "Strategies of Accusation and Self-Defence," 164.

101. Joan DeJean refers to this instability between author and narrator as the "jeu de je" in *Reinvention of Obscenity*, chap. 1.

102. Garasse, *Doctrine curieuse*, 843.

103. Viau, "Première journée," in *Oeuvres complètes*, 1:30.

104. On the longer tradition of Chrisitan humanism in France, see the essays by Bedouelle and Farge in *Biblical Humanism and Scholasticism in the Age of Erasmus*, 117–42; 143–66.

105. Viau asserts this a century before the cosmopolitan argument presented in Picard and Bernard's *Cérémonies et coutumes religieuses de tous les peoples du monde* (1723–37), analyzed in Hunt and Jacobs, *Book That Changed Europe*.
106. Horsley, "Strategies of Accusation and Self-Defence," 168.
107. Horsley, "Strategies of Accusation and Self-Defence," 174.
108. As summarized by Van Damme, *A l'épreuve libertine*, 85–89.
109. Letter 4 in Viau, *Œuvres complètes*, 19. Cited in Horsley, "Strategies of Accusation and Self-Defence," 176.
110. Horsley, "Strategies of Accusation and Self-Defence," 157–77.
111. Garrisson, *History of Sixteenth-Century France*, 319–20.
112. Koot, *Empire at the Periphery*.

2. LOCATING THE LIBERTINES

1. On confessional divisions among European settlers in New France, see Choquette, *Frenchmen into Peasants*, chap. 5; and Zuidema, *French-Speaking Protestants in Canada*, especially Robert Larin's chapter, "French Monarchy," 13–28.
2. Choquette, "Colony of 'Native French Catholics'?"
3. Greer, *People of New France*, 3:45–46. See also Wenzel, "La procedure criminelle au Canada"; and, for the foundational study of legal system in colonial New France, see Lachance, *Crimes et criminels en Nouvelle-France*.
4. Van Ruymbeke and Sparks, *Memory and Identity*, 12.
5. Cowan details how Jesuit missionaries forged a distinctively Atlantic demonology in these decades, integrating Indigenous theologies with European demonology in "Jesuit Missionaries and Accomodationist Demons."
6. Below I briefly explain the terms used to identify the peoples discussed in this chapter: I attempt to use the most precise term to accurately represent an individual's linguistic, geographic, ethnic, and political identity, based on the historical record, even if that is not the preferred term at the time period or today. Therefore, when speaking of a group of settlers born in the Netherlands, England, Ireland, Germany, and France, I use "European," although they rarely used this aggregate term, preferring linguistic, regional, or religious identities. I use "French" to identify individuals born in France who resided in France or the French colonies of Canada, although the term was also used by their American-born children, signifying linguistic identity rather than geographic origin. I use "Canadian," which approximates the gendered, geolocated terms *canadien* and *canadienne*, used to identify individuals born in America to parents of European ancestry who remained subject to French colonial law. Such individuals typically called themselves *canadiens* or *américains*. Colonial law and custom distinguished between European-born and American-born people of European ancestry with implications for property, colonial office, and military service that changed over these centuries. I use "Indigenous" to refer to individuals born in the Americas who belonged to one of over six hundred different linguistic groups that comprise the

First Nations in northern North America. During these centuries, however, these individuals shared no sense of a common Indigenous identity; they identified themselves by families, languages and within political-cultural nations, including the Inuit, Huron-Wendats, Abénakis, Algonquins, Atikamekws, Mi'kmaqs, Kanyen'kehà:kas of the Haudenosaunee Confederacy (Mowhawks), Naskapis and Innus (Montagnais in French colonial records), Wolastoqiyiks (Malécites), and Nehiyawaks (Crees). When available in the historical record, I favor these specific identities. Depending on the time and place, individuals with one European parent and one Indigenous parent are sometimes identified as canadien, sometimes as Indigenous, and sometimes as métis (defined as a state-recognized Nation by the Constitution Act of 1982).

7. Trigger, *Children of Aataentsic*, 303.

8. Anderson, *Betrayal of Faith*, 75.

9. Codignola, "Competing Networks."

10. Kerstetter, *Inspiration and Innovation*, 51.

11. Poirier emphasizes the masculinist preferences of most Jesuit missionaries, causing them to ignore or belittle Indigenous women's political influence, in *Religion, Gender, and Kinship*, 164-70.

12. Although maintaining these relationships was no easy feat. Anderson narrates the Catholic education of a young Innu boy, baptized in Angers, France, in 1621 as Pierre Antoine Pastedechouan, and the cultural dislocation that he experienced as a result in *Betrayal of Faith*.

13. Kostroun and Vollendorf, *Women, Religion*.

14. Sagard-Theodat, *Histoire du Canada et voyages*, 26.

15. Le Jeune, *Brève relation*, 1632; Reuben Thwaites, ed. and trans., *Jesuit Relations and Allied Documents*, 5:48.

16. Choquette, "Colony of 'Native French Catholics'?," 255.

17. Wood, *Archipelago of Justice*, 13.

18. Cahall, *Sovereign Council of New France*, 22–23.

19. Wood, *Archipelago of Justice*, 6.

20. Règlements généraux de police faits par le Conseil souverain de Québec et Jacques Duchesneau, intendant de justice, police et finances de la Nouvelle France, en vertu d'une commission donnée par le Roi le 5 juin 1675 et enregistrée au Conseil le 16 septembre 1675, May 11, 1676, BANQ, TPI, S28, P1314.

21. McIntire, "Protestant Christians," 95–96.

22. Larin, *Brève histoire* criticizes the historiography that underestimates the Protestant influence in New France after Richelieu's edict of 1627.

23. The *Jesuit Relations* were propaganda—inaccurate and prone to exaggeration—and designed to raise funds to support future missions, as analyzed in Greer's *Jesuit Relations*. Still these reports provide invaluable testimony regarding missionaries' perceptions and early modern French colonial policies in the Americas.

24. Sagard-Theodat, *Histoire du Canada et voyages*, 330.

25. Sagard-Theodat, *Histoire du Canada et voyages*, 382–83.

26. Lalemant, *Relation*, 86.

27. Arrêt ordonnant que Monsieur L'Évêque de Québec sera informé des paroles impures contre l'honneur de Dieu, de la Sainte Vierge et des Saints proférées par le sieur Jacques du Mareuil, lieutenant réformé du détachement des troupes de la Marine, February 1, 1694, BANQ TPI, S28, P5586.

28. Van Ruymbeke and Mentzner, *Companion to the Huguenots*, 101–3.

29. McIntire, "Protestant Christians," 96; Règlements généraux de police faits par le Conseil souverain de Québec, May 11, 1676, BAnQ, TPI, S28, P1314.

30. Zuidema, ed., *French-Speaking Protestants in Canada*.

31. On the Indigenous and European populations of seventeenth-century Québec, see Labelle and Peace, *From Huronia to Wendakes*, introduction and chap. 1.

32. See the modern edition presented by Réal Ouellet: Lahontan [and Gueudeville], *Dialogues avec un sauvage*. On the central role that Lahontan's writings played in forging European ideologies of the "noble s*v*ge," see Harvey, "Noble Savage and the Savage Noble," 162.

33. Although the Wendat historian Georges Sioui finds it a remarkably "accurate picture of aboriginal American theology" in *For an Amerindian Autohistory*, 68.

34. Havard, *Great Peace of Montréal*.

35. In the English translation of Lahontan's *New Voyages*,13. This dialogue is republished in French using "Adario" as the Huron leader's name.

36. White, *Middle Ground*, 183.

37. Havard, *Great Peace of Montréal*, 214.

38. Lahontan and Gueudeville, *Dialogues*, 1.

39. Lahontan and Gueudeville, *Dialogues*, 3.

40. Lahontan and Gueudeville, *Dialogues*, 7.

41. Lahontan and Gueudeville, *Dialogues*, 8.

42. Lahontan and Gueudeville, *Dialogues*, 9–10.

43. Lahontan and Gueudeville, *Dialogues*, 10.

44. Lahontan and Gueudeville, *Dialogues*, 13.

45. Lahontan and Gueudeville, *Dialogues*, 16.

46. Lahontan and Gueudeville, *Dialogues*, 27.

47. Boisvert, "L'influence protestante," 31–51.

48. Boisvert, "L'influence protestante," 49.

49. Muthu, *Enlightenment against Empire*, 24.

50. Arrêt renouvelant les défenses faites aux domestiques de quitter le services de leurs maîtres, sous les peines portées par les arrêts antérieurs, June 2, 1673, BANQ Québec, TPI, S28, P827.

51. Arrêt, June 2, 1673.

52. Arrêt, June 2, 1673.

53. For several similar cases, see Craven, "Canada," 186.

54. Arrêt, June 2, 1673.

55. Jugement condemnant Renault Chollet dit Laliberté à la peine de carcan, à 100 sols d'amende, et à porter l'écriteau, pour s'être absenté du service de son maître, le sieur Saintour, October 30, 1673, BANQ Québec, TP1, S28, P861.

56. Procès entre Jean Quenet, marchand bourgeois, plaignant, et son domestique, Charles Bellon, accusé de désertion et libertinage, December 16–18, 1715, BANQ Montréal, TL4, S1, D1833.

57. Charbonneau et al., *First French Canadians*, 25–27.

58. Procès entre Jean-Baptiste Hervieux, l'aîné, maître arquebusier, demandeur, et Jacques Thibierge, maître arquebusier, défendeur, pour le remboursement de journées de salaire et le retour d'un apprenti, November 29–December 1, 1715. BANQ Montréal, TL4, S1, D1819.

59. Procès, November–December 1715, BANQ Montréal, TL4, S1, D1819.

60. Gossard, "Breaking a Child's Will," 239–59.

61. On detention by royal fiat (king's orders, *lettres de cachet*), see Graham, "Lettres de cachet," in Dewald, *Europe*, 4:491–92, as well as later chapters of this text.

62. Paul, *Exilés au nom du roi*, 39.

63. Procès criminel contre Louis Bonin, caporal de la compagnie de Lanaudière et soldat congédié; et Denis Lemoine dit Parisien, 14 ans, soldat de la compagnie de Lanaudière en garnison à Québec, logé à la caserne Dauphone, et complices, accusés de vol. February 17–August 6, 1752, BANQ Québec, TL5, D1667.

64. Paul, *Exilés au nom du roi*, 28–29.

65. Paul, *Exilés au nom du roi*, 37.

66. Paul, *Exilés au nom du roi*, 76–78.

67. Archives nationales du Canada (ANC), Fonds des colonies, Series E, dossiers personnels, microfilm F-830, vol. 197.

68. ANC, Fonds des colonies, Series E, dossiers personnels, microfilm F-830, vol. 197.

69. ANC, Fonds des colonies, Series E, dossiers personnels, microfilm F-830, vol. 197.

70. Maurepas to M. de Beauharnois, May 7, 1740, in *Report Concerning Canadian Archives*, 281.

71. Le Beau, *Avantures*, cited in Paul, *Exilés au nom du roi*, 95–97. For a reliable scholarly edition of this text, see Le Beau, *Aventures*.

72. Le Beau, *Aventures*, 76.

73. Le Beau, *Aventures*, 83n27.

74. Le Beau, *Aventures*, 83.

75. Paul, *Exilés au nom du roi*.

76. Paul, *Exilés au nom du roi*, 94–96.

77. Paul, *Exilés au nom du roi*, 140.

78. Lessard, "Les faux-sauniers."

79. A *minot* was roughly equivalent to a bushel in the UK.

80. Paul, *Exilés au nom du roi*, 123.

81. On alcohol in colonial North America, see Mancall, *Deadly Medicine*.

82. Le Jeune, *Brève relation*, 48.

83. Le Jeune, *Brève relation*, 48.

84. Campbell, "Making Sober Citizens."

85. Le Jeune, *Relation de ce qui s'est passé*, 143.

86. Arrêt portant défense à toutes personnes de quelque qualité et condition qu'elles soient, de traiter ou de donner, directement ou indirectement, aucunes boissons enivrantes aux Sauvages (Amérindiens), sous peine d'une amende de 300 libres pour la première offense et du fouet ou bannissement pour la récidive, BANQ Québec, TPI, S28, P16 (Sepember 28, 1663); TPI, S28, P97 (April 17, 1664); TPI, S28, P368 (April 29, 1665); TPI, S28, P436 (January 5, 1667); TPI, S28, P641 (June 26, 1669); TPI, S28, P1306 (March 23, 1676); TPI, S28, P2196 (March 7, 1679); RI, P30 (May 22, 1683); BANQ Trois Rivières TL3, SII, P2500 (January 12, 1699); BANQ Québec TPI, S28, P5467 (January 18, 1700); TPI, S28, P7631 (April 16, 1703); EI, SI, P28 (September 9, 1707); TPI, S28, P8789 (July 6, 1709); EI, SI, P1271 (May 26, 1721); EI, SI, P3644 (August 4, 1745); R2, SI, DI, P15 (November 10, 1764). Lachance's survey of French colonial law in Québec, *Crimes et criminels*, ignores cross-cultural alcohol regulations entirely. On the English applications and transformations of French colonial laws in Québec, see Fyson, *Magistrates, Police and People*, on liquor laws, see 18, 20, 22–23,32, 37–38, 97, 178, 180, 211, 214–16, 218–19, 246, 260, 268–69, 273–74, 277–79, 302, 329, 335–38, 343, 346–48, 350–51.

87. Arrêt, September 1663. BANQ Québec, TPI, S28, P16.

88. Arrêt, September 1663.

89. Ordonnance contre ceux qui donnent, traitent ou vendent des boissons enivrantes aux sauvages (Amérindiens, January 5, 1667, BANQ Québec, TPI, S28, P436).

90. Déclaration de Jeanne Bouchard, femme de Martin Foisy, fermier de monsieur de Bourjolym au sujet de ce qui a été rapporté contre elle en ce qui concerne la traite de boissons avec les sauvages, January 29, 1667, BANQ Trois Rivières, TL3, SII, P456.

91. Arrêt portant permission à tous les français, habitants de la Nouvelle-France, de traiter des boissons aux sauvages (Amérindiens), et enjoignant ces derniers à en user sobrement, en vertu du désir de Sa Majesté, "que les sauvages vivent avec ses naturels sujets dans un esprit de douceur et d'union pour formenter l'alliance promise enre eux et la cimenter de mieux en mieux par leur continuel commerce et fréquentation," November 10, 1668, BANQ Québec, TPI, S28, P616.

92. Arrêt, November 10, 1668.

93. Enregistrement de la remonstrance du Gouverneur, de la réponse de l'Intendant et de l'écrit du sieur de Villeray sur la requête de Josias Boisseau, concernant les coureurs des bois, May 2, 1681, BANQ Québec, TPI, S28, P2928.

94. Podruchny, *Making the Voyageur World*, 17.

95. Delâge, *Bitter Feast*, 136. See also Conrad, "Disorderly Drinking."

96. Remontrances du procureur général qu'en dépit de l'arrêt du 24 mai 1679, portant défense de porter des boissons aux habitations des sauvages (Amérindiens) et dans les bois, les coureurs des bois ne se sont nullement gênés de le faire; par ailleurs

quelques libertins, coureurs des bois, pour s'attirer les pelleteries des sauvages, ont fait courir de faux bruits parmi les dits sauvages, à savoir qu'à Québec, Trois-Rivières et Montréal les marchandises étaient empoisonnées et que la pest était dans ces lieux, ce qui a empêché les 8ta8as (Outaouais) de descendre cette année et ainsi mit la colonie en état de périr; attendu qu'il passe l'heure de la levée ordinaire, le Conseil a été remis à mercredi à faire droit sur la dite remontrance, August 18, 1681, BANQ Québec, TP1, s28, P2999.

97. Remontrances, August 18, 1681.

98. Savary de Bruslons, *Dictionnaire universel*, 1:1549. 1 Quintal = 100 kg., roughly.

99. Savary de Bruslons, *Dictionnaire universel*, 1:1550.

100. Lahontan, *Mémoires de l'Amérique septentrionale*, 684.

101. Permission à tous particuliers de Québec de vendre des boissons en gros et en detail, et ordre au sujet des enseignes à la porte des cabarets, sous la requête de Laurent Normandin, Jean Robitaille, Jean Gastin (Gatin), Jacqueline De L'eau, veuve de feu d'Aubigny et François Janny (Janis), tant pour eux que pour les autres aubergistes et cabaretiers de Québec, February 6, 1713, BANQ Québec, TP1, s28, P9245. This permission was granted based upon the request made by Laurent Normandin, Jean Robitaille, Jean Gastin, Jacqueline De L'Eau (the widow of Aubigny), and François Janny "for themselves and the other innkeepers and cabaret owners of Québec."

102. On the peace treaty of 1720, see Havard, *Great Peace of Montréal*.

103. Ordonnance de l'intendant Bégon qui fait défense à tous, bourgeois ou habitants, de vendre ou troquer de l'eau-de-vie ou autres boissons, avec les Sauvages (Amérindiens) à peine de cinq cents livres d'amende, May 26, 1721, BANQ Québec EI, SI, D7A, P1271.

104. Ordonnace de l'intendant Bégon qui condamne Jacques Héry dit Duplanty, tonnelier à Montréal, convaincu d'avoir traité des boissons enivrantes aux Sauvages (Amérindiens), en 500 livres d'amende applicable à l'Hôtel-Dieu de Montréal, June 30, 1722, BANQ Québec, EI, SI, D8, P1399.

105. Le Beau, *Avantures*, 139.

106. Ordonnance du gouverneur de Beauharnois et de l'intendant Hocquart qui fait défense à tous cabaretiers et autres de la ville de Québec de donner de l'eau-de-vie, guildive et autres boissons enivrantes aux Sauvages (Amérindiens) sous peine de punition corporelle, August 4, 1745, BANQ Québec, EI,SI, D33, P3664.

107. Procès contre Jacques Adam, journalier, habitant du faubourg St-Joseph, accuse de vente de boisson aux sauvages, June 15–July 27, 1756, BANQ Montréal, TL4,SI, D6101. See also the interrogation of Adam, September 5, 1756, BANQ Québec, TL5, D1860.

108. Trigger, *Children of Aataentsic*, 358–359.

109. Conrad, "Disorderly Drinking."

110. Ferland, *Bacchus en Canada*.

111. Jaenen, *Role of the Church*, 13–14; Wood, *Archipelago of Justice*, 13.

112. Sentence après interrogatoire de Nicolas Daucy de Saint-Michel, lieutenant d'une compagnie du détachement de la Marine, et de Jean Forgeron dit Larose et Jean Filiau dit Dubois, soldats des compagnies du dit détachement, tous accusés du crime de sodomie, November 12, 1691, BANQ Montréal, TP1, S28, P2514.

113. Procès entre Olivier Quesnel, armurier, plaignant, et Marie Matou, épouse de Chamaillard, et Catherine Thunay, veuve de Filiatraut, épouse de Deniau, accusées d'avoir débauché Raymond Quesnel, son fils mineur, August 8, 1716, BANQ Montréal, TL4, S1, D1995.

114. Procès, August 8, 1716.

115. Tutelle des enfants mineurs de feu Marie Madeleine Mathoux [Marie Madeleine Mathon Labrie] et feu Jean Haudecoeur, son premier époux, et de René Deniau, son second époux, July 31, 1699, BANQ Montréal, CC601, S1, SS1, D103. In this document, regarding guardianship of Jeanne and her siblings, she is identified as nine years old.

116. Procès, February 19, 1717, BANQ Montréal, TL4, S1, D1995.

3. A COLONIAL LIBERTY?

1. For decades French explorers used interchangeably the terms "Mississippi," an Indigenous name for the powerful river at the heart of this territory, and "Louisiana," an appellation that honored the French monarch who sponsored settlements along the Gulf of Mexico, King Louis XIV.

2. The Mississippi colony was funded by John Law's paper money and joint-stock initiative, leading to widespread speculation and an investment bubble of staggering consequence. French and English colonial rivalries in North America contributed to the Seven Years' War, fought in the Americas, Europe, and India. For more on these global connections, see Havard and Vidal, *Histoire de l'Amérique française*, 130–33, 613–70.

3. Colonial liberties—those "libertés des colonies"—became a keyword in the French press and foreign ministry in the 1770s, particularly referencing British North American settlers' revolt against the British Crown. See, for example, Beaumarchais, *Observations*, 14. This chapter adapts that political term to consider the gendered and racialized dynamics of sexual relationships between European settlers and Indigenous and enslaved peoples in the colonies. Evidence of interracial sex as de facto policy is addressed in Melzer, "France's Colonial History"; Sleeper-Smith's classic *Indian Women and French Men*; Spear, "They Need Wives," 41; and Garrigus, *Before Haiti*, 40.

4. "Mémoire du Roy pour servir d'instruction au S. de l'Epinay," 20 October 1716, Archives Nationales d'Outre Mer (ANOM), 4DFC/9.

5. French merchants dramatically expanded participation in the Atlantic slave trade after 1702, when the Treaty of Utrecht allowed Britain and France to sell enslaved Africans in Spain's American colonies, as evidenced in the data tabulated by the Slave Voyages database: https://www.slavevoyages.org/voyage/database#tables (accessed August 30, 2022).

6. See Røge's persuasive analysis of empire's impact on French economic and political theory, *Economistes and the Reinvention of Empire*. Heath adopts quantitative methods to document the economic and cultural impact of the early modern French empire in metropolitan commerce. See initial research reports on Heath's website: https://blogs.baruch.cuny.edu/elizabethheath/?page_id=36 (accessed August 30, 2022).

7. Stoler, *Race and the Education of Desire*, 7.

8. Van Ruymbeke, "Dominion of True Believers," 90.

9. Shoemaker, *Strange Likeness*, 129.

10. In *Africans in Colonial Louisiana*, Hall observes that Blackness did not connote "slave" in early New Orleans, nor was whiteness a mark of privilege (130). See also Johnson, *Wicked Flesh*; and White, *Voices of the Enslaved*.

11. In *The Anatomy of Blackness*, Curran also emphasizes the important role played by scientific institutions and epistemologies in this process.

12. Shoemaker, "How Indians Got to Be Red"; Shoemaker, *Strange Likeness*.

13. Milne, *Natchez Country*.

14. Milne, *Natchez Country*, 214.

15. Forbes, *Africans and Native Americans*.

16. On this conflict, see Aubert, "'To Establish One Law'"; and Vidal, "Caribbean Louisiana," in Vidal, *Louisiana*, 21–43, 125–46. See also Belmessous, "Assimilation and Racialism," 322–49.

17. Historians of the French in America have occasionally accepted colonial laws as forceful facts imposed by an absolutist state, rather than evaluating them as artifacts of the relationships negotiated between Versailles and the colonies, the officials, settlers, Native allies, and enemies. On methodologies to approach law as an artifact of social relationships, see Friedman, "Legal Culture as Social Development," 29–44.

18. DuVal, *Native Ground*. See also Morrissey's *Empire by Collaboration*; and Milne, *Natchez Country*.

19. Fine-grained studies of French colonial law continue to be produced; see, for example, Christie et al., *Voices in the Legal Archives*.

20. Spear, *Race, Sex, and Social Order*; Morrissey, *Empire by Collaboration*; White, *Wild Frenchmen and Frenchified Indians*; Rushforth, *Bonds of Alliance*; Johnson, *Wicked Flesh*; Aubert, "To Establish One Law," and Vidal, "Caribbean Louisiana," in Vidal, *Louisiana*, 125–46; Clark, *Strange History*.

21. On the French king's inability to enforce key terms of the law of slavery in colonial Saint-Domingue, see Ghachem, *Old Regime and the Haitian Revolution*; on colonial legal challenges to absolutism see Wood, *Archipelago of Justice*.

22. Rapport de Deux Soldats Canadiens [les frères Talon de la Compagnie de Feuquerolles] qui ont fait le voyage de Delasalle au Mississipi et en sont revenus en 1698, ANOM, 4DFC/9.

23. These terms shaped modern racisms and geopolitical power relations. They are also words that wound, and categories that threaten to divide parents from their children. The term "mulatto" compares the offspring of a Black-white union to a mule, the sterile offspring of an interspecies intercourse between a horse and a donkey. The implication of this term is to render sex across the color lines as unnatural and sterile. In *To Be Free and French*, Semley reminds us that the "idea of the 'mulatto' is a profound reflection of the anxieties and violence around race, sexuality, and babies born of black women's bodies in slave-holding societies" (8).

24. On racial taxonomies in New Spain, see Cope, *Limits of Racial Domination*.

25. Greer et al., *Rereading the Black Legend*, 1–26.

26. See Joutel, *Journal historique*. This propaganda was effectively evaluated by Maltby's *Black Legend in England*. Allyson Poska convincingly demonstrates in *Gendered Crossings* that many Spanish women—nuns, elites, servants, workers—did travel to the Americas thus undermining one of the key assumptions organizing this "Black Legend." Most Spanish ships' passenger manifests include 25 to 30 percent female Spanish travelers.

27. Rapport de Deux Soldats Canadiens, 1698, ANOM, 4DFC/9.

28. Indeed, these individuals dominated commerce and diplomacy into the era of the American war for independence, as evidenced by the life histories of Molly Brant mentioned in Taylor's *American Revolutions* or Alexander McGillivray profiled in DuVal's *Independence Lost* (24–34).

29. Deslandes, "Alors que nos garçons"; Hyde, *Born of Lakes and Plains*.

30. Englebert and Teasdale, *French and Indians*.

31. Joutel, *Journal historique*, 215.

32. On French responses to American tattooing customs, see Balvay, "Tattooing."

33. Delâge, "L'influence des Amérindiens," 51–59.

34. Joutel, cited in Havard, "Virilité et 'ensauvagement,'" 57–74.

35. Greer, *Jesuit Relations*, 149.

36. Spear, *Race, Sex and Social Order*, 18.

37. Spear, *Race, Sex and Social Order*, 26.

38. Belmessous, "Etre français en Nouvelle-France," 525.

39. Henri Roulleaux de la Vente, 1716, as cited in Morrissey, *Empire by Collaboration*, 99.

40. Spear, *Race, Sex and Social Order*, 34.

41. Spear, *Race, Sex and Social Order*, 34.

42. Belmessous, "Etre français," 27; Governor Vaudreuil and the intendant Jaques Raudot to the minister, November 11, 1709, in *Rapport de l'Archiviste*, 420.

43. On this point, see Aubert, "Blood of France."

44. See René Le Conte's "Germans in Louisiana."

45. Jean-Baptiste du Bois Duclos, Sieur de Montigny to Pontchartrain, December 25, 1715, MPAFD, 2:205.

46. As cited in White, *Wild Frenchmen and Frenchified Indians*, 27–8.

47. Spear, *Race, Sex and Social Order*, 49.

48. Duclos to Pontchartrain, December 25, 1715.

49. Duclos to Pontchartrain, December 25, 1715.

50. Duclos to Pontchartrain, December 25, 1715.

51. Mémoire du Roy pour server d'instruction au S. de l'Epinay, October 20, 1716, ANOM, 4DFC/9.

52. On the colonial policy discussions that contributed to the Mississippi myth, see Berthiaume, "Louisiana, or the Shadow Cast."

53. On the imperial rivalries mobilized to control Peru, a fascination leveraged by renowned novelist of the eighteenth century, Françoise de Graffigny, in *Lettres d'une péruvienne* (1747), among others; see Mapp's *Elusive West*, 115–37.

54. Havard and Vidal, *L'histoire de l'Amérique française*, 230. See also the discussion of Saucier family, who relocated from Québec to Louisiana with the Iberville expedition of 1699 for migration motives and consequences in Belsom and de Ville, "Sauciers in 1726."

55. Hall, *Africans in Colonial Louisiana*, 5.

56. A declaration of the king published on January 8, 1719, condemned vagabonds and those without employment to transportation to the colonies to serve as indentured servants. The law read: "The Kings our predecessors have always paid singular attention to distancing Vagabonds, who have no other occupation than their libertinage, their procurement, and who often survive by the crimes and debauchery they commit." In *Recueil d'edits*, 48.

57. See Paul, *Exilés au nom du roi* on forced migrations to Louisiana and Québec.

58. Mémoire du Roy pour server d'instruction au S. de l'Epinay, 1717, ANOM, 4DFC/9. These funds were to be dedicated to building and manning ships to improve overseas communications, tranporting goods, and building civil and domestic structures within the American colony.

59. Havard and Vidal, *Histoire de l'Amérique française*, 130.

60. On the Law system, see John Law's *Observations*. Thiers revisited the subject in a text translated as *The Mississippi Bubble*. Murphy's *John Law* explores the Mississippi bubble of 1720 within the broader context of Law's writings and policies. Coleman considers Law as an economic theologian in "Spirit of Speculation."

61. Velde, "Government Equity and Money," 50.

62. Sayre, "Introduction," in *Memoir of Lieutenant Dumont*, 22.

63. Douthwaite, "Bad Economic Memories."

64. White, *Wild Frenchmen and Frenchified Indians*, 50–53.

65. "Déclaration concernant les condemnés aux galères, bannis, et vagabonds," January 8, 1719, Bibiliothèque Nationale de France, F 21308 (106). This decree initially included only the region of Paris and was extended to all of France in March 1719.

66. Buvat, *Journal de la Régence*, 438–9, cited in Hardy, "Transportation of Convicts," 213.

67. Usner, *Indians, Settlers, and Slaves*, 50.

68. Gravier, *Relation du voyage*, xlvii.

69. Caillot, *Company Man*, 35–40. He describes a cruel flirtation with Marguerite Le Coq, ending in a joke marriage in which all the ship's passengers, including several other "young ladies," took part, at Mlle Le Coq's expense. Erin Greenwald notes that, upon arrival in New Orleans, Marguerite Le Coq married a Québecois resident of the city, Joseph Larchevesque, in 1729. He died in 1732.

70. For example, the will of Marie Grissot, a midwife in Fort St. Louis, dated December 22, 1718, left the city's priests a sum valued at 144 livres and distributed another 200 livres among residents of Louisiana and France, including a small donation to a Rochefort orphanage. The bulk of her estate went to her eleven-year-old nephew, André Penigaud. See the Louisiana Digital Library, http://www .louisianadigitallibrary.org/cdm/compoundobject/collection/p15140coll60/id/15 /rec/3 (accessed August 30, 2022). Grissot had arrived in 1704 and developed extensive family connections in Louisiana when her relative Marie Catherine Prévost married André Penigaud (also s Penigault) in 1706. Penigaud was one of the King's carpenters who led the extensive efforts at shipbuilding on the Gulf Coast. For more on this family, see Higginbotham, *Old Mobile*, 376–78.

71. Cited by Greenwald, *Company Man*, 98, n211.

72. *Journal d'un voyage à la Louisiane*, 255–56.

73. Many thanks to Heidi Keller-Lapp, who shared chapters from her forthcoming book addressing the Ursuline convents in Québec, New Orleans, Martinique and Pondichery. See also Keller-Lapp, "Les *Guerrières de Dieu*."

74. Aubert, "Kinship, Blood," 181.

75. Dawdy, *Building the Devil's Empire*, 18–19.

76. Particularly as studied by Stoler, *Carnal Knowledge and Imperial Power*; and Hinderaker and Mancall, *At the Edge of Empire*.

77. In the British American context, see Block, *Rape and Sexual Power*.

78. "Harangue de lIllinois à la Compagnie des Indes," in *Recueil de Fevret de Fontette* 77r & v, Bibliothèque de l'Arsenal, MS 3724. MS B Tome II, 1719–27.

79. LaChance, "Free and Slave Populations," 220. LaChance estimates 4,600 Blacks, 2,500 whites, and 200 enslaved Indians. On the early population of the colony, see also Hall, *Africans in Colonial Louisiana*, 5–8.

80. DuVal, *Native Ground*, 60. Contemporary French observers estimated the indigenous population at fewer than 20,000, a dramatic fall from Spanish estimates a century earlier which estimated it at 300,000 to 1 million people.

81. White, *Voices of the Enslaved*.

82. Aubert, "Blood of France."

83. Aubert, "To Establish One Law."

84. *Edit du Roi*, article 9.

85. Geggus, *Before Haiti*, 56.

86. Palmer, *Intimate Bonds*.

87. Henochsberg, *Public Debt and Slavery*, 9.

88. King, *Blue Coat or Powdered Wig.*

89. Ghachem, *Old Regime and the Haitian Revolution*, 210.

90. Aubert, "To Establish One Law"; Vidal, "Caribbean Louisiana."

91. On this interaction, see Rushforth, *Bonds of Alliance.*

92. Rushforth, *Bonds of Alliance*, 355.

93. Aubert, "To Establish One Law," 41.

94. Aubert, "To Establish One Law," 23.

95. Spear, *Race, Sex and Social Order*, 64.

96. Vidal, "Caribbean Louisiana."

97. Prévost, *Manon Lescaut*, 6.

98. Prévost, *Manon Lescaut*, 28.

99. Prévost, *Manon Lescaut*, 26.

100. Prévost, *Manon Lescaut*, 28.

101. On narrative deception in this novella, Gossman's "Prévost's Manon" remains invaluable. On gender, see Miller's *Gender and Genre*; and Yalom, *How the French Invented Love*, chap. 4. For the money angle, see Douthwaite, "Bad Economic Memories"; and Knoop, "Over the Edge." In "Manon Lescaut's Countrymen," Moogk uses the novel as an entry into a discussion of French migration to Louisiana during the eighteenth century, but does not provide analysis of the Prévost text itself.

102. Prévost, *Manon Lescaut*, 145.

103. Joutel, *Journal historique*, x.

104. Prévost, *Manon Lescaut*, 160.

105. Prévost, *Manon Lescaut*, 163.

106. Prévost, *Manon Lescaut*, 163.

107. Prévost, *Manon Lescaut*, 165.

108. Prévost, *Manon Lescaut*, 166.

109. Prévost, *Manon Lescaut*, 167.

110. Prévost, *Manon Lescaut*, 169.

111. Prévost, *Manon Lescaut*, 168.

112. The governor's authority to match newly arrived women with settlers was widely recognized in colonial Louisiana despite the fact that such practices directly contravened canon law on marriage established with the Council of Trent, emphasizing that marriage required the consent of both parties. See Sperling, "Marriage at the Time."

113. Prévost, *Manon Lescaut*, 176.

114. Caillot, *Company Man.*

115. Caillot, *Company Man*, 111.

116. He was the Canadian-born son of Philippe de Rigaud Vaudreuil, governor-general of New France, mentioned above. Like his father and many administrators born in the Atlantic colonies, Pierre de Rigaud was a committed segregationist.

117. Pierre de la Rue (Bourges, France) to Vaudreuil (New Orleans), April 20, 1750 (fo. 210), Huntington Library, Vaudreuil Papers, Mss LO, Box 5.

118. De la Rue to Vaudreuil, April 20, 1750.

119. Ordre du commandement pour Mr. de Macarty major du pais des Illinois. (fo. 325), Huntington Library, Vaudreuil Papers, Mss LO, Box 6, August 8, 1751.

120. Ordre du commandement pour Mr. de Macarty.

121. Ordre du commandement pour Mr. de Macarty.

122. Ordre du commandement pour Mr. de Macarty.

123. Vidal, "Caribbean Louisiana," 140–41.

124. Rushforth, *Bonds of Alliance*.

125. Hall, *Africans in Colonial Louisiana*, 10.

4. LIBERTINES AND S*V*GES

1. Voltaire to Rousseau, August 30, 1755, http://tecfa.unige.ch/proj/rousseau/voltaire.htm (accessed August 31, 2022).

2. Voltaire to Rousseau, August 30, 1755.

3. Keal, *European Conquest*, 75–77.

4. Although the simple could be exceptionally expensive. See Martin's analysis of the marketing of natural cosmetics in *Selling Beauty*, chap. 6.

5. On Voltaire's diet, see Spary, *Eating the Enlightenment*, 370–75.

6. Voltaire to Rousseau, August 30, 1755.

7. On American conflicts as catalysts of the Seven Years' War, see Baugh, *Global Seven Years' War*, chap. 1.

8. Voltaire to Rousseau, August 30, 1755.

9. On the role played by Grotius and Vattel in forging the foundations of international law, see O'Connell, *Power and Purpose of International Law*, chap. 1. On the role of the Seven Years' War on Vattel's political theory, see Stapelbroek, "Vattel and the Seven Years' War."

10. Dziembowski interrogates the contours of this debate in *Un nouveau patriotisme français*, especially 256–62.

11. Cited in Osman, *Citizen Soldiers*, 77.

12. As evidenced in accounts by the French commander, Louis-Joseph de Montcalm; his successor, François Gaston, the Chevalier de Lévis; and Louis Antoine de Bougainville, who served as a captain under Montcalm. Summarized by Osman, *Citizen Soldiers*, 33–54; and Crouch, *Nobility Lost*, 65–94.

13. Such assessments were common throughout ministerial correspondence from Québec and Louisiana, even during periods of violence. These texts formed the evidentiary backbone for Parkman's analysis of the differences between French and British colonial styles in the seven-volume opus *France and England in North America*, which positioned French assimilation against British segregation, obscuring how much French colonial policy relied on segregation by the eighteenth century, documented in chapter 3 in this volume.

14. Eccles, "French Imperial Policy."

15. For example, Eccles, *French in North America*. On the enduring impact of French settlers in North America, see Blaufarb's *Bonapartists in the Borderlands*.

16. As evidenced in the ill-conceived invasions of Mexico in 1838 and 1861. Shawcross, *France, Mexico and Informal Empire*.

17. Voltaire, *Candide* (1758), chap. 23.

18. Dziembowski, *La Guerre de Sept Ans*, chap. 5.

19. Dziembowski, *La Guerre de Sept Ans*, chap. 5; Newbigging, "Propaganda, Political Discourse."

20. Shovlin, "Selling American Empire."

21. Crouch, *Nobility Lost*.

22. Crouch, *Nobility Lost*. In the wake of the loss of French America, the Canadian "citizen militia" provided the model for the reformed French military, as Osman argues in *Citizen Soldiers*, 54.

23. Nester, *Great Frontier War*, 230–32.

24. For an overview of these debates over Indigenous dress and customs within early America, see Deloria, *Playing Indian*; and Silver, *Our Savage Neighbors*.

25. Of course, identical qualities of so-called American warfare are still celebrated in elementary and high school textbooks on the American revolutionaries' success in tackling the British empire. Popular historical magazines still laud Francis Marion and his Partisans, which employed guerilla tactics and strategic use of terrain to compensate for lack of adequate supplies in their struggle against British forces in the American Revolution; for example, see Crawford, "Swamp Fox."

26. Crouch, *Nobility Lost*, 170–76.

27. Amply documented in Dechêne's *People, State, and War*.

28. Lépine, "Les stratégies militaires," 147.

29. See Osman's "Pride, Prejudice, and Prestige"; Forrest and Hagemann, *War, Demobilization, and Memory*; and Blaufarb, *French Army*.

30. Crouch, *Nobility Lost*, 127.

31. Summarized in the polemical Champigny, *Louisiane ensanglantée*.

32. For analysis of the perceived abandonment of French Acadiens and long-term imperial political consequences, see Hodson, *Acadien Diaspora*, 84–87.

33. See, for example, the breathless coverage of the French campaign in the siege of Forts George and Oswego in the *Mercure de France*, January 1, 1756, 221–38; and Lennox, *Homelands and Empires*.

34. Fréron, *Journal étranger*, 120.

35. With new editions published in 1703, 1728, 1735, and 1744.

36. This two-volume epistolary novel has been dismissed in French letters as merely derivative of Montesquieu's *Lettres persanes* (1721), which inspired so many exoticist imitators. See Green, "Montesquieu the Novelist." The summary statement on eighteenth-century French literature (1977) finds the novel interesting primarily for the blatant materialism of its morals. This neglects the wide circulation and influence that "Igli" wielded in French political theory. In addition to the multiple

editions of the work that testify to a certain audience, the book appears in the published library catalogs of leading men of letters and political policy, including M. le Maréchal Duc de Luxembourg, the Marquis de Courtanvaux, and Chrétien Guillaume Lamoignon-Malesherbes. See *Lettres iroquoises*.

37. So conclude the editors Griffin and Grinde of *Apocalypse de Chiokoyhikoy*, 219. These connections are further plumbed in Paschoud's *Le monde amérindien au miroir*.

38. Parmenter, "After the Mourning Wars," 39–76.

39. On the central role of the Iroquois in early American treaty negotiations by the eighteenth century, see Richter, *Trade, Land, Power*, 88–94.

40. Correspondence, governor-general of Louisiana, Huntington Library, Vaudreuil Papers, Mss LO, Boxes 1–8, 1742–54. The first concern expressed in the Louisiana governor-general's correspondence was to shore up those Indigenous alliances that would repel English traders establishing settlements in French North American territories.

41. Vaudreuil to Maurepas, November 4, 1745, as cited in Trudel, "Jumonville Affair," 353.

42. Some of the maps created for French forces can be viewed today at the Library of Congress, the Huntington Library, and the John Carter Brown Library, to name just a few. See, for example, Robert de Vaugondy's "Partie de l'Amérique Septentrionale qui comprend le cours de l'Ohio, la Nlle Angleterre, la Nlle. York, le New Jersey, la Pensylvanie, le Maryland la Virginie, la Caroline," from the *Atlas universel* (1757). See Petto, *When France Was King*.

43. This site, located near the present-day town of Farmington in southwestern Pennsylvania, is in the western foothills of the Appalachian Mountains, long perceived as the "natural" limit of the English colony.

44. For centuries Indigenous American accounts were characterized as as too "partisan." Explicitly excluded from Trudel's analysis ("Jumonville Affair") is how competing accounts and historiographies speak to the divergent national purposes which this affair served. Recent historians of the event have reconsidered and esteem the Indigenous American testimonies of the attack as essential evidence. Baugh, *Global Seven Years' War*, 62–64, 84–85.

45. Calloway, *Scratch of a Pen*, 100.

46. Contrecoeur to Duquensne, June 2, 1754, in *Précis des faits*, 107.

47. Cited in Contrecoeur to Duquesne, June 2, 1754, *Précis des faits*, 107ff.

48. White, *Middle Ground*.

49. Gordon, *Citizens without Sovereignty*.

50. Vattel, *Le droit des gens*, 2:343.

51. Vattel, *Le droit des gens*, 1:343–44.

52. Schumann and Schweitzer, *Seven Years' War*, 19.

53. Cited in Abbé de la Porte's *L'Observateur littéraire*, February 20, 1759, 1:262–63.

54. Bell, "Jumonville's Death," 39.

55. Bell, "Canon Wars," 724.

56. *L'Observateur littéraire*, 263.

57. *L'Observateur littéraire*, 265.

58. *L'Observateur littéraire*, 266.

59. Lesuire, *Les sauvages de l'Europe*, 58.

60. Lesuire, *Les sauvages de l'Europe*, 58.

61. Entry of May 27, 1754, in Jackson, *Diaries of George Washington*, 1748–65, 1:195, as cited in Anderson, *Crucible of War*, 53.

62. Anderson, *Crucible of War*, 58–59.

63. *Feuille hebdomadaire*, 60.

64. Montcalm, *Journal*, 53. This likely refers to cloudberries, grown in the marshes of the Québec colony. The berries were used to make a liqueur, Chicoutai, that is still in production.

65. Montcalm, *Journal*, 59. On the smallpox inoculation debates, see Rusnock, "Biopolitics," 59–66.

66. On this event, see Steele, *Betrayals*; and Hughes, *Siege of Fort William Henry*.

67. Nester, *French and Indian War*, 233–47. Nester identifies Indigenous warriors from the Abenaki, Algonquin, Fox, Huron, Iowa, Kickapoo, Iroquois, Menominee, Miami, Mi'kmaq, Mississauga, Nipissing, Ojibwe, Onondaga, Ottawa, Potawatomi, Sac, Atikamekw, and Winnebago nations.

68. Ewing, "Eyewitness Account," 308.

69. Quoted in the contemporary British report conserved at the Huntington Library. See Steele, "Suppressed Official British Report," 344.

70. Ewing, "Eyewitness Account," 313.

71. Steele, "Suppressed Official British Report," 347.

72. Lozier, "Lever des chevelures," 513–42.

73. Steele, "Suppressed Official British Report," 349.

74. Ewing, "Eyewitness Account," 313.

75. Steele, "Suppressed Official British Report," 351.

76. On the archaeological record of the fort and this battle, see Starbuck, *Legacy of Fort William Henry*.

77. Ewing, "Eyewitness Account," 314.

78. Ewing, "Eyewitness Account," 314.

79. Ewing, "Eyewitness Account," 315.

80. Steele, "Suppressed Official British Report," 351.

81. Anderson, *Crucible of War*, 196–98.

82. On this historiography, see Steele, *Betrayals*.

83. Cooper, *Last of the Mohicans*, 9.

84. Cooper, *Last of the Mohicans*, 210.

85. Cooper, *Last of the Mohicans*, 154.

86. Cooper, *Last of the Mohicans*, 182.

87. This scandal is treated in Bosher, "French Government's Motives." Bosher surveys the ample evidence created by a rigorous process of judicial inquiry.

88. Dziembowski, *La guerre de sept ans*, chap. 14.

89. On the personal politics surrounding King Louis XV's consort, Madame de Pompadour, see Lever, *Madame de Pompadour*. On the comparison of Pompadour to Angélique Péan, see Frégault's analysis in *La guerre de la conquête*.

90. *Jugement rendu souverainement*, 8.

91. *Mémoire pour Michel-Jean-Hugues Péan*.

92. Rémillard, "Renaud d'Avène des Méloizes," http://www.biographi.ca/fr/bio/renaud _d_avene_des_meloizes_angelique_4f.html (accessed August 30, 2022).

93. Parkman, *France and England*, 305–16, 511–23.

94. Coté, *Joseph-Michel Cadet*.

95. Voltaire to Cramer, ca. December 20, 1763, http://www.e-enlightenment.com .ezproxy.lib.ou.edu/item/voltfrvf110114a1c/?srch_type=letters&all=affaire+du +canada&lang_main=all&r=10 (accessed August 30, 2022).

96. *Jugement rendu souverainement*, 78.

97. Gay, *Voltaire's Politics*, 296–97n56.

98. Moufle d'Angerville, *Vie privée de Louis XVI*, 4 :71.

99. Crouch, *Nobility Lost*, 32–34.

100. Bib. Arsenal, Bastille Mss, 12,200 fo. 69.

101. Bosher, "French Government's Motives," 73.

102. Bosher, "French Government's Motives," 78.

103. Vattel, *Le droit des gens*, 2:329.

104. Le Trosne, *Discours sur l'état*.

105. On this point, see the conclusion penned by Sylvie Dépatie and Catherine Desbarats to Dechêne's magisterial *People, State, and War*, 327–31.

106. Swann, *Politics and the Parlement*, 197.

5. A RACE OF LIBERTINES

1. Garrioch, *Making of Revolutionary Paris*, 99.

2. Reglemens que le Roy veut être executés dans l'Hôpital Général de Paris pour la correction des enfants de famille et pour la punition des femmes débauchées qui y seront renfermez," and "Mémoire sur les mendicants, vagabonds et gens sans aveu, BNF, Joly de Fleury 1309, fols. 6 and 8.

3. *Recueil des déclarations*, III.

4. Argenson, *Rapports inédits*, 105.

5. Argenson, *Rapports inédits*, 318. Regarding a young libertine's detention in 1711 at the request of his mother, Dame Dussy, d'Argenson observed that the young man was released and reimprisoned for "his disorder and his indocility," and that violence, brutality mixed with fury, characterized his behavior.

6. Argenson, *Rapports inédits*. On May 29, 1705, d'Argenson made inquiries to determine if the so-called Marquis de Puget was actually a member of the nobility,

but determined that the individual spent all his time with *procureurs* (the term could mean prosecutors or pimps, depending on context) or women of ill repute, leading Argenson to determine that he "is a libertine and a cheater" (172). On May 8, 1707: Claude Leleu contracted a marriage against his father's wishes, and the police pursued him as a libertin. But, as the son was thirty-five years old, and the marriage had been contracted according to church and state law, d'Argenson determined it was better to leave him his liberty and allow the family quarrel to play out in the courts (204–5).

7. Garrioch examines some of these fraying seams in *Huguenots of Paris*.

8. Farge and Foucault, *Le désordre des familles*; Emmanuelli, "Ordres du roi."

9. Choudhury, "Carnal Quietism." The Jesuit thesis proved compelling and resulted in the French king banning the Jesuit order from France in 1764. See Delon, *Encyclopedia of the Enlightenment*, 1:742.

10. MacMahon, *Enemies of the Enlightenment*.

11. On the philosophes as cultural targets, see McMahon, *Enemies of the Enlightenment*.

12. On the regency's reputation for libertinage, see Wynn, "Libertinage." On the crapulous example set by King Louis XV and the political consequences, see Swann, *Politics and the Parlement*, 45–47.

13. Réguis served as the parish priest of the Barret-de-Bas parish in the diocese of Gap in 1765. In 1770 he moved to the cathedral Notre-Dame du Hamel in Lisieux. *Recueil des travaux*, 12–13.

14. On Abbé Réguis and Catholic conservative critiques of early capitalism, see Roche, *History of Everyday Things*, 205.

15. On the luxury debates and global commerce, see Shovlin, *Political Economy of Virtue*; and Kwass, *Contraband*.

16. Dziembowski, *Guerre de Sept Ans*, chap. 5; Newbigging, "Propaganda, Political Discourse," 101–10.

17. In *There Are No Slaves in France*, Peabody illuminates one of these debates regarding the Edict of October 1716, which regulated the conditions by which enslaved people could enter the French kingdom (16–18). See also the contributions in Christie, Gauvreau, and Gerber, *Voices in the Legal Archives*.

18. Caraccioli's *Le livre à la mode*.

19. Diderot, *Oeuvres*, 1:262–64.

20. On Greuze's innovation in founding "a distinct genre, the painting of sentiment," see Barker, *Greuze and the Painting of Sentiment*, 3.

21. Diderot, *Oeuvres*, 1:263–64.

22. Benabou, *La prostitution*, 35.

23. Based on decades of observations of charges of insult brought before the Paris commissaires and provincial intendants in Provence, Ile-de-France, and Languedoc. See also Farge, *Fragile Lives*, on insult and police charges (114–22).

24. Quétel asserts in his study of the lettres de cachet in eighteenth-century Caen that, "in the semantic universe of the lettres de cachet, *libertinage* very precisely

signifies sexual debauchery, and the feminine form of the word *libertine* is practically a synonym for occasional prostitute" (*De Par le Roi*, 140). In Paris this was true for women. But, regarding men's behavior, *libertine* connoted exclusively sexual transgressions only by the 1770s.

25. Benabou, *La prostitution*, 35–36.

26. As noted in Farge and Foucault's analysis of the petitions conserved at the Bastille prison archives in *Le désordre des familles*.

27. On the absorption of canon law into French law, see Lange, "Droit canon et droit français."

28. Benabou, *La prostitution*, 22–23; *Code de l'hôpital-général*, 51–2.

29. Benabou, *La prostitution*, 24–25.

30. Such laws stood in contrast to community expectations: in *Sex in an Old Regime City*, Hardwick's research highlights how community leaders involved young men as well as women in developing responses to youth sexuality and pregnancy outside of marriage (20–22).

31. On sexual innuendo and women in the guilds, see Lanza, *From Wives to Widows*, 180.

32. Hardwick traces several such cases in *Sex in an Old Regime City* (59–61, 124–25, 148). I am grateful to Prof. Hardwick for sharing archival photographs of several of cases conserved in the Archives départementales du Rhône et de la métropole de Lyon (ADR, 1657–1787), in which young women registered legal complaints against the fathers of their children who had refused to marry them. ADR BP, February 6, 1657; BP3541, February 16, 1685, and January 16, 1673; BP3549, July 3, 1731; BP3573 March 19, 1787.

33. Emmanuelli, "Ordres du roi." The archives for the intendant of Provence conserved 1287 detention orders for the period 1745–19. Of these 81.9 percent were requested by the family. Ninety-nine cases identified libertinage as the motivation for requesting these orders from the king, with *inconduite* (76), prostitution (17), *dérèglements et la débauche* (13), concubinage (12), adultery (5), and rape (2), 374. Quétel notes that or 732 king's orders emanating from the intendant based in Caen, libertinage accounts for 23 percent of orders requested for men, and 50 percent of orders requested to detain women (*De Par le Roi*, 132).

34. On the rule of law in early modern Europe, see Breen, "Law, Society, and the State."

35. Richer, *Essai*, 68–70. This anecdote relates that a French soldier, arrested in Spain for eating meat on a Friday, was sent back in chains to Nantes for judgment when the ship was seized by Algerian pirates, and the French soldier took the opportunity to work with his captors. Richer credits this anonymous French soldier with devising the plan for the Ottoman siege of La Goulette, present-day Tunis, in 1574.

36. Richer, *Essai*, 68–69.

37. English travelers to France would have disputed Richer's assessment that the French flouted Catholic dietary laws. Tobias Smollett wrote in particularly disparaging terms of the impossibility of locating meat to eat during his travels in France (*Travels through France and Italy*, 109).

38. On the renaissance dispute over the French Church, see Nicholls, "Gallican Liberties and the Catholic League"; and Parsons, *Church in the Republic*. On the religious debates that shaped French law and legal institutions, see Van Kley, *Religious Origins*.

39. Davis, *Defining Culinary Authority*, 98–105.

40. Benabou, *La prostitution*, 21–25.

41. Benabou, *La prostitution*; Kushner, *Erotic Exchanges*.

42. Deniel-Ternant, *Ecclésiastiques en débauche*, 3.

43. *Mémoires de la Bastille*, 191.

44. Extensive scholarship emphasizes the overlap between these institutions, meaning that violent criminals were incarcerated alongside mentally ill, impoverished, and political prisoners. See Foucault's influential *Discipline and Punish*; and Ranum, *Paris in an Age*, 278, 320–24.

45. But only temporarily. In *Empire and Underworld*, Spieler documents how the South American outpost of French Guyana emerged as the tropical detention destination in the years after the 1789 Revolution.

46. Sade was accused of poisoning girls with candies adulterated with cantharides in Marseille in 1772 in a predatory scheme to sexually assault and torture them. The judges of the Parlement of Aix found both Sade and his valet guilty of poisoning and sodomy, and both men were executed in effigy after they fled France for Italy. Sade returned clandestinely that year and lived sequestered on the family estate of Lacoste. Then, in 1774, the City of Lyon began an investigation of Sade for the violent assault of several children employed as servants in the household. Sade's family requested his confinement in 1777; he remained in the Chateau de Vincennes prison for the following six years, transferred to the Bastille prison, then finally was committed to the asylum at Charenton. He was released in 1789 under the revolutionary government's amnesty for all prisoners detained on king's orders. Sade was arrested again in 1801 as a pornographer and detained in the Charenton hospital with inmates suffering from mental illness, notably directing theatrical performances of the inmates. Quétel, *De Par le Roi*. On cantharides and the Marseilles Affair, see Lever, *Sade*, 202–3; On the family's use of lettres de cachet to shield Sade from public trials for his crimes, see Bongie, *Sade*, 100, 114–16, 125, 141, 147, 190, 217, and 233.

47. On high-profile detentions, see Desnoireterres, *Grimod de la Reynière et son groupe*, 139–50. See also Chaussinand-Nogaret, *Mirabeau*.

48. On the monarch's authority to order detention, see Chassaigne, *Les lettres de cachet*; Funck-Brentano, *Les lettres de cachet à Paris*; and Fling, "Mirabeau."

49. Cohen, "Savoir pragmatique," 6.

50. Cohen, "Savoir pragmatique," 8–9.

51. Archives civiles, Police: Ordres du roi. Correspondance et enquêtes, Series C in the Archives de la Bouche du Rhône (hereafter ADBR).

52. Intendants were appointed by the King, in posts created after 1640 to centralize the royal state. Hamscher, *Royal Financial Administration*, 254–55.

53. ADBR, Series C, boxes 4118–4166. See box 4117 for correspondence between the intendant of Provence and the royal secretary of state for the Maison du roi, 1765–1789.

54. Emmanuelli, "Ordres du roi." Detention sites requested by families: most of the Provençal fortresses are represented here, as are the region's monasteries and convents, and municipal refuges. Families requested that their errant member be sent to the Chateau d'If, the island fortress in the Marseille harbor 23.2 percent of the time. The fortress on the Ile Ste Marguerite in the Cannes harbor was chosen 15 percent of the time.

55. Strayer, *Lettres de Cachet*, chap. 1.

56. Quétel, *De Par le Roi*, 132.

57. Quétel, *De Par le Roi*, 132–38.

58. Malesherbes to Intendant Senac de Meilhan, August 12, 1775; circular letter from Baron de Breteuil to all intendants, October 25, 1784, ADBR, C 4117.

59. Strayer, *Lettres de Cachet*, 145–46.

60. Emmanuelli, "Ordres du roi," 370–71.

61. Les minutes du commissaire de police, Louis Henri Auret de la Grave, August 29, 1764, Archives Nationales (AN), Y/15961.

62. Les minutes du commissaire de police, Louis Henri Auret de la Grave, August 29, 1764.

63. Les minutes du commissaire de police, Louis Henri Auret de la Grave, August 29, 1764.

64. Les minutes du commissaire de police, Louis Henri Auret de la Grave, August 4, 1765, AN, Y/15963.

65. Les minutes du commissaire de police, Louis Henri Auret de la Grave, August 4, 1765.

66. Les minutes du commissaire de police, Louis Henri Auret de la Grave, August 4, 1765.

67. Les minutes du commissaire de police, Louis Henri Auret de la Grave, December 24, 1765, AN, Y/15963.

68. Les minutes du commissaire de police, Louis Henri Auret de la Grave, December 24, 1765.

69. Les minutes du commissaire de police, Jacques Dupuy, August 12, 1778, AN, Y/12797.

70. Les minutes du commissaire de police, Jacques Dupuy, August 13, 1778, AN, Y/12797.

71. Les minutes du commissaire de police, Jacques Dupuy, August 13, 1778.

72. Archives civiles, Police: Ordres du roi, Correspondance et enquêtes, September 1778, ADBR, C/4121, Bailly dossier.

73. Archives civiles, Police: Ordres du roi, Correspondance et enquêtes, September 22, 1778, ADBR, C/4121, Bailly dossier.

74. Archives civiles. Police: Ordres du roi, Correspondance et enquêtes, December 8, 1778, ADBR, C/4121, Bailly dossier.

75. Les minutes du commissaire de police, Louis Henri Auret de la Grave, August 18–19, 1763, AN, Y/15960/B.

76. Contemporaries testify to the widespread reliance on Church-sponsored orphanages in the eighteenth century. Indeed, all five of the children conceived by Jean-Jacques Rousseau and his partner, Thérèse Levasseur, were quickly deposited at the Hopital des Enfants Trouvés in the Faubourg Saint-Jacques neighborhood of Paris. Rousseau observed that "this arrangement seemed to me so good, so sensible, so legitimate that, if I did not boast of it openly, this was solely out of consideration for their mother" (*Confessions*, 348).

77. Les minutes du commissaire de police, Louis Henri Auret de la Grave, August 19, 1763, AN, Y/15960/B.

78. Les minutes du commissaire de police, Louis Henri Auret de la Grave, October 19, 1764, AN, Y/15961.

79. The *Almanach royal* includes a notice of M. Gaignant, prosecutor at the Grand Conseil since 1737, living on the rue des grands Augustins (201).

80. Les minutes du commissaire de police, October 19 1764.

81. Les minutes du commissaire de police, Jacques Dupuy, January 10, 1778, 9 p.m., AN, Y/12796.

82. Les minutes du commissaire de police, Jacques Dupuy, January 10, 1778, 9 p.m.

83. Archives civiles, Police: Ordres du roi, Correspondance et enquêtes, ADBR, C/4121.

84. Bagnoly dossier, Archives civiles, Police: Ordres du roi, Correspondance et enquêtes, ADBR, C/4121.

85. Les minutes du commissaire de police, Jacques Dupuy, February 3, 1778, 9 a.m., AN, Y/12796.

86. Les minutes du commissaire de police, Jacques Dupuy, February 3, 1778, 9 a.m.

87. Les minutes du commissaire de police, Jacques Dupuy, February 3, 1778, 9 a.m.

88. Phillips, "Women and Family Breakdown."

89. Farge, *Un ruban et des larmes*. It is a case of unusual length and detail, in which a Parisian husband details hi wife's adultery in a public accusation rare in the historical record.

90. Les minutes du commissaire de police, Jean Baptiste Dorival, December 18, 1774, AN, Y/12469.

91. Musset, *Le régime des biens*.

92. Kushner, "Adultery and the Ideal."

93. Les minutes du commissaire de police, Jacques Dupuy, January 8, 1779, AN, Y/12799.

94. Les minutes du commissaire de police, Jacques Dupuy, January 24, 1779, AN, Y/12799.

95. Minutes du Grand Criminel, Dossiers de procès jugés à l'éxtraordinaire, July 1779 AN, Y/10400 A & B. The case was thrown out on July 28, 1779.

96. Minutes du Grand Criminel, Dossiers de procès jugés à l'éxtraordinaire, July 1779.

97. Farge, *Un ruban et des larmes*, 77.

98. Farge, *Un ruban et des larmes*, 77.

98. The memoir of Elisabeth Vigée-Lebrun, *Souvenirs*, provides rich anecdotal evidence of this world. See also the evidence and analysis provided in Berlanstein's *Daughters of Eve*.

100. Kushner, *Erotic Exchanges*; Shovlin, *Political Economy of Virtue*.

101. Les minutes du commissaire de police, Jacques Dupuy, June 6, 1778, AN, Y/12797.

102. In *Sex in an Old Regime City*, Hardwick documents how communities policed young men's sexuality (109).

103. Les minutes du commissaire de police, Jacques Dupuy, January 12, 1778, AN, Y/12796.

104. Les minutes du commissaire de police, Jacques Dupuy, November 20, 1778, AN, Y/12798.

105. Desan and Merrick, *Family, Gender and Law*.

106. Bajolet dossier, Archives civiles, Police: Ordres du roi, Correspondance et enquêtes, ADBR, C/4121.

107. Les minutes du commissaire de police, Jacques Dupuy, January 25, 1779. AN, Y/12799.

108. Les minutes du commissaire de police, Jacques Dupuy, January 25, 1779.

109. Carra, *Mémoires historiques*, II.

110. Vigarello, *Histoire du viol*.

111. Les minutes du commissaire de police, Jacques Dupuy, August 3, 1778, 3 p.m., AN, Y/12797.

112. Caraccioli, *Dictionnaire critique*, 1:369.

113. See passages in Rousseau, *Emile*, excerpted in Bell and Offen, *Women, the Family, and Freedom*, 1:43–49. See also Hageman, "Woman's Reputation."

114. *Code ou Nouveau règlement*, xiv; [Restif de la Bretonne,] *Le Pornographe*.

115. Le Fébure, *Traitement gratuit*.

116. Benabou, *La prostitution*, 26–27

117. Benabou, *La prostitution*, 26–27.

118. Farge and Foucault address familial strategies to preserve honor in *Le desordre des familles*, 203–8.

119. Kushner, *Erotic Exchanges*, 91.

120. Vattel, *Le droit des gens*, 1:123.

121. Miller, *Feudalism, Venality, and Revolution*.

1. Les minutes du commissaire de police, Louis Henri Auret de la Grave, August 3, 1778, 3 p.m., AN, Y/15959.
2. Les minutes du commissaire de police, Louis Henri Auret de la Grave, December 8, 1762, AN Y/15959.
3. Gossard, "Breaking a Child's Will."
4. I encountered the Royer case while researching the Parisian culinary guilds; see Davis, *Defining Culinary Authority*, 199n77.
5. Petition dated January 26, 1764, Les minutes du commissaire de police, Louis Henri Auret de la Grave, 1763, AN, Y/15959.
6. Farge and Foucault, *Le désordre des familles*.
7. Peabody, *There Are No Slaves*; Wood, *Archipelago of Justice*.
8. Monographs that survey the French empire typically conclude in 1763: for example, Banks, *Chasing Empire across the Sea*; and Royot, *Divided Loyalties*.
9. See Dubois, *Colony of Citizens*; Godechot, *France and the Atlantic Revolution*.
10. Godefoy, *Kourou and the Struggle*.
11. Choiseul to Froger de l'Eguille, naval commander at Rochefort, December 26, 1763, Service Historique de la Défense (SHD), Rochefort, 1E 174 (MI 87).
12. Dawdy's *Building the Devil's Empire* addresses Franco-American resistance to Spanish officials who attempted to enstate treaty-established authority over Louisiana in 1763–64. Similar resistance to English authorities simmered throughout Québec in the 1760s, according to Fyson, *Magistrates, Police and People*.
13. Garrigus, *Before Haiti*; Dubois, *Colony of Citizens*.
14. *Ordonnance concernant les jeunes gens*.
15. 6 April 1764, Archives départementales du Calvados, C/314, quoted in Quétel, *De Par le Roy*, 139.
16. Paul, *Exilés au nom du roi*.
17. Raymond, *On the Eve of Conquest*.
18. Letter cited in Vallée, *Avantures*, 122n5.
19. Choiseul to Froger de l'Eguille, July 1, 1764, SHD, Rochefort, 1E 174 (MI 87), no. 41.
20. Barbotin, *La Désirade*.
21. Schaeffer, *Marquis de Sade*, 168.
22. Mirabeau, *Oeuvres de Mirabeau*; Fling, "Mirabeau"; Desnoireterres, *Grimod de la Reynière*; Strayer, *Lettres de Cachet and Social Control*.
23. Choiseul to Froger de l'Eguille, July 31, 1763, SHD, Rochefort, 1E 174 (MI 87).
24. Choiseul to Froger de l'Eguille, July 22, 1763, received August 3, 1763, SHD, Rochefort, 1E 174 (MI 87).
25. Aubert, *Dictionnaire de la noblesse*, 12:701.
26. Turmeau de la Morandière, *Appel aux étrangers*, 75; Turmeau de la Morandière, *Representations*.
27. Turmeau de la Morandière, *Représentations*, v–vi.

28. See Kushner's analysis of Turmeau de la Morandière in *Erotic Exchanges*, 80, 138.

29. Turmeau de la Morandière, *Représentations*, 8–10.

30. Turmeau de la Morandiere, *Appel des etrangers*, ix–x.

31. Turmeau de la Morandière, *Appel des etrangers*, xii.

32. See the important recent intervention in the discussion of the physiocrats provided in Charbit, "Political Failure."

33. Sauvy, "Lesser Known French Demographers."

34. Fish, "Population Trends in France."

35. Turmeau de la Morandière, *Appel des etrangers*, xxi.

36. Choiseul to Froger de l'Eguille, SHD, Rochefort, IE 174 (MI 87), no. 415.

37. Choiseul to Froger de l'Eguille, SHD, Rochefort, IE 174 (MI 87), no. 175.

38. Turmeau, *Appel des étrangers*, 142.

39. Turmeau, *Appel des étrangers*, 118.

40. Fougère, *Des indésirables à la Désirade*.

41. Archives Départementales de Calvados (AD-C), C 314. See Chatel, *Inventaire des Archives Départementales*, 95.

42. Strayer, *Lettres de Cachet and Social Control*, 31–38.

43. Les minutes du commissaire de police, Louis Henri Auret de la Grave, 1763, AN, Y/15959.

44. Froger de l'Eguille to Choiseul, February 27, 1765, AN, Séries Colonies B/121/2.

45. Entry register for the hospital of the marine, 1764–65, SHD, Rochefort, 2FI 59.

46. Choiseul to Froger de l'Eguille, March 26, 1765, AN, Colonies B/121/2.

47. Villejouin to Choiseul, August 3, 1763, AN, Colonies C10/D/2.

48. Choiseul to Froger de l'Eguille, October 11, 1763, SHD, Rochefort, IE 174 (MI 87), no. 387.

49. Choiseul to Froger de l'Eguille, December 29, 1763, SHD, Rochefort, IE 174 (MI 87), no. 605.

50. Choiseul to Froger de l'Eguille, January 16, 1764, SHD, Rochefort, IE 175 (MI 88), no. 737.

51. Fougère, *Des indésirables à la Désirade*, 87.

52. Choiseul to Froger de l'Eguille, January 16, 1764.

53. Villejouin to Choiseul, November 12, 1763, AN, Colonies C/10D/2.

54. Villejouin to Choiseul, November 13, 1763, AN, Colonies C/10D/2.

55. Fougère, *Des indésirables à la Désirade*, 92–3.

56. *Gentleman's Magazine*, 509.

57. *Gentleman's Magazine*, 509.

58. *Gentleman's Magazine*, 509.

59. Baudry to Choisuel, September 22, 1765, ANOM, Col. E 19.

60. Letter dated July 1765, ANOM, C/10/D2.

61. Villejouin to Choiseul, July 1765, ANOM, C/10/D2.

62. Villejouin to Choiseul, July 1765.

63. Jean Dubucq to Choiseul, August 1765, ANOM C/10/D2.

64. Jean Baptiste Alliot to Choiseul, July 1765, ANOM, C/10/D2.

65. Tyler Stovall thoughtfully interrogates this dynamic in *White Freedom*; see especially chap. 3.

66. Fougère, *Des indésirables à la Désirade*, 105–6.

67. *Report Concerning Canadian Archives*, 1:395.

68. Petition to the Duke of Praslin, minister and secretary of state and the Department of Colonies, March 1770, ANOM, Col E 91, ark:/61561/up424khfflw (accessed August 5, 2021). The Corbeau family of watchmakers in Douai requested colonial detention for young Louis, who was "given to all genres of libertinage, who cannot conduct himself without dishonoring them and dishonoring himself, in seeking to keep himself in his libertine and lazy life by these illicit paths, typical pitfalls of incorrigible libertines."

69. ANOM, Col. E 102, ark:/61561/up424olnmjr (accessed August 5, 2021). In 1772, the Curty family asked the King to arrest Nicolas Curty, a wool worker, and consign him to the depot for colonial troop recruits on the Ile de Ré, "to prevent the unhappy results of his libertinage." In a letter dated June 26, 1772, the secretary of state for war, the Marquis de Monteynard, instructed his subordinates to determine whether or not the young man "was of the size and the constitution proper to serve, and that his parents have consigned the necessary money to furnish the costs of his subsistence during the trip."

70. Lalanne to Versailles, February 2, 1788, AN, C/10/D/2. Letter signed by Lalanne identifying those *gens de couleur* belonging to the king who had been relocated to Désirade: seven men, ten women.

71. Des Essarts, *Choix de nouvelles causes célèbres*, 3:358–416.

72. *L'esprit des journaux*, 184.

73. *L'esprit des journaux*, 185.

74. Des Essarts, *Choix de nouvelles causes célèbres*, 3 :386–87.

75. *Esprit des journaux*, 190.

76. *Esprit des journaux*, 196.

77. Cited in Quétel, *De Par le Roy*, 139.

78. Petit et al., *Histoire des galères*.

79. Spieler, *Empire and Underworld*.

80. *Gazette de commerce*, 546.

81. *Gazette de commerce*, 546.

82. *Gazette de commerce*, 546.

83. *Gazette de commerce*, 546.

84. *Gazette de commerce*, 546.

7. RACIALIZING LIBERTINES

1. Indigenous Taino islanders, decimated by violence and disease during European invasions of Hispaniola, had called this land "Ayiti," meaning "mountainous." European colonists brought thousands of enslaved Americans and Africans there

throughout the sixteenth and seventeenth centuries, before dramatically expanding the African slave trade in the eighteenth century (Geggus, "Naming of Haiti"; Eddins, "First Ayitian Revolution," *Age of Revolutions*). Enslaved people maintained the collective memories of resistance to Europeans and attributed Taino names and identities to the men and women who took up arms in the revolutionary era to destroy systems of slavery and imperial administrations across the Atlantic.

2. Garraway provides powerful analysis of French-language literature regarding Saint-Domingue in *Libertine Colony*.

3. A process narrated by Garrigus in *Before Haiti*.

4. The historian François Blancpain notes the Spanish did not approve the division of Hispaniola until 1777 (*Haïti et la République domincaine*; see also Sepinwall, *Haitian History*, 22).

5. With the 1660 treaty of Basse-Terre, the governor of Martinique dispossessed the Carib residents of Martinique, as Wilson notes ("Surviving European Conquest").

6. Tertre admits that, among early settlers, there were some "atheists and several libertines" who made fortunes in the islands only to return to France where they "exhausted all their earnings in the ports and harbors of France with debaucheries and scandals that brought shame on the islands and their inhabitants" (*Histoire générale des isles*, 466–67). And the municipal authorities termed maroons "libertines" in the "Arrêt du Conseil de St. Christophe," January 12, 1682, in "Projet de règlement," May 20, 1682, fol. 3. On enslaved runaways, or marronnage in the colony, see Eddins, "Runaways, Repertoires, and Repression." On the relationship between the French law of slavery in the Code Noir and the maroon communities in Saint-Domingue, see Fick, *Making of Haiti*, 53–54.

7. Wimmler addresses the economic and political policies that built French colonial Saint-Domingue in *Sun King's Atlantic*, chap. 2.

8. Garraway, *Libertine Colony*, 25.

9. Rushforth, "Gaoulet Uprising of 1710."

10. Aubert, "Blood of France," 442–43.

11. Peabody, *There Are No Slaves*, 32.

12. On this point, I follow the analysis developed by Ghachem, *Old Regime and the Haitian Revolution*, 47–55.

13. Rawley with Behrendt, *Transatlantic Slave Trade*, 58–9.

14. Ghachem addresses the anxieties and assumptions written into the French laws governing colonial slavery, or the Code Noir (*Old Regime and the Haitian Revolution*; see 29–76). On the process preceding the publication of the Code Noir, see Palmer, "Origins and Authors."

15. Palmer, "Origins and Authors."

16. *Code Noir*, 1. On the impact of the Code Noir on European Jewish subjects, see Arbell, "Jewish Settlements"; and, on Jewish residents of Saint-Domingue, see Garrigus, "New Christians/'New Whites.'"

17. *Code Noir*, article 6.

18. The law of slavery did not articulate racial categories until the 1724 Code Noir applied to the Louisiana colony. See Aubert, "To Establish One Law."

19. Garrigus, "New Christians, New Whites," 317.

20. *Code Noir*, article 9.

21. *Code Noir*, article 9.

22. Taber notes that the provision, though rarely used, became one tool employed by families to avoid the "freedom tax" imposed in 1761 ("Mystery of Marie-Rose").

23. Perceptively analyzed by Beik, *Absolutism and Society*.

24. *Code Noir*, article 57.

25. Ghachem, *Old Regime and the Haitian Revolution*, 122–23.

26. Ghachem, *Old Regime and the Haitian Revolution*, 210.

27. Zvi Loker, "Jewish Communities in Saint-Domingue."

28. Labat, *Nouveau voyage*, 1:36–37. The term *mulâtre* in French, roughly equivalent to the Spanish and Portuguese *mulato* and English "mulatto," speaks to increasingly specific racial categories, and relies on a specious comparison of "interracial" human and equine reproduction. The cross-breeding of horses and donkeys results in mules, a sterile offspring with qualities of both parents. The term "mulatto" is both pejorative and an unreliable indicator of an individual's parentage.

29. Aubert, "Blood of France,.."

30. Labat, *Nouveau voyage*, 1:32.

31. Herbal abortifacients played a significant role in limiting enslaved women's childbearing. See Weaver, *Medical Revolutionaries*; and Schiebinger, "Agnatology and Exotic Abortifacients," 323, 326–30.

32. Labat, *Nouveau voyage*, 1:32–33.

33. Labat, *Nouveau voyage*, 1:33.

34. Under these circumstances, all sexual relationships between free and enslaved people took on a coerced quality, as Morgan explains in *Laboring Women*, chap. 2; see also Block, "Sexual Coercion in America."

35. Garrigus, *Before Haiti*.

36. Noted by Stoler as a core concept in modern European empires in southeast Asia as well in *Carnal Knowledge and Imperial Power*.

37. As argued by Morgan, *Laboring Women*. See also Fuentes, *Dispossessed Lives*, 8–12, regarding eighteenth-century Barbados; Berry, *Price for Their Pound of Flesh*, 11, in the early United States; and Turner, *Contested Bodies*.

38. ANOM, COL C8 A 17 F 361, August 30, 1710.

39. ANOM, COL C8 B 9, No. 61, December 1727.

40. ANOM, COL C8 B 9, No. 61, December 1727.

41. *Code Noir*, article 6.

42. Correspondence, December 21, 1727, ANOM, COL C8 B 9, No. 60.

43. Correspondence, December 22, 1727, ANOM, COL C8 B 9, No. 60.

44. Garrigus, *Before Haiti*, 51–82.

45. Particularly notable in the work of the kingdom's leading natural historian, Georges-Louis Leclerc, Count of Buffon, *Natural History*. See also Curran, *Anatomy of Blackness*.

46. These debates form the heart of Garrigus's *Before Haiti*.

47. Exemplified in the anxious sociolegal commentary offered by Médéric Louis Elie Moreau de Saint-Méry, discussed below. Many multiracial subjects went on to illustrious careers in the military and the arts. Gallaher's *General Alexandre Dumas* details the biography of Thomas-Alexandre Dumas, the son of a French nobleman and an enslaved woman, raised in Jérémie, Saint-Domingue who went on to serve as a general in the Revolutionary army (12–13). His son Alexandre Dumas penned some of the most popular novels of the nineteenth century, including *The Count of Monte Cristo* (1844–46), *The Three Musketeers* (1844), and *The Man in the Iron Mask* (1847). Joseph Boulogne, the Chevalier de Saint-Georges, a champion fencer and musician who also served in the revolutionary army as *chef de brigade*, was the son of the French governor of Guadeloupe and an enslaved woman. Banat, *Chevalier de Saint-Georges*, 5–6.

48. Gerber, *Bastards*, 184–92.

49. Trouillot, "Motion in the System."

50. Indeed, this characterization seems to have been part of the process by which race laws took shape in the aftermath of the Seven Years' War. See Garrigus, *Before Haiti*, 51–82.

51. Gerber, *Bastards*.

52. Painstakingly analyzed by Julien Raimond at the time; see Raimond, *Observations*.

53. Rogers and King, "Housekeepers, Merchants, Rentières," 396.

54. Palmer, *Intimate Bonds*.

55. Palmer, *Intimate Bonds*, 16.

56. Palmer, *Intimate Bonds*, 136.

57. Burnard and Garrigus, *Plantation Machine*, chap. 4.

58. Scott, *The Common Wind*, 42–43.

59. Garrigus, *Before Haiti*, 163–64.

60. Peabody, *There Are No Slaves*, 106–20.

61. Palmer, *Intimate Bonds*, 139.

62. Palmer, *Intimate Bonds*, 139.

63. On the broader context for French and French colonial port towns, see Brandon, Frykman, and Røge, *Free and Unfree Labor*, 1–18.

64. In addition to works cited above, see Pruitt, "'Opposition of the Law.'"

65. Palmer, *Intimate Bonds*, 147.

66. Cited in Palmer, *Intimate Bonds*, 148.

67. Frostin, *Les révoltes blanches*, 307.

68. Palmer, *Intimate Bonds*, 147–48; Gordon-Reed, *Hemingses of Monticello*, 347–49.

69. Ghachem, *Old Regime and the Haitian Revolution*, 93.

70. Ghachem, *Old Regime and the Haitian Revolution*, 94.

71. Ghachem, *Old Regime and the Haitian Revolution*, 95.

72. Ghachem, *Old Regime and the Haitian Revolution*, 95.

73. *Archives de la Bastille*, 450.

74. *Ordonnance portant creation d'un corps*, 3.

75. Garrigus, *Before Haiti*, 122.

76. Frostin, *Les révoltes blanches*, 297.

77. The white colonial militia included those free men whose fathers were white, and whose mothers were one-quarter African. Another militia was to unite free men of color with French metropolitan soldiers.

78. St. Méry, *Loix et constitutions*, vol. 4, AN Col, C9 A, rec 125.

79. Burnard and Garrigus, *Plantation Machine*, 184.

80. Durand de Distroff, August 4, 1767. Cited in Frostin, *Les révoltes blanches*, 297.

81. Tacky's Revolt in 1761 in Jamaica and the Berbice Rebellion of 1763–64 constituted the most important instances of anticolonial movements incorporating antislavery ideologies. See Brown, *Tacky's Revolt*; and Kars, *Blood on the River*.

82. Garrigus, *Before Haiti*, 95–99.

83. Funck-Brentano, *Les lettres de cachet*, 380.

84. Funck-Brentano, *Les lettres de cachet*, 380.

85. *Mémoires de la Bastille*, 3:258.

86. Gerber, "Bastardy, Race, and Law," 579.

87. Gerber, "Bastardy, Race, and Law," 598.

88. Gerber, "Bastardy, Race, and Law," 598.

89. Palmer, *Intimate Bonds*, 143.

90. Peabody, *There Are No Slaves*, 121–34.

91. Petit, *Traité sur le gouvernement*, 1:111. Cited in Frostin, *Les révoltes blanches*, 307.

92. Petit, *Dissertations sur le droit public*, 464.

93. King, *Blue Coat or Powdered Wig*, 197.

94. King, *Blue Coat or Powdered Wig*, 181.

95. Garrigus, *Before Haiti*, 195–226.

96. Ably summarized in Fabella's chapter "Empire Founded on Libertinage."

97. Moreau de St. Méry, *Description*, 1:33.

98. Moreau de St. Méry, *Déscription*, 1:49.

99. Henochsberg, *Public Debt and Slavery*, 9.

100. Cormack, "Revolution and Free-Colored Equality,"

8. ARISTOCRATS AND LIBERTINES

1. Beaumarchais, *La folle journée*, 3. On the performance of this play in Paris and across the French empire, see Clay, *Stagestruck*, 229.

2. *The Barber of Seville*, written in 1773, was first performed in 1775 by the actors of the Comédie-Française. See David Coward's translation of Beaumarchais, *Figaro Trilogy*.

3. Beaumarchais, *La folle journée*, xviii.

4. Beaumarchais, *La folle journée*, xlvi.

5. In *Paulin de Barral.* Salamand identifies Barral as one of the likely models for the Vicomte de Valmont, the fictional archetypal libertine of Pierre Choderlos de Laclos's novel *Dangerous Liaisons* (1782).

6. These rumors and innuendo regarding the prior king found a wide audience, particularly in Bachaumont's *Mémoires secrets.*

7. We might attribute it to the initial ideological waves initiated by the Atlantic Revolutions in both Holland and British North America, supported by the French Crown, that transformed public and legal opinions regarding political rights and duties. For two very different perspectives on the "Atlantic Revolutions" and the consequences in 1780s France, see Palmer, *Age of the Democratic Revolution*; and Polasky, *Revolutions without Borders.*

8. On Beaumarchais's career, see Lever's monumental biography, *Pierre-Augustin Caron de Beaumarchais.*

9. Beaumarchais, *La folle journée*, 199.

10. Burwick, *History of Romantic Literature*, 85.

11. According to analysis provided by the Comédie-Française Registers: https://www .cfregisters.org/en/the-data/basic-tool (accessed September 2, 2022).

12. Museum Fine Arts Boston: Gallerie des modes—Suzanne from Figaro; chapeaux Figaro, St. Domingue. See also Gallerie des modes et costumes français, https:// gallica.bnf.fr/ark:/12148/btv1b53192297k/f17.item (accessed September 2, 2022).

13. Maza, "Diamond Necklace Affair."

14. Beaumarchais, *La folle journée*, xiii–xv.

15. Hunter, *New Comedy of Greece and Rome.*

16. Beaumarchais, *La folle journée*, 165.

17. Beaumarchais, *La folle journée*, 165.

18. See Smith, *French Nobility*, 12–13, 177.

19. Boureau, *Lord's First Night.*

20. See Voltaire, *Le Droit du Seigneur*, performed January 18, 1762, by the Comédiens françois as "L'Ecueil du sage."

21. Maza, *Servants and Masters*, 90–93.

22. Every year hundreds of women reported such assaults before the Paris commissaires, and to the provincial and municipal authorities across France and the American colonies. Vigarello, *Histoire du viol.*

23. Marraud, *La noblesse de Paris.*

24. Schaeffer, *Marquis de Sade*, 234–37.

25. See Kushner, *Erotic Exchanges*, 7, for an insightful discussion of social status and sexualities in eighteenth-century France.

26. Choudhury, "Women, Gender, and the Image," 188.

27. Reconciling the theory of royal absolutism with France's patchwork of legal customs and codes proved a central objective of Montesquieu's *Spirit of the Laws.* On the challenge posed to these traditions, see Swann and Félix, *Crisis of the Absolute Monarchy.*

28. This phenomenon is identified and theorized in the essays collected in Goodman, ed., *Marie Antoinette*; and Weber, *Queen of Fashion*.

29. Goodman, ed., *Marie Antoinette*; Thomas, *Wicked Queen*. On the Diamond Necklace Affair and its political consequences, see Hardman, *Marie Antoinette*, 97–121.

30. Persuasively recounted in Sarah Maza's *Private Lives and Public Affairs*, 167–212.

31. Walton, *Policing Public Opinion*, 142–43, details Marie Antoinette's public oath in 1790 to "raise her son to be loyal to public liberty and the laws of the nation."

32. Desmoulins, "Fable," in *Satyre*, 10.

33. Thomas, "Heroine of the Crime."

34. On the rumors and innuendo that targeted the queen, see Hunt, *Family Romance*, chap. 4.

35. *Les nouveaux projets*, 3.

36. *La ligue aristocratique*, 3–4.

37. *La ligue aristocratique*, 4.

38. *Le Ministère*, 8. Heavily footnoted, this passage included the following aspersions against most of Marie-Antoinette's closest courtiers: "[Note: well-deserved epithet, given the lusty caresses given in these rooms, to the swollen Péguigny, & St. Maigrin, Coffé & Mailly as well as Guéméné, Polignac, & de la Motte, &c after the lascivious pleasures taken in the gardens with the debached Dilon, Coigny, & Bezenval, Vaudreuil, Campan & Bazin, as with the insolent Abbé de Vermont and the novice commis of War, &c.]."

39. *La vie et les crimes*, 6.

40. On revolutionary attacks on patriarchal authority and monarchy, see Hunt, *Family Romance*.

41. Manuel, *La police de Paris dévoilée*.

42. See Heuer's analysis of these debates in *Family and the Nation*.

43. Blaufarb, *Great Demarcation*.

44. Desan, *Family on Trial*, 216.

45. Plumauzille, *Prostitution et révolution*.

46. Cage, *Unnatural Frenchmen*.

47. McMahon, *Enemies of the Enlightenment*, 78–80.

48. Burke, *Reflections on the Revolution*.

49. In *Religion and Revolution in France*, Aston provides ample evidence to contest Raynal's polemical portrait (20–22).

50. Raynal, *Tableau philosophique*, 11.

51. Raynal, *Tableau philosophique*, 23.

52. See Kaiser, "Nobles into Aristocrats."

53. Typified in historical and literary treatments of the Old Regime after 1804. See, for example, the recent group biography of seven aristocrats in the 1780s: Craveri, *Last Libertines*.

54. On the political force of pornography in this era, see Hunt, "Pornography and the French Revolution."

55. Chaussinand-Nogaret, *Mirabeau*, Ch. 2.

56. [Mirabeau,] *Des lettres de cachet*. Despite the title's assertion that this was a "posthumous" work, Mirabeau lived another decade, and his father, a respected man of letters in the field of political economy, remained alive until 1789.

57. Bouwers, *Public Pantheons*, 94–95.

58. Mirabeau, *Des lettres de cachet*, 1:253.

59. Mirabeau, *Des lettres de cachet*, 1:253.

60. Mirabeau, *Des lettres de cachet*, 1:253.

61. Mirabeau, *Des lettres de cachet*, 1:85.

62. Petit, *Histoire des galères*, 68.

63. Jandeaux, "La Révolution face aux 'victimes du pouvoir arbitraire,'" 33–60; Quétel, *De par le Roy*, 25–206.

64. Shapiro and Markoff, *Revolutionary Demands*, 278, 289, 382, 386.

65. In *Lawyers and Citizens*, Bell details the development of the *parlementaires* as an anti-absolutist wing of French lawyers and judges (129–47). Timothy discusses the political orientation of lawyers elected to the Estates-General/National Assembly in 1789 in *Becoming a Revolutionary*, 36–41.

66. "Declaration des droits de l'homme et du citoyen," https://www.conseil -constitutionnel.fr/le-bloc-de-constitutionnalite/declaration-des-droits-de-l-homme -et-du-citoyen-de-1789 (accessed September 2, 2022).

67. Jandeaux, "La Révolution face aux 'victimes du pouvoir arbitraire,'" 38, AN, D/V/3.

68. Jandeaux, "La Révolution face," 39.

69. Jandeaux, "La Révolution face," 33–60.

70. Jandeaux, "La Révolution face," 34.

71. Jandeaux, "La Révolution face," 34.

72. Jandeaux, "La Révolution face," 53; citing *Archives parlementaires*, 12:203.

73. Edelstein, *Terror of Natural Right*.

74. Burke, *Reflections on the Revolution*, 19.

75. Burke, *Reflections on the Revolution*, 21.

76. Burke, *Reflections on the Revolution*, 45.

77. Burke, *Reflections on the Revolution*, 108–9.

78. Spang, *Stuff and Money*.

79. *La Police et les Municipalités*, vol. 10 of *Encyclopédie méthodique*, 384–85.

80. *Jacobellis v. Ohio*, 378 U.S. 184 (1964). Underscoring the transatlantic connections I am tracing here, the case concerned Nico Jacobellis, a movie theater owner in Cleveland Heights, Ohio, who had exhibited Louis Malle's film *Les Amants* and was convicted and fined on charges of distributing pornographic material. The U.S. Supreme Court found that the film was not pornographic, finding in favor of Jacobellis and reversing the earlier judicial decisions.

81. On the surveillance of homosexuality in eighteenth-century France, see Merrick, *Sodomites, Pedarasts, and Tribades*; and Rey, "Police et sodomie à Paris."

82. *La Police et les Municipalités*, vol. 10 of *Encyclopédie méthodique*, 384–85.

83. *La Police et les Municipalités*, vol. 10 of *Encyclopédie méthodique*, 384–85.

84. *La Police et les Municipalités*, vol. 10 of *Encyclopédie méthodique*, 384–85.

85. The Gallica database identifies fourteen plays published between 1792 and 1795 that employ *libertin/e* or *libertinage* in characters' dialogue.

86. *Journal des théâtres et des fêtes*, 280.

87. Marat, *Les chaines de l'esclavage*, 84–85.

88. Marat, *Les chaines de l'esclavage*, 85.

89. [Giovane,] *Plan pour faire servir*, 60.

90. Andries, "Almanacs," 214.

91. Grimod de la Reynière, *Moins que rien*, 70.

92. *Epines otées*.

93. *Epines otées*, 204.

94. *Epines*, 205.

95. *Gazette des nouveaux tribunaux*, 150.

96. *Gazette des nouveaux tribunaux*, 151.

97. *Gazette des nouveaux tribunaux*.

98. *Gazette des nouveaux tribunaux*, 155

99. *Choix des causes célèbres*, 62.

100. Beffroy, *La constitution de la lune*, 73.

101. Beffroy, *La constitution de la lune*, 73.

102. Beffroy, *La constitution de la lune*, 74.

103. Bourdon, *Bourdon*, 6.

104. [Duperron,] *Vie secrette*, 26. On Robespierre and women's political support, see Sepinwall, "Robespierre, Old Regime Freminist?"; and Schusterman, "All of His Power."

105. Schaeffer, *Marquis de Sade*, 427–30.

106. Kozul, "Le voyage sadien en Italie," 480; citing Sade, *Œuvres complètetes*, 8:588.

107. Kozul, "Le voyage sadien en Italie," 480.

108. Fradinger, "Riveted by the Voice," 53.

109. Herluison, *Le fanatisme du libertinage*, letter 2, 2.

110. Cage, *Unnatural Frenchmen*, chaps. 2 and 3.

111. Plumauzille, *Prostitution et Revolution*.

112. [Dupin,] *La Prusse galante*, 124.

113. [Dupin,], *La Prusse galante*, 124.

114. [Dupin,] *La Prusse galante*, 125.

115. Brown documents the turmoil of this transition in *Ending the French Revolution*.

116. Rapports de police, Section de la Butte des Moulins (St. Roch), December 21, 1790, Archives de la Préfecture de Police (APP), AA/81.

117. Rapports de police, Section de la Butte des Moulins (St. Roch), December 24, 1790, APP, AA/81.

118. Trouillet, *Le Palais-Royal*.

119. Rapports de police, Section de la Butte des Moulins (St. Roch), April 11, 1791, APP, A/83.

120. The Scioto river runs through the center of present-day Ohio in the United States.

121. *Chronique de Paris*, April 15, 1791.

122. Tuetey, *Répertoire général*, v. 2, 235.

123. Antoine Joseph Gorsas, *Le courrier des 83 départements*, vol. 23, no. 15, 36.

124. Procès-verbaux, Section de la Butte des Moulins (St. Roch), April 11 and 22, 1791, APP, A/83.

125. Jacques Pierre Brissot de Warville also mentions the hopes for the Scioto region in his travels to America (*Nouveau voyage*). See also Chasseboeuf de Volney, *Tableau du climat*.

126. Deloria, *Playing Indian*.

127. Deloria, *Playing Indian*, 41.

128. Desan, "Transatlantic Spaces of Revolution"; Buel *Joel Barlow*, 115.

129. The Delaware, Shawnee, and Cherokee nations resided in the Scioto River valley in the late 1780s and 1790s. Weslager, *Delaware Indians*, 243.

130. Lezay-Marnésia, *Letters Written*.

131. Desan, "Transatlantic Spaces of Revolution," 468.

132. Desan addresses the retraction of women's rights to divorce, property ownership and inheritance under the Civil Code in *Family on Trial*, chap. 8.

133. Dubois, *Avengers of the New World*.

EPILOGUE

1. See White, *Natural Rights*, chap. 6, which compares William Blake and Jean-Paul Marat's discussions of slavery as a metaphor for all inequality.

2. Popkin, "Colonial Media Revolution," 7.

3. *Observations d'un habitant des colonies*, 41. For an orientation to Grégoire and his influence in revolutionary antiracism, see Sepinwall, *Abbé Grégoire*.

4. Raimond, *Observations*, 19.

5. Fick, *Making of Haiti*.

6. Ghachem, *Old Regime and the Haitian Revolution*, 299.

7. Colwill, "Freedwomen's Familial Politics"; "Fêtes de l'hymen," 125–55.

8. Ghachem, *Old Regime and the Haitian Revolution*, 304.

9. Barbé-Marbois, *Réflexions*, 1:162.

10. Thanks to recent scholarship, historians know a great deal more about Haiti (formerly Saint-Domingue) and Martinique during the immediate postrevolutionary period. See, especially, Sepinwall, *Haitian History*; Hector and Hurbon, *Genèse de l'Etat haïtien*; Stieber, *Haiti's Paper War*; and Schloss, *Sweet Liberty*.

11. For example, Patrice Leconte's *Ridicule* (1996) and Edouard Molinaro's *Baumarchais the Scoundrel* (1996). However, the tropes of sexually aggressive aristocrats populate recent historical films and television produced in Europe and North America, including *La Révolution* (2020), in which a virus infects the nobility, causing them

to murder their social inferiors, and *Versailles* (2015–18), which is set in a hedonistic version of Louis XIV's court. Ubisoft's *Assassin's Creed Unity*, set in Revolutionary France, sidesteps this republican narrative, much to the dismay of socialist and communist politicians, including Jean-Luc Mélenchon, who castigated the game as "propaganda against the people" in an interview with the Irish *Independent* in 2014. John Lichfield, "French Left Loses Its Head over *Assassin's Creed* Unity," *Independent*, November 17, 2014, https://www.independent.ie/entertainment /games/french-left-loses-its-head-over-assassins-creed-unity-30752098.html.

12. Linton, *Choosing Terror*, 83–85, 240–41.
13. Gaffield, *Haitian Declaration of Independence*.
14. Vastey, *Colonial System Unveiled*, 124.
15. Desmangles, *Faces of the Gods*, 43.
16. Vastey, *Colonial System Unveiled*, 145.

BIBLIOGRAPHY

ARCHIVAL AND MANUSCRIPT MATERIALS

Archives départementales de la Bouche du Rhône (ADBR), Marseille and Aix-en-Provence, France
  Series C: Provincial Administration
Archives de département du Rhône et de la métropole de Lyon, Lyon, France
  BP 3540–3573: Sénéchaussée criminel (1657–1787)
Archives nationales de France (AN), Paris, France
  Colonies B/116/1: Governance of Caribbean Colonies (1763)
  Colonies B/116/2: Governance of Caribbean Colonies (1763)
  Colonies B/121/1: Table of King's Orders for St. Domingue (1765)
  Colonies B/121/2: Table of King's Orders for Désirade (1765)
  C/10D/2: Governance of Caribbean Colonies: St. Croix, St. Vincent, Désirade (1763–89)
  Series Y: Paris Police Commissaires' Eighteenth-Century Examination Reports and Correspondence
Archives nationales d'outre mer (ANOM), Aix-en Provence, France
  4DFC/9: Louisiana—Memoirs, Reports (1698–1769)
  Col A//8: Collection of Edicts (1760s)
  110APC/1: Dessalles Papers (late eighteenth century)
Archives nationales du Canada (ANC), Ottawa
  Fonds des colonies, Series E: Fonds des colonies, dossiers personnels
Archives de la préfecture de police (APP), Paris, France
  Series AA: Police records, 1660–1820
Bibliothèque et Archives Nationales de Québec (BaNQ), Québec City, Canada
  Series TP1: Sovereign Council Judgments
  Series TL5: Judiciary and Notarial Records, 1638–1900
Bibliothèque et Archives Nationales de Québec (BaNQ), Vieux Montréal, Canada
  Series TL4: Royal Jurisdiction of Montréal

Bibliothèque et Archives Nationales de Québec (BaNQ), Trois-Rivières, Canada

Bibliothèque de l'Arsenal, Paris, France

    Archives de la Bastille

      MS 3724. MS B Tome II, 1719–27. *Recueil de Fevret de Fontette*

Bibliothèque Nationale de France (BNF), Paris, France

    MSS NAF: Manuscripts (Nouvelles Acquisitions Françaises)

      MSS NAF-4156. Bonnefons, J.-C. *Voyage au Canada dans le nord de l'Amérique septentrionale fait depuis l'an 1751 à 1761*, ms s.l, s.d.

      MSS F 21308 (106). "Déclaration concernant les condemnés aux galères, bannis, et vagabonds," January 8, 1719

Huntington Library, San Marino, California

    Loudun Collection: Vaudreuil Papers, MSS LO Boxes 1–8

Louisiana Digital Library,

    http://www.louisianadigitallibrary.org/cdm/compoundobject/collection /p15140coll60/id/15/rec/3

Mississippi Provincial Archives: French Dominion, (MPAFD). 5 vols. Edited by Dunbar Rowland, A. G. Sanders, and Patricia Galloway. Jackson MS: Press of the Mississippi Archives and History, 1927–84.

Service Historique de la Défense (SHD), Rochefort, France

    1E 174–182 Correspondence between the Court and Rochefort (1763–67)

    2F1 58–60 Register of Entries to the Naval Hospital (1762–68)

PUBLISHED WORKS

Abbéville, Claude d'. *Discours et congratulations à la France sur l'arrivée des Pères Capuchins en l'Inde nouvelle de l'Amérique Meridionale en la terre du Brasil.* Paris: Chez Denis Langloys, 1613.

Abé, Takao. *The Jesuit Mission to New France: A New Interpretation in the Light of the Earlier Jesuit Experience in Japan.* Leiden: Brill, 2011.

Abler, Thomas. "Iroquois Cannibalism: Fact not Fiction." *Ethnohistory* 27, no. 4 (Autumn 1980): 309–16.

Adam, Antoine. *Les libertins au XVIIe siècle.* Paris: Buchet Chastel, 1964.

———. *Théophile de Viau et la libre pensée française en 1620.* Geneva: Slatkine, [1935] 2008.

Agmon, Danna. *A Colonial Affair: Commerce, Conversion, and Scandal in French India.* Ithaca NY: Cornell University Press, 2017.

Allen, David, Mark S. Roberts, and Allen S. Weiss, eds. *Sade and the Narrative of Transgression.* Cambridge: Cambridge University Press, 1995.

Almanach royal. Paris: Le Breton, 1766.

Anderson, Emma. *The Betrayal of Faith: The Tragic Journey of a Colonial Native Convert.* Cambridge MA: Harvard University Press, 2007.

Anderson, Fred. *Crucible of War: The Seven Years' War and the Fate of Empire in British North America, 1754–1766.* New York: Vintage, 1991.

Andries, Lise. "Almanacs: Revolutionizing a Traditional Genre." In *Revolution in Print: The Press in France, 1775–1800*, edited by Robert Darnton and Daniel Roche, 203–22. Berkeley: University of California Press, 1989.

Arbell, Mordechai. "Jewish Settlements in the French Colonies in the Caribbean (Martinique Guadeloupe, Haiti, Cayenne) and the 'Black Code.'" In *The Jews and the Expansion of Europe to the West, 1450–1800*, vol. 2, edited by Paolo Bernardini and Norman Fiering, 287–313. New York: Berghahn, 2001.

Archives de la Bastille. Paris: n.p., 1789.

Argenson, Marc-René de Voyer de Paulmy, comte d'. *Rapports inédits du lieutenant de police, René d'Argenson*. Edited by Paul Cottin. Paris: Plon, 1891.

Arrest de la Cour de Parlement. Paris: Chez Antoine Vitray, 1623.

Aston, Nigel. *Religion and Revolution in France, 1780–1804*. Washington DC: Catholic University of America Press, 2000.

Aubert, Francois-Alexandre, de La Chesnaye Des Bois. *Dictionnaire de la noblesse*. Paris: n.p., 1778.

Aubert, Guillaume. "'The Blood of France': Race and the Purity of Blood in the French Atlantic World." *William and Mary Quarterly* 61, no. 3 (July 2004): 439–78.

———. "Kinship, Blood, and the Emergence of the Racial Nation in the French Atlantic World, 1600–1789." In *Blood and Kinship: Matter for Metaphor from Ancient Rome to the Present*, edited by Christopher H. Johnson, Bernhard Jussen, David Warren Sabean, and Simon Teuscher, 175–95. Oxford: Berghahn, 2013.

———. "To Establish One Law and Definite Rules: Race, Religion, and the Transatlantic Origins of the Louisiana Code Noir." In *Louisiana: Crossroads of the Atlantic World*, edited by Cecile Vidal, 21–43. Philadelphia: University of Pennsylvania Press, 2013.

Aurélie, Julia. "Frédéric Lachèvre, chantre ou pourfendeur du libertinage?" *Revue des deux Mondes* (June 2007): 44–54.

Bachaumont. *Mémoires secrets pour server à l'histoire de la République des lettres en France depuis 1762 jusqu'à nos jours; ou Journal d'un Observateur*. 36 vols. London: John Adamson, 1783–89.

Balvay, Arnaud. "Tattooing and Its Role in French-Native American Relations in the Eighteenth Century." *French Colonial History* 9 (2008): 1–14.

Banat, Gabriel. *The Chevalier de Saint-Georges: Virtuoso of the Sword and Bow*. Hillsdale NY: Pendragon, 2006.

Banks, Kenneth. *Chasing Empire across the Sea: Communications and the State in the French Atlantic, 1713–1763*. Montréal: McGill-Queen's University Press, 2006.

Barbierato, Federico. *The Inquisitor in the Hat Shop: Inquisition, Forbidden Books, and Unbelief in Early Modern Venice*. Burlington VT: Ashgate, 2012.

Barbé-Marbois, François. *Réflexions sur la colonie de Saint-Domingue: ou Examen approfondi des causes de sa ruine et des mesures adoptées pour la rétablir*. Paris: Garnery, 1796.

Barbotin, Maurice. *La Désirade: une île de la Guadeloupe, son histoire étonnante*. Basse-Terre: Société de l'histoire de la Guadeloupe, 2010.

Barker, Emma. *Greuze and the Painting of Sentiment*. Cambridge: Cambridge University Press, 2005.

Bartlett, Katharine T., and Rosanne Kennedy. *Feminist Legal Theory: Readings in Law and Gender*. Boulder CO: Westview, 1991.

Bataillon, Marcel. "L'Amiral et les 'nouveaux horizons' français." *Bulletin de la Société de l'Histoire du Protestantisme Français* (1974): 41–52.

Baugh, Daniel. *The Global Seven Years' War, 1754–1763: Britain and France in a Great Power Contest*. London: Routledge, 2014.

Beaumarchais, Pierre Caron de. *La folle journée, ou Le mariage de Figaro*. Paris: L'Imprimerie de la Société Littéraire et typographique, 1785.

———. *The Figaro Trilogy*. Translated by David Coward. Oxford: Oxford University Press, 2003.

———. *Observations sur le mémoire justicatif de la Cour de Londres*. n.p., 1779.

Bedouelle, Guy, and James K. Farge. *Biblical Humanism and Scholasticism in the Age of Erasmus*. Edited by Erika Rummel. Leiden: Brill, 2008.

Beffroy de Reigny, Louis-Abel. *La constitution de la lune: rêve politique et moral*. Paris: Troublé, 1793.

Beik, William. *Absolutism and Society in Seventeenth-Century France: State Power and Provincial Aristocracy in Languedoc*. Cambridge: Cambridge University Press, 1985.

———. *A Social and Cultural History of Early Modern France*. Cambridge: Cambridge University Press, 2009.

Bell, David A. "Canon Wars in Eighteenth-Century France: The Monarchy, the Revolution, and the 'Grands Hommes de la Patrie.'" *MLN* 116, no. 4 (September 2001): 705–38.

———. "Jumonville's Death." In *The Age of Cultural Revolutions: Britain and France, 1750–1820*, edited by Colin Jones and Dror Wahrman, 33–61. Berkeley: University of California Press, 2002.

———. *Lawyers and Citizens: The Making of a Political Elite in Old Regime France*. Oxford: Oxford University Press, 1994.

Bell, Susan Groag, and Karen M. Offen, eds. *Women, the Family, and Freedom: The Debate in Documents*. Stanford CA: Stanford University Press, 1983.

Belmessous, Saliha. "Assimilation and Racialism in Seventeenth- and Eighteenth-Century French Colonial Policy." *American Historical Association* 110, no. 2 (April 2005): 322–49.

———. "Etre français en Nouvelle-France: Identité française et identité coloniale aux dix-septième et dix-huitième siècles." *French Historical Studies* 27, no. 3 (2004): 507–40.

Belsom, Jack, and Winston de Ville. "The Sauciers in 1726: Year of Decision for a Colonial Louisiana Family." *Louisiana History* 29, no. 2 (Spring 1988): 183–89.

Benabou, Erica. *La prostitution et la police des moeurs au XVIIIe siècle*. Paris: Perrin, 1987.

Benbassa, Esther. *The Jews of France: A History from Antiquity to the Present*. Translated by M. B. DeBevoise. Princeton NJ: Princeton University Press, 1999.

Benot, Yves, ed. *Les Lumières, l'esclavage, la colonisation*. Paris: La Découverte, 2005.

Bergin, Joseph. *Crown, Church, and Episcopate under Louis XIV*. New Haven CT: Yale University Press, 2004.

———. *The Politics of Religion in Early Modern France*. New Haven CT: Yale University Press, 2014.

Berlanstein, Lenard. *Daughters of Eve: A Cultural History of French Theater Women from the Old Regime to the Fin de Siècle*. Cambridge MA: Harvard University Press, 2001.

Berman, Harold J. *Law and Revolution II: The Impact of the Protestant Reformations on the Western Legal Tradition*. Cambridge MA: Harvard University Press, 2006.

Bernardini, Paolo, and Norman Fiering, eds. *The Jews and the Expansion of Europe to the West, 1450–1800*. Vol. 2. New York: Berghahn, 2001.

Berrong, Richard. "The Nature and Function of the 'Sauvage' in Jacques Cartier's *Récits de Voyage*." *Romance Notes* 22, no. 2 (Winter 1981): 213–17.

Berry, Daina Ramey. *The Price for Their Pound of Flesh: The Value of the Enslaved, From Womb to Grave, in the Building of a Nation*. Boston: Beacon, 2017.

Berthiaume, Pierre. "Louisiana, or the Shadow Cast by Colonial Myth." *Dalhousie French Studies* 58 (Spring 2002): 10–25.

Blackburn, Carole. *Harvest of Souls*. Montréal: McGill-Queen's University Press, 2000.

Blanc, Olivier. *Les libertines: Plaisir et liberté au temps des lumières*. Paris: Perrin, 1997.

Blancpain, François. *Haïti et la République domincaine: une question de frontiers*. Matoury: Ibis Rouge Editions, 2008.

Blaufarb, Rafe. *Bonapartists in the Borderlands: French Exiles and Refugees on the Gulf Coast, 1815–1835*. Tuscaloosa: University of Alabama Press, 2005.

———. *The French Army, 1750–1820: Careers, Talent, Merit*. Manchester: Manchester University Press, 2002.

———. *The Great Demarcation: The French Revolution and the Invention of Modern Property*. Oxford: Oxford University Press, 2016.

———. "Noble Privilege and Absolutist State Building: French Military Administration after the Seven Years' War." *French Historical Studies* 24, no. 2 (Spring 2001): 223–46.

Block, Sharon. *Rape and Sexual Power in Early America*. Chapel Hill NC: Omohundro Institute / University of North Carolina Press, 2006.

———. "Sexual Coercion in America." In *The Oxford Handbook of American Women's and Gender History*, edited by Ellen Hartigan-O'Connor and Lisa G. Materson, 265–90. Oxford: Oxford University Press, 2019.

Boisvert, France. "L'influence protestante chez Lahontan." *Revue d'histoire et de philosophie religieuses* 84, no. 1 (2004): 31–51.

Boitano, John. *Polemics of Libertine Conversion in Pascal's* Pensées: *A Dialectics of Rational and Occult Libertine Beliefs*. Tubingen: Gunter Narr Verlag, 2002.

Bond, Bradley G., ed. *French Colonial Louisiana and the Atlantic World*. Baton Rouge: Louisiana State University Press, 2005.

Bongie, Laurence. *Sade: A Biographical Essay*. Chicago: University of Chicago Press, 1998.

Bosher, J. F. "The French Government's Motives in the Affaire du Canada, 1761–1763." *English Historical Review* 96, no. 378 (January 1981): 59–78.

Bossuet, Jacques Benigné. *Histoire des variations des églises protestantes*. 2 vols. Paris: Veuve de Mabre-Cramoisy, 1688.

Boucher d'Argis, Antoine-Gaspard. "Law of Nature, or Natural Law" (1755). The Encyclopedia of Diderot & d'Alembert Collaborative Translation Project. Translated by Susan Rosa. Ann Arbor: Michigan Publishing, University of Michigan Library, 2002, http://hdl.handle.net/2027/spo.did2222.0000.021 (accessed December 15, 2018).

Boulle, Pierre. "Eighteenth-Century French Policies toward Senegal: The Ministry of Choiseul." *Canadian Journal of African Studies / Revue Canadienne des Etudes Africaines* 4, no. 3 (1970): 305–20.

Bourdon, *Bourdon, de l'Oise, à ses collègues et à ses concitoyens*. Paris: Langlois fils, 1794.

Boureau, Alain. *The Lord's First Night: The Myth of the Droit de Cuissage*. Translated by Lydia Cochrane. Chicago: University of Chicago Press, 1998.

Bouwers, E. *Public Pantheons in Revolutionary Europe: Comparing Cultures of Remembrance, c. 1790–1840*. London: Palgrave Macmillan, 2012.

Brandon, Pepijn, Niklas Frykman, and Pernille Røge, eds. *Free and Unfree Labor in Atlantic and Indian Ocean Port Cities (1700–1850)*. Cambridge MA: Cambridge University Press, 2019.

Brazeau, Brian. *Writing a New France, 1604–1632: Empire and Early Modern French Identity*. Burlington VT: Ashgate, 2009.

Breen, Michael H. "Law, Society, and the State in Early Modern France." *Journal of Modern History* 83, no. 2 (June 2011): 346–86.

Brissot, Jacques Pierre, de Warville. *Nouveau voyage dans les Etats-Unis de l'Amérique septentrionale, fait en 1788*. 3 vols. Paris: Buisson, 1791.

Brock, Michelle, Richard Raiswell, and David R. Winter, eds. *Knowing Demons, Knowing Spirits in the Early Modern Period*. London: Palgrave Macmillan, 2018.

Brown, Howard G. *Ending the French Revolution: Violence, Justice, and Repression from the Terror to Napoleon*. Charlottesville VA: University of Virginia Press, 2006.

Brown, Vincent. *Tacky's Revolt: The Story of an Atlantic Slave War*. Cambridge MA: Harvard University Press, 2020.

Buel, Richard, Jr. *Joel Barlow: American Citizen in a Revolutionary World*. Baltimore MD: Johns Hopkins University Press, 2011.

Buffon, Georges-Louis Leclerc, comte de. *Histoire naturelle, generalle et particulière*. 12 vols. London: n.p., 1749–64.

Burke, Edmund. *Reflections on the Revolution in France*. Oxford: Oxford University Press, [1790] 2009.

Burnard, Trevor, and John Garrigus. *The Plantation Machine: Atlantic Capitalism in French Saint-Domingue and British Jamaica*. Philadelphia: University of Pennsylvania Press, 2016.

Burton, William. *The Most Delectable and Pleasant History of Clitiphon and Leucippe*. London: Thomas Creede, 1597.

Burwick, Frederick. *A History of Romantic Literature*. Hoboken NJ: Wiley Blackwell, 2019.

Buvat, Jean. *Journal de la Régence, 1715–1723*. 2 vols. Paris: Plon, 1865.

Cabrol, Camille. *Essai sur l'histoire de la Réforme à Clairac. Des Origines à l'édit de Tolerance (1530–1787)*. Cahors: Imprimerie A. Coueslant, 1900.

Cage, E. Claire. *Unnatural Frenchmen: The Politics of Priestly Celibacy and Marriage, 1720–1815*. Charlottesville: University of Virginia Press, 2015.

Cahall, Raymond Du Bois. "The Sovereign Council of New France: A Study in Canadian Constitutional History." PhD diss., Columbia University, 1915.

Cahill, Ann J. "Unjust Sex vs. Rape." *Hypatia* 31, no. 4 (Fall 2016): 746–61.

Caillot, Marc-Antoine. *A Company Man: The Remarkable French-Atlantic Voyage of a Clerk for the Company of the Indies*. Edited by Erin M. Greenwald. Translated by Teri F. Chalmers. New Orleans LA: Historic New Orleans Collection, 2013.

Callanan, Keegan. "Liberal Constitutionalism and Political Particularism in Montesquieu's *The Spirit of the Laws*." *Political Research Quarterly* 67, no. 3 (September 2014): 589–602.

Calloway, Colin. *The Scratch of a Pen: 1763 and the Transformation of North America*. Oxford: Oxford University Press, 2007.

Calvin, John. *Contre la secte phantastique et furieuse des libertins. Qui se nomment spirituelz*. Geneva: 1545.

Campbell, Robert. "Making Sober Citizens: The Legacy of Indigenous Alcohol Regulation in Canada, 1777–1985." *Journal of Canadian Studies* 42, no. 1 (2008): 105–26.

Caraccioli, Louis-Antoine de. *Dictionnaire critique, pittoresque et sentencieux*. Lyon: Duplain, 1768.

———. *Le livre à la mode*. Paris: Imprimerie de Printemps, 1759.

Carey, Daniel, and Lynn Festa, eds. *The Postcolonial Enlightenment: Eighteenth-Century Colonialism and Postcolonial Theory*. Oxford: Oxford University Press, 2009.

Carra, Jean-Louis. *Mémoires historiques et authentiques de la Bastille*. London: Buisson, 1789.

Catterall, Douglas, and Jodi Campbell, eds. *Women in Port: Gendering Communities, Economies, and Social Networks in Atlantic Port Cities, 1500–1800*. Leiden: Brill, 2012.

Cavaillé, Jean-Pierre. *Les déniaisés: irréligion et libertinage au début de l'époque moderne*. Paris: Classiques Garnier, 2013.

———. *Dis/simulations. Jules-César Vanini, François La Mothe Le Vayer, Gabriel Naudé, Louis Machon et Torquato Accetto. Religion, morale et politique au XVIIe siècle*. Paris: Champion, 2002.

———. "Libérer le libertinage: Une catégorie à l'épreuve des sources." *Annales. Histoire, sciences sociales* (2009): 45–78.

———. "Le 'libertinage érudit': fertilité et limites d'une catégorie historiographique." Les Dossiers du Grihl. Accessed July 20, 2021. http:journals.openedition.org /dossiersgrihl/4827.

Champigny, Jean Bochart, Col. Chevalier de. *La Louisiane ensanglantée*. London: Fleury Mesplet, 1778.

Charbit, Yves. "The Political Failure of an Economic Theory: Physiocracy." Translated by Arundhati Virmani. *Population* 57, no. 6 (November–December 2002): 855–83.

Charbonneau, Hubert, Bertrand Desjardins, Andre Guillemette, Yves Landry, Jacques Légaré, and Francois Nault. *The First French Canadians: Pioneers in the St. Lawrence Valley*. Translated by Paulo Colozzo. Cranbury NJ: Associated University Presses, 1993.

Chareyre, Philippe. "Le roi, les protestants et l'édit: applications, variations." *Bulletin de la Société de l'Histoire du Protestantisme Français* 145 (April–June 1999): 401–11.

Chasseboeuf de Volney, Constant François. *Tableau du climat et du sol des Etats-Unis d'Amérique: suivi d'éclaircissements sur la Floride, sur la colonie française au Scioto, sur quelques colonies canadiennes, et sur les sauvages. Enrichi de quatre planches gravées*. 2 vols. Paris: Courcier, 1803.

Charlevoix, Pierre-François-Xavier. *Histoire et description générale de la Nouvelle France*. Paris: Giffart, 1744.

Chassaigne, André. *Les lettres de cachet sous l'Ancien Régime*. Paris: Rousseau, 1903.

Chatel, Eugène, ed. *Inventaire des Archives Départementales de Calvados, antérieures à 1790*. Paris: Dupont, 1877.

Chaussinand-Nogaret, Guy. *Mirabeau*. Paris: Seuil, 1982.

Cheney, Paul. *Cul de Sac: Patrimony, Capitalism, and Slavery in French Saint-Domingue*. Chicago: University of Chicago Press, 2017.

Choix des causes célèbres jugées dans les tribunaux de Paris, depuis l'origine de la Révolution. Paris: Perlet, 1793.

Choquette, Leslie. "A Colony of 'Native French Catholics'? The Protestants of New France in the Seventeenth and Eighteenth Centuries." In *Memory and Identity: The Huguenots in France and the Atlantic Diaspora*, edited by Bertrand van Ruymbeke and Randy Sparks, 255–66. Columbia: University of South Carolina Press, 2003.

———. *Frenchmen into Peasants: Modernity and Tradition in the Peopling of French Canada*. Cambridge MA: Harvard University Press, 1997.

Choudhury, Mita. "Carnal Quietism: Embodying Anti-Jesuit Polemics in the Catherine Cadière Affair, 1731." *Eighteenth-Century Studies* 39, no. 2 (Winter 2006): 173–86.

———. "Women, Gender, and the Image of the Eighteenth-Century Aristocracy." In *The French Nobility in the Eighteenth Century: Reassessments and New Approaches*, edited by Jay M. Smith, 167–89. University Park PA: Penn State University Press, 2006.

Christie, Nancy, Michael Gauvreau, and Matthew Gerber, eds. *Voices in the Legal Archives in the French Colonial World*. New York: Routledge, 2020.

Chronique de Paris. 15 avril 1791.

Clark, Emily. *The Strange History of the American Quadroon: Free Women of Color in the Revolutionary Atlantic World*. Chapel Hill: University of North Carolina Press, 2015.

Clark, Henry C. *Compass of Society: Commerce and Absolutism in Old Regime France*. Lanham KY: Lexington, 2007.

Clark, William, Jan Golinski, and Simon Schaffer, eds. *The Sciences in Enlightened Europe*. Chicago: University of Chicago Press, 1999.

Clay, Lauren. *Stagestruck: The Business of Theater in Eighteenth-Century France and Its Colonies.* Ithaca NY: Cornell University Press, 2013.

Code de l'hôpital-général de Paris, ou Recueil des principaux édits, arrêts, déclarations et réglements qui le concernent, ainsi que les maisons & hôpitaux réunis à son administration. Paris: veuve Thiboust, 1786.

Le Code Noir ou recueil des règlements rendus jusqu'à présent. Translated by John Garrigus. Paris: Prault, 1767.

Code ou Nouveau règlement sur les lieux de prostitution dans la ville de Paris. London: n.p., 1775.

Codignola, Luca. "Competing Networks: Roman Catholic Ecclesiastics in French North America, 1610–58." *Canadian Historical Review* 80, no. 4 (December 1999): 539–84.

Cohen, Déborah. *La nature du peuple: les formes de l'imaginaire social (XVIIIE–XXIE siècles).* Paris: Champ Vallon, 2010.

———. "Savoir pragmatique de la police et preuves formelles de la justice: deux modes d'appréhension du crime dans le Paris du XVIIIe siècle." *Crime, Histoire & Sociétés / Crime, History & Societies* 12, no. 1 (2008): 5–23.

Coleman, Charly. "The Spirit of Speculation: John Law and Economic Theology in the Age of Lights." *French Historical Studies* 42, no. 2 (April 2019): 203–38.

Colwill, Elizabeth. "Fêtes de l'hymen, fêtes de la liberté: Matrimony and Emancipation in Saint-Domingue, 1793." In *The World of the Haitian Revolution*, edited by David Patrick Geggus and Norman Fiering, 125–55. Bloomington: Indiana University Press, 2009.

———. "Freedwomen's Familial Politics: Marriage, War, and Rites of Registry in Post-Emancipation Saint-Domingue." In *Gender, War, and Politics: The Wars of Revolution and Liberation—Transatlantic Comparisons, 1775–1820*, edited by Karen Hagemann, Gisela Mettele, and Jane Rendall, 71–89. London: Palgrave Macmillan, 2010.

Comédie-Française Registers. Accessed August 29, 2022. https://www.cfregisters.org /en/the-data/basic-tool.

Conrad, Maia. "Disorderly Drinking: Reconsidering Seventeenth-Century Iroquois Alcohol Use." *American Indian Quarterly* 23, nos. 3–4 (Summer–Autumn 1999): 1–11.

Cooper, James Fenimore. *The Last of the Mohicans: A Narrative of 1757.* London: J. Miller, 1826.

Cope, Douglas. *The Limits of Racial Domination: Plebeian Society in Colonial Mexico City, 1660–1720.* Madison: University of Wisconsin Press, 1994.

Cormack, William S. "Revolution and Free-Colored Equality in the *Iles du Vent* (Lesser Antilles), 1789–1794." *Journal of the Western Society for French History* 39 (2011). http://hdl.handle.net/2027/spo.0642292.0039.015 (accessed November 3, 2022).

Cossic-Péricarpin, Annick, and Emrys D. Jones, eds. *La Représentation et la reinvention des espaces de sociabilité durant le long XVIIIe siècle.* Paris: Editions Le Manuscrit, 2021.

Coté, André. *Joseph-Michel Cadet, 1719–1781: Négociant et munitionnaire du roi en Nouvelle France.* Québec: Editions du Septentrion, 1998.

Cowan, Mairi. "Jesuit Missionaries and Accomodationist Demons." In *Knowing Demons, Knowing Spirits in the Early Modern Period*, edited by Michelle D. Brock, Richard Raiswell, and David R. Winter, 211–38. London: Palgrave Macmillan, 2018.

Craven, Paul. "Canada, 1670–1935: Symbolic and Instrumental Enforcement in Loyalist North America." In *Masters, Servants, and Magistrates in Britain and the Empire, 1562–1955*, edited by Douglas Hay and Paul Craven, 175–218. Chapel Hill: University of North Carolina Press, 2004.

Craveri, Benedetta. *The Last Libertines*. Translated by Aaron Kerner. New York: New York Review of Books, 2020.

Crawford, Amy. "The Swamp Fox." *Smithsonian Magazine*, June 30, 2007. https ://www .smithsonianmag.com/history/the-swamp-fox-157330429/.

Crébillon, Claude-Prosper Jolyot de, fils. *Le Sopha: conte morale*. Gaznah: Imprimerie du Très-Pieux, très-Clément & Très-Auguste Sultan des Indes, L'an de l'Hegire, 1120 [1742].

Crouch, Christian Ayne. *Nobility Lost: French and Canadian Martial Cultures, Indians and the End of New France*. Ithaca NY: Cornell University Press, 2014.

Curran, Andrew. *The Anatomy of Blackness: Science and Slavery in an Age of Enlightenment*. Baltimore MD: Johns Hopkins University Press, 2011.

Cusset, Catherine. *No Tomorrow: The Ethics of Pleasure in the French Enlightenment*. Charlottesville: University of Virginia Press, 1999.

Dabhoiwala, Faramerz. *The Origins of Sex: A History of the First Sexual Revolution*. Oxford: Oxford University Press, 2012.

Danley, Mark H., and Patrick J. Speelman, eds. *The Seven Years' War: Global Views*. Leiden: Brill, 2012.

Darnton, Robert. *The Forbidden Best-Sellers of Pre-Revolutionary France*. New York: W. W. Norton, 1996.

Darnton Robert, and Daniel Roche, eds. *Revolution in Print: The Press in France, 1775–1800*. Berkeley: University of California Press, 1989.

Davis, Jennifer J. *Defining Culinary Authority: The Transformation of Cooking in France, 1650–1830*. Baton Rouge LA: Louisiana State University Press, 2013.

Dawdy, Shannon Lee. *Building the Devil's Empire: French Colonial New Orleans*. Chicago: University of Chicago Press, 2009.

Dayan, Joan. *Haiti, History, and the Gods*. Berkeley: University of California Press, 1998.

Dechêne, Louise. *People, State, and War under the French Regime in Canada*. Montréal: McGill-Queen's University Press, 2021.

DeJean, Joan. *Libertine Strategies*. Columbus OH: Ohio State University Press, 1981.

———. *The Reinvention of Obscenity: Sex, Lies, and Tabloids in Early Modern France*. Chicago: University of Chicago Press, 2002.

Delâge, Denis. *Bitter Feast: Amerindians and Europeans in Northeastern North America, 1600–64*. Translated by Jane Brierley. Seattle: University of Washington Press, 1995.

———. "L'influence des Amérindiens sur les Canadiens et les Français au temps de la Nouvelle-France." *Lekton* 2, no. 2 (Autumn 1992): 51–59.

Delon, Michel, ed. *Encyclopedia of the Enlightenment*. New York: Routledge, 2001.

Deloria, Philip. *Playing Indian*. New Haven CT: Yale University Press, 1999.

Démeunier, Jean-Nicolas. *L'Esprit des usages et des coutumes des différens peoples, ou observations tirées des voyageurs et des historiens*. London: Pissot, 1776.

Deniel-Ternant, Myriam. *Ecclésiastiques en débauche (1700–1790)*. Paris: Champ Vallon, 2017.

Denton, Chad. *Decadence, Radicalism, and the Early Modern French Nobility: The Enlightened and Depraved*. Lanham MD: Lexington, 2016.

Desan, Suzanne. *The Family on Trial in Revolutionary France*. Berkeley: University of California Press, 2004.

———. "Transatlantic Spaces of Revolution: The French Revolution, *Sciotomanie*, and American Lands." *Journal of Early Modern History* 12 (2008): 467–505.

Desan, Suzanne, Lynn Hunt, and William Max Nelson, eds. *The French Revolution in Global Perspective*. Ithaca NY: Cornell University Press, 2013.

Desan, Suzanne, and Jeffrey Merrick. *Family, Gender, and Law in Early Modern France*. University Park PA: Penn State University Press, 2009.

Des Essarts, Nicolas Toussaint Le Moyne. *Choix de nouvelles causes célèbres*. 15 vols. Paris: Moutard, 1785.

Deslandes, Dominique. "'. . . alors que nos garçons se marieront à vos filles & nous ne ferons qu'un seul peuple': Religion, genre et déploiement de la souveraineté française en Amérique aux XVIe–XVIIIe siècles-une problématique." *Revue d'histoire de l'Amérique française* 66, no. 1 (été 2012): 5–35.

Desmangles, Leslie G. *The Faces of the Gods: Vodou and Roman Catholicism*. Chapel Hill: University of North Carolina Press, 2000.

Desmoulins, Camille, ed. *Satyre, ou choix des meilleures pièces de vers qui ont précédé et suivi la Révolution*. Paris : n.p. 1789.

Desnoireterres, Gustave. *Grimod de la Reynière et son groupe: d'après des documents*. Paris: Didier et Cie, 1877.

Désy, Pierrette. "L'homme-femme (Les berdaches en Amérique du Nord)." In *Libre— politique, anthropologie, philosophie*, 57–102. Paris: Payot, 1978.

Dewald, Jonathan, ed. *Europe, 1450–1789: Encyclopedia of the Early Modern World*. New York: Scribner & Sons, 2004.

Dewar, Helen. *Disputing New France: Companies, Law, and Sovereignty in the French Atlantic, 1598–1663*. Montréal: McGill-Queen's University Press, 2022.

Le Dictionnaire de l'Académie Française. Paris: Coignard, 1694.

Le Dictionnaire de l'Académie Française. Paris: Brunet, 1762.

Diderot, Denis. *Oeuvres de Denis Diderot Salons*. Vol. 1. Paris: Brière, 1821.

———. *Supplément au voyage de Bougainville*. In *Diderot: Political Writings*, edited by John Hope Mason and Robert Wokler, 31–76. Cambridge: Cambridge University Press, 1992.

Diderot, Denis, and Jean le Rond d'Alembert. *Encyclopédie ou Dictionnaire raisonné des sciences, des arts et des métiers*. Paris: Le Breton, 1755.

Dorigny, Marcel, and Bernard Gainot, eds. *Atlas des esclavages de l'Antiquité à nos jours*. Paris: Autrement, 2017.

Doughty, A. G. *Report Concerning Canadian Archives*. Ottawa: Dawson, 1905.

Douthwaite, Julia. "How Bad Economic Memories Are Made: John Law's System in *Les lettres persanes, Manon Lescaut*, and 'The Great Mirror of Folly.'" *L'esprit créateur* 55, no. 3 (Fall 2015): 43–58.

Doyle, William, ed. *The Oxford Handbook of the Ancien Regime*. Oxford: Oxford University Press, 2014.

Dubois, Laurent. *Avengers of the New World: The Story of the Haitian Revolution*. Cambridge MA: Belknap Press of Harvard University Press, 2004.

———. *A Colony of Citizens: Revolution and Slave Emancipation in the French Caribbean, 1787–1804*. Chapel Hill: University of North Carolina Press, 2004.

Duggan, Anne. "Epicurean Cannibalism, or France Gone Savage." *French Studies: A Quarterly Review* 67, no. 4 (2013): 463–77.

Dumont de Montigny, Jean-François-Benjamin. *The Memoir of Lieutenant Dumont, 1715–1747: A Sojourner in the French Atlantic*. Edited by Gordon M. Sayre and Carla Zecher. Translated by Gordon M. Sayre. Chapel Hill: University of North Carolina Press, 2012.

Dupas, Mathieu. "La sodomie dans l'affaire Théophile de Viau: questions de genre et de sexualité dans la France du premier XVIIe siècle." Dossiers de GRIHL 2010. Accessed August 29, 2022. http://journals.openedition.org/dossiersgrihl/3934.

[Duperron, L.] *Vie secrète, politique et curieuse de M. J. Maximilen Robespierre*. Paris: Prévost, 1794.

[Dupin, Etienne.] *La Prusse galante ou Voyage d'un jeune homme à Berlin, traduit de l'allemand*. Paris: Jacquin, Desenne, Duprat, 1800.

DuVal, Kathleen. *Independence Lost: Lives on the Edge of the American Revolution*. New York: Random House, 2016.

———. *Native Ground: Indians and Colonists in the Heart of the Continent*. Philadelphia: University of Pennsylvania Press, 2007.

Dziembowski, Edmond. *La Guerre de Sept Ans*. Paris: Tempus Perrin, 2018.

———. *Un nouveau patriotisme français, 1750–1770*. Oxford: Voltaire Foundation, 1998.

Eccles, William. "French Imperial Policy for the Great Lakes Basin." In *The Sixty Years War for the Great Lakes, 1754–1814*, edited by David Curtis Skaggs and Larry L. Nelson, 21–42. East Lansing: Michigan State University, 2001.

———. *The French in North America, 1500–1783*. London: Fitzhenry & Whiteside, 2010.

Eddins, Crystal. "The First Ayitian Revolution." Age of Revolutions, May 18, 2020. https://ageofrevolutions.com/2020/05/18/the-first-ayitian-revolution/.

———. "Runaways, Repertoires, and Repression: Marronnage and the Haitian Revolution, 1766–1791." *Journal of Haitian Studies* 25, no. 1 (Spring 2019): 4–38.

Edelstein, Dan. *The Terror of Natural Right: Republicanism, the Cult of Nature, and the French Revolution*. Chicago: University of Chicago Press, 2009.

Edit du Roi, touchant la Police de l'Amérique Française. Paris: n.p., 1687.

Ellingson, Ter. *The Myth of the Noble Savage.* Berkeley: University of California Press, 2001.

Elliott, J. H. *Empires of the Atlantic World: Britain and Spain in America, 1492–1830.* New Haven CT: Yale University Press, 2006.

Emmanuelli, F.-X. "'Ordres du roi' et lettres de cachet en Provence, à la fin de l'Ancien Régime. Contribution à l'histoire du climat social et politique." *Revue historique* (October–December 1974): 357–392.

Encyclopédie méthodique. Paris: Panckoucke, 1791.

Englebert, Robert, and Guillaume Teasdale. *French and Indians in the Heart of North America, 1630–1815.* Lansing: Michigan State University Press, 2013.

Epines otées de dessus le tombeau de Louis XVI, roi de France et de Navarre, ou Réfutation d'un ouvrage intitutlé 'Une fleur sur le tombeau de Louis XVI, etc.' par M. L'Abbé Moutet. Bruxelles: n.p. 1793.

L'esprit des journaux. Vol. 5. Bruxelles: De l'Imprimerie du Journal, 1776.

Evreux, Père Yves d'. *Voyage dans le Nord du Brésil fait dans les années 1614 et 1614.* Paris: Librairie Franck, 1864.

Ewing, Tabetha. *Rumor, Diplomacy, and War in Enlightenment Paris.* Oxford: Voltaire Foundation, 2014.

Ewing, William. "An Eyewitness Account by James Furnis of the Surrender of Fort William Henry." *New York History* 42, no. 3 (July 1961): 307–16.

Fabella, Yvonne. "'An Empire Founded on Libertinage': The *Mulâtresse* and Colonial Anxiety in Saint-Domingue." In *Gender, Religion, and Race in the Colonization of the Americas,* edited by Nora Jaffary, 109–24. Burlington VT: Ashgate, 2007.

Farge, Arlette. *Fragile Lives: Violence, Power, and Solidarity in Eighteenth-Century Paris.* Translated by Carol Shelton. Cambridge MA: Harvard University Press, 1993.

———. *Un ruban et des larmes: un procès en adultère au XVIIIe siècle.* Paris: De Conti, 2011.

Farge, Arlette, and Michel Foucault. *Le désordre des familles: lettres de cachet des Archives de la Bastille au XVIIIe siècle.* Paris: Gallimard, 1982.

Féraud, Jean-François. *Le dictionnaire critique de la langue française.* Marseille: Chez Jean Mossy, 1787.

Ferland, Catherine. *Bacchus en Canada: boissons, buveurs, et ivresses en Nouvelle France.* Québec: Septentrion, 2010.

Feuille hebdomadaire de la généralité de Limoges 10, no. 14 (18 Mai 1785).

Fick, Carolyn. *The Making of Haiti: The Saint-Domingue Revolution from Below.* Knoxville: University of Tennessee Press, 1990.

Fish, W. B. "Population Trends in France." *Geography* 25, no. 3 (September 1940): 107–20.

Fisher, David Hackett. *Champlain's Dream.* New York: Simon & Schuster, 2007.

Fling, Fred. "Mirabeau, A Victim of the Lettres de Cachet." *American Historical Review* 3, no. 1 (October 1897): 19–30.

Forbes, Jack D. *Africans and Native Americans: The Language of Race and the Evolution of Red-Black Peoples.* Urbana: University of Illinois Press, 1993.

Forrest, Alan. *The Death of the French Atlantic: Trade, War, and Slavery in the Age of Revolution.* Oxford: Oxford University Press, 2020.

Forrest, Alan, and Karen Hagemann, eds. *War, Demobilization and Memory: The Legacy of War in the Era of Atlantic Revolutions.* London: Palgrave Macmillan, 2016.

Forrestal, Alan, and Eric Nelson, eds. *Politics and Religion in Early Bourbon France.* New York: Palgrave Macmillan, 2009.

Foucault, Didier. *Histoire du libertinage: des goliards au marquis de Sade.* Paris: Perrin, 2007.

Foucault, Michel. *Discipline and Punish: The Birth of the Prison.* Translated by Alan Sheridan. New York: Vintage, 1995.

———. *The History of Sexuality.* Vol. 1. Translated by Robert Hurley. New York: Knopf, [1976] 2012.

Fougère, Eric. *Des indésirables à la Désirade: histoire de la déportation de mauvais sujets, 1763–1767.* Matoury, Guyane: Espaces Outre-mers, 2008.

Fradinger, Moira. "Riveted by the Voice: The Sadean City at Silling." *French Forum* 30, no. 2 (Spring 2005): 49–66.

Frégault, Guy. *La guerre de la conquête.* Montréal: Fides, 1955.

Fréron, ed. *Journal étranger.* Paris: Michel Lambert, March 1756.

Friedman, Lawrence. "Legal Culture as Social Development." *Law & Society Review* 4, no. 1 (August 1969): 29–44.

Frostin, Charles. *Les révoltes blanches à Saint-Domingue aux XVIIe et XVIIIe siècles.* Paris: Editions de l'Ecole, 1975.

Fuentes, Marisa. *Dispossessed Lives: Enslaved Women, Violence, and the Archive.* Philadelphia: University of Pennsylvania Press, 2016.

Funck-Brentano, Frantz. *Les lettres de cachet à Paris, étude suivie d'une liste des prisonniers de la Bastille.* Paris: 1904.

Fyson, Donald. *Magistrates, Police, and People: Everyday Criminal Justice in Québec and Lower Canada, 1764–1837.* Toronto: University of Toronto Press, 2006.

Gaffield, Julia, ed. *The Haitian Declaration of Independence: Creation, Context, and Legacy.* Charlottesville: University of Virginia Press, 2016.

Gallaher, John G. *General Alexandre Dumas: Soldier of the French Revolution.* Carbondale: Southern Illinois University Press, 1997.

Gallerie des modes et costumes français. Paris: n.p., 1778–85.

Garnot, Benoît. "La législation et la répression des crimes dans la France moderne." *Revue Historique* (Jan-Mars 1995): 75–90.

———. *On n'est point pendu pour etre amoureux . . . le liberté amoureuse au XVIIIe siècle.* Paris: Belin, 2008.

Garasse, François. *La doctrine curieuse des beaux esprits de ce temps, ou pretendus tels, contenant plusieurs maximes pernicieuses à la religion, à l'Estat et aux bonnes mœurs, combattue et renversée par le P. François Garassus.* Paris: S. Chappelet, 1623.

———. *Les Recherches des Recherches et autres oeuvres de Me. Etienne Pasquier.* Paris: Sébastien Chappelet, 1622.

Garraway, Doris. *The Libertine Colony: Creolization in the Early French Caribbean.* Durham NC: Duke University Press, 2005.

Garrigus, John. *Before Haiti: Race and Citizenship in French Saint-Domingue.* London: Palgrave Macmillan, 2006.

———. "New Christians/'New Whites': Sephardic Jews, Free People of Color, and Citizenship in Saint-Domingue, 1760–1789." In *The Jews and the Expansion of Europe to the West, 1450–1800,* vol. 2, edited by Paolo Bernardini and Norman Fiering, 314–34. New York: Berghahn, 2001.

Garrioch, David. *The Huguenots of Paris and the Coming of Religious Freedom.* Cambridge: Cambridge University Press, 2014.

———. *The Making of Revolutionary Paris.* Berkeley: University of California Press, 2002.

Garrison, Ch. "Paul de Viau: Capitaine Huguenot et frère du poète Théophile, 1621–1629." *Bulletin historique et littéraire (Société de l'Histoire du Protestantisme Français)* 41, no. 6 (juin 1892): 281–306.

Garrisson, Janine. *A History of Sixteenth-Century France, 1483–1598: Renaissance, Reformation, and Rebellion.* London: Palgrave, 1995.

Gautier, Théophile. *Les grotesques.* Paris: Michel Lévy frères, 1873.

Gay, Peter. *Voltaire's Politics.* Princeton NJ: Princeton University Press, 1959.

Gazette de commerce. Paris: Prault, 1781.

Gazette des nouveaux tribunaux. Edited by Bouchard and Drouet. Paris: Veuve Desaint, 1793.

Geggus, David. *Before Haiti: Race and Citizenship in French Saint-Domingue.* New York: Palgrave Macmillan, 2006.

———. "The Naming of Haiti." *New West Indian Guide/Nieuwe West-Indische Gids* 71, nos. 1–2 (1997): 43–68.

Geggus, David, and Norman Fiering, eds. *The World of the Haitian Revolution.* Bloomington: Indiana University Press, 2009.

Gentleman's Magazine. London, 1763.

Gerber, Matthew. *Bastards: Politics, Family, and Law in Early Modern France.* Oxford: Oxford University Press, 2012.

———. "Bastardy, Race, and Law in the Eighteenth-Century French Atlantic: The Evidence of Litigation." *French Historical Studies* 36, no. 4 (Fall 2013): 571–600.

Ghachem, Malick. *The Old Regime and the Haitian Revolution.* Cambridge: Cambridge University Press, 2012.

[Giovane, Julie, baronne von Mudersbach.] *Plan pour faire servir les voyages à la culture des jeunes gens qui se vouent au service de l'Etat dans la carrière politique.* Vienna: Veuve Alberti, 1797.

Gisler, Antoine. *L'esclavage aux Antilles françaises (XVII-XIXe siècles).* Paris: Karthala, 1981.

Godechot, Jacques. *France and the Atlantic Revolution of the Eighteenth Century, 1770–1799.* Translated by Herbert H. Rowan. New York: Free Press, 1965.

Godefoy, Marion F. *Kourou and the Struggle for a French America.* London: Palgrave Macmillan, 2015.

Goodbar, Robert, ed. *The Edict of Nantes: Five Essays and a New Translation*. Bloomington MN: National Huguenot Society, 1998.

Goodman, Dena, ed. *Marie Antoinette: Writings on the Body of a Queen*. New York: Routledge, 2003.

Gordon, Daniel. *Citizens without Sovereignty: Equality and Sociability in French Thought, 1670–1789*. Princeton NJ: Princeton University Press, 1994.

Gordon-Reed, Annette. *The Hemingses of Monticello: An American Family*. New York: W. W. Norton, 2008.

Gossard, Julia. "Breaking a Child's Will: Eighteenth-Century Parisian Juvenile Detention Centers." *French Historical Studies* 42, no. 2 (April 2019): 239–59.

———. *Young Subjects: Children, State-Building, and Social Reform in the Eighteenth-Century French World*. Montréal: McGill-Queens University Press, 2021.

Graham, Lisa Jane. "Lettres de cachet." In *Europe, 1450–1789: Encyclopedia of the Early Modern World*, vol. 4, edited by Jonathan Dewald, 491–92. New York: Scribner & Sons, 2004.

Gossman, Lionel. "Prévost's Manon: Love in the New World." *Yale French Studies*, no. 40 (1968): 91–102.

Goubert, Pierre. *The Ancien Régime: French Society, 1600–1750*. Translated by Steve Cox. New York: HarperCollins, 1974.

Graffigny, Françoise de. *Lettres d'une péruvienne*. Paris: A Peine, 1747.

Gravier, Gabriel. *Relation du Voyage des Dames Ursulines de Rouen à la Nouvelle Orléans*. Paris: Maisonneuve, 1872.

Green, F. C. "Montesquieu the Novelist and Some Imitations of the 'Lettres Persanes.'" *Modern Language Review* 20, no. 1 (January 1925): 32–42.

Greer, Allan. *The Jesuit Relations: Natives and Missionaries in Seventeenth-Century North America*. Boston: Bedford/St. Martin's, 2000.

———. *The People of New France*. Toronto: University of Toronto Press, 1997.

Greer, Margaret, Walter D. Mignolo, and Maureen Quilligan, eds. *Rereading the Black Legend: The Discourse of Religious and Racial Difference in the Renaissance Empires*. Chicago: University of Chicago Press, 2008.

Griffin, Robert, and Donald A Grinde, Jr., eds. *Apocalypse de Chiokoyhikoy, Chef des Iroquois*. Québec: Les presses de l'université de Laval, 1997.

Grimod de la Reynière, *Moins que rien, suite de Peu de chose*. Lausanne: n.p., 1793.

Hachard, Marie Madeleine. *Voices from an Early American Convent: Marie Madeleine Hachard and the New Orleans Ursulines* Edited by Emily Clark. Baton Rouge: Louisiana State University Press, 2007.

Hageman, Jeanne. "A Woman's Reputation: Madame de Saint-Chamond Responds to Rousseau." *Dalhousie French Studies* 59 (Summer 2002): 32–41.

Hagemann, Karen, G. Mettele, and J. Rendall, eds. *Gender, War, and Politics: The Wars of Revolution and Liberation—Transatlantic Comparisons, 1775–1820*. London: Palgrave Macmillan, 2010.

Hall, Gwendolyn Midlo. *Africans in Colonial Louisiana: The Development of Afro-Creole Culture in the Eighteenth Century.* Baton Rouge: Louisiana State University Press, 1992.

Hamscher, Albert. *The Royal Financial Administration and the Prosecution of Crime in France, 1670–1789.* London: Rowman & Littlefield, 2012.

Hardman, John. *Marie Antoinette: The Making of a French Queen.* New Haven CT: Yale University Press, 2019.

Hardwick, Julie. *Family Business: Litigation and Political Economies of Daily Life in Early Modern France.* Oxford: Oxford University Press, 2009.

———. *Sex in an Old Regime City: Young Workers and Intimacy in France, 1660–1789.* Oxford: Oxford University Press, 2020.

———. "Women 'Working' the Law: Gender, Authority, and Legal Process in Early Modern France." *Journal of Women's History* 9, no. 3 (Autumn 1997): 28–49.

Hardy, James, Jr. "The Transportation of Convicts to Colonial Louisiana." *Louisiana History* (Summer 1966): 207–20.

Harper, Kyle. *Slavery in the Late Roman World, AD 275–425.* Cambridge: Cambridge University Press, 2011.

Hartigan-O'Connor, Ellen, and Lisa G. Materson, eds. *The Oxford Handbook of American Women's and Gender History.* Oxford: Oxford University Press, 2019.

Harvey, David Allen. "The Noble Savage and the Savage Noble: Philosophy and Ethnography in the *Voyages* of the Baron de Lahontan." *French Colonial History* 11 (2010): 161–91.

Hauser, Raymond E. "The Berdache and the Illinois Indian Tribe during the Last Half of the Seventeenth Century." *Ethnohistory* 37, no. 1 (Winter 1990): 45–65.

Havard, Gilles. "'Les forcer à devenir Cytoyens': Etat, sauvages et citoyenneté en Nouvelle France (XVIIe–XVIIIe siècles)." *Annales HSS* (2009): 985–1018.

———. *The Great Peace of Montréal of 1701: French-Native Diplomacy in the Seventeenth Century.* Translated by Phyllis Aronoff and Howard Scott. Montréal: McGill-Queen's University Press, 2001.

———. "Virilité et 'ensauvagement': le corps du coureur de bois (XVIIe et XVIIIes)." *Clio: Femmes, Genre, Histoire* no. 27 (2008) : 57–74.

Havard, Gilles, and Cécile Vidal. *Histoire de l'Amérique française.* Paris: Flammarion, 2006.

Hay, Douglas, and Paul Craven, eds. *Masters, Servants, and Magistrates in Britain and the Empire, 1562–1955.* Chapel Hill: University of North Carolina Press, 2004.

Head, David, ed. *Encyclopedia of the Atlantic World, 1400–1900: Europe, Africa, and the Americas in an Age of Exploration, Trade, and Empires.* Santa Barbara CA: ABC-CLIO, 2018.

Heath, Elizabeth. "Visualizing Colonial Trade and Commodities in Early Modern Paris." Paper presented at the 44th Annual Conference of the Western Society for French History, November 2016.

Hector, Michel, and Laënnec Hurbon. *Genèse de l'Etat haïtien (1804–1859)*. Paris: Editions de la Maison des sciences de l'homme, 2009.

Henochsberg, Simon. "Public Debt and Slavery: The Case of Haiti (1765–1915)." Master's thesis, Ecole d'Economie de Paris, 2016.

Herluison, Grégoire-Pierre. *Le fanatisme du libertinage confondu: ou Lettres sur le Célibat des Ministres de l'Eglise*. Paris: Chez Leclerc, 1791.

Heuer, Jennifer. *Family and the Nation: Gender and Citizenship in Revolutionary France, 1789–1830*. Ithaca NY: Cornell University Press, 2005.

Higginbotham, Jay. *Old Mobile: Fort Louis de la Louisiane, 1702–1711*. Tuscaloosa: University of Alabama Press, 1977.

Hilliard d'Auberteuil, Michel René. *Considérations sur l'état présent de la colonie française de Saint-Domingue*. 2 vols. Paris: Grangé, 1776.

Hinderaker, Eric, and Peter C. Mancall. *At the Edge of Empire: The Backcountry in British North America*. Baltimore MD: Johns Hopkins University Press, 2003.

Hodes, Martha, ed. *Sex, Love, Race: Crossing Boundaries in North American History*. New York: New York University Press, 1999.

Hodson, Christopher. *The Acadien Diaspora: An Eighteenth-Century History*. Oxford: Oxford University Press, 2012.

Holder, R. Ward. *John Calvin in Context*. Cambridge: Cambridge University Press, 2019.

Holt, Mack. *The French Wars of Religion, 1562–1629*. Cambridge: Cambridge University Press, 2005.

Hopkins, Donald. *The Greatest Killer: Smallpox in History*. Chicago: University of Chicago Press, 2002.

Horsley, Adam. "Le Président libertin: The Poetry of François Maynard after the Trial of Théophile de Viau." *Early Modern French Studies* 37, no. 2 (2015): 93–107.

———. *Libertines and the Law: Subversive Authors and Criminal Justice in Early Seventeenth-Century France*. Oxford: Oxford University Press, 2022.

———. "Strategies of Accusation and Self-Defence at the Trial of Théophile de Viau (1623–25)." *Papers on French Seventeenth-Century Literature* 44, no. 85 (2016): 157–77.

Hughes, Ben. *The Siege of Fort William Henry: A Year on the Northeastern Frontier*. Yardley PA: Westholme, 2011.

Hunt, Lynn. *The Family Romance of the French Revolution*. Berkeley: University of California Press, 1992.

———. "The Global Financial Origins of the French Revolution." In *The French Revolution in Global Perspective*, edited by Suzanne Desan, Lynn Hunt, and William Max Nelson, 32–43. Ithaca NY: Cornell University Press, 2013.

———. "Pornography and the French Revolution." In *The Invention of Pornography: Obscenity and the Origins of Modernity, 1500–1800*, edited by Lynn Hunt, 301–40. New York: Zone, 1993.

Hunt, Lynn, ed. *The Invention of Pornography, 1500–1800: Obscenity and the Origins of Modernity*. New York: Zone, 1993.

Hunt, Lynn, and Margaret Jacobs. *The Book That Changed Europe: Picart and Bernard's Religious Ceremonies of the World*. Cambridge MA: Harvard University Press, 2010.

Hunter, Richard L. *The New Comedy of Greece and Rome*. Cambridge: Cambridge University Press, 1985.

Hyde, Anne. *Born of Lakes and Plains: Mixed-Descent People and the Making of the American West*. New York: W. W. Norton, 2022.

Jackson, Donald, ed. *The Diaries of George Washington, vol. 1, 1748–65*. Charlottesville VA: University of Virginia Press, 1976.

Jaenen, Cornelius J. *The Role of the Church in New France*. Ottawa: Canadian Historical Association, 1985.

Jaffary, Nora, ed. *Gender, Religion, and Race in the Colonization of the Americas*. Burlington VT: Ashgate, 2007.

Jandeaux, Jeanne-Marie. "La Révolution face aux 'victimes du pouvoir arbitraire': L'abolition des lettres de cachet et ses consequences." *Annales historiques de la Révolution française*, no. 368 (Avril–Juin 2012): 33–60.

Journal des théâtres et des fêtes nationales. Paris: 1794.

Journal d'un voyage à la Louisiane, fait en 1720 par M. ***, capitaine de vaisseau du Roi. The Hague: Musier, Fils et Fournier, 1768.

Johnson, Christopher H., Bernhard Jussen, David Warren Sabean, and Simon Teuscher, eds. *Blood and Kinship: Matter for Metaphor from Ancient Rome to the Present*. Oxford: Berghahn, 2013.

Johnson, Jessica Marie. *Wicked Flesh: Black Women, Intimacy, and Freedom in the Atlantic World*. Philadelphia: University of Pennsylvania Press, 2020.

Jones, Colin, and Dror Wahrman, eds. *The Age of Cultural Revolutions: Britain and France, 1750–1820*. Berkeley: University of California Press, 2002.

Jore, Léonce. "Les établissements français sur la côte occidentale d'Afrique de 1758 a 1809." *Outre-Mers: Revue d'histoire* (1965): 9–252.

Joutel, Henri. *Journal historique du dernier voyage que feu M. de La Sale fit dans le golfe de Mexique*. Paris: Etienne Robinot, 1713.

Jugement rendu souverainement et en dernier ressort dans l'affaire du Canada par Messieurs les lieutenant général de police, lieutenant particulier et conseillers au Chatelet et siège présidial de Paris. Paris: Bourdet, 1763.

Jurney, Florence Ramond. "Médias et inégalités genrées sur fond d'affaire DSK." *Women in French Studies* 22 (2014): 60–71.

Kaiser, Thomas. "Nobles into Aristocrats, or How an Order Became a Conspiracy." In *The French Nobility in the Eighteenth Century: Reassessments and New Approaches*, edited by Jay M. Smith, 189–226. University Park PA: Penn State University Press, 2012.

Kaplan, Benjamin J. "Dutch Particularism and the Calvinist Quest for 'Holy Uniformity.'" In *The Reformation: Critical Concepts in Historical Studies*, vol. 3, edited by Andrew Pettegree, 286–301. London: Routledge, 2004.

Kars, Marjoleine. *Blood on the River: A Chronicle of Mutiny and Freedom on the Wild Coast*. New York: New Press, 2020.

Keal, Paul. *European Conquest and the Rights of Indigenous Peoples: The Moral Backwardness of International Society*. Cambridge: Cambridge University Press, 2003.

Keller-Lapp, Heidi. "Les *Guerrières de Dieu* in the French Ursuline Missionary Archives." *Journal of Early Modern History* 21 (2017): 91–115.

Kerstetter, Todd. *Inspiration and Innovation: Religion in the American West*. Oxford: Wiley & Sons, 2015.

Kessler, Amalia D. *A Revolution in Commerce: The Parisian Merchant Court and the Rise of Commercial Society in Eighteenth-Century France*. New Haven CT: Yale University Press, 2008.

Kettering, Sharon. "Political Pamphlets in Early Seventeenth-Century France: The Propaganda War between Louis XIII and His Mother, 1619–1620." *Sixteenth-Century Journal* 42, no. 4 (Winter 2011): 963–80.

———. *Power and Reputation at the Court of Louis XIII: The Career of Charles d'Albert, duc de Luynes (1578–1621)*. Manchester: Manchester University Press, 2008.

King, Stewart. *Blue Coat or Powdered Wig: Free People of Color in Pre-Revolutionary Saint-Domingue*. Athens: University of Georgia Press, 2001.

Knight-Baylac, Marie-Hélène. "Gorée au XVIIIe siècle: L'Appropriation du sol." *Revue française d'histoire d'outre-mer* 64, no. 234 (1977): 3–56.

Knoop, Christine. "Over the Edge of the Mental Map: On the Narrative Functions of Wilderness in Abbé Prévost's *Manon Lescaut*." *Romance Studies* 30, no. 1 (January 2012): 36–47.

Koot, Christian J. *Empire at the Periphery: British Colonists, Anglo-Dutch Trade, and the Development of the British Atlantic, 1621–1713*. New York: New York University Press, 2011.

Kostroun, Daniella, and Lisa Vollendorf. *Women, Religion, and the Atlantic World (1600–1800)*. Toronto: University of Toronto Press, 2009.

Kozul, Mladen. "Le voyage sadien en Italie: La Révolution française comme politique libertines dans *l'Histoire de Juliette*." *Eighteenth-Century Fiction* 10, no. 4 (July 1998): 467–81.

Kushner, Nina. "Adultery and the Ideal of the Good Woman: Infidelity in Eighteenth-Century France." Paper presented at the American Historical Association, January 2017, Denver CO.

———. *Erotic Exchanges: The World of Elite Prostitution in Eighteenth-Century Paris*. Ithaca NY: Cornell University Press, 2013.

Kwass, Michael. *Contraband: Louis Mandrin and the Making of a Global Underground*. Cambridge MA: Harvard University Press, 2014.

Labat, Jean-Baptiste. *Nouveau voyage aux iles de l'Amérique*. The Hague: n.p., 1724.

Labelle, Kathryn Magee, and Thomas Peace. *From Huronia to Wendakes: Adversity, Migration, and Resilience, 1650–1900*. Norman: University of Oklahoma Press, 2014.

Lachance, André. *Crimes et criminels en Nouvelle-France*. Montréal: Boreal Express, 1984.

LaChance, Paul. "The Growth of the Free and Slave Populations of French Colonial Louisiana." In *French Colonial Louisiana and the French Atlantic World*, edited by Bradley Bond, 204–43. Baton Rouge: Louisiana State University Press, 2005.

Lachèvre, Frédéric. *Le libertinage au XVIIe siècle. Mélanges: trois grands procès de libertinage.* 15 vols. Geneva: Slatkine Reprints, [1909–28] 1968.

———. "Un mémoire inédit de François Garassus adressé à Mathieu Molé pendant le procès de Théophile." *Revue d'histoire littéraire de la France* 18, no. 4 (1911): 900–939.

Laclos, Pierre Choderlos de. *Dangerous Liaisons.* Translated by Douglas Parmée. Oxford: Oxford University Press, 2008.

Ladurie, Emmanuel Le Roy. *The Ancien Regime: A History of France, 1610–1774.* Hoboken NJ: Wiley-Blackwell, 1998.

Lafitau, Joseph-François. *Moeurs des sauvages amériquains.* Paris: n.p., 1724.

Lahontan, Louis-Armand de Lom d'Arce [and Nicolas Gueudeville]. *Dialogues avec un sauvage: suivi de Conversations de l'auteur avec Adario, sauvage distingué.* Edited by Réal Ouellet. Québec: Lux, [1704] 2010.

———. *Mémoires de l'Amérique septentrionale, ou la suite des voyages de M. le baron de Lahontan.* La Haye: Chez les Frères l'Honoré, 1704.

———. *Nouveaux voyages de M. le baron de Lahontan, dans l'Amérique septentrionale.* 2 vols. La Haye: Chez les Frères l'Honoré, 1703.

Lalement. *Relation de ce qui s'est passé en la Nouvelle France, les années 1663 & 1664. In The Jesuit Relations and Allied Documents.* Vol. 49. Edited by Ruben Gold Thwaites. Cleveland OH: Burrows Brothers, 1899.

La Morlière, *Angola, histoire indienne.* Agra [Paris]: n.p. 1746.

Lanavère, Alain. "Théophile de Viau, imitateur des anciens." *XVIIe siècle* (avril 2011): 397–422.

Lange, Tyler. "Droit canon et droit français à travers l'activité du Parlement de Paris à l'époque des Réformes." *Revue historique de droit français et étranger* 91, no. 2 (Avril–Juin 2013): 243–261.

Lanza, Janine. *From Wives to Widows in Early Modern Paris: Gender, Economy, and Law.* Aldershot: Ashgate, 2007.

Larin, Robert. *Brève histoire des protestants en Nouvelle-France et au Québec, XVIe–XIXe siècles.* Québec: Editions de la Paix, 1998.

———. "The French Monarchy and Protestant Immigration to Canada before 1760; The Social, Political, and Religious Contexts." In *French-Speaking Protestants in Canada,* edited by Jason Zuidema. 13–28. Leiden: Brill, 2011.

Law, John. *Observations on the New System of the Finances of France: Particularly, on the Repurchase of Paying off the Annuities, and on Credit and Its Use, in Two Letters to a Friend.* London: n.p., 1720.

Le Beau, Claude. *Aventures du Sieur Claude Le Beau.* Québec City: Presses de l'université Laval, 2011.

Le Conte, René. "The Germans in Louisiana in the Eighteenth Century." Translated by Glenn R. Conrad. *Louisiana History* 8, no. 1 (Winter 1967): 67–84.

Le Fébure, Guillaume-René. *Traitement gratuit, pour le mal vénérien administré aux adultes de l'un & l'autre sexe, & aux enfans dans Versailles.* Paris: Desprez, 1775.

Le Jeune, Paul. *Brève relation du voyage de la Nouvelle France, fait au mois d'Avril dernier, 1632.* In *The Jesuit Relations and Allied Documents.* Vol. 5. Edited by Ruben Gold Thwaites. Cleveland OH: Burrows Brothers, 1899.

———. *Relation de ce qui s'est passé en la Nouvelle France, en l'année 1636.* In *The Jesuit Relations and Allied Documents.* Vol. 10. Edited by Ruben Gold Thwaites. Cleveland OH: Burrows Brothers, 1899.

Lennox, Jeffers. *Homelands and Empires: Indigenous Spaces, Imperial Fictions, and Competition for Territory in Northeastern North America, 1690–1763.* Toronto: University of Toronto Press, 2017.

Lépine, Luc. "Les stratégies militaires françaises et britanniques en Nouvelle-France." In *La Guerre de Sept Ans en Nouvelle-France*, edited by Laurent Veyssières and Bertrand Fonck, 133–154. Québec: Septentrion, 2016.

Leroy, P. E., and J. P. Oddos. *La vie a Troyes sous Louis XIII.* Troyes: n.p., 1984.

Léry, Jean de. *Histoire d'un voyage faict en la terre de Bresil.* Geneva: n.p., 1578.

———. *History of a Voyage to the Land of Brazil.* Translated by Janet Whatley. Berkeley: University of California Press, 1990.

Lessard, Rénald. "Les faux-sauniers et le peuplement de la Nouvelle-France." *L'Ancêtre: Bulletin de la Société de généologie de Québec* 14, no. 3 (novembre 1987): 83–95.

Lestringant, Frank. "The Philosopher's Breviary: Jean de Léry in the Enlightenment." Translated by Katherine Streip. *Representations* (Winter 1991): 200–211.

Lesuire, Robert-Martin. *Les sauvages de l'Europe.* Berlin: n.p., 1750.

Le Trosne, Guillaume François. *Discours sur l'état actuel de la magistrature, et sur les causes de sa décadence, prononcé à l'ouverture des Audiences du Bailliage d'Orléans, le 15 Novembre 1763.* Paris: Panckoucke, 1763.

Lever, Evelyne. *Madame de Pompadour.* Paris: Perrin, 2003.

Lever, Maurice. *Pierre-Augustin Caron de Beaumarchais.* 3 vols. Paris: Fayard, 1999–2004.

———. *Sade: A Biography.* Translated by Arthur Goldhammer. New York: Farrar, Strauss & Giroux, 1993.

Lezay-Marnésia, Claude François de. *Letters Written from the Banks of the Ohio.* Edited with an introduction by Benjamin Hoffmann. Translated by Alan J. Singerman. University Park PA: Penn State University Press, 2017.

La ligue aristocratique ou les catilinaires françoises, par un member deu Comité patriotique du Caveau. Palais-Royal: Imprimerie de Josseran, 1789.

Lingis, Alphonse. "The Society of the Friends of Crime." In *Sade and the Narrative of Transgression*, edited by David Allen, Mark S. Roberts, and Allen S. Weiss, 100–121. Cambridge: Cambridge University Press, 1995.

Linton, Marisa. *Choosing Terror: Virtue, Friendship, and Authenticity in the French Revolution.* Oxford: Oxford University Press, 2015.

Little, David. *Religion, Order, and Law*. Chicago: University of Chicago Press, 1970.

Loker, Zvi. "Were There Jewish Communities in Saint-Domingue (Haiti)?" *Jewish Social Studies* 45, no. 2 (1983) : 135–46.

Lozier, J.-F. "Lever des chevelures en Nouvelle-France: La politique française du paiement des scalps." *Revue d'histoire de l'Amérique française* 56, no. 4 (2003): 513–42.

MacMahon, Darrin. *Enemies of the Enlightenment: The French Counter-Enlightenment and the Making of Modernity*. Oxford: Oxford University Press, 2002.

Maire, Catherine. *De la cause de dieu à la cause de la nation: Le jansenisme au XVIIIe siècle*. Paris: Gallimard, 1998.

Maltby, William. *The Black Legend in England: The Development of Anti-Spanish Sentiment, 1558–1660*. Durham NC: Duke University Press, 1971.

Mancall, Peter. *Deadly Medicine: Indians and Alcohol in Early America*. Ithaca NY: Cornell University Press, 1995.

Manuel, Pierre. *La police de Paris dévoilée*. Paris: Garnery, 1793.

Mapp, Paul. *The Elusive West and the Contest for Empire, 1713–1763*. Chapel Hill: University of North Carolina Press, 2011.

Marat, Jean-Paul. *Les chaines de l'esclavage: ouvrage destiné à développer les noirs attentats des princes contre les peuples*. Paris: Imprimerie Marat, 1792.

Marraud, Mathieu. *La noblesse de Paris au XVIIIe siècle*. Paris: Editions du Seuil, 2000.

Marshall, Bill. *The French Atlantic: Travels in Culture and History*. Liverpool: University of Liverpool Press, 2009.

Martin, Jacqueline, and Tony Storey. *Unlocking Criminal Law*. New York: Routledge, 2013.

Martin, Morag. *Selling Beauty: Cosmetics, Commerce, and French Society, 1750–1830*. Baltimore MD: Johns Hopkins University Press, 2009.

Marzagalli, Silvia. "The French Atlantic and the Dutch, Late Seventeenth–Late Eighteenth Centuries." In *Dutch Atlantic Connections, 1680–1800*, edited by Gert Oostindie and Jessica V. Roitman, 101–18. Leiden: Brill, 2014.

———. "The French Atlantic World in the Seventeenth and Eighteenth Centuries." In *The Oxford Handbook of the Atlantic World: 1450–1850*, edited by Nicholas Canny and Philip Morgan, 103–18. Oxford: Oxford University Press, 2011.

Maubert de Gouvest, Jean-Henri. *Lettres iroquoises*. London: n.p., 1781.

Maza, Sarah. "The Diamond Necklace Affair." In *Marie Antoinette: Writings on the Body of a Queen*, edited by Dena Goodman, 73–98. New York: Routledge, 2003.

———. *Private Lives and Public Affairs: The Causes Célèbres of Prerevolutionary France*. Los Angeles: University of California Press, 1993.

———. *Servants and Masters in Eighteenth-Century France: The Uses of Loyalty*. Princeton NJ: Princeton University Press, 1983.

McIntire, C. T. "Protestant Christians." In *The Religions of Canadians*, edited by Jamie S. Scott, 75–130. Toronto: University of Toronto Press, 2012.

McKim, Donald K., ed. *The Cambridge Companion to Calvin*. Cambridge: Cambridge University Press, 2004.

McMahon, Darrin. *Enemies of the Enlightenment: The French Counter-Enlightenment and the Making of Modernity.* Oxford: Oxford University Press, 2002.

Melzer, Sara. *Colonizer or Colonized: The Hidden Stories of Early Modern French Culture.* Philadelphia: University of Pennsylvania Press, 2012.

———. "France's Colonial History: From Sauvages into Civilized French Catholics." In *Colonizer or Colonized: The Hidden Stories of Early Modern French Culture,* edited by Sara Melzer, 91–122. Philadelphia: University of Pennsylvania Press, 2012.

Mémoire pour Michel-Jean-Hugues Péan, accusé, contre M. le procureur général du roi en la commission, accusateur. Paris: n.p. 1763.

Mémoires de la Bastille. London: n.p. 1789.

Merrick, Jeffrey. *Sodomites, Pedarasts, and Tribades in Eighteenth-Century France: A Documentary History.* University Park PA: Penn State University Press, 2019.

Miller, Nancy K. *Gender and Genre: An Analysis of Literary Femininity in the Eighteenth-Century Novel.* New York: Columbia University Press, 1974.

Miller, Stephen. *Feudalism, Venality, and Revolution: Provincial Assemblies in Late-Old Regime France.* Manchester: Manchester University Press, 2020.

Milne, George Edward. *Natchez Country: Indians, Colonists, and the Landscapes of Race in French Louisiana.* Athens: University of Georgia Press, 2015.

Le Ministère de Monsieur de Calonne dévoilé, 1789. http://catalogue.bnf.fr/ark:/12148/cb36588061v (accessed November 3, 2022).

[Mirabeau, Honoré Riquetti, comte de.] *Des lettres de cachet et des prisons d'état: ouvrage posthume, composé en 1778.* 2 vols. Hambourg: n.p., 1782.

———. *Le libertin de qualité, ou Confidences d'un prisonnier au Château de Vincennes.* Stamboul: n.p., 1784.

———. *Oeuvres de Mirabeau: Des lettres de cachet.* Paris: Decourchant, 1835.

Montaigne, Michel de. *Essays.* Edited and translated by M. A. Screech. New York: Penguin, 2003.

Montcalm de Saint-Véran, Louis-Joseph, marquis de. *Journal du Marquis de Montcalm.* Québec: Imprimerie L.-J. Demers, 1895.

Montesquieu, Charles de Secondat, baron de. *The Persian Letters.* Translated by C. J. Betts. New York: Penguin, [1721] 1973.

———. *The Spirit of the Laws.* Edited by Anne M. Cohler, Basia Carolyn Miller, and Harold Samuel Stone. Cambridge: Cambridge University Press, 1989.

Moogk, Peter. "Manon Lescaut's Countrymen: Emigration from France to North America before 1763." *Proceedings of the Meeting of the French Colonial Historical Society* 16 (1992): 24–44.

Moote, A. Lloyd. *Louis XIII, the Just.* Berkeley: University of California Press, 1989.

Moreau de St. Méry, Louis Elie. *Déscription topographique, physique, civile, politique, et historique de la partie française de l'isle Saint-Domingue.* 2 vols. Paris: Dupont, 1797–98.

———. *Loix et constitutions des colonies françaises de l'Amérique sous le vent.* 6 vols. Paris: Quillau, 1784–85.

Morgan, Jennifer L. *Laboring Women: Reproduction and Gender in New World Slavery.* Philadelphia: University of Pennsylvania Press, 2004.

Morrissey, Robert Michael. *Empire by Collaboration: Indians, Colonists, and Governments in Colonial Illinois Country.* Philadelphia: University of Pennsylvania Press, 2015.

Moufle d'Angerville, Barthelemy-Francois-Joseph. *Vie privée de Louis XVI ou principaux événements, etc.* London: n.p., 1781.

Mouritsen, Henrik. *The Freedman in the Roman World.* Cambridge: Cambridge University Press, 2011.

Muir, Edward. *The Culture Wars of the Late Renaissance: Skeptics, Libertines, and the Opera.* Cambridge MA: Harvard University Press, 2007.

Murphy, Antoine. *John Law: Economic Theorist and Policy-Maker.* Oxford: Oxford University Press, 1997.

Musset, Jacqueline. *Le régime des biens entre époux en droit normand du XVIe siècle à la Révolution française.* Caen: Presses universitaires de Caen, 1997.

Muthu, Sankar. *Enlightenment against Empire.* Princeton NJ: Princeton University Press, 2003.

Nagy, Peter. *Libertinage et Révolution.* Translated by Christiane Grémillon. Paris: Gallimard, 1975.

Nelson, Eric. *The Jesuits and the Monarchy: Catholic Reform and Political Authority in France (1590–1615).* Burlington VT: Ashgate: 2005.

Nester, William. *The Great Frontier War: Britain, France, and the Imperial Struggle for North America, 1607–1755.* Westport CT: Praeger, 2000.

Newbigging, William James. "Propaganda, Political Discourse, and French Public Opinion in the Seven Years' War." *Proceedings of the French Colonial Historical Society* 19 (1994): 101–10.

Nicholls, Sophie. "Gallican Liberties and the Catholic League." *History of European Ideas* 40 (2014): 940–64.

Norrie, Alan. *Crime, Reason, and History: A Critical Introduction to Criminal Law.* Cambridge: Cambridge University Press, 2014.

Les nouveaux projets de la cabale dévoilés, ou lettre du prince de Lambesc au marquis de Belsunce. Caen: Imprimerie de la Municipalité, 1789.

Observations d'un habitant des colonies sur le "Mémoire en faveur des gens de couleur..." Adressé à l'Assemblée nationale par M. Grégoire. December 16, 1789. http://catalogue .bnf.fr/ark:/12148/cb36400171p.

O'Connell, Mary Ellen. *The Power and Purpose of International Law.* Oxford: Oxford University Press, 2011.

Olivier-Martin, François. *Histoire du droit français des origines à la Révolution.* Paris: Domat Montchrestien, 1948.

Ordonnance concernant les jeunes gens de mauvaise conduite que Sa Majesté permet d'envoyer à l'isle de la Désirade. Paris, July 15 1763.

Ordonnance portant creation d'un corps de troupes-légeres, désigné sous le nom de premiere legion de S. Domingue, rendue par M. le comte d'Estaing, Gouverneur-Général, &c., le 15 Janvier 1765. Cap Français: chez Marie, 1765.

Osman, Julia. *Citizen Soldiers and the Key to the Bastille.* New York: Palgrave Macmillan, 2015.

——. "Pride, Prejudice, and Prestige: French Officers in North America during the Seven Years' War." In *The Seven Years' War: Global Views,* edited by Mark H. Danley and Patrick J. Speelman, 191–212. Leiden: Brill, 2012.

Otto, Beatrice K. *Fools Are Everywhere: The Court Jester around the World.* Chicago: University of Chicago Press, 2001.

Palmer, Jennifer. *Intimate Bonds: Family and Slavery in the French Atlantic.* Philadelphia: University of Pennsylvania Press, 2016.

Palmer, R. R. *The Age of the Democratic Revolution: A Political History of Europe and America, 1760–1800.* 2 vols. Princeton NJ: Princeton University Press, [1959, 1964] 2014.

Palmer, Vernon Valentine. "The Origins and Authors of the Code Noir." *Louisiana Law Review* 56, no. 2 (Winter 1996): 363–407.

Paquette, Gabriel. *Enlightened Reform in Southern Europe and its Atlantic Colonies, 1750–1830.* New York: Routledge, [2009] 2016.

Parker, David. *La Rochelle and the French Monarchy: Conflict and Order in Seventeenth-Century France.* London: Royal Historical Society, 1980.

Parkman, Francis. *France and England in North America.* 7 vols. New York: Library of America, [1865] 1983.

Parmenter, Jon. "After the Mourning Wars: The Iroquois as Allies in Colonial North American Campaigns, 1676–1760." *William and Mary Quarterly* 64, no. 1 (January 2007): 39–76.

Parsons, Jotham. *The Church in the Republic: Gallicanism and Political Ideology in Renaissance France.* Washington DC: Catholic University of America, 2004.

Paschoud, Adrien. *Le monde amérindien au miroir des Lettres édifiantes et curieuses.* Oxford: Voltaire Foundation, 2000.

Paul, Josiane. *Exilés au nom du roi: les fils de famille et les faux-sauniers en Nouvelle-France, 1723–1749.* Québec: Editions du Septentrion, 2008.

"Paul de Viau: Capitaine Huguenot et frère du poète Théophile, 1621–1629." *Bulletin historique et littéraire (Société de l'Histoire du Protestantisme Français)* 41, no. 6 (juin 1892): 281–306.

Peabody, Sue. *There Are No Slaves in France: The Political Culture of Race and Slavery in the Ancien Regime.* Oxford: Oxford University Press, 1996.

Pesantubbee, Michelene. *Choctaw Women in a Chaotic World.* Albuquerque: University of New Mexico Press, 2005.

Petit, Emilien. *Dissertations sur le droit public des colonies françoises, espagnoles et angloises, d'après les lois des trois nations comparées entr'elles.* Geneva: n.p. 1778.

——. *Traité sur le gouvernement des esclaves.* 2 vols. Paris: n.p., 1777.

Petit, Jacques-Gay, and Michelle Perrot, eds. *Histoire des galères, bagnes, et prisons, XIIIe–XXe siècles: Introduction à l'histoire pénale de la France.* Paris: Privat, 1995.

Pettegree, Andrew, ed. *The Reformation: Critical Concepts in Historical Studies.* London: Routledge, 2004.

Petterson, James. *Poetry Proscribed: Twentieth-Century (Re)Visions of the Trials of Poetry in France.* Lewisburg PA: Bucknell University Press, 2008.

Petto, Christine Marie. *When France Was King of Cartography: The Patronage and Production of Maps in Early Modern France.* Plymouth KY: Lexington, 2007.

Peureux, Guillaume, ed. *Lectures de Théophile de Viau: les poésies.* Rennes: Presses universitaires de Rennes, 2008.

Phillips, Roderick. "Women and Family Breakdown in Eighteenth-Century France: Rouen, 1780–1800." *Social History* 1, no. 2 (May 1976): 197–218.

Pichichero, Christy L. *The Military Enlightenment: War and Culture in the French Empire from Louis XIV to Napoleon.* Ithaca NY: Cornell University Press, 2017.

Pintard, René. *Le libertinage érudit dans la première moitié du XVIIe siècle.* 2 vols. Paris: Boivin, 1943.

Plumauzille, Clyde. *Prostitution et révolution: Les femmes publiques dans la cité républicaine.* Paris: Champ Vallon, 2016.

Podruchny, Carolyn. *Making the Voyageur World: Travelers and Traders in the North American Fur Trade.* Lincoln: University of Nebraska Press, 2006.

Poirier, Lisa J. M. *Religion, Gender, and Kinship in Colonial New France.* Syracuse NY: Syracuse University Press, 2016.

Polasky, Janet. *Revolutions without Borders: The Call to Liberty in the Atlantic World.* New Haven CT: Yale University Press, 2015.

Popkin, Jeremy. "A Colonial Media Revolution: The Press in Saint-Domingue, 1789–1793." *Americas* 75, no. 1 (January 2018): 3–25.

———. *You Are All Free: The Haitian Revolution and the Abolition of Slavery.* Cambridge: Cambridge University Press, 2010.

Popkin, Richard. *The History of Skepticism: From Savonarola to Bayle.* Oxford: Oxford University Press, 2003.

Porte, Abbé de la. *L'Observateur littéraire.* Amsterdam: Chez Michel Lambert, 1759.

Poska, Allyson. *Gendered Crossings: Women and Migration in the Spanish Empire.* Albuquerque: University of New Mexico Press, 2016.

Prévost, Antoine François. *Manon Lescaut.* Translated by Angela Scholar. Oxford: Oxford University Press, [1731] 2009.

Pritchard, James. *In Search of Empire: The French in the Americas, 1670–1730.* Cambridge: Cambridge University Press, 2004.

Pruitt, Dwain C. "'The Opposition of the Law to the Law': Race, Slavery, and the Law in Nantes, 1715–1778." *French Historical Studies* 30, no. 2 (Spring 2007): 147–74.

Pyle, Ransford Comstock. *Family Law.* Boston: Cengage, 1993.

Quatremer, Jean. *Sexe, mensonges et médias.* Paris: Plon, 2012.

Quétel, Claude. *De Par le Roi: Essai sur les Lettres de Cachet.* Toulouse: Privat, 1981.

Raimond, Julien. *Observations sur l'origine et les progrès du préjugé des colons blancs contre les hommes de couleur; sur les inconvéniences de le perpétuer; la nécessité . . . de le détruire*. Paris: Belin, 1791.

Ranum, Orest. *Paris in an Age of Absolutism: An Essay*. University Park PA: Penn State University Press, 2004.

Rawley, James A. with Stephen Behrendt, *The Transatlantic Slave Trade: A History*. Lincoln: University of Nebraska Press, 2005.

Raymond, Charles, chevalier de. *On the Eve of Conquest: The Chevalier de Raymond's Critique of New France in 1754*. Edited and translated by Joseph Peyser. East Lansing: Michigan State University Press, 1997.

Raynal, Guillaume-Thomas, Abbé. *Histoire philosophique et politique des établissements et du commerce des Européens dans les des deux Indes*. Amsterdam: n.p., 1770–80.

———. *Tableau philosophique de la Révolution de France en 1789*. Marseille: n.p., 1790.

Recueil des déclarations, édits, lettres patentes, et arrêts du Conseil d'Etat du Roi, enregistrés au Parlement de Dijon. Dijon: Augé, 1700.

Recueil d'edits, declarations, et arrest de Sa Majesté, concernant l'administration de la justice & la police des colonies françaises de l'Amérique et les Engagés. Paris: Chez les libraires associés, 1765.

Recueil des travaux. Evreux: Imprimerie de Charles Hérissey, 1894.

Régent, Frédéric. *La France et ses ésclaves: De la colonisation aux abolitions, 1620–1848*. Paris: Grasset, 2007.

Réguis, Abbé François-Léon. *La voix du Pasteur: discours familiers d'un curé à ses paroissiens*. Paris: Claude Bleuet, 1766.

Rémillard, Juliette. "Renaud d'Avène des Méloizes, Angélique-Geneviève." Dictionnaire biographique du Canada. Accessed August 29, 2022. http://www.biographi.ca/fr/bio/renaud_d_avene_des_meloizes_angelique_4f.html.

Requemora, Sylvie. "Voyage et libertinage, ou l'usage du genre hodéporique comme 'machine à déniaiser' dans la littérature française du XVIIe siècle." *Annali d'Italianistica* 21 (2003): 116–36.

[Restif de la Bretonne.] *Le Pornographe, ou Idées d'un honnête homme sur un project de règlement pour les prostituées, propre à prévenir les malheurs qu'occasionne le 'publicisme' des femmes, avec des notes histoiriques et justicatives*. Paris: Nourse/Delalain, 1769.

Rey, Michel. "Police et sodomie à Paris au XVIIIe siècle: Du péché au désordre." *Revue d'histoire moderne et contemporaine* 29 (1982): 113–24.

Riddell, Walter. *The Rise of Ecclesiastical Control in Québec*. PhD diss., Columbia University, 1916.

Richer, Adrien. *Essai sur les grands évènemens par les petites causes, tiré de l'histoire*. Paris: Gueffier fils, 1760.

Richter, Daniel. *Trade, Land, Power: The Struggle for Eastern North America*. Philadelphia: University of Pennsylvania Press, 2013.

Riley, James C. *The Seven Years War and the Old Regime in France: The Economic and Financial Toll*. Princeton NJ: Princeton University Press, 1986.

Riou, Daniel. "Théophile de Viau et les paradoxes de l'affirmation poétique de soi: 'Il faut écrire à la moderne.'" In *Lectures de Théophile de Viau*, edited by Guillaume Peureux, 43–62. Rennes: Presses universitaires de Rennes, 2008.

Roberts, Penny. *A City in Conflict: Troyes during the French Wars of Religion*. Manchester: Manchester University Press, 1996.

Roche, Daniel. *France in the Enlightenment*. Translated by Arthur Goldhammer. Cambridge MA: Harvard University Press, 1998.

———. *History of Everyday Things: The Birth of Consumption in France, 1600–1800*. Translated by Brian Pearce. Cambridge: Cambridge University Press, 2000.

Røge, Pernille. *Economistes and the Reinvention of Empire: France in the Americas and Africa, 1750–1802*. Cambridge: Cambridge University Press, 2019.

Rogers, Dominique. "Raciser la société: un projet administratif pour une société domingoise complexe (1760–1791)." *Journal de la Société des américanistes* 95, no. 2 (2009): 235–60.

Rogers, Dominique, and Stewart King. "Housekeepers, Merchants, Rentières: Free Women of Color in the Port Cities of Colonial Saint-Domingue, 1750–1790." In *Women in Port: Gendering Communities, Economies, and Social Networks in Atlantic Port Cities, 1500–1800*, edited by Douglas Catterall and Jodi Campbell, 357–98. Leiden: Brill, 2012.

Rosellini, Michèle. "La composition des *Oeuvres poétiques* de Théophile de Viau." In *Lectures de Théophile de Viau: Les poésies*, edited by Guillaume Peureux, 231–55. Rennes: Presses universitaires de Rennes, 2008.

Rossellini, Michelle, and Philippe Caron, eds. *Théophile de Viau: Oeuvres poétiques*. Neuilly: Atlande, 2009.

Rousseau, Jean-Jacques. *Confessions*. Edited by Patrick Coleman. Translated by Angela Scholar. Oxford: Oxford University Press, [1782–89] 2008.

Rouyer, Muriel. "The Strauss-Kahn Affair and the Culture of Privacy: Mistreating and Misrepresenting Women in the French Public Sphere." *Women's Studies International Forum* (2013): 1–10. http://dx.doi.org/10.1016/j.wsif.2013.07.004.

Royot, Daniel. *Divided Loyalties in a Doomed Empire: The French in the West from New France to the Lewis and Clark Expedition*. Newark: University of Delaware Press, 2007.

Ruff, Julius R. *Crime, Justice, and Public Order in Old Regime France*. New York: Routledge, 1984.

Rufus, Jean Jacques. *Lettres cherakeesiennes*. Rome [Holland]: De l'imprimerie du Sacré College de la propaganda, 1769.

Rushforth, Brett. "The Gaoulet Uprising of 1710: Maroons, Rebels, and the Informal Exchange Economy of a Caribbean Sugar Island." *William and Mary Quarterly* 76, no. 1 (January 2019): 75–110.

Rushforth, Brett. *Bonds of Alliance: Indigenous and Atlantic Slaveries in New France.* Chapel Hill: University of North Carolina Press / Omohundro Institute, 2012.

Rusnock, Andrea. "Biopolitics: Political Arithmetic in the Enlightenment." In *The Sciences in Enlightened Europe*, edited by William Clark, Jan Golinski, and Simon Schaffer, 49–68. Chicago: University of Chicago Press, 1999.

Saba, Guido. *Théophile de Viau: un poète rebelle.* Paris: Presses universitaires de France, 1999.

Saba, Guido, ed. *Œuvres complètes.* Paris: Nizet, 1984.

———. *Oeuvres poétiques.* Paris: Nizet, 1987.

———. *Oeuvres poétiques; et Les amours de Pyrame et Thisbé.* Paris: Classiques Garnier, 2008.

Saba, Guido, Alvin Eustis, and Claire Gaudiani, eds. *La poésie française du XVIIe siècle: textes et contextes.* Charlottesville VA: Rookwood, 2004.

Sadlier, Darlene J. *Brazil Imagined: 1500 to the Present.* Austin: University of Texas Press, 2008.

Sagard-Theodat, Gabriel. *Histoire du Canada et voyages que les Freres mineurs Recollets y on t Fait pour le conversion des infidèles depuis l'an 1615. Avec un dictionnaire de la langue huronne.* Paris: Libraire Tross, 1866.

Saint-Amand, Pierre. *The Libertine's Progress: Seduction in the Eighteenth-Century French Novel.* Translated by Jennifer Curtiss Gage. London: Brown University Press, 1994.

Salamand, George, ed. *Paulin de Barral, Libertin dauphinois: Un débauché à la veille de la Révolution française, avec les Mémoires (1764–1784) de Marie-Séraphine Guillaud de la Motte, comtesse Paulin de Barral.* France: La Pensée Sauvage, 1989.

Sandberg, Brian. *Warrior Pursuits: Noble Culture and Civil Conflict in Early Modern France.* Baltimore MD: Johns Hopkins University Press, 2010.

Sauvy, A. "Some Lesser-Known French Demographers of the Eighteenth Century: De la Morandière, de Caveirac, Cerfvol and Pinto." *Population Studies* 5, no. 1 (1951): 3–22.

Savary de Bruslons, Jacques. *Dictionnaire universel de commerce.* 3 vols. Amsterdam: Chez les Jansons, à Waesberge, 1726–32.

Schaeffer, Neil. *The Marquis de Sade: A Life.* Cambridge MA: Harvard University Press, 2000.

Schiebinger, Londa. "Agnatology and Exotic Abortifacients: The Cultural Production of Ignorance in the Eighteenth-Century Atlantic World." *Proceedings of the American Philosophical Society* 149, no. 3 (September 2005): 316–43.

Schloss, Rebecca Hartkopf. *Sweet Liberty: The Final Days of Slavery in Martinique.* Philadelphia: University of Pennsylvania Press, 2009.

Schmitz, Neil. *White Robe's Dilemma: Tribal History in American Literature.* Amherst: University of Massachusetts Press, 2001.

Schneider, Zoe. *The King's Bench: Bailiwick Magistrates and Local Governance in Normandy, 1670–1740.* Rochester NY: University of Rochester Press, 2008.

Schröder, Peter, ed. *Concepts and Contexts of Vattel's Political and Legal Thought.* Cambridge: Cambridge University Press, 2021.

Schumann, Matt, and Karl W. Schweitzer. *The Seven Years War: A Transatlantic History*. New York: Routledge, 2008.

Schusterman, Noah C. "All of His Power Lies in the Distaff: Robespierre, Women, and the French Revolution." *Past & Present* 233, no. 1 (May 2014): 129–60.

Scott, Jamie S., ed. *The Religions of Canadians*. Toronto: University of Toronto Press, 2012.

Scott, Julius. *The Common Wind: Afro-American Currents in the Age of the Haitian Revolution*. London: Verso, 2018.

Scott, Rebecca, and Jean Hébrard. *Freedom Papers: An Atlantic Odyssey in the Age of Emancipation*. Cambridge MA: Harvard University Press, 2012.

Scoular, Jane. "What's Law Got to Do with It? How and Why Law Matters in the Regulation of Sex Work." *Journal of Law and Society* 37, no. 1 (March 2010): 12–39.

Séguin, Robert Lionel. *La vie libertine en Nouvelle France au XVIIe siècle*. 2 vols. Ottawa: Leméac, 1972.

Semley, Lorelle. *To Be Free and French: Citizenship in France's Atlantic Empire*. Cambridge: Cambridge University Press, 2017.

Sepinwall, Alyssa Goldstein. *The Abbé Grégoire and the French Revolution: The Making of Modern Universalism*. Berkeley: University of California Press, 2005.

———. *Haitian History: New Perspectives*. New York: Routledge, 2012.

———. "Robespierre, Old Regime Feminist? Gender, the Late Eighteenth Century, and the French Revolution Revisited." *Journal of Modern History* 82, no. 1 (March 2010): 1–29.

Sévigné, Marie de Rabutin-Chantal, marquise de. *Lettres de Madame de Sévigné*. Paris: Firmin Didot, 1843.

Shawcross, Edward. *France, Mexico, and Informal Empire in Latin America, 1820–1867*. New York: Palgrave Macmillan, 2018.

Shoemaker, Nancy. "How Indians Got to Be Red." *American Historical Review* 102, no. 3 (June 1997): 625–44.

———. *A Strange Likeness: Becoming Red and White in Eighteenth-Century North America*. Oxford: Oxford University Press, 2004.

Shoemaker, Peter W. *Powerful Connections: The Poetics of Patronage in the Age of Louis XIII*. Newark: University of Delaware Press, 2007.

Shovlin, John. *The Political Economy of Virtue: Luxury, Patriotism and the Origins of the French Revolution*. Ithaca NY: Cornell University Press, 2007,

———. "Selling American Empire on the Eve of the Seven Years War: The French Propaganda Campaign of 1755–1756." *Past and Present*, no. 206 (February 2010): 121–49.

Silver, Peter. *Our Savage Neighbors: How Indian War Transformed Early America*. New York: W. W. Norton, 2007.

Sioui, Georges. *For an Amerindian Autohistory: An Essay on the Foundations of a Social Ethic*. Montréal: McGill-Queen's University Press, 1995.

Skaggs, David Curtis, and Larry L. Nelson, eds. *The Sixty Years War for the Great Lakes, 1754–1814*. East Lansing: Michigan State University Press, 2001.

Sleeper-Smith, Susan. *Indian Women and French Men: Rethinking Cultural Encounter in the Western Great Lakes*. Amherst: University of Massachusetts Press, 2001.

Smith, Jay M., ed. *The French Nobility in the Eighteenth Century: Reassessments and New Approaches*. University Park PA: Penn State University Press, 2012.

Smith, Linda Tuhiwai. *Decolonizing Methodologies: Research and Indigenous People*. London: Zed, 1999.

Smith, William. *A Dictionary of Greek and Roman Antiquities*. London: John Murray, 1875.

Smollet, Tobias. *Tobias Smollet Travels through France and Italy*. Edited by Frank Felsenstein. Oxford: Oxford University Press, 1979.

Spang, Rebecca. *Stuff and Money in the Time of the French Revolution*. Cambridge MA: Harvard University Press, 2015.

Spary, Emma. *Eating the Enlightenment: Food and the Sciences in Paris, 1670–1760*. Chicago: University of Chicago Press, 2013.

Spear, Jennifer. *Race, Sex and Social Order in Early New Orleans*. Baltimore MD: Johns Hopkins University Press, 2009.

———. "They Need Wives: Métissage and the Regulation of Sexuality in French Louisiana, 1699–1730." In *Sex, Love, Race: Crossing Boundaries in North American History*, edited by Martha Hodes, 35–59. New York: New York University Press, 1999.

Sperling, Jutta. "Marriage at the Time of the Council of Trent." *Journal of Early Modern History* 8, nos. 1–2 (2004): 67–108.

Spieler, Miranda. *Empire and Underworld: Captivity in French Guiana*. Cambridge MA: Harvard University Press, 2012.

Spink, J.S. *French Free Thought from Gassendi to Voltaire*. London: Bloomsbury, [1960] 2013.

Stanwood, Owen. *The Global Refuge: Hueguenots in an Age of Empire*. Oxford: Oxford University Press, 2019.

Stapelbroek, Koen. "Vattel and the Seven Years' War." In *Concepts and Contexts of Vattel's Political and Legal Thought*, edited by Peter Schröder, 101–20. Cambridge: Cambridge University Press, 2021.

Starbuck, David R. *The Legacy of Fort William Henry: Resurrecting the Past*. Lebanon NH: University Press of New England, 2014.

Steele, Ian K. *Betrayals: Fort William Henry and the "Massacre."* Oxford: Oxford University Press, 1990.

———. "Suppressed Official British Report of the Siege and 'Massacre' at Fort William Henry." *Huntington Library Quarterly* 5, no. 2 (Spring 1992): 339–52.

Steintrager, James. *The Autonomy of Pleasure: Libertines, License, and Sexual Revolution*. Columbia: Columbia University Press, 2016.

Stieber, Chelsea. *Haiti's Paper War: Post-Independence Writing, Civil War, and the Making of the Republic, 1804–1954*. New York: New York University Press, 2020.

Stoler, Ann Laura. *Carnal Knowledge and Imperial Power*. Berkeley: University of California Press, 2010.

———. *Race and the Education of Desire: Foucault's* History of Sexuality *and the Colonial Order of Things*. Durham NC: Duke University Press, 1995.

Stone, Bailey. *The French Parlements and the Crisis of the Old Regime*. Chapel Hill: University of North Carolina Press, 1986.

Stovall, Tyler. *White Freedom: The Racial History of an Idea*. Princeton NJ: Princeton University Press, 2021.

Strayer, Brian. *Lettres de Cachet and Social Control in the Ancien Regime, 1659–1789*. New York: Peter Lang, 1992.

Swann, Julian. *Exile, Imprisonment, or Death: The Politics of Disgrace in Bourbon France, 1610–1789*. Oxford: Oxford University Press, 2017.

———. *Politics and the Parlement of Paris Under Louis XV, 1754–1774*. Cambridge: Cambridge University Press, 1995.

Swann, Julian, and Joël Félix. *The Crisis of the Absolute Monarchy: France from Old Regime to Revolution*. Oxford: Oxford University Press, 2013.

Swenson, Geoffrey. "Legal Pluralism in Theory and Practice." *International Studies Review* 20, no. 3 (September 2018): 438–62.

Taber, Robert. "The Mystery of Marie-Rose: Family, Politics and the Origins of the Haitian Revolution," Age of Revolutions, January 6, 2016. https://ageofrevolutions .com/2016/01/06/the-mystery-of-marie-rose-family-politics-and-the-origins-of -the-haitian-revolution/.

Tackett, Timothy. *Becoming a Revolutionary: The Deputies of the French National Assembly and the Emergence of a Revolutionary Culture*. Princeton NJ: Princeton University Press, 1996.

Taylor, Alan. *American Revolutions: A Continental History, 1750–1804*. New York: W. W. Norton, 2016.

Tertre, Jean-Baptiste du. *Histoire générale des isles de S. Christophe, de la Guadeloupe, de la Martinique, et autres dans l'Amérique*. Paris: n.p., 1654.

Thiers, Adolphe. *The Mississippi Bubble: A Memoir of John Law*. New York: Townsend, 1859.

Thomas, Chantal. "The Heroine of the Crime: Marie-Antoinette in Pamphlets." In *Marie Antoinette: Writings on the Body of a Queen*, edited by Dena Goodman, 99–116. New York: Routledge, 2003.

———. *The Wicked Queen: The Origins of the Myth of Marie Antoinette*. Translated by Julie Rose. Princeton NJ: Princeton University Press, 2001.

Thwaites, Reuben J. *The Jesuit Relations and Allied Documents: Travels and Explorations of the Jesuit Missionaries in New France, 1610–1791*. 71 vols. Cleveland OH: Burrows Brothers, 1898.

Tocqueville, Alexis de. *The Ancien Régime and the French Revolution*. Edited by John Elster. Translated by Arthur Goldhammer. Cambridge: Cambridge University Press, 2011.

Tooker, Elizabeth. *An Ethnography of the Huron Indians, 1615–1649*. Syracuse NY: Syracuse University Press, 1991.

Traer, James. "From Reform to Revolution: The Critical Century in the Development of the French Legal System." *Journal of Modern History* 49 (1977): 73–88.

Trigger, Bruce. *Children of Aataentsic: A History of the Huron People to 1660.* Montréal: MQUP, [1976] 1987.

Trouillet, Rodolphe. *Le Palais-Royal: Un demi-siècle des folies, 1780–1830.* Paris: Editions Bernard Giovanangeli, 2010.

Trouillot, Michel-Rolf. "Motion in the System: Coffee, Color, and Slavery in Eighteenth-Century Saint-Domingue." *Review (Fernand Braudel Center)* 5, no. 3 (Winter 1982): 331–88.

Trousson, Raymond, ed. *Romans libertins du XVIIIe siècle.* Paris: Laffont, 1993.

Trudel, Marcel. "The Jumonville Affair." Translated by Donald H. Kent. *Pennsylvania History: A Journal of Mid-Atlantic Studies* 21, no. 4 (October 1954): 351–81.

Tuetey, Alexandre. *Répertoire général des sources manuscrites de l'histoire de Paris pendant la Révolution française.* Paris: Imprimerie Nouvelle, 1892.

Turmeau de la Morandière, Denis Laurian. *Appel aux étrangers dans nos colonies.* Paris: Dessain Junior, 1763.

———. *Principes politiques sur le rappel des protestants en France.* Paris: Valleyre, 1764.

———. *Representations a Monsieur le Lieutenant general de police de Paris, sur les courtisannes a la mode & les Demoiselles du bon ton.* Paris: Imprimerie d'une Société des gens ruinés par les femmes, 1760.

Turner, James Grantham. *Libertines and Radicals in Early Modern London: Sexuality, Politics, and Literary Culture, 1630–1685.* Cambridge: Cambridge University Press, 2007.

———. *Schooling Sex: Libertine Literature and Erotic Education in Italy, France, and England, 1534–1685.* Oxford: Oxford University Press, 2002.

Turner, Sasha. *Contested Bodies: Pregnancy, Childrearing, and Slavery in Jamaica.* Philadelphia: University of Pennsylvania Press, 2017.

Usner, Daniel. *Indians, Settlers, and Slaves in a Frontier Exchange Economy: The Lower Mississippi Valley before 1783.* Chapel Hill: University of North Carolina Press, 1992.

Vallée, Andréanne. *Avantures du Sieur Claude Le Beau, avocat en Parlement. Voyage curieux et nouveau parmi les sauvages de l'Amérique Septentrionale.* Québec City: Presses de l'Université Laval, 2011.

Vallée, Geoffroy. *La Béatitude des Chrétiens.* n.p., 1574.

van Damme, Stéphane. *L'épreuve libertine: morale, soupçon et pouvoirs dans la France baroque.* Paris: CNRS, 2008.

van den Belt, Henk. *The Authority of Scripture in Reformed Theology: Truth and Trust.* Leiden: Brill, 2008.

van den Brink, Gjisbert, and Harro Höpfl, eds. *Calvinism and the Making of the European Mind.* Leiden: Brill, 2014.

Van Kley, Dale. *The Religious Origins of the French Revolution: From Calvin to the Civil Constitution of the Clergy, 1560–1791.* New Haven CT: Yale University Press, 1999.

van Ruymbeke, Bertrand. "A Dominion of True Believers Not a Republic for Heretics: French Colonial Religious Policy and the Settlement of Early Louisiana." In *French*

Colonial Louisiana and the Atlantic World, edited by Bradley G. Bond, 83–94. Baton Rouge: Louisiana State University Press, 2005.

van Ruymbeke, Bertrand, and Randy J. Sparks, eds. *Memory and Identity: The Huguenots in France and the Atlantic Diaspora*. Columbia: University of South Carolina Press, 2003.

van Ruymbeke, Bertrand, and Raymond Mentzner, eds. *A Companion to the Huguenots*. Leiden: Brill, 2016.

van Veen, Mirjam, and J. Spohnholz. "Calvinists vs. Libertines: A New Look at Religious Exiles and the Origins of 'Dutch' Tolerance." In *Calvinism and the Making of the European Mind*, edited by Gjisbert van den Brink and Harro Höpfl, 76–99. Leiden: Brill, 2014.

Vastey, Jean Louis, baron de. *The Colonial System Unveiled*. Translated by Chris Bongie. Liverpool: Liverpool University Press, 2016.

Vattel, Emer de. *Le droit des gens, ou principes de la loi naturelle appliquée à la conduite et aux affaires des nations et des souverains*. 2 vols. London: n.p., 1758.

Velde, François. "Government Equity and Money: John Law's System in 1720s France." Heraldica, 2004. http://www.heraldica.org/econ/law.pdf (accessed August 29, 2022).

Veyssières, Laurent, and Bertrand Fonck, eds. *La Guerre de Sept Ans en Nouvelle-France*. Québec: Septentrion, 2016.

Viau, Theophile. *Les œuvres de Théophile, divisée en trois parties*. Paris: Pepingué, 1662.

Vidal, Cécile. "Caribbean Louisiana: Church, *Métissage*, and the Language of Race in the Mississippi Colony during the French Period." In *Louisiana: Crossroads of the Atlantic World*, edited by Cecile Vidal, 21–43. Philadelphia: University of Pennsylvania Press, 2013.

Vidal, Cécile, ed. *Louisiana: Crossroads of the Atlantic World*. Philadelphia: University of Pennsylvania Press, 2014.

La vie et les crimes de Philippe, duc d'Orléans. n.p., 1793.

Vigarello, Georges. *Histoire du viol (XVI–XXe siècles)*. Paris: Editions du Seuil, 1998.

Vigée-Lebrun, Elisabeth. *Souvenirs de Madame Louise-Elisabeth Vigée-Lebrun*. 3 vols. Paris: Fournier, 1835–37.

Voltaire. *Le Droit de Seigneur*. Paris: Duchesne, 1763.

Vyverberg, Henry. *Human Nature, Cultural Diversity, and the French Enlightenment*. Oxford: Oxford University Press, 1989.

Walton, Charles. *Policing Public Opinion in the French Revolution: The Culture of Calumny and the Problem of Free Speech*. New York: Oxford University Press, 2009.

Weaver, Karol. *Medical Revolutionaries: The Enslaved Healers of Eighteenth-Century Saint Domingue*. Urbana: University of Illinois Press, 2006.

Weber, Caroline. *Queen of Fashion: What Marie Antoinette Wore to the Revolution*. New York: Picador, 2006.

Wells, Charlotte. "Loathsome Neighbors and Noble Savages: The 'monde inversé' of Antoine de Montchrétien." *L'Esprit Créateur* 48, no. 1 (Spring 2008): 96–106.

Wenzel, Eric. "La procedure criminelle au Canada sous le régime français (1670–1760): un exemple d'adaptation de la norme juridique à l'époque du premier empire colonial." *Revue historique de droit français et étranger* 93, no. 1 (January–March 2015): 103–14.

Weslager, C. A. *The Delaware Indians: A History.* New Brunswick NJ: Rutgers University Press, 1972.

Weuves le jeune. *Réflexions historiques & politiques sur le commerce de France, avec ses colonies de l'Amérique.* 8 vols. Paris: Cellot, 1780.

White, R. S. *Natural Rights and the Birth of Romanticism in the 1790s.* London: Palgrave Macmillan, 2005.

White, Richard. *The Middle Ground: Indians, Empires, and Republics in the Great Lakes Region, 1650–1815.* Cambridge: Cambridge University Press, 1991.

White, Sophie. *Wild Frenchmen and Frenchified Indians: Material Culture and Race in Colonial Louisiana.* Philadelphia: University of Pennsylvania Press, 2012.

———. *Voices of the Enslaved: Love, Labor, and Longing in French Louisiana.* Chapel Hill: University of North Carolina Press / Omohundro Institute, 2019.

Wilson, Samuel M. "Surviving European Conquest in the Caribbean." *Revista de Arqueología Americana* (January–June 1997): 141–60.

Wimmler, Jutta. *The Sun King's Atlantic: Drugs, Demons and Dyestuffs in the Atlantic World, 1640–1730.* Leiden: Brill, 2017.

Wintroub, Michael. *A Savage Mirror: Power, Identity and Knowledge in Early Modern France.* Stanford CA: Stanford University Press, 2006.

Woo, Kenneth. "Nicodemism and Libertinism." In *John Calvin in Context*, edited by R. Ward Holder, 287–96. Cambridge: Cambridge University Press, 2019.

Wood, Laurie. *Archipelago of Justice: Law in France's Early Modern Empire.* New Haven CT: Yale University Press, 2020.

Wright, Anthony D. *The Divisions of French Catholicism, 1629–1645: "The Parting of the Ways."* Burlington VT: Ashgate, 2011.

Wynn, Thomas. "Libertinage." In *The Cambridge History of French Literature*, edited by William Burgwinkle, Nicholas Hammond, and Emma Wilson, 412–19. Cambridge: Cambridge University Press, 2011.

Yalom, Marilyn. *How the French Invented Love.* New York: HarperCollins, 2012.

York, Christine. "Translating the New World in Jean de Léry's *Histoire d'un voyage fait en la terre du Brésil.*" In *Charting the Future of Translation History*, edited by Georges Bastin and Paul Bandia, 293–308. Ottawa: University of Ottawa Press, 2006.

Zecher, Carla. "Marc Lescarbot Reads Jacques Cartier: Colonial History in the Service of Propaganda." *L'Esprit Créateur* 48, no. 1 (Spring 2008): 107–19.

Zim, Rivkah. "'La nuit trouve enfin la clarté': Captivity and Life Writing in the Poetry of Charles d'Orléans and Théophile de Viau." *European Journal of Life Writing* 2 (October 2013): 79–109.

Zuidema, Jason, ed. *French-Speaking Protestants in Canada: Historical Essays.* Leiden: Brill, 2011.

INDEX

Page numbers in italics indicate illustrations

emigration, forced, 64, 90, 169, 170, 188

England, 27, 33, 113, 124, 177

English settlers. *See* British settlers

Enlightenment era, 107, 139

enslaved labor, 79, 83, 194, 195, 205

enslaved people, 95–97, 192, 195–97, 199–202, 249–50, 295n1

enslaved women, 89, 95–96, 195–96, 199–200, 211–12, 297n47

errant family members: colonial laws and policies, 64–65; detention of, 137, 141, 142; episodes related to, 144–47; identified as libertine, 64–67; sending to New France, 64–67

Estissac, Duke of, 166

European settlers: about, 16, 23, 52; American-born, 87; of Antilles, 200; emigration of, 49; objections of, 209; physical labor required of, 67; and segregation solution, 93–94; sexual domination, 200; type of women suitable for, 87

European women, 86, 88, 91, 92

excessive liberties, 98, 201, 203, 218, 228

extramarital sex: about, 5; double standards regarding, 236; and inheritance rights, 212; and libertines, 175; and nobility, 218; and people of color, 203; prosecution for, 138; and religious codes, 197

familial detention, 133, 136, 138, 140, 149–50, 162–63

family law, 50, 74, 97, 226, 238

family order, 11, 133, 137, 139, 140, 142

The Father's Curse (Greuze), *135*

female sexuality, 55, 262n72

feudal rights, 217, 220, 221

Figaro, 217–20, 222, 228

filial disobedience, 135, 166

The First Day (Viau), *39*

Fleuriau, Aimé-Benjamin, 204, 206

forced emigration, 64, 90, 169, 170, 188

Fort Edwards, 121, 122, 123

Fort William Henry, 120–25

Fournier, André, 151–52

France: Admiralty Ordinance in, 205, 206; Atlantic empire, 167–68; as the best-loved empire, 123; Church teachings in, 46; cosmopolitanism, 24; and demand for island exile, 179–80; legal reforms in, 12–13; map of, *43, 132*; and military losses, 109, 126, 130; natural law theory in, 13–14; non-Catholic subjects of, 14; people of color registration in, 204, 207; perceived population crisis in, 174–77; Protestant population in, 23, 37, 40; recovering economic strength of, 178; social ills of, 175, 199; Topinambours in, 40, *41*

freedom of thought, 7, 36

freedom tax, 207, 208, 296n22

freed slaves, 7, 8, 105, 196, 214

freethinkers, 7, 36, 44, 55, 113

free trade, 202

French Atlantic, 6–7, 13–18, 20, 23–24, 27, 30, 40, 47, 51, 67, 80, 81, 87, 90, 105, 110, 168, 191, 222, 247, 253, 259n22

French colonies: about, 14; and enslaved people, 95; and July 1763 decree, 172; and law of slavery, 185; manumission in, 97; and race issues, 198, 208; and religious diversity issues, 177, 178; slavery reforms in, 213; transporting errant sons to, 67

French court, 9, 19, 21, 24, 46, 224

French Crown: about, 3, 5, 9; assertion of preeminence, 37; criticism of, 227–28; and detention solution, 179–83; and Edict of Nantes, 23–25; manumitted slaves as natural subjects of, 96; policies, 11, 57, 64,

beverages, 71; and debauchery, 75, 144, 145, 161, 287n24; defined, 175, 235, 261n56; detention for, 63, 64, 287n33; discourses of, 193; domestic, 236; and enslaved women, 89; and population decline, 174, 176; of runaway slaves, 200; and sex and marriage, 74, 75; as a stage of life, 66; and venereal diseases, 160, 162. *See also* libertines; libertinism

libertine behavior and life: about, 4, 5, 11; and Catholic Church, 239–40; concern for, 202; definition of, 77; during detention, 183–84; importance of, 49; and legal pluralism, 5. *See also* arbitrary detention

libertine category, 3, 6, 9, 11, 14, 16, 255; in Caribbean, 199–203; and colonial exile, 168–70; and cultural hybridity, 193; in France, 133–34, 162; and French Revolution, 218, 223, 234–35, 243; and legalization of divorce, 237–38; in Louisiana colony, 80; in Québec settlements, 50, 76; in Seven Years' War, 108–9, 111; and Viau trial, 21, 22, 47, 50

libertine literature, 3, 10, 14–15, 17, 97–98, 113, 156–57, 218, 261n56, 262n76, 263n82

libertines: about, 2–3; adult, 150–53; among early settlers, 295n6; as a "bad subject," 4, 6; Caribbean, 199–201, 202–3; colonial phenomenon, 131; conclusion about, 249–55; contested uses of, 40, 42, 56; cosmopolitan, 14–15; court cases related to, 1, 15, 19; and crimes, 136, 138, 140, 178; and debauchery, 161–62; defined, 7–15, 21; detention of, 137, 140–41; and disorder in Paris, 143–44; and disorder in provinces, 141–43; docile, 37; enslaved people called as, 200; episodes related

to, 144–47; errant men identified as, 64–67; and excessive love of liberty, 9–10; and extramarital sex, 175; and idleness, 132, 133; indecent spectacle of, 243–44; and insubordinate behavior, 138–39; an island of, 168–74; and law in revolutionary imagination, 224–28; in legal debates, 241; and legal reforms, 235–43; limit on, 97; neighbors, 160–62; of New France, 50–57, 64; nobles, 218–22; Old Regime, 222; and parental authority, 4, 133, 137, 139–40, 142, 163; plays about, 236; and political systems, 251–55; as quasi-criminals, 22, 50, 108, 247, 255; race of, 136–40, 197–99, 202–3; Racinet-Valmont case, 147–49; redeeming of, 174–78; and religion, 8–9, 13, 25, 40, 53, 85, 100, 103, 134, 201, 227; revolutionary, 232–35; at royal court, 223–24; as sect of reformers, 8–9; and Seven Years' War, 109–11; and sex and marriage, 74–76; sons and daughters, 149–50; spouses, 153–55; stereotype of, 218; as subversive figures, 49; as a term for servants, 61; as threat, 9, 18, 103; and transgressive sex, 87; views about, 25, 171; as worst offenders, 184

libertinism, 51, 55, 74, 218, 222, 237

lieutenant général de police in Paris, 98, 132, 170

Lignier, François, 159–60

liquor. *See* alcohol

Louisiana colony: about, 77–78; Code Noir of, 96; conclusion about, 104–5; founding of, 78; French-Indigenous marriage in, 85–92; libertine category in, 80; and Manon Lescaut, 97–104; map of, *78*; and race, 79–81; segregation in, 92–94; and sexual alliances, 81–85, 93. *See also* Mississippi colony

Louis XIII, 25, 26, 28, 30, 33, 40
Louis XIV, 71, 191, 218, 227, 252, 304n11
Louis XV, 134, 218, 227
Louis XVI, 223, 224
Luynes, Duke of, 30, 33

Macarty, Chevalier, 103–5
Manon Lescaut (novel). See *Histoire du Chevalier des Grieux et de Manon Lescaut* (Prévot)
manumission, 96–97, 196–97, 204, 207–8, 212, 250
Marat, Jean-Paul, 236–37
Marie-Antoinette, 223, 300n38
The Marriage of Figaro (play), 218–22, 228
Marseille, 32, 149, 159
Martinique island, 16, 171, 191, 194, 200, 215
masters and servants, 61–68
masturbation, 12, 14
Maubert de Gouvest, Jean-Henri, 113
Maurepas, Count of, 64, 65, 67
mercantilism, 51. *See also* global trade
Mezy, Marie Jeanne, 159–60
migrants, 67, 79, 90, 96, 110, 197
military losses, 109, 126, 130
Mirabeau, Honoré Gabriel Riquetti, Count of, 140, 228–29, 232
missionaries. *See* Catholic missionaries
Mississippi colony, *78*, 80, 104, 112, 234, 275nn1–2
mixed-race people: about, 80, 82, 97; and inheritance rights, 211–13; children, 198, 207, 296n28; objections to mixed-race marriages, 88. *See also* interracial sex; people of color
Molé, Mathieu, 21, 38, 42–47
monopolies, 18, 90, 126–27, 202
Montaigne, Michel de, 29–30
Montcalm, Louis-Joseph de, 119–25, 128–29
Montmorency, Duke of, 26, 43, 44

Montréal, 54, 57, 58, 62, 72–74, 76, 120, 123
Moreau de Saint-Méry, Médéric Louis Elie, 212, 214

Napoleon I, 2 franc coin, *254*
Narbonne, Pierre Charles, 66–67
Natchez revolt, 79–80
National Assembly, 226, 229, 231–33, 241, 250
Native Americans, 6, 15. *See also* Indigenous nations of the Americas; Indigenous people
natural law theory, 13–14, 163, 188, 241
New France: about, 26, 29; Catholicism as new religion of, 53; colonial migration to, 174; corruption in, 129, 130; drinks and treaties, 68–74; and François Bigot, 126; French Crown's rule over, 54; and Lahontan's dialogues, 57–60; libertines of, 50–57, 64; and masters and servants, 61–68; Saint Lawrence River Valley map, *50*; sending errant sons to, 64–67; and sex and marriage, 74–76
New Orleans, 90–93, 99–101
New Spain, 82, 83, 209, 259n22
nobility, social order: 2, 36, 111, 117, 124–25, 218–24, 234, 247

Odéon Theater, 217, 219
Ohio River valley, 114, 115
Old Regime France, 12, 17, 76, 236, 261n55, 262n68
Old Regime law, 226, 228, 231, 238, 261n54
one king, one faith, one law ideal, 13, 14, 38, 134
Orléans, Louis Philippe II, Duke of, 224
Orléans, Philippe II, Duke of, 133
oscillation principle of law, 13, 73, 249, 261n64

Palais-Royal, 243–44, 246
parental authority, 4, 133, 137, 139–40, 163, 247
Paris, 19, 28–31, 39, 43, 47, 64, 65–66, 91, 94, 98, 132, 138, 145–48, 152–53, 157–58, 160, 162–63, 165–66, 169, 175, 187, 199; disorder in, 143–44; in French Revolution, 231, 240, 243–47, 252; policing of, 98, 132–33, 136, 138–41, 143–46, 148, 152; theater in, 217–19
Parlement of Paris, 20, 43, 44, 158, 186, 238
Paulin, Pierre-François, count of Barral, 218
peace treaties, 57, 58, 68, 72, 110, 112, 114, 126, 168, 202
Péan, Michel Jean-Hugues, 127, 129
people of color, 95, 202–9, 212–13, 215, 247, 252. See also interracial sex; mixed-race people
Petit, Jean (libertine minor), 145–46
physiocracy, 176
Picard, Catherine, 154–55
pimping, 1, 2, 139, 162, 242
Piochot, Marie Louise, 150–51
Pollet, Antoine, 146–47
polygamy, 14, 262n72
popular sovereignty, 112, 116
pornography, 156, 223, 240
Port-au-Prince, 206, 210
Prévot, Antoine-François, abbé, 97
property ownership, 202, 208, 250, 303n132
property rights, 81, 196, 226, 247, 248
prostitutes. See sex workers
prostitution: about, 1, 74, 91; decriminalization of, 242; increase in, 242; and Manon Lescaut, 97, 99; and Parisian youth, 132; prohibition of, 138, 162. See also sex workers

Protestants, 14, 21, 23, 25–26, 28, 33–34, 37, 40, 48, 49, 51, 53–55, 57, 60, 63–64, 77, 96, 139, 174, 177, 197, 218
proxy wars, 108, 111, 115, 120
public order, 39, 138, 141, 231, 235, 236

quasi-crime, 5, 15–16, 22, 50, 108, 138, 193, 221, 222, 235, 247, 255, 260n53
Québec: about, 13, 15–17, 56; Lahontan's comments on, 57–58; libertine category in, 50; religious practice in, 52–53; salt-and tobacco-smugglers to, 67–68; selling alcoholic beverages in, 72; Sovereign Council in, 54, 61–63, 69–71. See also New France
Quesnel, Olivier, 75–76

race: 18, 78–83, 86–88, 103–5, 168, 192–94, 197–99, 202–8; and inheritance rights, 211–13; and sexual relations, 92, 94–97
racial hierarchy, 189, 203–5, 207–11, 214, 215
racial prejudice, 78, 86, 87, 194, 205, 209, 250
racial segregation, 80, 87, 89, 92–94, 212
Racinet, Jeanne Julie Gabrielle, 147–49
Racinet-Valmont case, 147–49
racism, 86, 204, 277n23
Raffron, Marie-Madelaine Christine, 160–61
Ralé, Joseph, 152–53
rape, 1, 2, 4, 74, 95, 199, 200, 221
Raymond v. Casse, 212
Récollets, 52, 55. See also Catholic missionaries
Reflections on the Revolution in France (Burke), 232–33
reformed religion, 8, 23, 54, 56
Réguis, Abbé, 134, 136
religious codes, 139, 197, 199

religious dissent, 9, 12, 24, 60, 134, 264n2

religious diversity, 25, 38, 53, 177, 178

religious heterodoxy, 9, 42, 50, 74, 77, 201

religious identities, 48, 195, 269n6

religious liberties, 9, 21, 22, 37, 255

religious orthodoxy, 9, 54, 134, 137, 138, 195

religious skepticism, 6, 56, 134, 225, 265n14

religious tolerance, 21, 23–25, 45, 48, 54, 262n75

religious wars, 23, 25, 27, 56

Republican legislators, 219, 225, 226, 228, 239, 250–51

revolutionary politics, 245, 246

rogue colonialism, 93, 98, 112

Rousseau, Jean-Jacques, 12, 107, 108, 113, 162, 244

royal absolutism. See absolutism

royal administrators, 170, 179, 180

royal court, 20, 23, 32, 39, 223–24, 256

royal directives, 6, 58, 67, 89, 142, 168

Royer, Jean, 165–67, 170, 179

rumor, 71, 138, 223, 224, 251

s*v*ges, 19, 29–30, 38, 68–71, 84, 86, 99, 103, 104, 244, 264n1; and Seven Years' War, 108, 109, 112–23. See also Indigenous nations; Indigenous people

Sade, Marquis de, 2, 140, 172, 221, 240–41

Sagard, Gabriel, 52, 53, 55

Saint-Domingue: about, 18, 95, 168; and category of "race," 193; and Code Noir, 194; inheritance suits in, 211–13; interracial sex in, 213–14; law of slavery in, 210–11; map of, 192; militia's role in defense of, 208–9;

and people of color, 203–6, 215; as secure site for exiles, 171; and war for independence, 248

Saint-Michael, Nicolas Daussi de, 75

savages. See s*v*ges

Scioto Company, 245–46

seduction, 3, 27, 42, 74, 219, 221, 223, 236

segregation. See racial segregation

Senegal, 16

Senneville, Gilles François de Ganneau de, 65

servants: in American colonies, 62; contracted, 62; and crimes, 61; king's orders for, 63–64; libertine as a term for errant, 61; and masters, 61–68; punishment for, 61–63; social hierarchy, 61, 62

settlers. See European settlers

Seven Years' War: about, 107, 108; and Affaire du Canada, 126–30; conclusion about, 130; and Canadian soldiers, 204–5; and Fort William Henry massacre, 120–25; and Indigenous allies, 109, 112–20; and law of nations, 108–12, 116, 122, 126, 130; and libertines, 109–11

sex and marriage, 74–76

sexual activities, 12, 17, 44, 51, 175

sexual alliances. See sexual relations

sexual assaults, 1, 2, 166, 199, 200, 257n1

sexual behavior, 10, 13–15, 60, 199, 228, 241–42

sexual deviance, 12, 74, 75, 92, 100, 260n50

sexual domination, 1, 200, 217, 220, 222

sexual liberties, 4, 85, 93, 111, 218

sexually transmitted diseases. See venereal diseases

sexual morality, 55, 97

sexual promiscuity, 10, 137, 147, 149, 162

sexual relations: about, 14; and Code
Noir, 95–96, 195–97, 200; with
Indigenous women, 81–85, 89, 93;
with enslaved women, 92, 94–97;
clerical hypocrisy regarding, 60; and
revolutionary era, 240, 246
sexual revolution, 97
sexual violence, 4, 198, 199
sex workers, 1, 90–92, 94, 101, 144, 152,
176, 213, 242, 244, 251
slavery and slave trade: abolition,
249, 251, 254; about, 7, 17, 18, 78;
European men's role in, 212–13; and
excessive liberties, 201; Catholic
holidays, 200; race and sex, 78,
94–97; reforms of, 213–15; restoration
of, 248
smugglers, 64, 67–68, 76, 90–91, 170–71
social conservatives, 225–26
social ills, 175, 199, 214
social order: about, 6, 11, 29, 50, 138, 188;
and adultery, 157–58; and Church's
orders, 103; and hierarchy, 2, 12, 55,
61–62, 107, 224; and parental authority, 163; and penal system, 232; and
racial segregation, 87; and religious
skepticism, 225; and subordinates,
185, 225; threats to, 56, 77, 86; types
of, 137–38
social systems, 58, 102, 111
sodomy, 20, 22, 44, 74–75, 240, 288n46
Sovereign Council (Martinique), 194
Sovereign Council (Québec), 49, 54,
61–63, 69–71
Sovereign Council (Saint-Domingue),
194, 210
Spain, 14, 32, 83, 139
Spanish empire, 82, 83
Spanish settlers, 191, 198
Strauss-Kahn trials, 1–2, 4–5
syphilis. *See* venereal diseases

Talon brothers, 82, 83, 84
Thomas, Antoine-Léonard, 117–19
travel narratives, 99
Treaty of Paris, 64, 110, 126, 202
Trois-Rivières, 54, 70
Tupinambá, 29–30, 40, *41*
Turmeau de la Morandière, Denis-
Laurian, 174–78

vagrancy and vagabonds, 64, 91, 92, 132,
140–41, 278n56
Valmont, Dame (Marie Antoinette
Blanchard), 147–49
Vastey, Jean-Louis de, 252, 254, 255
Vattel, Emer de, 109, 116, 130, 163
Vaudreuil, Philippe de Rigaud, Marquis
de, 87
Vaudreuil-Cavagnial, Pierre de Rigaud,
Marquis de, 103, 104, 114, 123, 126,
128
venereal diseases, 1, 42, 137, 159–60, 162,
238
Viau, Théophile de: acquittal of, 20–21,
46–47; arrest of, 43–44; charges
against, 42, 44–46; conclusion about,
47–48; conversion to Catholicism,
34, 40; and cosmopolitanism, 31; as
a courtier, 39–40; and crimes, 20,
43, 44, 55; death of, 47; and Duke
of Luynes, 30, 33; and Duke of
Montmorency, 26; early life of, 25;
education of, 25–26; exile of, 26–27,
30, 39; and François Garasse, 21–22,
32–33, 36–38, 40, 42, 45–46; and
French Crown, 33; and Louis XIII,
33; narrative poetry of, 28–29, 33–36;
popularity of, 30–31; in prison, 20,
33, 38, 42; travel account of, 39–40;
views on Catholicism, 24; writings
about s*v*ges, 30. *See also* Jesuits;
Huguenots

Viau trial: from 1623 to 1625, 19–20; about, 19–20; conclusion about, 47–48; evidence in, 46–47; and libertine category, 21, 22; opening of, 44–46

Villejouin, Gabriel Rousseau de, 173, 179–85, 187

Voltaire, François-Marie Arouet, 107–8, 110, 113, 128

voyageurs, 103, 104. *See also* fur trade

warfare, 68, 80, 108, 109, 111, 120

Washington, George, 115, 117–18

whiteness, 79, 88, 89, 276n10

witness testimony, 2, 20, 46, 138

women. *See* Black women; European women; Indigenous women

Printed in the USA
CPSIA information can be obtained
at www.ICGtesting.com
LVHW041209191223
766481LV00026B/144